EVERYBODY'S POLITICAL WHAT'S WHAT?

EVERYBODY'S POLITICAL WHAT'S WHAT?
BY BERNARD SHAW

NEW YORK

DODD, MEAD & COMPANY

1945

Published October, 1944
Second Printing, October, 1944
Third Printing, November, 1944
Fourth Printing, January, 1945

THIS BOOK IS COMPLETE AND UNABRIDGED. IT IS
MANUFACTURED UNDER WARTIME CONDITIONS IN CON-
FORMITY WITH GOVERNMENT REGULATIONS CONTROL-
LING THE USE OF PAPER AND OTHER MATERIALS

PRINTED IN THE UNITED STATES OF AMERICA

CONTENTS

v

31231

CONTENTS

CONTENTS

EVERYBODY'S POLITICAL WHAT'S WHAT?

CHAPTER I

IS HUMAN NATURE INCURABLY DEPRAVED?

IF it is, reading this book will be a waste of time, and it should be exchanged at once for a detective story or some pleasant classic, according to your taste. For though the book is in a sense a detective story inasmuch as it is an attempt to track down some of the mistakes that have landed us in a gross misdistribution of domestic income and in two world wars in twentyfive years, yet if we have neither the political capacity nor the goodwill to remedy them, we had better not torment ourselves uselessly by making ourselves conscious of them. Better cling to our delusions and keep our hope and selfrespect, making the most of our vices and follies before they destroy us.

I grant that the case against us seems strongly fortified by the fact that just now the nations are engaged in a horrible reciprocity of slaughter and destruction. You have only to read Gulliver's Travels to learn from the king of Brobdingnag how English history may on its bare facts lead to the conclusion that mankind is incorrigibly villainous. When Swift threw off the mask of the king, he described a Utopia ruled by horses, in which men were vermin and were not called men but Yahoos. Yet Swift did not know the whole truth of the condition of mankind, nor did Goldsmith, though his Deserted Village shews how he concluded that "honor sinks where commerce long prevails."

Not until the nineteenth century, when Karl Marx tore the reports of our factory inspectors from our unread bluebooks and revealed Capitalism in all its atrocity, did Pessimism and Cynicism reach their blackest depth. He proved up to the hilt that capital in its pursuit of what he called Mehrwerth, which we translate as Surplus Value (it includes rent, interest, and commercial profit), is ruthless, and will stop at nothing, not even at mutilation and massacre, white and black slavery, drugging and drinking, if they promise a shilling per cent more than the dividends of philanthropy. Before Marx there had been plenty of Pessimism. The book of Ecclesiastes in the Bible is full of it. Shakespear in King Lear, in Timon of Athens, in Coriolanus, got to it and stuck there. So did Swift and Goldsmith. But none of them could document the case from official sources as Marx did. He thereby created that demand for "a new world" which not only inspires modern Communism and Socialism but in 1941 became the platform catchword of zealous Conservatives and Churchmen.

They all agree that you cannot have a new sort of world without a new sort of Man. A change of heart they call it. But the Bible tells us that the heart of Man is deceitful above all things and desperately wicked. And history seems to confirm the Bible. The deeper we dig into it the more evidence we find that not only ancient Greece and Rome but half a dozen earlier civilizations as advanced and imposing as our own collapsed. Apparently the changes needed to save them were repudiated by the unchanging human heart, convincing the Pessimists that the demand for a new world has not the faintest chance of being supplied by our generations of Yahoos, now busy slaughtering and murdering one another in a war which is fundamentally not merely maniacal but nonsensical.

Nevertheless if this book is to be worth writing or reading I must assume that all this pessimism and cynicism is a delusion caused, not only by ignorance of contemporary facts but, in so far as they are known, by drawing wrong conclusions from them. It is not true that all the atrocities of Capitalism are the expression of human vice and evil will: on the contrary, they are largely the product of domestic virtue, of patriotism, of philanthropy, of enterprise, of progressiveness, of all sorts of socially valuable qualities. The unscrupulous misers and grabbers have no public opinion on their side. The result may be hell on earth; but it is a hell paved with good intentions. Capitalism is not an orgy of human villainy: it is a Utopia that has dazzled and misled very amiable and public spirited men, from Turgot and Adam Smith to Cobden and Bright. The upholders of Capitalism are dreamers and visionaries who, instead of doing good with evil intentions like Mephistopheles, do evil with the best intentions. With such human material we can produce a dozen new worlds when we learn both the facts and the lessons in political science the facts teach. For before a good man can carry out his good intentions he must not only ascertain the facts but reason on them.

This is a counsel of perfection. All we can actually do is to get as much information as we can and act on it to the best of our fallible judgment. And our information is fallible too: it may, for instance, be honest and accurate, but out-of-date. Information that was quite substantial in 1066 for William the Conqueror may be completely obsolete for a Prime Minister in the twentieth century. If education has not kept pace with the changing facts the Prime Minister may be a walking anachronism. Most of our Prime Ministers are. If the information dates from 1500, when the feudal barons had largely killed one another off and the facts, becoming commercial, appealed as such to the Welsh adventurer who consummated the baronial slaughter by killing Richard the Third and succeeding him as king, the schools founded then will be mercantile, middle class, anti-feudal, and even regicidal. Ministers educated in them will challenge Conservative Premiers as leaders of a Liberal Opposition, starting a tradition that they represent progress and individual liberty as against conservatism and feudal serfdom. When the resultant industrial revolution reaches a point at which the capital needed for a start in big business rises from hundreds of pounds to millions, the employers lose their mastery and are enslaved by the financiers as salaried managers, thus becoming employees; and with this new change in the facts we have the scions of the newly proletarianized middle class denouncing Liberalism as iniquitous and ruinous, and Ruskin College and its like educating Labor leaders to hurl Marxisms at the heads of the feudal Conservatives and the Liberal mercantilists alike.

The trouble about these evolutions is that our human habits and ideas do not change synchronically with the facts. In the eleventh century England was feudalized by the Norman Conquest, with the land owned by the king, and the barons holding their estates from him on strenuous public conditions. By the nineteenth century this system had evolved (or degenerated) into a three-class system, the land being virtually owned by its inheritors or purchasers, cultivated by a proletariat too numerous to fetch more than bare subsistence in the labor market, and managed by a middle class selling its commercial and professional ability to the landlords at supply-and-demand prices, all three being politically "free" but in fact in complete bondage economically. Nevertheless the great public schools established by dominant ecclesiastics and feudal monarchs in the fourteenth and fifteenth centuries, which set the fashion for the later schools founded by rich merchants, continue to teach the feudal system and the Church creeds in England today. Even their limitation to Latin as the language of literature, religion, diplomacy and law survives, defying the fact that vernacular Latin died a natural death fifteen centuries ago.

The technique and tradition of secondary education established in this way still dominates our educational system. I once ventured to criticize it in the presence of a Winchester master. He proudly adduced as a proof of the modernity and intellectual leadership of his school that it had just actually introduced a mathematical master, thus reaching in the twentieth century the point reached by Archimedes two thousand years ago.

When the development of commerce forced the universities to add political economy to their curriculum, it was tolerated and even welcomed as proving that a business policy of entire selfishness, politely called individualism, would automatically produce continuous employment at subsistence wages for the whole population, headed by a superior class in sufficient affluence to accumulate capital and maintain culture; and this also petrified into a tradition and is still taught as it was when it was invented by the French Physiocrats two centuries ago. It never was true: what it really produced automatically were the horrors of poverty brought to light by Karl Marx, against which Humanitarians of all parties agitated for Factory Acts, and Trade Unions too powerful to be persecuted as criminal conspiracies.

The time lag in education thus varies from a hundred years to two thousand, and produces the quaint phenomenon known as the Old School Ties, meaning the government of modern States by Cabinets in which the outlooks on society of Noah and Samuel, of William the Conqueror and Henry the Seventh, of Cromwell and Tom Paine, of Adam Smith and Robert Owen, of Jesus and Charles Darwin, are all jumbled up in incalculable confusion. When confronted as they are today with upstart foreign dictators who have read Karl Marx in the light of bitter personal experience of proletarian poverty and persecution, and therefore know the worst of the world they are living in, the resulting misunderstandings are tragic as well as comic, and in either case disastrous. To the Old School Ties the dictators seem ignorant uneducated rebels. To the dictators the Ties seem sordid exploiters who live by robbing the poor, and intend to go on doing it by hook or crook, mostly crook.

And both factions have the best intentions, and believe they are ceasing to do evil and learning to do well.

Sometimes the parties are more dangerous when they profess agreement than when they contradict. When Mr H. G. Wells drafted a new Declaration of Rights, and submitted it for general discussion, I found myself in perfect agreement with it. That was perhaps to be expected; but I found myself in equally perfect agreement with all the other parties to the discussion as well, including persons who regard my political aims as subversive and even diabolical.

This apparently millennial harmony was shattered by the Prime Minister, Mr Winston Churchill, who said, in reply to certain sceptics who were pressing him for a more explicit declaration of our war aims, that "if you try to set forth in a catalogue what will be the exact settlement of affairs you will find that the moment you leave the area of pious platitude you will descend into the arena of heated controversy."

With this deadly sentence Mr Churchill knocked down all the skittles with a single throw, leaving us in the region of abstraction, in which we appear a united nation. Such unanimity is useful in war time, when we all have to fight for our lives whether we like it or not; but anyone who supposes that it will continue when the war is over, and we have to start rebuilding and cleaning up, is deluded by phrases as useless for legislative purposes as algebraical symbols which represent quantities but give no information as to quantities of what.

As long as we describe the virtues we are to practise and the vices we are to eschew in abstract terms every sane thinker, from Confucius and Moses to Jesus and Mahomet, and from these to the Pope and the President of the National Secular Society, agrees with us wholeheartedly. But the moment we come down to tin tacks and raise the question whether some specific stroke of conduct is virtuous or vicious, allowable or criminal, the agreement vanishes; and we are plunged into controversies which may be carried to the extreme of sanguinary crusades. We all agree as to the sanctity of legal marriage; but the Yesmen include the Kulin polygamist who has conferred his caste on a hundred daughters of rich men by marrying them very temporarily for a consideration, the Moslem who draws the line at four wives, the Hollywood hero or heroine of many divorces, and the Irish couples bound together in an indissoluble monogamy. These varieties must either oppress one another unbearably or agree to differ; and that is not always possible. Smokers and non-smokers cannot be equally free in the same railway carriage.

To get enough real agreement to make a body of common law possible we must have not only psychological homogeneity: the homogeneity must also be scientific. As Mr Wells puts it, common law presupposes common knowledge. For legislative purposes it also presupposes common conclusions drawn from that knowledge. The Pitcairn islanders know as much as the British, but do not bother about high civilization because they look to the second coming of

Christ in the near future to establish the kingdom of heaven on earth. My study of vaccination has convinced me that it is an ignorant delusion, and its imposition often a shocking tyranny; but many writers who have the same opportunities as I of finding out all about it are persuaded that the nation will be wiped out by confluent smallpox if vaccination be not sternly enforced on everyone at frequent intervals. In Russia they are all Communists with a beautiful Wellsian constitution; but the official economists, believing that their most urgent need is for more factories, more power stations, and more railways, oppose and coerce the people who want more silver watches. And what are the hyperaesthetic and furiously energetic people who want to work sixteen hours a day, spend tens of thousands a year, retire at 40, and die worn-out at 60, to do with the anaesthetic people who want to work four hours a day for three hundred a year, retire at 60, and die at 90, when both of them come face-to-face with a Government advanced enough to be intensely jealous of shaking social stability by any serious inequality of income among its citizens?

There is also the difficulty that the clearest knowledge of what needs to be done does not carry with it the knowledge of how to do it. Dickens describes our governing classes as perfect masters of the art of How Not To Do It. But then, thinking themselves very well off as they are, they do not want to do it. Rulers who honestly and intensely want to do it make disastrous messes of their jobs because they do not know how to do them. When Mahomet divided the calendar into twelve lunar months he meant well, and proceeded not on obsolete theories but on visible astro-physical scientific facts. Yet the seasonal caravans soon went all wrong because his knowledge, sound enough as far as it went, did not go far enough.

However, we need not go way back to the seventh century for examples. During the ten years after the Bolshevik Revolution of 1917 in Russia the Communist government, though up-to-date and even ahead of it in social theory and knowledge of the facts, made so many legislative and administrative mistakes that the survival of the Communist State and even of the Russian people still seems miraculous and providential. The Bolsheviks knew what they wanted but did not know how to get it. And if the heads of our Old School Ties could be emptied of everything political they learnt at school or at home, and refitted with Lenin's mental furniture and faculty, they would make all his mistakes over again, and bring the country even nearer to starvation and ruin without any guarantee that the circumstances would allow us to pull through as Lenin did.

There is nothing to be done but fence off as many of the pitfalls and signpost as many of the right roads as we can.

Suppose we begin with the Land Question. It is so fundamental that if we go wrong on it everything else will go wrong automatically.

CHAPTER II

THE LAND QUESTION

WHAT is the common sense view of the agricultural land question as it seems to townsmen born and bred? It is that a farmer should own the land he cultivates. If this land is not his own and he may not drive trespassers off it with the law at his back, what security can he have for the possession and consumption of his harvest? So by all means let him own his plot against all comers. The cultivators will then thrive according to their industry, their temperance, their honesty: in short, their good character and aptitude for their difficult technical job. If under these circumstances a man and his family are not well-to-do, it is reasonably safe to conclude that either he has mistaken his calling and should try city life, or else there is a screw loose in his character, and his poverty and failure "serve him right." Such is the simple morality of the earth's pioneer cultivators. It works well enough in regions where there is still equally fertile land free for everybody without paying a landlord for it.

What we are suffering from at present is the persistence of this primitive morality now that the facts contradict it flatly at every point. Modern cultivators are not pioneers: they cannot find an acre of land of equal fertility free within their reach, nor indeed any land at all. Yet farmers who have to work sixteen hours a day to pay their rent, their taxes, and the interest on their mortgages, still tell you gravely that they are independent, that they are their own masters, that they enjoy the priceless benefit of political freedom, and that foreign governments which have abolished private property in land must be such monsters and bloodthirsty tyrants that it is our duty to civilization to make war on them and root out their horrible doctrines from the mind of man. They learn this at home and in school, and have it dinned into them by the press, by the wireless, by Parliament, by the judges, and by the platform speeches they listen to at election times.

And they mean well. They honestly believe that they are standing up for the social foundation of all private and public honor and virtue when they are really voting for idleness, waste, vicious luxury, parasitism, poverty, overwork, and all the other evils that follow selfish private property in the ultimate sources of public welfare. But let us not rush into political pessimism and declare that they are only getting what they deserve for their stupid wickedness. Bring them up as collective farmers paying rent to the State for the common good as they now pay taxes to it, and precisely the same ethical impulses that now make them bigoted Conservatives will make Bolshevists of them. Russia has proved it.

To understand the matter we must begin by grasping the fact that land is neither unlimited in quantity nor equally valuable everywhere. It varies from acre to acre between frontages in the city of London which are valued by the foot, and Saharas on which human life cannot subsist. Within the British islands there are places where at low tide the inhabitants pick up coal and take it home in their prams for nothing, and mines from which, after 20 years' expensive tunnelling, coal is hewn and transported laboriously from miles out under the sea. There are lands flowing with milk and honey, lands oozing oil, lands stuffed with diamonds or gold nuggets, el Dorados of all sorts, side by side with deserts of waterless sand, malarious swamps, and jungles haunted by venomous snakes and man eating leopards. In the loveliest landscapes of western Ireland and Scotland there are stony fields on which the hardest labor will not support the cultivator unless he can get a yearly job as harvest laborer elsewhere. On suburban roads the house rents vary from mile to mile by the amount of the fare by tram, bus, or railway to the nearest market or business centre. If rents vary as they do from shillings a week to thousands a year, it is because the earth varies in fertilities, proximities, advantages and disadvantages of all descriptions. These are not views of the land question: they are facts. Women bringing up their children on a war allowance of £2 a week and paying fourteen shillings a week rent are facts also.

If the land of a country be divided up into separate plots and made the property of its occupiers, the final result will not be that individuals will be rich in proportion to their industry, honesty, sobriety and capacity. Some of them will be longlived and fabulously rich;

others will be fever-stricken and half-starved, or on the road as destitute tramps, with the rest somewhere on the scale between these extremes. Almost immediately the unlucky ones will abandon their barren sands and swamps and offer to cultivate the land of the lucky ones for a better subsistence, giving up the rest of the product to the owner as rent. The lucky ones thus become not only a rich class, but, if they like, an idle one. Enough of them will like it to constitute them a class of ladies and gentlemen, and set up a tradition that it is disgraceful to have to work for a living or even to carry a parcel through the street. Walking instead of riding or being driven in carriages involves loss of caste.

Besides, when all the land has been appropriated, the subsequently born will have no land, and will become a new helot class called the proletariat, living by the sale of their labor to the cultivators, or, as tenant farmers or craftsmen, paying rent for the land they occupy. When more proletarians are born than the cultivators can profitably employ, the price of proletarian labor falls to a point at which it will barely support a life shortened by slow starvation.

In this state of things the proprietors are the only people who have more money than they need spend. They have practically all the spare money in the country. Spare money is called capital; and the proprietors, already called landlords, and "living by owning," become capitalists, and lend their capital to men of business for a rent called interest exactly as they have leased their lands. Class monopoly of capital follows class monopoly of land as inevitably as winter follows autumn.

Let us go into the history of the matter for a moment. William the Conqueror is interesting even eight centuries after his death, as an example of the advantage of cross breeding between the classes. He was not an inbred nobleman: he was a duke's bastard and the grandson of a vulgar tanner. And he was able enough to collect an army of Norman adventurers and conquer England. Being a Feudalist and Royalist he divided the land into great estates to be fortified with castles distributed among his French comrades-in-arms, or left in the hands of Saxon holders who gave him no trouble, to make what they could out of them on condition that they undertook the military defence of the country, the administration of justice in their domains, the financing of the royal establishments, and generally, the discharging of their local share of civilization subject to their fealty to himself as king, and the inheritance of their estates at their deaths in undivided integrity by a single male heir capable of assuming all their responsibilities. Being a baptized Catholic he built churches and abbeys as well as castles, and gave the estates they stood on to the clergy on condition that they took charge of the spiritual welfare of the people.

It was quite a reasonable arrangement under the circumstances, and kept the country in order for a while in an agricultural society of barons, bishops, farmers and serfs. But only for a while. Only as long as the facts corresponded roughly to the plan of feudalism. And facts will not, like plans, stay put. Kings and barons, however able, are only mortal men; and ability does not always pass from father to son: it often dies with its possessor. Yet the feudal system, instead of providing for the selection of able persons to succeed the kings and barons, only stipulated that the successor should be a male. And to the question "Which male?" it replied "The dead man's eldest son." This avoided fights for the succession; but it was no guarantee of the new ruler's competence as civil judge and military chieftain. William's eldest son was a failure and did not succeed him, though he actually made war on his father in France and defeated him. Among the barons there were many such failures who did succeed their fathers and either made a disastrous mess of it or drifted along doing what the other barons did. The few who were neither failures nor nincompoops, and were in effect local kings, strove for the control of the country, and even for the throne, against the central king. The system had the seeds of civil war in it from the first.

It also created a class of younger sons for whom it made no provision, and who in England were commoners brought up to baronial habits and expenditure without incomes to pay for them. They had either to live on the bounty of their elder brothers or obtain national employment as army officers and diplomats or Church livings and bishoprics. Their descendants had to live by practising professions, which was such a come-down that within my own recollection the fact that doctors accepted money for their services was treated as a disgraceful secret, and you paid your doctor as furtively as you tipped a butler. The barrister's gown still has little back pockets, relics of the time when you slipped his fee into his pocket behind his back. Finally the younger sons' descendants had to condescend, first to wholesale business, then to clerkship, then to retail trade, then to manual craftsmanship, and at last to unskilled labor, whence it comes that you find quite commonly that an English laborer is an inveterate snob who regards himself as an aristocrat under a cloud, and votes always for the Conservative candidate at elections whilst dukes and marquesses are supporting the Labor Party in the House of Lords.

The feudal system found itself confronted not only with its disinherited cadets but with the five per cent or so of commoners who by natural political or commercial ability acquired spiritual power or material riches (purchasing power) as cardinals and merchant princes. The cardinals, organized in a Catholic Church, were deeply vowed to holy poverty and humility; but they found these virtues insufficient without a backing of temporal power, and had to join the strife for control of the State, siding sometimes with the barons and sometimes with the king, but necessarily always against the heretics, an intellectual class not provided for in the system.

As for the merchant princes, they built cities which became petty States competing with both Church and King for power. Charles Martel, a great feudal soldier chieftain of the 8th century in France, virtually its king, had a short way with cities. He simply destroyed them as he destroyed dens of thieves. But later kings could not do without the money of the cities and had to tolerate them. With that money, the burgesses bought land and built cities on it. They hired armies of proletarians to fight for them against Crown, Church and peerage. They strove continually to abolish all the feudal conditions attached to property in land, and make it a commodity to be traded in like the portable products of their factories. Now trade in land was not much use to them without trade in labor, which was immovably attached to the feudal estates by serfage and "settlement," so that the serfs could not desert the estates and sell their labor (that is, sell themselves) to the merchant princes in the cities. Labor, like land, had to be made a trade commodity to be bought and sold like any other commodity. Thus the commercial class came into politics as the champions of personal freedom.

But it was only freedom in the abstract; for when the serfs escaped from the estates and church glebes and crowded into the cities they glutted the labor market and cheapened themselves to such a degree that poverty, excessive toil, and cruel subservience to the monopolists of capital at last forced them to become bitterly conscious of themselves under the general name of The Proletariat as a class for which there is no hope under either Feudalism or Capitalism. Slowly they began to organize themselves, first in trade unions fiercely persecuted by the landlords, the money lords, and the Church, and later in alliance with bodies of doctrinaire Socialists, both aiming at "The Dictatorship of the Proletariat," the Socialists providing the intellectual leadership and the trade unions the money.

This development achieved the miracle of uniting the city men and the landed gentry into a plutocracy standing solid against proletarianism. Marx met the challenge in 1861 by his slogan "Proletarians in all lands, unite," and declared The Class War for the abolition of private property with its unearned incomes, and the political organization of society as a Co-operative Commonwealth of workers.

The two Parties came to blows in 1871 in the sanguinary suppression of the Paris Commune by the plutocrats, followed fifty years later by the triumph of the proletariat in Russia in 1920. In 1939 in Spain the proletariat was defeated again. Meanwhile, however, the plutocrats, who had begun by furiously opposing any interference by the government in their moneymaking activities, had their minds changed on this point by the proletarian economists, who shewed that the fullest development of modern production was beyond the means of private enterprise and could be achieved only by the authority and financial resources of the State. If they could retain their control of the State and use it for their own enrichment instead of for the general good, thus combining socialist production with plutocratic distribution, they could make fortunes undreamt-of by their competitive forbears. A movement grew up to steal the thunder of the Socialists and substitute State Capitalism for private Capitalism whilst maintaining private property with all its privileges intact, and buying off the proletariat with doles and higher wages. This movement was called Fascism in Italy, and National Socialism (or, for short, Nazi-ism) in Germany, in both of which countries it captured and financed proletarian leaders and put them in command of the government: namely, Benito Mussolini and Adolf Hitler. In England and America, where it was much less lucid, it was called The New Deal and the New Order, thus securing a footing in both the democratic and plutocratic camps, but at the cost of a war with Italy and Germany for European hegemony; for when the new Fascist dictators invited the western States to join them in a grand attack on proletarian Russia they were rebuffed as dangerous and subversive revolutionaries, whereupon the two dictators desperately undertook jointly the subjection not only of Russia but of recalcitrant Britain and America as well. The only considerable ally they gained was Japan, leaving them in the position of having to fight both the Communists and the plutocracies in a paradoxical but terribly formidable combination to destroy them.

That is roughly the present historical situation. Now let us return
to tin tacks.

Though I am in theory a Communist, and by profession a playwright, I am in fact and in rank a landlord, and an absentee landlord
at that; for my estate is in Ireland. When I inherited it I was a responsible married adult; and had I lived under William he would
have expected me to administer justice between my tenants like a
cadi under a palm tree, to lead them to battle in his wars, to control
and direct the cultivation of my land, and to bear my share of
financing him in various ways. I dare say I could have done this at
least as well as some of his barons; but the first things I discovered
were that my estate did not belong to me at all, and that I had no
power to control it or direct its management. Instead of the title deeds
I received a bundle of mortgages and a packet of pawn tickets.

I was not greatly surprised: for my uncle, from whom I inherited,
had died shabby and almost indigent, the medical practice he had
purchased and once lived prosperously by in attendance on the
county squires having been ruined by the conversion of the country
houses and parks into rows of small houses inhabited by city clerks
with salaries of fifteen shillings a week. The wages of his one faithful
servant were seventeen years in arrear; and his gold watch had been
pawned, leaving him to count pulses by a silver one which he had
presented me with many years before, and was afterwards obliged to
borrow from me. I had been with him when he bought the gold
watch for £30. He had pawned it for £3–10–0, and for years clung
to the right to redeem it by borrowing the interest on that sum
from my mother.

Inheriting this right, I took the ticket to the pawnbroker and redeemed the watch. I then took it to a place in London where I
handed it in for sale by auction. It sold for £3–10–0, which I duly
got back less the auctioneer's commission. Having made no profit on
the transaction, and lost the commission, I accepted this result as
typical and dropped all the other pawn tickets into the waste-paper
basket. I then bought the estate which was supposed to be my property from the mortgagees by paying them off, and thus became in
effect myself the mortgagee and the real proprietor. This I could not
have done had I not had other resources unconnected with the estate.

But that is not the end of the story. I had never understood why
the estate had always been described as "a nice little one." The land
was no longer used for agriculture, but for residences and places of
business: in short, it had become part of a town. The lessees had sub-

let it, and the sublessees had done the same with it in bits and scraps to such an extent that though I could point to certain houses as being "on my property" I had no control over them nor any power to improve them in any way; but I could exact from this or that lessee or sublessee a head rent or quit rent or what not, representing only a fragment of the value of the site. There were only three houses really in my hands and under my control; and their condition was so ruinous that when I attempted to have one of them put into habitable repair it collapsed the moment the builders touched it. It had been mortgaged to its full value and beyond. My uncle could not afford to repair it, nor could the tenant; and it was not the mortgagee's business to meddle with it as long as his interest was paid.

In short, the property was a nice little one because I could do nothing with most of it except make its inhabitants pay me without letting me in for any of the contingent powers and responsibilities imposed by the feudal system. I am not a judge, ruler, custodian, soldier, civil servant, director, controller, nor anything else of the smallest use to the country. The powers of life and death which Henry II attached to my lands, and which he would have exercised over me if I had neglected or abused them (if he had been strong enough) have gone; but so also have the duties. Nothing remains but a nice little property, which I can sell or mortgage to any stranger who never lent a hand at the Battle of Hastings or the Strongbow raid nor can shew any evidence of caring two straws for the public weal.

This development of a feudal barony into a nice little property and of a responsible public servant into an irresponsible parasite became possible and inevitable when the feudal world of agriculture and chivalry became a world of commerce and competition.

Some of the big estates yet survive; and where great cities have grown up upon them their owners have become enormously rich, and still exercise powers which may be described as powers of life and death, as they can turn the farmer and his laborers into the street and replace them by sheep, by shopkeepers, by rich sportsmen addicted to deer shooting, or by anybody who will pay more for the use of their land than any farmer can afford. Thus we have the nice big properties as well as the nice little ones, the owners being equally irresponsible. They may be philanthropists more or less; but there is nothing in their social training to prevent them being luxuriously voracious, and everything to encourage them in that direction. It becomes demonstrably not only their individual interest but their social duty to rackrent their land and invest their capital at the highest interest obtainable.

This immunity from the moral law distinguishes property in land so effectively from ordinary property that lawyers call them real property and personal property. The distinction is supposed to have been abolished by the legislation of 1925, which made an end of feudal primogeniture; but it holds good all the same. The landlord is licensed to possess a gun as his personal property, but only on condition that though he may shoot certain animals and birds at certain seasons and under certain circumstances, he may not shoot me with it, whereas if I build up a big business on his land or make my home there he may take the whole business from me or turn me out at the end of my lease without the least regard to my interests.

That this state of things does not provoke a general massacre of landlords may seem surprising to those who grasp it in its enormity. It actually has from time to time. Before the Land Purchase Acts took effect in Ireland, Ribbon Lodges were formed by the Irish peasantry to shoot landlords as such. The French Revolution had for its cutting edge the burning of the great landlords' country houses (the chateaux) by the peasants. The same tactics had a main share in the establishment of the Irish Free State. In Russia the Bolshevik government established in 1917, abolished private property in land (real property) as an institution, and has made any attempt to exercise it a criminal offence.

But the system does not always work so unbearably as to drive people who have been brought up to regard it as honest to rebellion and assassination. When a landless man agrees to take a plot from a landlord at so much a year, he does so voluntarily on his own initiative, content if he can make the sort of living he is accustomed to out of it, and thinking it as natural to pay for his land as for his umbrella. He does not understand the land question, and often looks forward to becoming a land proprietor himself; for there is always land enough in the market for people with money enough to buy it. Even if the purchaser has not money enough he can still purchase land and borrow the price on mortgage.

The difference between buying an umbrella from its maker and leasing land from someone who found it readymade was no secret among the political economists. Revolting peasants could only sing "When Adam delved and Eve span Where was then the gentle man?" But the educated French Physiocrats went into the matter scientifically. French reformers before the Revolution, notably the father of Mirabeau, were proposing the abolition of taxes on commodities, and the substitution of a single tax on land as a means of nationalizing rent. This proposal was laughed out of countenance by Voltaire, who pointed out that it would leave the rent of capital untouched, and that whilst the landlord would starve the banker would be richer than ever. The proposal was, however, revived a century later with extraordinary eloquence by the American Henry George, whose volume entitled Progress and Poverty had a wide circulation, and incidentally drew my attention to the subject. But by that time the land question had developed into a capital question of such magnitude that Voltaire's criticism was stronger than ever; for it was evident that if the State confiscated rent without being prepared to employ it instantly as capital in industry, production would cease and the country be starved. Consequently a movement had begun, called Socialism, advocating the organization of industry by the State for the benefit of the whole people. When this alternative to Capitalism appeared, the official economists became much less candid on the subject of rent.

Meanwhile, a Frenchman had written an essay entitled "What is Property? It is Theft." Easygoing people said "How silly!" Serious people said "How wicked! How dishonest!" But the Frenchman (named Proudhon) was neither silly nor dishonest. He had analysed the situation, and discovered that the landlord and capitalist, in as much as they consume without producing, inflict precisely the same injury on the community as a thief does. That great and intensely respectable Englishman John Ruskin put the same point when he reminded us that there are only three possible ways of making a living: 1, working, 2, begging, 3, stealing.

Are our landlords therefore thieves? William Morris, the greatest of our English Communists, replied bluntly "Yes: damned thieves. They live by robbing the poor." But De Quincey, the greatest Tory wit, called the landlords country gentlemen, adding "Who more worthy?" Marx called them bourgeoisie, which is now out of date, as the poorer bourgeoisie has been proletarianized by big business, and the richer absorbed by the plutocracy. Cairnes, a leading English economist, described them as "drones in the hive." For my own part I do not call myself a thief. My intentions are not dishonest; and I did not institute, nor have I any power to change, the legalized system under which I became a landlord whether I liked it or not; but I have devoted all my political life to rubbing in the aforesaid fact that I inflict on my tenants exactly the same economic injury as a burglar, pickpocket, shoplifter, highwayman, or any other sort of robber. I am not a robber baron because I am not a baron; but a robber I certainly am in effect; for I make my tenants yield up to me a part of their hardearned incomes without doing them, or having ever done them, any service whatever. That this is not my fault, and has been to some extent my misfortune, does not make their rents any easier to pay. That in paying off the mortgagees I bought my powers of exploitation with hard cash is equally irrelevant: the burglar has to pay for his jemmy.

How, then, is the nation to get rid of me? To shoot me, as the late Lord Leitrim's tenants got rid of him, would only substitute my next of kin for myself in the proprietorship. For the State or the municipality to seize my land and throw me into the street would need a Bolshevik revolution to legalize it, and a new public department for the management of all the estates in the country ready in full working order to take over from me. For the first rule in transferring private property to public property is, obviously, that the Government shall not confiscate any item of property, in land or capital, that it is not ready to put to immediate use as productively as before. If a field is not cultivated it will not only grow thistles but spread them to the neighboring cultivated fields.

The solution in my separate single case is simple enough. As soon as the municipality of the city in which my property is situated needs my land for, say, an electric power station, for public baths, for schools, for a tramway terminus, for the police or the fire brigade, for a new town hall, post office, labor exchange, or what not, all it need do is to purchase it from me at its rateable value, and obtain the price by levying a rate on all the rateable values in the city including my own. Thus my bit of land would become public property at the expense of the whole body of landlords, I bearing no more than my fair share of the expropriation instead of being ruined by it whilst my fellow landlords get off scot free. There would be nothing unusual about the transaction: people are accustomed to the sale and purchase of land and to rates varying by a penny or so in the pound from year to year. I would have to find some new investment for the purchase money, or, were I an occupier, a new house to live in or trade in; but the public would not bother about that: it happens to somebody every day.

This apparently customary transaction need only be repeated often enough to transfer all the land of the town from private to public ownership and exterminate the local landlords as such painlessly. It

is equally possible as between the national government and the
holders of great estates. Near by where I live, a private company
purchased such an estate and built a Garden City on it. Its cost was
not raised by a public rate: it was subscribed by private speculators.
I was one of them, and am accordingly now a British landlord as well
as an Irish one. But if the government should conclude at any future
time that it can make a better use of the city for the national welfare
than I and my fellow shareholders are making of it for our private
profit, it can easily buy it from us and obtain the money by a tax on
the incomes of all the landlords in the country. Here again the transaction has only to be repeated often enough to effect the complete
nationalization of the land without departing from the usual routine
of business, without revolutionary legislation, and without mention
of the word Nationalization, or the word Compensation, which is
abhorrent to doctrinaire nationalizers.

The only alternative legal process is the resumption of the land by
the King under a vestige of feudal law which still remains, though in
abeyance and mostly forgotten. The last King to exercise it to any
considerable degree was Henry the Fifth five hundred years ago.
William the Third made some use of it two hundred and fifty years
ago. But it rests on the assumption that the King is a feudal king,
which lost all its old correspondence to contemporary facts in 1649.
And in most of the European countries today, and throughout
America, north and south, there is no king.

The revolutionary alternative is to declare the land public property and behead all the landlords who do not leave the country in
time, as was done in the French Revolution in the eighteenth century, or shoot the few who actively object, and leave the rest to shift
for themselves as best they can with their incomes cut off and their
houses taken from them, as in Russia in 1917. But in both instances
the new governments established by the revolution could do nothing
with the agricultural land but divide it between the peasants, few of
whom were capable of developing its potential productiveness. The
Russian farmers who made money on their plots and ploughed with
their own horses, employing other peasants hired as laborers, were
denounced as "kulaks" and thrown out of their farms as exploiters
and profiteers, with the result that their farms went to waste and
ruin. The Soviet Government soon had to hunt up the derelict
kulaks and replace them on their farms as violently as they had
expelled them. But they were so few that there were still about
ninety miserably cultivated plots with their owners living on them

in wood cabins with room enough for one lousy family bed, one stove, and a strip of mud floor, to every ten farms cultivated up to kulak standard, which was still far below the possibilities. And both ordinary peasants and kulaks, finding that when they produced enough to have some money to spare the Soviet Government took it in taxes which were really an economic rent, just like the old landlords, killed their horses and cattle and destroyed their seeds rather than have the Government distrain upon these for taxes. The Cossacks actually produced artificial famines in this way and had to be left to starve in consequence.

The Soviet Government finally had to get rid of peasant proprietors, competent and incompetent alike, and substitute collective farms and garden cities, which were an immediate and enormous success. With such an object lesson before the eyes of the world there is clearly no excuse for persistence in the old plan of leaving our agriculture in the hands of uneducated peasants and miseducated country gentlemen, all competing instead of co-operating, and each expected to be his own agricultural chemist, live stock biologist, financier, statistician, practical man of business and accountant: in short, such a paragon of versatility combined in one person with the Admirable Crichton as was never imagined by the wildest romancer. Farming is staff work, not individual work; and no country gentleman or yeoman or peasant can be a staff in himself, though on a collective farm staffs are a matter of course.

The economic future of the land is with collective farms and garden cities; and no person whose notion of land reform is to turn all the crude agricultural estates into little peasant properties and leave cities as they are (there are many such simpletons) should be allowed to meddle with politics in any capacity. It is however psychologically advisable to plan collective farms and garden cities in such a fashion that every house should have attached to it a private plot to play in or grow flowers and vegetables, or keep one's own cow or what not?

This concession to privacy has been found necessary in the U.S.S.R. in spite of the success of the collective farms. It provides for domesticity, which is not the same thing as agriculture, though at present the farmhouse must serve most incongruously as dwelling house; and workers are expected to live in mills, in forges, over their shops, and in some countries actually in factories. This is an intolerable state of things. The land question is one of private life as well as economic productive life. Private life produces babies, who are more vitally important than crops and factory output. Housekeeping is an indispensable industry. No doubt family habits will be greatly modified as communal arrangements prove more convenient than private ones. For example, all the objections to the farmer having to dwell in his farmhouse, the miller in his mill, and the operative in his factory, apply equally to the cook having to live in her kitchen and the scullery maid in her scullery. The kitchen range and the washing-up sink will go the way of the spinning wheel and the hand loom; and clubs and restaurants, hotels and hostels, hospitals and schools, will increase real privacy as fast as they increase communal organization.

Parentage, a very onerous industry, has already for the greater part shifted from the actual fathers and mothers at home to the teaching staff in the school: that is, from the amateur to the professional.

Socialists are so preoccupied with changes in this direction that they are apt to overlook the contrary current. When we discuss the Industrial Revolution we think of how water power and steam power abolished the handloom and drove the proletariat out of the cottages into the factories, where division of labor made it impossible for any worker to learn more than a moment of the long process of collecting raw material, manufacturing it, and marketing the result. This played the very devil with the laboring classes: in the factory towns they became robots with the feelings of human beings. They lived in pestilential slums; and their children died like flies whilst the riches and luxury of the landlords and capitalists increased "by leaps and bounds" as Gladstone expressed it at the Exchequer. It seemed that mankind must always work in factories and mills and mines because the power that drove the spinning jenny and the steam hammer could not be distributed, and was beyond the means of anyone but capitalists.

But we now know that water power and steam power can be converted into electric power and distributed from house to house like water or gas, and used in a cottage by a child to light itself to bed or by a craftsman to harness Niagara to his machine tools. I remember using tallow candles which needed trimming with a scissors called a snuffers to light me to bed, and smelly oil burners to read by in the evenings. I have had a tooth cavity scraped out with a spike. I have lived to have my teeth (when I had any) drilled by electricity, my hair cut by electricity, my rooms not only lighted but swept and dusted by electricity turned on from a tap in the wall.

The first statesman to see more in this than a nine days wonder was the Russian Lenin. He saw that the way to revolutionize Russia was to electrify Russia; and as fast as the electrification could be effected Russian steppes and Asiatic deserts became flourishing slumless civilized cities, and her wild tribesmen cultivated artisans.

Here again the western world thought only of the huge electric enterprises of the U.S.S.R., of the Dnieper dam, of the new canals, of the factories built of steel and glass turning out scores of tractors every day: all the work of regimented bodies of workers under direction and discipline. Until the classic investigation by the Sidney Webbs was published we did not know, and even then did not notice that the individual craftsman, the smith, the cabinet-maker, the potter, the weaver, was rising from the dead in Russia under the Socialism which was supposed to be extinguishing him. What we did notice was that housekeeping with mechanized kitchens and vacuum cleaners gave the lie to the old statement that "a woman's work is never done" and thereby altered that balance between home life and communal life which had turned so strongly against privacy under the yoke of capitalism.

Consequently no greater mistake can be made by a modern states-man than to let himself be obsessed by the collective side of the land question. Important as that is, Wayland the smith, working "for his own hand" and settling his accounts with the State through the tax collector only, may come to be a much bigger factor in politics than the bureaucrat in a totalitarian State factory to whose rule the in-corrigibly individualistic Englishman looks forward with so much misgiving.

My own misgivings are in the opposite direction. My craft of playwright can be exercised singlehanded on a desert island; and the effect is that authors are harder to organize even for their own pro-tection than hogs. On paper they are models of every virtue: in business they are inveterate anarchists, quarrelsome, sentimental, un-able to debate without losing their tempers, and treating differences from their opinion as personal insults. Journalism, being a social activity, civilizes them; but the romancers who sit alone and arrange the world out of their own heads, uncontradicted and unedited, never, unless they have a strong sense of humor, learn how to live in political society, and have to be indulged by statesmen as visitors from another world. The explanation seems to be that freedom from economic pressure makes room for an excessive development of in-dividuality in people who have any individuality to develop and are not, like soldiers, specially trained not to think for themselves.

Authors are not free from pecuniary cares, very far from it; but nobody who had any regard for his pecuniary interests would adopt
literature as a profession. There are religious orders in which the rule
is so completely monastic that every penny the members would own
as laymen belongs to the order. They may not even choose the
fashion of the clothes they wear. But their daily bread is secure; and
wherever they go they are entitled to at least three days hospitality
from the order. I asked a friend of mine who belonged to such an
order what bad effects, if any, it had on its votaries. He thought a
moment, and said "Well, it develops one's individuality so frightfully that at forty years of age every member is a confirmed crank."
It will be interesting to see whether Communism will change the
Russians into a nation of robots or a nation of cranks.

Finally I must insist that the crux of the land question is the classical theory of Economic Rent, dubbed by Ferdinand Lassalle the
Iron Law of Wages. Like the roundness of the earth it is unfortunately not obvious. It is so opposed to moral common sense and so
complicated mathematically, that I could find fifty experts in the
tensor calculus more easily than five statesmen who think of the land
question habitually in terms of the law of rent. It is the *pons asinorum*
of economic mathematics. Our politicians cannot draw their conclusions from it any more than Shakespear could draw his from the okapi
or the axolotl: they simply do not know of its existence. Karl Marx,
by an absurd reference to it in Das Kapital, proved that he did not
understand it. John Ruskin, after a very promising beginning as an
economist by his contrast of exchange values with human values,
was stopped dead by it. Yet Marx and Ruskin had more brains and
keener interest in social questions than three or four average Cabinets or three or four million average voters. It is the rock on which
Liberal Cobdenism has been broken and Socialism built in the
struggle between plutocracy and democracy. We are in the thick of
that struggle at present; and as it is a necessary part of my business
to advertize my own writings I am tempted to add that nobody who
has not read my paper on the Economic Basis of Socialism in Fabian
Essays should be allowed to write, speak, vote or agitate politically
in any fashion in this unhappy country.

Those who suspect that the Iron Law is an invention of my own
to bolster up socialism can qualify themselves in the orthodox
academic manner by mastering, for the theory of rent, Ricardo's
Principles of Political Economy and Taxation, written before
Socialism had found a name in England, and, for the cognate theory

of exchange value, the Theory of Political Economy by Stanley Jevons, which corrected the mistake of Adam Smith, Ricardo and Karl Marx on this subject.

CHAPTER III

THE BRITISH PARTY SYSTEM

PRACTICALLY nobody in these islands understands the Party System. Britons do not know its history. They believe that it is founded in human nature and therefore indestructible and eternal. When I point out that it does not exist in our municipalities they think that I am ignorant or crazy, and assure me that there are Conservative parties and Progressive parties in the municipal councils and corporations "just the same as" in Parliament, and always will be by the immutable law of political human nature.

What are the facts? Let me put them in the form of a little historical drama, as that comes easiest to me and is the most amusing.

Scene: Althorp, the residence of the Spencers, Earls of Sunderland. Present King William the Third, aged 45, of glorious pious and immortal memory, and his host Robert Spencer, the second Earl, ten years older, famous even at the courts of Charles II and James II for his complete unscrupulousness and political ingenuity. Period 1695.

ROBERT. Your Majesty has done me a tremendous honor in visiting my humble residence. As I cannot pretend to have deserved it I apprehend that there is some way in which I can be of service to your Majesty.

WILLIAM. There is. I am at my wits' end. I want advice. I am expected to save the Protestant religion in Europe from the Scarlet Woman of Rome. I am expected to save your country and my own country from the Bourbons. I am expected to do everything for everybody. And I am expected to do it all without money and without a standing army. I cannot plan my campaigns for a year ahead because this damnable British Parliament, which is elected to govern England, only wants what all Englishmen want: that is, not to be governed at all. It may leave me at any moment without a penny and without a soldier. France's best general, who has won all her battles for her, has just died and left King Louis in the hollow of my hand. And this is the moment your parliament chooses to threaten me with a peace. It is intolerable. Damn your parliament! I will go back to Amsterdam: better be a real Stadtholder than a sham king. They want liberty, these pigheaded squires and knights of the shire. Well, let them have their liberty: liberty to be broken on the wheel to please the Pope, liberty to be the vassals of France, liberty to go to the devil their own way and not be interfered with by any king or council. I shall fling the crown in their faces and shake the dust of England off my feet unless you can shew me a way of making Parliament do what I tell it to do.

ROBERT. I cannot do that; but I can shew you a way to prevent Parliament from doing anything at all except vote supplies and stave off the next election as long as it can.

WILLIAM. Can you? The only supplies I care about are supplies of men and money to save the Protestant north from that fat Bourbon bigot. If I cannot have them your crown is no use to me. You can have James back again. You know where to find him: in Louis' pocket. I daresay you are in correspondence with him, double-faced schemer that you are.

ROBERT. I am what the times have made me; and I keep in correspondence with everybody: one never knows what will happen next. But I wish I could get your Majesty's mind off the Protestant north and the army for a moment. I wish I could convince you that what you have to fight here is not King Louis, but the British Parliament.

WILLIAM. Well, do I not know it? Am I not telling you so?

ROBERT. Keep to that, your Majesty. Is it agreed, too, that I am a schemer?

WILLIAM. Oh, it is: it is: by God it is!

ROBERT. Would your Majesty condescend so far as to say, a fairly successful schemer?

WILLIAM. A devilishly subtle one, I should say. What then?

ROBERT. I have a scheme for dealing with Parliament, though I have never yet found a king subtle enough to understand it.

WILLIAM. Try me.

ROBERT. You, sir, are the last king on earth to understand it. But I will lay it at your royal feet. Just now you choose your ministers on their merits and capacities without regard to their parties, a Whig here, a Tory there, each in his department which you call his Cabinet, and the assembly of them forming your council, which may be called *your* Cabinet.

WILLIAM. Just so. What fault have you to find with that?

ROBERT. My advice to your Majesty is that in future you choose all your ministers from the same party, and that this party shall always be the party which has a majority in the House of Commons.

WILLIAM. You are mad. Who ever heard of such a thing?

ROBERT. All things must have a beginning, sir. Think it over.

WILLIAM. I am thinking it over. And I remember what you have forgotten.

ROBERT. What is that, your Majesty?

WILLIAM. That the majority in the House of Commons at present is a Whig majority.

ROBERT. I have not forgotten it, sir. You must at once get rid of all your Tory ministers and replace them by Whigs.

WILLIAM. But, man alive, I am a Tory. Are you out of your senses?

ROBERT. Some day the Tories will have a majority and will defeat the Whig government on some measure. You will then immediately dissolve Parliament; and when the Tories come back from the general election with a majority you will choose Tory ministers only.

WILLIAM. But what is the purpose of this absurdity? You talk as coolly as if you were talking sense. Why are you talking nonsense?

ROBERT. If your Majesty will only deign to do what I advise, I pledge my word—

WILLIAM [*sceptically*]. Hmm!

ROBERT. Pardon: I should have said I pledge my reputation as a schemer. Well, I pledge it that from the moment when your Majesty adopts this plan no member of the House of Commons will ever again vote according to his principles or his convictions or his judgment or his religion or any other of his fancies. The people will think that he is voting on toleration, on peace or war, on whether the crown shall go to the elector of Hanover if your sister-in-law's children continue to die, on the enclosure of commons or billeting or the window tax or what not; but the real question on which he will always be voting is whether or no his party shall remain in office or he himself have to spend half his property on another election with the chance of losing his seat if his opponent has a few thousand pounds more to spend than he.

WILLIAM. Dont be a fool, Robert. I should be the slave of the majority no matter how they voted. And what has all this to do with the army and the money to pay for it?

ROBERT. There would be only one way of voting about the war or about anything; and you could always count on it. No majority,

Whig or Tory, dare vote for surrender to our natural enemies the French, or to the Pope.

WILLIAM. The Pope is on my side.

ROBERT. Fortunately only a few of us know that curious fact. Your best card in England is always No Popery.

WILLIAM. You are laying a trap for me. You want to make the majority in the Commons the real ruler and make the monarch a puppet. And as the majority is always led by the nose by some ambitious schemer with the gift of the gab like yourself, he would be able to dictate to me as if he were the king and I a nobody.

ROBERT. I shall never be a dictator while you live, because you, sir, will never be a nobody. But I give you this further pledge. That if you do as I advise, you will have nothing to fear from the boldest and ablest adventurer, were he Cromwell himself, or Lilburne the Leveller. He will spend half his life and most of his means in getting into Parliament; and when he at last arrives there he will have no time to think of anything but how to get into your Majesty's Cabinet. When he intrigues his way to the top of that, he will be a master of the Party game and of nothing else. He will feed out of your Majesty's hand. And the people will imagine they are free because they have a parliament. Then you can fight all Europe all the time to your heart's content.

WILLIAM. I dont understand it and dont believe it. But as I cannot go on as at present, not knowing where my next regiment or my next penny is to come from, I will try your plan until I have driven Louis back to his pigstye. And if the plan fails I will have your head off by hook or crook.

ROBERT. You shall, sir. It has been on my weary shoulders too long.

Twentyfive years elapse. William and Sunderland, having died in the same year, have been eighteen years in their coffins. Queen Anne is dead; and George the First is King. Sunderland's son Charles, aged 45, is a member of the Whig Government. Robert Walpole, aged 44, though a notable Whig Parliamentarian, leads the Opposition to the Peerage Bill. As it happens, they meet one morning in St. James's Park, where they are taking the air. Walpole is inclined to pass on with a wave of the hand; but Sunderland is determined to engage him in conversation and will not be shaken off. After the usual commonplaces he comes to his point.

SUNDERLAND. I wish I could have your support for this Peerage Bill of mine. Frankly, I fear you will defeat me if you oppose it. Why not come to my aid? It is not a Party question: we are all

Whigs, and all equally interested in it.

WALPOLE. How do you make that out?

SUNDERLAND. Well, is it not as plain as a pikestaff? We Whigs are above all Parliament men: to us British liberty means the supremacy of Parliament. Parliament has two rival powers to fear: the king and the voting mob. My sainted father, a grain or two of whose political genius I may claim to have inherited, rescued us from the tyranny of the mob by the Party System. He made you what you are: the greatest Party leader in the world: you owe your eminence to his invention.

WALPOLE. It costs a lot of money. Every man has his price.

SUNDERLAND. All the more reason for making sure of the cash for us, and not for the mob. But what about Parliament's other rival, the King?

WALPOLE. The king question was settled seventyone years ago.

SUNDERLAND. Nay, my dear Walpole, you cannot kill kingship with a single chop of the axe in Whitehall. The Restoration brought back the House of Lords, and the King's power to pack it by making as many new peers as he pleased at any moment. The sole purpose of the Peerage Bill is to destroy that power. It will make it impossible for the king ever to make a single peer in excess of the present number. Surely you agree.

WALPOLE. Do I? I think not. Your sainted father persuaded King William that the Party System would give him the control of Parliament. But it really gave the parliamentary majority the control of the king. That ought to suit you very well, because you have the control of the majority until I get it back again, as I shall do when I defeat your Bill.

SUNDERLAND. But why defeat us on this Bill, which is as much in your interest as in mine? You can choose some other issue.

WALPOLE. It is not as much in my interest as in yours. You are a peer: I am a commoner. You want to make the Lords supreme by breaking the king's power over them. I want the king to keep his power over the Lords, and the Commons to keep its power over the King. I can see through and through your game. I have English brains, not Dutch ones.

SUNDERLAND. You are too clever for me, I see. But consider. You are a Commoner; but you will not always be a Commoner. You will soon be one of us. You know there is an earldom waiting for you to stretch out your hand and take it.

WALPOLE. Yes, provided the King keeps his power to make me an earl. Your Bill might deprive him of that power.

SUNDERLAND. Pooh! There is always a vacancy.

WALPOLE. Even so, an earldom would be the end of me. I do not look forward to being kicked upstairs. The House of Lords is the springboard from which you plunged into politics at 21. For me it is the shelf on which I shall be laid by at three score and ten.

SUNDERLAND. That may be so in your personal case. But take the larger view. Consider the interests of the country. The Upper House, with all its faults, stands between England and the mob of rich commercial upstarts who want to make money out of her: money, money and still more money. You are not an upstart: you are a country gentleman.

WALPOLE. Yes; and you are up to the neck in this commercial South Sea madness. It will be your ruin. I warn you: it will be the end of you politically within a year from now.

SUNDERLAND. You are impossible. [Brusquely] Good morning. [He walks quickly away, leaving Walpole to finish his walk alone].

Had the third earl of Sunderland been able to humbug British Walpole as successfully as his father humbugged Dutch William, the Reform Act of 1832 might not have got through without a civil war; and when the new Labor Party took office a century later it might have been left without representation in the Lords. As it is, the Lords have always finally to give way under the threat of new creations. The last word is with the Commons: in fact with the plutocracy. And that is how the matter stands at present.

For vivid sketches of what the Party System comes to in practice nowadays, turn to the description of it in a novel entitled Bleak House, and more thoroughly in another entitled Little Dorrit, both written by Charles Dickens, ex-reporter in the gallery of the House of Commons and on the hustings. Then study the parliamentary experiences of scientific publicists like John Stuart Mill and Sidney Webb, and the careers of Charles Bradlaugh, Keir Hardie, Ramsay MacDonald, and all the other intransigents who made their way into Parliament and were extinguished there. Compare the sterility of Parliament in everything but postprandial oratory with the extension of municipal socialism by the municipalities, where there are no Cabinets, no royal selection, no general elections except at immovably fixed dates: in short, no possibility of the Party System.

Nobody who does not see through Sunderland's trick and understand its history should be trusted with any parliamentary vote or function, or even allowed to mention Democracy in public.

This lands us in the unexpected conclusion that government by Parliaments modelled on the British Party System, far from being a guarantee of liberty and enlightened progress, must be ruthlessly discarded in the very fullest agreement with Oliver Cromwell, Charles Dickens, John Ruskin, Thomas Carlyle, Adolf Hitler, Pilsudski, Benito Mussolini, Stalin, and everyone else who has tried to govern efficiently and incorruptly by it, or who has studied its operation with a knowledge of its history and that of the Industrial Revolution. Contrast what it has done with what an efficient and entirely public spirited government might and should have done during the two centuries of its deplorable existence, or with what the Russian Soviet government has done in twenty years, and all our Whig Macaulayism drops dead before the facts.

Nevertheless the parliamentary growth must not be pulled up by the roots. Stalin and Hitler, the most thoroughgoing disciples of Cromwell and Dickens in this matter, are also the most convinced that government can make no great change until a long propaganda and inculcation of its principles and hopes has persuaded the mass of the people, if not to understand them critically, at least to follow the flags and echo the catchwords of its advocates. A club of political philosophers can never become a government without years of contact with the commonalty through books, pamphlets, and above all, as Hitler maintains, by speeches at public meetings, now enormously reinforced by broadcast talks from the studio to the fireside. That was how the Bolsheviks, beginning as a Marxist club, became the Communist government in Russia through the support of the peasants and peasant soldiers, neither of them Communists, but all more or less talked and pamphleteered and journalized into believing that the Bolsheviks were the boys to give them land and peace. In this way, too, Adolf Hitler became an autocrat in Germany, politically supported by millions of Germans whom he had talked and written into believing that he was, in fact, Messiah. If government is to be effective it must be popular with the governed and generally acceptable. It must have Vogue. The vogue may be unintelligent and ignorantly idolatrous; but it must exist and be worked up by agitation.

I do not mean that Mr and Mrs Everybody should be allowed to elect Mr and Mrs Anybody as rulers, though our democratic politicians still seem to think so. Since women were enfranchised we have tried this plan and found that it produces not only stagnant

Conservatism but retrogression checked only by the common sense of the plutocrats it idolizes. Yet Parliament must survive as a congress of plaintive and plangent Anybodies with unlimited license to complain, to criticize, to denounce, to demand, to suggest, to supply and discuss firsthand information, to move resolutions and take a vote on them: in short, to keep the Government abreast of public sentiment.

This is very much what parliaments and congresses do at present. In the British House of Commons for instance, when a war, forcing the Parties to coalesce, suspends the Party System, the backbenchers on both sides are unmuzzled and become useful. Outside parliament Nationalist non-party public meetings and demonstrations of all sorts are convened and organized by Mr Anybody-who-Can; and his right to such activities, and to the use of the streets and public places for them, should be jealously preserved; for if grievances and desires are not made known fairly vociferously ("ventilated"), the Government cannot be expected to remedy and consider them. They provide a sounding board for the Initiative which seethes continually in the unofficial mass of citizens. The wisest rulers are not always the most inventive: they are mostly old enough to have shot their bolts inventively and lost their taste for novelty. The young men must have a platform to shout from; for a government must know what the young Calvins, Napoleons, Hitlers, and Ataturks have to say, and how far they are converting the public or being hissed by it.

Without such contact the ruling sages may get dangerously out of touch with the spirit of the age.

But these assemblies of agitators and petitioners must not be legislators. Such plausible pseudo-democratic devices as the legislative Initiative and Referendum, which offer Mr and Mrs Everyman a direct immediate power to bind and loose, must be ruled out, because even when they know exactly what they want they do not know how to get it, just as they may want a motor car, but cannot make the blue print which the engineer must have before he can construct one for them. Legislation must be by "the quality," not by the mob.

When using such convenient terms as the quality and the mob it must never be forgotten that they do not indicate two classes of entirely different persons. They are the same persons. In literature and drama, for instance, I belong to the quality. In mathematics, athletics, mechanics, I am one of the mob, and not only accept and obey authority but claim a neighborly right to be told what to do

by those who know better than I do. The best of us is nine hundred
and ninetynine per cent mob and one per cent quality; and the vulgar ailment called Swelled Head afflicts only those whose minds are
so preoccupied with the few things they know that there is no room
left for the innumerable things they dont know. I do some things
very well; but my self-esteem is crushed by the multitude of things
at which I am a hopeless duffer. In championing the rights of the
mob I champion my own.

Who is to choose and appoint the quality? At present the King is
supposed to where there is a king, or the President where there is a
president; but nobody believes that the King of Italy had any real
alternative when he chose Benito Mussolini, Field-Marshal Hinden-
burg when he chose ex-corporal Hitler, or Queen Victoria when she
chose Palmerston or Gladstone. Even the United States President,
who has more freedom to choose than any king because he is himself chosen by plebiscite, cannot choose Mr Anybody. He must
choose among the prominent; and prominence is won by self-
assertion taking advantage of favorable circumstances and the
chapter of accidents; so that we may say that our rulers are partly
self-chosen and partly the result of Darwinian natural selection: that
is, of pure luck. In this way we sometimes hit on great leaders like
Lincoln, Brigham Young, Ferdinand Lassalle, or Kemal Ataturk (to
say nothing of living examples) all of whom were self-asserted. They
gained their following through the idolatry produced by the force
of their personalities rather than by their wisdom; for many energetic and ambitious persons have obtained prominence and power
with very little wisdom.

What about the periods, sometimes very long ones, during which
no such leaders arise, and the business of the State has nevertheless
to be carried on without a moment's pause? Such government is not
impossible under feudalism, where authority is legally hereditary,
nor under plutocracy where it is virtually hereditary to a great
extent. Under both, dunderheads are not only not excluded but very
frequently selected as rulers. When they have an established system,
which we call a Constitution, to work to, they can make shift for
long periods without wreckage. But the fundamental answer is that
Nature does as a matter of fact constantly supply a sufficient percentage of persons with the requisite mental power. The problem is
how to select the capable; for the capable are always there. In ancient Rome the Antonine emperors chose their successors, with much
better results than under succession by heredity. But except under

conditions of considerable activity which bring rulers to the test of battle the ablest successor is not always obvious. Even so able a ruler as Cromwell could think of nobody better than his son to succeed him as Lord Protector; and the result was a complete and almost instantaneous failure. Napoleon's attempt to found a Bonapartist dynasty was a ludicrous failure. A dynasty may select a dynasty, as when the Welsh Tudors selected the Scottish Stuarts to govern England; but the fourth Stuart king was a simpleton, and was ousted by a Dutchman who married his daughter.

We must get rid of the tradition of heredity altogether. We have only to study the lives, not of "great men," but of their fathers, mothers, sons, and daughters, to learn that political ability is inherited in such infinitesimal instalments that an extraordinary parent may have very ordinary children, and so capriciously that a very ordinary couple produce a genius. In a democracy we should all start from zero, no matter who or what our relatives. Our present notions are disordered and inconsistent. A proposal to make the Presidency of the United States of America hereditary would shock the Americans; yet they take it as a matter of course that the management of a business should descend from father to son. We should not dream of allowing the King to dictate what the nation shall do ten years after his death; yet we allow private citizens to make fantastic, unjust, bigoted, or even spitefully wicked disposals of their possessions after their deaths by will, and give these wills the force of law. But we do not make a man a judge because his father was a judge, nor give him a diploma as a qualified surgeon because his father had one, nor put him in command of the army because his father was a field-marshal. A century ago army officers (Burgoyne and Wellington for instance) claimed promotion as a purchasable privilege of their rank in the aristocracy, and would have regarded a claim based on successful services as the act of a cad; but today any other claim would be ridiculed as the pretension of a snob. These inconsistencies and contradictions are the accidents of an imperfectly organized society in which people have to be allowed to do what they please with their property when there is no other control over it. As social organization progresses and develops, and transactions that are now private become more and more public affairs, conditions now undreamt-of will be attached to our personal activities and liberties. We shall soon get used to them; and meanwhile, if we dont like them we must lump them.

Since we must give authority to those who are capable of it if we are to save civilization, our pseudo-democratic tradition of government by committees and their majorities brings us up sharply against the fact that majority rule is unnatural because capable rulers are always a minority, though, given fair play, Nature produces enough of them to give the ruled their choice. It also destroys responsibility. A minister of State who accepts and undertakes a public duty on the understanding that if he fails he will be impeached and possibly shot, or at least discharged and discredited, is a responsible minister. But a minister who has only to do what he can persuade a majority in Parliament or in committee to agree to has no responsibility; and neither has anyone else, because majorities cannot be shot except by their own consent, nor can they be demoted, as they have no rank.

One of the best descriptions of this no-thoroughfare is to be found in the autobiography of Adolf Hitler entitled Mein Kampf. When he began his work of organizing National Socialism in Germany in 1919 at the age of 30 he found himself a member of a committee of six nobodies with hardly a spare shilling in their collective treasury. Being entirely irresponsible they could do nothing but talk to one another. Adolf's six years training as a soldier had taught him that bodies of men cannot be made effectively active without authority combined with responsibility, neither of which is possible under majority government: a fact we conceal from ourselves by the simple and familiar expedient of calling it responsible government instead of irresponsible government. The Führer was not imposed on by this sort of humbug: hard experience and his ability to learn from experience had taught him better. When he was made chairman of a committee he stayed away from the committee meetings and acted while the rest talked. When he became head of the movement on his personal merits (or demerits if you dislike him) and had to appoint a staff, he gave his officers military authority and held them militarily responsible for their use of it. When he had risen in fourteen years by this method from being an obscure last recruit to a little knot of six persons to being the official leader of sixty millions, and Chancellor for life of the German realm, he kept up his vocal propaganda by occasionally making speeches through the microphone to the sixty millions from the Reichstag; but the Reichstag did not govern: the authority and responsibility were the Führer's; and in his hands and on his head were real authority and responsibility. After five years of this the sixty millions still adored him and made him Commander-in-Chief of their fighting forces.

Let us take this living contemporary instance as the extreme to which authority and responsibility can be pushed in practice. The opposite extreme is represented by the British Parliament in peace time, when authority, responsibility, and activity are reduced to the minimum, and a fortnight's work takes about thirty years unless a war forces Parliament to abandon the Party System, and make desperate efforts to do thirty years work in a fortnight. Our problem is to find the most eligible degree between these two extremes.

We must reject the Hitler plan because, though it works successfully in the army, it gives one man more authority and responsibility than one man can bear. If he is weak he is corrupted by his power: if he is strong he is demented by it, and, like Alexander, Hitler, and Napoleon, tries to add the world to his dominions, thus becoming at worst a scourge and a tyrant and at best an explorer and adventurer like Julius Caesar or William the Conqueror. The more conquests and adventures and social experiments he undertakes the more he has to delegate and distribute his authority for lack of time to be everywhere and attend to everything. His sub-governors get corrupted or demented in their degree; and finally the system, becoming intolerable, provokes a revolution or a *laisser-faire* reaction towards anarchy, whether the supreme boss is Cromwell, Louis XIV, the Kaiser, or Herr Hitler. The brooms sweep clean when they are new; but when they are spoiled or worn-out the place becomes an Augean stable.

What safeguards are available against these contingencies? Obviously to begin with, election and re-election of rulers for sufficiently short periods to keep them conscious of their dependence on the submissive approval of their subjects. Take the case of the President of the United States of North America! Although his office was brought into existence by a successful revolution against the tyranny of the British Government personified in King George III, he was, on Hitlerian principles, given more absolute authority than King George ever possessed. No defeat in committee or Congress can remove him. But his authority lasts only four years. Byron's description of George III as "a poor blind mad and despised old king" can never apply to him. If any Act of his is unconstitutional there is an appeal against it to the Supreme Court. In certain matters he has to obtain the consent of at least two thirds of the senate, which must for instance approve his choice of the secretaries who form his council. The separate States of the Union have Governors who are similarly authorized and restricted, similarly responsible and parliament-ridden, trusted and mistrusted, free in respect of religion, sex and color, and limited by age and nationality, place and length of residence. Altogether a queer jumble of precautions against tyranny with measures to provide the security of law and order.

In future we shall have to put more brains into our Constitution making. We must throw our idolization of Parliament and our slogans about British and American liberty and Britons never being slaves into the dustbin. Yet we shall discover that what we need is not only to reform our old parliament but to establish several new ones. Political decisions must not be the whims or phobias of men demented by absolute authority like those of Nero or Tsar Paul (to say nothing of later examples) with no remedy short of their assassination by their bodyguards or courtiers. Such decisions must be made in council with competent assessors in the light of the best advice and widest information available. We shall need regional councils, vocational councils, industrial councils, co-operative consumers' councils, financial councils, educational councils, planning and co-ordinating councils, councils for supernational affairs, all in constant session, as well as parliamentary congresses (at not too frequent intervals) to ventilate national grievances and contribute any political suggestions Mr Everyman may be capable of. This is what it has come to in ultra-democratic Russia under the inexorable necessities of human nature and circumstances.

The Russian system is not really a revolutionary departure from our own. We are governed more by trade unions, co-operative societies, professional associations of doctors and lawyers, the judicial bench, the committees of the Privy Council, the bureaucracy, and by Boards of all sorts than by the Houses of Parliament. The Treasury wields the Power of the Purse far more constantly and potently than the House of Commons; and the Foreign Office declares war and sends us helplessly to the trenches without consulting Parliament, which is simply told next day as in the Four Years War, or an hour too late as in the present war, what has been irrevocably done over its head and behind its back. The abdication of King Edward VIII was arranged and consummated without a word to the House of Commons or its constituencies. The Prison Commissioners shut the public out of their prisons and can make them much more cruel than concentration camps, as Dartmoor is, at their pleasure.

A change from our system to the Russian system would be no change at all as far as the multiplicity of governing bodies is concerned. Such bodies cannot be abolished: they are necessary and should be controlled and co-ordinated in the interest of the general welfare, and staffed from panels of competent and responsible persons. At present they are a jumble of casual growths, often unpopular because some of them are out-of-date, led by Party politicians, and operated by petty tyrants, ignorant halfwits, or incurable stick-in-the-muds who are virtually irremovable. But they need not be. In Russia the governing bodies are purged and the slackers "liquidated" (the word covers shooting in grave cases) pretty promptly when they are found out. What the Russians can do we can do.

The need for qualification, responsibility, and co-ordination asserts itself in voluntary association and commercial enterprise as urgently as in State business. Capitalist, Fascist and Communist States need them equally, though only in Communist States is it possible to prevent their corruption by private interests. But in any case their introduction need not involve a catastrophic upset of all our institutions. The well-to-do citizen, who mostly imagines that national institutions, being those of his beloved country, must be already perfect, would hardly be conscious of the change. At most he would echo the French proverb: "the more it changes the more it remains the same." Dreamers of "new worlds" should not forget this. If they do they will be heavily disillusioned.

As the need is not a new one, and clearly involves an educational system and a testing system, it will be asked why Liberal tradition runs so strongly against tests of all sorts that we have been occupied during the last few centuries more with their abolition than their enforcement or introduction. The answer is that the tests have so far failed to establish equality of opportunity and leave "the career open to the talents," both of which conditions are essential in democracy. Some of them were amazingly irrelevant: for instance, the restriction of membership of the College of Physicians to members of the Church of England. The British King must be Protestant, and must repudiate the Roman Church at his coronation explicitly, and all the oriental creeds implicitly, though most of his subjects are Jews, Moslems, Hindus, Buddhists, Jains, Roman Catholics, Atheists or Agnostics, each regarding the others as heretics, heathens, pagans, idolaters, or any equally disparaging epithet. Jews and Atheists were formerly excluded from the British Parliament. Clergymen of the Church of England are excluded from the House of Commons, though its prelates sit in the House of Lords. The whole business became so absurd that the abolition of tests, and the opening of all the professions and public services to Dissenters, Jews, Atheists, and sectarians of all sorts not positively criminal like Thuggee and

Voodoo, got deeply rooted in the Liberal program.

Unfortunately the reaction against the religious tests produced an anti-clerical movement which is reducing itself to absurdity as completely as the religious tests did. In Russia declared militant atheists only are admitted to the Communist Party (the only tolerated Party) which virtually nominates the Soviets. There is nothing new in such exclusion: it is the system of the Catholic Church, and indeed of all the Churches. Its effect was that the Russian Communist Party, aiming at the complete elimination of priestcraft, made itself a priesthood. To eliminate orthodoxy it set up the most intolerant orthodoxy in the world. To get rid of the religious orders it instituted the League of the Godless, with medals of its emblems just like the medals of the Seven Sorrows or the Sacred Heart: you may see them oftener in Russia than scapulars in Ireland. Europe, having led the way from the Ages of Faith to the Ages of Scientific Scepticism and Humanism, is finding that nothing can save her civilization but a new democratic faith, intolerant not only of rival creeds but of rival parties. Conservative England, convinced by the arguments of Macaulay, to its credit not only enfranchised the Jews but made a Jew Prime Minister. But Germany, carrying forward Liberalism to National Socialism under proletarian leadership, finds itself not only persecuting Jews but exterminating them.

It is always so. Popular Liberalism, which is in practice a policed Anarchism, throws government out through the door only to see it come back through the window. Despotic kings and tsars, executed as such, are replaced by Lord Protectors, by Presidents and Chancellors, by Prime Ministers, Leaders, Doges, and Duces whose little fingers are thicker than the loins of the monarchs. Liberalism and Freethought, far from finding their culmination and final triumph in Socialism, will have a losing fight at first under the dictatorship of the proletariat. But they are not dead. They are only in a cataleptic trance, and will resurge mightily when Socialism produces the leisure without which there can be no real liberty, and people supporting themselves comfortably on twentyfour hours work a week demand freedom of enterprise and freedom of thought in their leisure.

Now let us leave Democracy at large for a while, and return to our examination of parliaments as they exist in Britain today.

CHAPTER IV

THE PARLIAMENTS OF THE POOR

IF what is wrong with the House of Commons is the Party System and what is right with the municipalities is their freedom from the Party System, need we do anything more than abolish the Party System in Parliament and leave the municipalities as they are?

Unfortunately the municipalities are paralysed by a tyranny as effective as and more degrading than the Party System: to wit, the poverty of the ratepaying majorities who elect the municipal councillors. It defeats every object of the theoretical democracy to which they owe their votes. Let me describe a typical scene in which I myself played a part.

One of my first experiences as a member of a London vestry, arranging the civic life of a quarter of a million people, was a sitting at which the rates had to be struck for the current year. The committee in charge of finance put before us statements of the cost of the public services involved, and the rate necessary to cover it. I, being a greenhorn, naturally expected that this would be the rate recommended by the committee. But no: when the needed rate was fourteen pence in the pound, the recommended rate was a shilling. No explanation of this deliberate plunge into insolvency being forthcoming, I moved an amendment to make the rate fourteen pence.

The effect was appalling. A bearded elderly vestryman near me cried like an infant, and, with his tears falling fast on the table, reproached me for having no bowels of compassion for the poor. The less desperate or better-off members maintained a gloomy silence. They knew that I was acting reasonably; but they voted against me so unanimously that I never meddled in the rate question again, but left them to their doom, whatever that might be.

It came soon enough. A Local Government Act was passed which changed the vestry into a Borough Council and obliged us to have our accounts audited by the Local Government Board instead of by ourselves. It was discovered that our bank account was overdrawn by £70,000, which the new auditor, without even saying "if you have tears prepare to shed them now," ordered us to pay off immediately, at the cost of a rate which would have turned us all out at the next election. I forget how it was settled, as I was absent at the time. I believe our abject entreaties gained us time enough to spread the sacrifice over some years. Even as it was, the rate jumped up by sixpence in the pound; and the "ratepayers' candidates" were swept from power in the next election.

Now this matter of the rates was so simple that it would be absurd to conclude that the difference between my action and that of my bearded colleague who wept and raved at me was the difference between a high political intelligence and a relatively low one. He could not write plays and books; but he knew as well as I did that a shilling could not buy fourteen pence worth of goods. The difference was that he was a poor man living in a state of chronic pecuniary emergency, and I a securely rich one, practically unconscious of the rates except for the few moments in every year during which I was signing a cheque for them without troubling to look at the poundage. Had I been as poor as he I should no doubt have wept as he wept and voted as he voted. My conclusion was that if a property qualification of a thousand a year had been in force both for vestrymen and voters, the vestry would have been quite solvent, more efficient, and far less at the mercy of its officials, who despised it and regarded its meetings as a nuisance which should be reduced to two a year or less. The same members who sat silent in stunned assent when they had to vote for an item of £20,000 for electrical machinery, would hold all-night sittings to rage furiously over an item of three and sixpence for refreshments.

Only assemblies of persons who are economically carefree, chosen by constituents equally unintimidated, can be looked to for the imagination and daring which modern public business demands.

And let it not be supposed that Parliament is free from the dread of poverty because the majority of its members can lay their hands on a hundred pounds more easily than an average ratepayer on five. Under Capitalism that independence is a product of proletarian poverty. At present the newspapers are printing family budgets in which the income is forty shillings a week and the rent fourteen. Yet all the complaints are of the smallness of the income, not of the enormity of the share of it taken by the landlord through his rent collector, backed by the bailiffs, the brokers, the police, and the whole British army, navy, and air force if the rent is refused. Every purchase made out of the remaining shillings has to cover the rent paid by the vendor. The riches of the members of Parliament and the peers consist of the fourteen shillings plus the sums by which the workers' wages fall short of the prices obtained by their employers for the results of their labor. The legislators can cure the relative poverty of their constituents only by ruining themselves unless they possess the industrial genius needed to increase the productivity of labor sufficiently to feather both nests at one stroke. When the possibilities in this direction have been exhausted there is nothing for the proletariat but slavery mitigated only by doles to keep alive the goose that lays the golden eggs or a complete political capsize establishing the Dictatorship of the Proletariat.

Meanwhile the rich dread poverty even more than the poor, who are used to it. Even millionaires can never be sure that they will not die paupers. Their incomes may be extinguished by bankruptcy, by discoveries and inventions, or, even when all their securities are gilt-edged, by the enormous taxation and inflation involved by modern wars. The dread of this makes continual preoccupation with their private interests compulsory, and makes perfect public integrity suicidal. Both rich and poor have common cares and opposed interests.

This is the result of Plutocracy; and the remedy is Democracy. We have just seen that in our central and local parliaments, dominated by Plutocracy and Poverty (which mathematicians may call Negative Plutocracy), Democracy is inevitably defeated. Let us look farther into the matter.

CHAPTER V

DEMOCRACY: THE NEXT STEP

DEMOCRACY means the organization of society for the benefit and at the expense of everybody indiscriminately and not for the benefit of a privileged class.

A nearly desperate difficulty in the way of its realization is the delusion that the method of securing it is to give votes to everybody, which is the one certain method of defeating it. Adult suffrage kills it dead. Highminded and wellinformed people desire it; but they are in a negligible minority at the polling stations. Mr Everybody, as Voltaire called him—and we must now include Mrs Everybody and Miss Everybody—far from desiring the great development of public organization and governmental activity which democracy involves, has a dread of being governed at all, an intense dislike of being taxed, and a strong objection to being dictated to by a Government official even when the alternative is to be enslaved and plundered by people like himself without responsibility or authority. His mind, when it is capable of ranging beyond his personal, family, and business affairs, is full of the romance of war and chivalry, and his imagination with hero worship of his favorite platform orator or of famous military and naval commanders who have slaughtered the greatest number of foreigners. He is for any negative law that stands between him and the power of the State: for Magna Carta, Habeas Corpus, Trial by Jury, freedom of his own speech and his own newspaper and the public meetings of his own Party, which he reluctantly extends to other people provided they share his views and preferences; but a hint at any positive legislation sends him rushing to the polling station in his irresistible numbers to vote against it. Only by humbugging him to the top of his bent can he be governed at all. It has therefore always been necessary to humbug him more or less; but to the extent to which he has been able to make Parliament really representative of him his enfranchisement has made democracy impossible. With all his prejudices and superstitions and romantic illusions he knows himself too well to vote for himself. All the same he would resent having his vote taken from him. It remains to be seen how far the handful of real democrats can humbug him into voting for his own emancipation.

In 1920 Sidney and Beatrice Webb, our leading authorities on the subject, demonstrated very convincingly in a book entitled A Constitution for the Socialist Commonwealth that a single parliament, even if not Party ridden, cannot possibly govern a civilization as complicated as ours. Jack of all trades is master of none. The Webbs proposed the establishment of two parliaments: one political, the other social. Their arguments and the facts were unanswerable: consequently the problem of how not to do it was solved as usual by simply taking no notice of the proposal. Now it is easy to ignore a book or its writers; and if it were not for the facts this would be the end of the affair. But if the facts are ignored too long things will begin to break. And one of the facts is that if all the problems of society, political, commercial, legal, cultural and artistic are dealt with by a single body, and a vote in the election of such a body is therefore to be an omnibus vote cast every five years or so by Mr Everyman, he is much to be pitied. Conceive his perplexities at a general election! "I have just" he cries "been convinced by the Labor candidate that if the mines are nationalized I shall be able to buy my

coals for half what I am paying at present. But he has promised
Smith next door that he will vote for revision of the Prayer Book;
and I couldnt stand that: flat atheism I call it. The Conservative
candidate says he will die in the last ditch in defence of the Prayer
Book; but he owns half the coal mines in Durham and wont hear of
cheapening coal. And they tell me he is an Anglo-Catholic, which
is no better to my mind than Popery; for I, thank God, am a
staunch Protestant. I agree to all the Liberal candidate says about
liberty and getting rid of all these snooping inspectors coming and
interfering in my business with their regulations and Government
control and all that; but the man is a Republican and has the cheek
to say so; and I am for King and Country. The Independent seems
to me the most likeable of the lot; but he wants to have a negotiated
peace and make us all the slaves of Hitler. Besides, he hasnt a dog's
chance against the Party men; and I dont like having my vote
wasted. There was a Communist up last time; and he forfeited his
deposit. Robinson voted for him; and I tell you he did look a fool.
Fortunately this is a free country and I neednt vote unless I like. I
just wont vote at all. At the club each chap will think I have voted
for his pet candidate. Anyhow this election business is all rot: they
get your vote for one thing and then do just the opposite once
theyre in. Look at the gold standard! Look at Peace with Honor at
Munich! Pah!"

The proposal of the Webbs would get the Prayer Book and the
coal mines into separate compartments, and a good many other
questions along with them; but the success of the new Soviet system
in Russia has now carried the problem far beyond solution · by
two parliaments. Mr Everyman in Russia has dozens of governing
bodies to divide his votes between; and the candidates are people
whom he knows, and whose sons could marry his daughters or his
daughters their sons without loss of caste. Mr British Everyman
thinks he is governed by two authorities only: the House of Commons, elected by his vote, and the House of Lords, which he hopes
will soon be abolished, though it is far more representative of him,
coming into the world as it does like himself by the accident of birth.
Really he is governed by as many authorities as the Russians: by his
Trade Union or Professional Association, by his Co-operative Society, by his Employers' Federation, by his Church, by his bankers,
by his employers and by his landlords. Most of these have practically irresponsible powers over him to which no responsible State
department dare pretend. The common man can be deprived of

his employment and turned loose on the street to starve or live on the dole by his private employer without reason given or remedy available. The doctor can be disqualified and ruined, the lawyer struck off the rolls, the priest or parson unfrocked, the stockbroker or jobber shut out of the Exchange, if he runs counter to regulations to which his consent has never been asked. He may not obtain registration as a qualified member of any profession or skilled trade except through examinations and apprenticeships over which he has no control. The dictatorships of the trades and professions make short work of his aspirations to liberty: they tax him and control him at every turn; yet any proposal to bring these controllers under State control sets him shrieking that his liberty is being destroyed. He sings at the top of his voice that he will never never be a slave because, having no experience of real freedom, he does not know what it is.

It is not, however, the multiplicity of the authorities that is objectionable: on the contrary the more separate and specialized authorities we have, the more we escape from the ridiculous One Man One Vote of the Party System to the democratic ideal of One Subject One Vote. But there must be some public control of authorities to secure the welfare of the community against the scandalous tyrannies they become in the absence of any such control. And if Democracy is to be a central principle it must have a central organ. The organ may have a hundred stops, each with its separate row of pipes; but somebody must play the organ; and, though Mr Everyman may be quite incapable of handling the keyboard, whoever does handle it must play music that Mr Everyman likes or someday he will smash up the organ, kill the organist, and starve for want of music unless and until a new organ is built and a new organist found, both perhaps very inferior to the old ones. If Mr Everyman builds it and tries to play it, it will certainly be worse. If he is not consulted in the affair it may be used against his interests instead of democratically, and as in that case he will not like the music, the new organ will finally share the fate of the old one. Is there any way of avoiding this recurring deadlock and stalemate?

Of course there is. But before I put it into Mr E.'s head I must clear out a good deal of rubbish to make room for it. And I must do justice to the gentleman to begin with. In a recent fiction by Mr H. G. Wells, Mr E. is represented by a certain Mr Albert Edward Tewler. In a recent play of mine Miss E. is represented by a certain Miss Begonia Brown. Both are of the poorer middle class. Tewler is a narrow minded and ignorant idiot for whose powers of comprehension Kentish Town is too large. Begonia wins prizes at County Council schools and has boundless selfrespect; but her ardent patriotism consists in her readiness to die in defence of her native Camberwell against Peckham. (Londoners will get the measure of Tewler and Begonia from this; but for others I must explain that Kentish Town, Camberwell and Peckham are only contiguous suburbs of the same metropolis.) Begonia becomes the first female Prime Minister, too late for inclusion in the play.

Now it is obviously not true that all the inhabitants of London, much less of the British Isles, are Tewlers and Begonias. The mind of H. G. Wells is larger than Tewler's, and Bernard Shaw's more cosmopolitan than Begonia's. Behind Wells and Shaw is a considerable class of persons intelligent enough to buy their books and enjoy reading them, or at least criticizing them. They are at present only an intelligentsia; but they contain material for a genuine aristocracy ready to our hand. But as they are much less numerous than the enfranchised Tewlers and Begonias, and are misunderstood, mistrusted, dreaded and hated by them besides being despised as intellectuals in the richer commercial suburbs and tolerated by the upper ten only as superior servants and entertaining geniuses ("society clowns") outside politics, it is impossible for them to be elected to leading positions in public affairs.

Also as their ability enables them to win a tolerably comfortable income and position by private practice they have every inducement to keep aloof from the vulgar turmoil and squalor of politics and form a private aristocracy, letting the suffering proletariat and the political plutocracy go hang. Thus the utmost refinements and elegancies of civilization were enjoyed by the French intelligentsia in the eighteenth century and by the mandarins of China in the nineteenth whilst criminals broken on the wheel or sliced into a thousand pieces were presented as edifying public spectacles in the streets of Paris and Pekin. Today, though when indicted persons refuse to plead, as members of the Irish Republican Army usually do, we no longer lay them on the flags of the prison yard and pile weights on them until they are pressed to death or consent to plead, and though, when we sentence a prisoner to receive ninety lashes, we call them ten but inflict them with a ninetailed "cat", our criminal code is still horribly cruel and thoughtless, and could be called brutal and barbarous if any animal or primitive tribe could be convicted of maintaining such institutions as Dartmoor or Mountjoy convict prisons. Thirteen years in Dartmoor is much more cruel than breaking on the wheel; but as it is out of sight of the Intellectuals they can ignore it. And they do. There is one public service which forces them into contact with it: jury service. As one of the intelligentsia myself I was subject to this until old age disqualified me. Far from claiming it as a right, I strained every artifice to keep my name off the jury list, successfully, as it happened. In this I was thoroughly representative of my class. The Intellectuals are not forbidden to take part in the political life of the nation. They are only too anxious to keep out of it. Occasionally some notorious murder moves them to a squeamish protest against capital punishment; but the moment the Home Secretary is induced to reprieve the murderer and hides him or her for life in Dartmoor or some similar inferno they are quite satisfied and the case drops out of the newspapers for ever.

The evolutionary appetite, however, is not subject to adult suffrage. It specializes a proportion of the Intellectuals for commonwealth affairs just as it specializes people for poetry, painting, music, law, medicine, religion, fighting, sport and crime.

From Confucius and Lao Tse, Socrates and Plato, Jesus, Gautama and Mahomet, Luther, Knox and Calvin, to Robert Owen, Lassalle, Marx, Engels, Bentham, Richard Wagner, Ruskin, Morris, Stuart Mill, the Fabians, Lenin, Trotsky and Stalin, the Apostolic succession of revolutionists has never ceased. But though they have converted little congregations, and even been adopted as the founders of civilizations like Christendom and Islam, or governed cities for a while like Calvin in Geneva, the change has been only nominal: the new governments are as savage as the old. The worshippers of Jesus establish the Spanish Inquisition and wage the Thirty Years War in his name; and the mililtant Nazis of Germany imagine themselves good Nietzscheans and are led by a disciple of Wagner, whose last word to the world was Wisdom through Compassion (*durch Mitleid wissend*). It remains true, as I have said somewhere, that the conversion of savages to Christianity is really a conversion of Christianity to savagery.

I do not see any way out of this difficulty as long as our democrats persist in assuming that Mr Everyman is omniscient as well as ubiquitous, and refuse to reconsider the suffrage in the light of facts and commonsense. How much control of the Government does Mr Everyman need to protect himself against tyranny? How much is he capable of exercising without ruining himself and wrecking civilization? Are these questions really unanswerable? I think not.

I grant that Mr E. must be empowered to choose his rulers, were it only to save him from being ruled unbearably well. But how much choice should he have? May he choose a golden calf, as he did in the Sinai desert, or a cat as he did in Egypt, or a tribal idol as the sect called Jehovah's Witnesses now do, or Titus Oates, or Lord George Gordon, or Horatio Bottomley, to say nothing of idols now living? Surely not: we might as well let an Infant School loose among the poisons in a druggist's shop, or unbar the cages of all the animals in the Zoo. There is quite enough choice between qualified people to give Mr E. all the control that is good for him.

This is so obvious that when democracy began with parliaments we guarded them by a property qualification which secured at least some elementary education for our legislators; but they abused their power so disastrously in their class interest that it was discarded in favor of no qualification at all, which was a jump out of the frying pan into the fire which is consuming us at present.

It is a matter of simple natural history that humans vary widely in political competence. They vary not only from individual to individual but from age to age in the same individual. In the face of this flat fact it is silly to go on pretending that the voice of the people is the voice of God. When Voltaire said that Mr Everybody was wiser than Mr Anybody he had never seen adult suffrage at work. It takes all sorts to make a world; and to maintain civilization some of these sorts have to be killed like mad dogs whilst others have to be put in command of the State. Until the differences are classified we cannot have a scientific suffrage; and without a scientific suffrage every attempt at democracy will defeat itself as it has always done.

Classification then is the first step toward genuine democracy; and here accordingly it must have a chapter to itself.

CHAPTER VI

KNOWING OUR PLACES

MANY years ago I began investigating classification by asking H. M. Stanley, the journalist who explored Africa in search of Livingstone, what proportion of his men he found capable of leadership when he had to leave them in charge of his expedition for a while. He replied instantly and positively "Five per cent." I pressed him as to whether this was an offhand guess or an exact figure. He said, again without hesitation, that it was an exact figure. Taking it as such for want of a better estimate we may postulate that out of our population of forty millions two million persons are capable of some degree of government.

Immediately the question arises "What degree?" Stanley found that one in twenty could be left in charge of his African command. But if that job had needed a Julius Caesar he certainly would not have had his choice of one man in every twenty, or even one man in a thousand, but one man in the whole known world, which is another way of saying that he would have had no choice at all. Pope Julius II could have found plenty of painters to decorate the Sistine Chapel, but only one Michael Angelo. Our first King James had dozens of playwrights at his disposal but only one Shakespear; and after Shakespear's death his degree became extinct. James II could not have found a Shakespear for love or money.

Between these supreme cases in which a single superman occurs once in fifteen human lifetimes or so and Stanley's everyday five-percenters lie many vocations and many degrees of ability in them. I dare not claim to be the best playwright in the English language; but I believe myself to be one of the best ten, and may therefore perhaps be classed as one of the best hundred.

Outside his natural vocation the greatest genius may be simply feeble minded. In the theatre I am a highly efficient person: in an astronomical observatory I should be sacked at the end of the first week, or else set to dust and polish the telescopes, which I should do worse than any good housemaid. Now the success of any business depends on its operators being vocationally the right persons in their natural places; for a College of Music cannot be successfully conducted by a tone deaf staff nor an Academy of Painting by a color blind one, as some experiments in that direction have proved. Quite the biggest and most difficult business in the world is the organization and administration of a modern democratic State, which must find a remunerative use for every citizen and never put him off with a dole. Managed by the right persons in the wrong places, or the wrong persons in the right places, it will get into a disastrous mess and have to be rescued forcibly by some Napoleonic adventurer foolish enough to be ambitious yet able enough, as Mussolini put it, to clean up an Augean stable.

And here we must make another distinction. Sixty years ago,

walking one Sunday in Hyde Park, where any social reformer or religious apostle may collect a crowd by simply stopping and addressing the empty air, I came upon a certain Captain Wilson, now, I fear, forgotten, who was preaching a gospel which he called Comprehensionism, and urging his listeners to become Comprehensionists. But a world of Comprehenders might and probably would be a world of duffers. Comprehension is quite distinct from executive faculty. The men of action, skilled and ready in practice, are seldom comprehensive thinkers. The world is full of active solicitors who have no sense of law, doctors for whom biology might as well not exist, priests without a ray of religion, journalists thoughtlessly repeating stock phrases in customary collocations, boards of directors who do nothing but what was done last time, skilled workmen who know little more about their jobs than the machines they are handling, as well as Chancellors of the Exchequer who, convinced that the more a country exports the richer it is, hold that the ideal height of prosperity for a nation is to produce nothing for its own consumption and everything for foreign trade. I think it was Palmerston, our greatest Secretary for Foreign Affairs, who said "If you wish to be thoroughly misinformed about a country, consult a man who has lived there for thirty years and speaks the language like a native."

Utopians must not conclude that nobody should be allowed to practise any trade or profession which he or she does not thoroughly understand. They might as well hold that a baby should not be put to its mother's breast until it is completely instructed in food metabolism. A great part of our business has to be done by people who do not understand what they are doing, but can do it without understanding it. They may or may not be doing it in the best way; but it has to be done somehow; and the worst way is better than no way at all. For example, parents at present have to see to it that their families are fed. Accordingly some most affectionate mothers feed their infants on gin and red herrings, and their husbands on butchers' meat and fermented or distilled drinks in the full persuasion that without these they could not keep up their strength. They should be taught better in the elementary schools. But meanwhile children and husbands must be fed somehow. Red herrings and gin, beef and beer, may be worse than cereals, vegetables, and soft drinks; but they are better than nothing.

Instruction, however, is limited by the capacity to digest it. Also by the time at the learner's disposal, and the necessity for choosing the most profitable subjects to employ it on. The most gifted genius cannot study everything. I am a competent playwright; but nothing would make a competent mathematician of me. I can manipulate a calculating machine, and I daresay I could be taught to use a table of logarithms just as I use a ready reckoner. But my time is better employed in writing plays and books. Everything else I must leave undone or get somebody else to do it for me, or, if I do it myself, do it by rule of thumb, using the method without pretending to understand it. In literature and drama, I am a celebrity: in an aeroplane factory I should be a mental defective. When I contemplate what I know and have done (not that I ever do) I have a high opinion of myself. When I contemplate what I dont know and cannot do (which I am often forced to do) I feel as a worm might if it knew how big the world is.

But please do not infer that being a hopeless duffer mathematically and mechanically I cannot comprehend mathematics and physics in all their immense democratic importance. Lightning calculators and great inventors may have no such comprehension. Newton was so great a mathematician that when he invented the infinitesimal calculus he kept it secret as an unprofessional dodge until Leibniz invented it also and was highly praised for it. Yet Newton was as credulous as a child in the nursery in his elaborate study of historical chronology. It is by confusing the practitioner with the comprehensionist that we have come to believe in England that metaphysicians and philosophers are fools, and practical men safe guides. Certainly the practical men know where they are, but not always whither we are going, whereas the thinkers who know whither we are going do not always know where we are.

Democracy will have to reckon not only with differences of vocation but with degrees of ability within the vocation. When child welfare came to be systematically studied, it was soon found that the author of the popular song "They say there is no other can take the place of mother" knew very little about mothers and children. On the other hand when William Morris said that whoever may be the best people to be in charge of the nation's children there can be no doubt that the parents are the very worst, he was overstating his case. It is always necessary to overstate a case startlingly to make people sit up and listen to it, and to frighten them into acting on it. I do this myself habitually and deliberately.

When certain people took up the welfare of children as a neglected branch of vital public work (they were not all Mrs Pardiggleses) the facts soon forced them to classify mothers in three divisions: (*a*) the mothers who could bring up their own children (or other peoples') better than anyone else could or would, (*b*) the mothers who could do it well enough with some instruction and guidance, and (*c*) the mothers who were totally and incorrigibly incapable of rearing children properly at all, this last including not only those who bring their children up to be thieves and prostitutes, or who are uncontrollably violent and cruel, but those who spoil children by being stupidly or jealously fond of them. There are also to be considered for the moment the parents who are so poor that they are forced to set their children to earn a little money by long hours of drudgery instead of having them duly educated and recreated. This, however, is a matter to be dealt with by Factory Acts and Education Acts, or by a better distribution of the nation's income. The rough threefold division into average, superaverage and subaverage is a natural division, and will persist in spite of any development of factory legislation or Socialism.

As criticism of our institutions has spread and concerned itself less and less with individual grievances and more and more with social organization, a similar rough division into ordinary persons, blockheads and geniuses has cropped up in all directions. In the medical profession, in which a practitioner with an obsolete diploma conferred fifty years ago may undertake the most modern operations or apply treatments long discarded in the medical schools, we find that the doctors are like the mothers: most of them able to get through difficult cases with guidance from consultants who form a professional aristocracy at the top, and a percentage at the bottom who should never be allowed into a sick person's room, as their presence there greatly diminishes the patient's chance of recovery. There are Old Bailey barristers who are famous for the number of their clients who, however innocent, have been hanged; preachers whose sermons, however brief, are unbearable; generals whose promotion is a guarantee of defeat; shopkeepers whose inevitable doom is bankruptcy; and the unsuccessful in the lump, as well as the celebrities and the averages. Nothing can alter the natural difference of degree in specific human faculties.

In a society like ours, where private property in the sources of production has produced a monstrous misdistribution of the national income, resulting in a caste system which closes all the vocations to persons outside the level of income considered proper to them, a great deal of the incompetence and failure which afflict us is not really natural: it is the effect of the social pressure which is continually forcing square pegs into round holes. One of my grandfathers was clever with his hands. His "study" was fitted like a carpenter's shop. He built his own boats, and would have been a valuable member of society as a craftsman living by his talent. Unfortunately his station was that of a country gentleman, forbidden to make money by his gift of manual dexterity. For the management of his landed estate he had not the smallest aptitude. He did not even live on it: as sport was not good there he moved to another and wilder county, where he hunted and shot and fished (in the boat he built for himself) consummately; for he could ride any horse, however unmanageable, and was a dead shot with any sort of firearm. Meanwhile all he did as a landlord was to leave his estate in charge of an agent, and mortgage it until it was completely insolvent. He was not naturally incompetent or inactive, very much the reverse: he was a square peg in a round hole. In a sensibly organized society he would have had a useful and prosperous career as a craftsman. As a member of the landed gentry he was—what he was.

One of my greatgrandfathers did much better by practising an extraordinary social imposture. To all appearances he was a country gentleman intermarrying with the best county blood in Ireland. Yet all the time he was amassing riches by secretly carrying on the business of a pawnbroker in one of the poorest quarters in Dublin. His life should have been chronicled by Samuel Smiles as an example of Self Help. How he contrived to have a greatgrandson so utterly destitute of his qualities as I am remains a biological mystery. I should hardly have weathered my early years of rejection by the publishers but for what was left of the profits of his pawnbroking.

But leaving out of account these cases, which will disappear if and when society is more sensibly organized, and all the square pegs will not only find square holes but be forced by social pressure into them instead of out of them, there will still be an irreducible minimum of variation in executive skill in all the vocations to be dealt with. I am not putting this forward as a new discovery: for all States, democratic or plutocratic, act on it by instituting apprenticeship, examinations, articles, diplomas, registers, rules, ordinations, fellowships and other devices for confining practice in the trades and professions to persons who have qualified themselves by years of study and exercise to act as skilled mechanics, doctors, dental surgeons, lawyers, parsons, accountants, architects and the rest.

But there are dangerous gaps in these ring fences created round the vocations. For instance, a person of first rate commercial ability who has built up a business employing thousands of proletarians in the production of vitally necessary goods or services, may leave it to a relative, usually a son, whose ability is second rate, third rate, or even negative; so that the business, though it runs on in its own established grooves for a time, cannot adapt itself to new processes or changing social conditions, and finally dies of obsolescence. In socialized business this cannot occur: nobody now dreams of allowing posts in the national service to be filled by heredity except the throne, which, if left uncertain or subject to any sort of competition, might produce a civil war at every royal decease; and the throne cannot be gambled away from hand to hand in a single night, or left to any relative or favorite acquaintance of its owner as a private business can.

The worst gap in the ring fences is the omission of Comprehension from the list of skilled vocations. It is assumed that anyone can conduct a business just as it is assumed that anyone can choose the right Prime Minister. The result is that very few of our businesses are managed by persons who understand them comprehensively; and Prime Ministers capable of a comprehensive policy are very rare birds indeed. Mr Everyman may try his hand at either job and do his damndest in both.

But there is a special democratic requirement in the case of the Everyman family which makes any attempt to restrict their political activities rouse fierce opposition. When the law becomes an instrument of oppression, as laws often do, especially before they have been amended in the light of experience of their working, it is the Everymans who know where the shoe pinches. For them there must be congresses in which they can squeal their complaints, agitate for their pet remedies, move resolutions and votes of confidence or the reverse, draft private bills and call on the Government to adopt and enact them, and criticize the Government to their utmost with impunity. And as such congresses must be attended by the rulers, who could not possibly conduct the business of the country if they had to listen to Mr E. and Mrs E. and Miss E. "ventilating their grievances" for longer or oftener than a few weeks every two years, a day-to-day ventilation and agitation must be effected by the newspapers and pamphlets, which should have the same privileges as the congresses. Thus what we call freedom of congress, freedom of speech, freedom of agitation, freedom of the press are democratic necessities. As they should be as representative of the Everymans as it is possible to make them, congresses should be picked up haphazard like a jury or by some other method that makes party selection impossible. The legislators and rulers should, on the contrary, be as unrepresentative of Everyman as possible, short of being inhuman.

The Everyman Congress will give us everything desirable that Parliament gives us at present. In depriving it of powers that Parliament does not really possess and never has nor can possess, we shall lose nothing. The supremacy of our Cabinet is as complete as that of the Russian Politbureau or Sovnarkom (or whatever they call their Cabinets of political and industrial thinkers and statesmen in these days of changing names). But the mischief is that as Parliament can give this power to whom it pleases without any scientific tests of political capacity to guide it, we get Cabinets and even Prime Ministers who are windbags and do-nothings, religious bigots, rich plutocrats as such, resolute Conservatives and reactionaries, dangerous undesirables, illiterate anti-intellectuals, and ludicrous misfits of all sorts. The problem remains, how to limit Mr Everyman's choice to the politically competent, classified and graded according to their degrees of such competence. This we cannot do until we know who the competent people are. We must therefore begin by somehow making registers of persons mentally capable of functioning efficiently as parish councillors, district and county councillors, city aldermen, or Secretaries of State for home affairs, treasury finance, foreign affairs, and so on. Such registers had better be called panels, as we are now all familiar with panel doctors and can easily go on to panel Prime Ministers.

But this again we cannot do without anthropometric measurements and tests. Our present method of testing fitness for legislative work is by majority of votes in localities varying so widely in population and character that no common measure of competence can be obtained that way. For the highest positions we have selection by the Prime Minister recommending a suitable person to the King. But as neither the Prime Minister nor the King can know all the eligible people in the community their choice is limited to their circle of acquaintance, which is much smaller than the number of available qualified persons. It is obviously not applicable to the permanent public services, which have to be recruited in many thousands from masses of people utterly unknown in Downing Street or Buckingham Palace. For them, after a long trial of jobbery at the top and the press gang at the bottom, we have been driven to the Chinese system of literary examination, supplemented by medical tests and personal interviews. Of late, intelligence tests of a simple kind have come into fashion; but they are extensions of the examination system and leave it undisturbed.

Have we really any alternative to the examination system now that we are up against the democratic necessity for a census of political capacity and a hierarchy of panels founded on it? This also shall have a chapter to itself, later on.

CHAPTER VII

EQUALITY

DEMOCRACY means Equality; but what does Equality mean? Obviously it does not mean that we are all alike in political faculty or indeed any faculty. Nature inexorably divides us into a mass of persons differing in aptitudes and ability, with a percentage of nincompoops and a percentage of geniuses. But as their bodily needs are the same their food and clothes and lodging can be rationed equally; and they are all equally indispensable. The cabin boy needs more food and wears his clothes out faster than the ageing admiral; but the same income will provide for either of them: they are both equally necessary to the work of the fleet; and their common civilization is a necessary part of the civilization of the nation and indeed of the world. Admirals of the same rank are paid alike whether they are Byngs or Nelsons; and cabin boys, quick or slow, clever or stupid, are paid alike also. All civilized communities consist mostly of classes within which wages and salaries are the same, the figures varying from class to class according to their customary standard of living, but not from individual to individual, however varied their characters and talents. Differences in character and talent cannot be assessed in terms of money: for instance, nobody can suppose that because Mr Joseph Louis, world-champion heavyweight boxer, can earn more in fifteen three-minute rounds than Einstein in fifteen years, his exertions are a hundred and eighty thousand times as valuable as Einstein's. Nobody challenged to fix the incomes of the two on their merits could do so: it would be like trying to measure in money the difference between the relative value to a family of a frying-pan and a bible.

The prices of frying-pans and bibles are fixed, not according to their merits, but to their marginal cost of production: that is, production under the least favorable circumstances. Bibles are cheaper than bottles of brandy, and suits of clothes than diamond rings, though their value is infinitely greater. The remedy is for the Government to control production in the order of its social desirability so that nobody shall be able to buy a diamond ring while children are going naked or in rags, and to see that the citizens shall pay no more for their goods than their averaged cost of production. But before this pitch of socialism, or civilization, or scientific humanism, or whatever you choose to call it, is reached, the Government will have to provide the country with cabin boys and admirals; and consequently to fix their prices. Now it is easy for a democratic statesman to jump to the conclusion that as we all cost the same to feed, clothe, and house decently no matter how our abilities vary, the simple solution is to give us all the same share of the national income. But this will bring him up against the fact that it costs more to produce an admiral *as such* than a cabin boy as such, though their needs as human beings are the same. If we reduce them to a common denominator we shall get a superfluity of cabin boys and no admirals. The cost of production of a worker as such varies with the sort of worker required. In Japan the cost of a cotton operative as such is a penny an hour. In Lancashire it is twenty pence. In Tsarist Russia the cost of production of a common laborer as such was twenty-four shillings a month. Within the British Commonwealth we have black African workers who are expected by pink settlers to be grateful for a hut, a scrap of garden, the privilege of being British subjects, instruction in Christianity by missionaries, and eight shillings a month pocket money.

Now legislators and administrators, managers and scholars, lawyers and doctors and clergymen, artists and philosophers, are not to be had on these terms: they cost education, culture, gentle nurture, privacy, decency, and some leisure. When the Soviet Government in Russia started with the intention of giving all workers an equal share of the national income their labor was producing, it found that they were not producing enough to give each of them more than the pittance earned by the cheapest labor under the Tsardom. It had either to increase the national income to such an amount as would enable it to pay every worker on the professional scale, which was not immediately possible, or else do without an educated public service, which meant pulling the linchpin out of the

Communist cart and collapsing in hopeless bankruptcy. Equality of income had therefore to be dropped until the national dividend could be raised to the professional level. This level is attainable, and is within sight of being attained; but meanwhile Russia has a bureaucracy and a professional class with incomes ten times greater than the hewers of wood and drawers of water.

The statesman aiming at equal distribution of income will find that he must fix a wage figure at wnich no talent or genius can be wasted through lack of the means for its fullest cultivation. As this figure will at first exceed that arrived at by dividing the total national income by the number of people in the country, he must maintain the incomes of the bureaucracy and the professions at the fixed figure as a first charge on the national income. The rest he must distribute as best he can with equality of income as his goal, using every device to increase the national income and using the increase to level up the lowest wage to the grade above it until all the grades are levelled up to the fixed figure, and equality of income attained, virtually if not mathematically.

For mathematical equality is not an end in itself. The politicians with whom Stalin lost patience when he derided them as Equality Merchants were not only clamoring for it before it was possible, but failing to foresee that when achieved it will have lost its present urgency. Even in capitalist society there is a level at which it ceases to matter. The difference between a class income of a couple of hundred pounds a year or less and a couple of thousand or more is disastrous, because the physically vigorous and habitually industrious two hundred class is cut off by its poverty from cultivating its natural stores of leadership and talent; and the thousands class, debilitated by parasitic idleness, is equally cut off from interbreeding with the workers. But as between the class incomes of five thousand a year and fifty thousand (the millionaire figure), this restriction of eugenic selection does not exist. Education in them is the same. The career is equally open to the talents. They associate on terms of equality: they belong to the same clubs: they eat the like food, wear the like clothes, live in the same squares and streets in the same fashionable end of the town. Some of them may have five houses and others only two; but they can live in one at a time only. They employ the same lawyers and the same doctors; and they buy at the same shops. In short, they are intermarriageable. There is so little personal advantage in being ten times as rich as one's next-door neighbor that millionaires like Carnegie and Pierpont Morgan,

Ford and Morris, give away their surpluses and found Rockefeller
Trusts, Pilgrim Trusts, and the like, to get rid of their unneeded
money and "do good" with it. A legacy of twenty thousand pounds,
which is the golden dream of a poor man, makes a rich one swear
because it gives him the trouble of claiming and investing it. Consequently, when the entire population is brought up to our five thousand level, the main objects of equality of income will be secured; and
the Government, though it must still take care that no class gets
poorer, need not prevent any individual becoming richer if he or she
can, and thinks it worth the trouble. Such an ambition may even be
encouraged when it acts as an incentive to increase production. In
the U.S.S.R. it was found impossible to increase production, or even
maintain it, until piece-work and payment by results was established
in spite of the Equality Merchants. When democratic Socialism has
achieved sufficiency of means, equality of opportunity, and national
intermarriageability for everybody, with production kept in its
natural order from necessities to luxuries, and the courts of justice
unbiased by mercenary barristers, its work will be done; for these,
and not a mathematical abstraction like equality of income are its
real goal. The present stratification of society will be levelled up
until the largest possibilities of human nature are no longer starved;
but it will still be human nature with all its enterprises, ambitions,
and emulations in full swing, and with its pioneering superior persons, conservative average persons, and relatively backward inferiors
in their natural places, all fully fed, educated up to the top of their
capacity, and intermarriageable. Equality can go no farther.

CHAPTER VIII

THE PROPOSED ABOLITION OF CLASSES

CIVILIZATION involves division of labor. A solitary man has to be
Jack of all trades. The question "What are you?" has no meaning for
Robinson Crusoe: all he can say is that he is a man. But in society
he is tinker tailor soldier sailor rich man poor man apothecary or
thief according to his occupation. In modern civilization there are
many more denominations; and when denominations have different
incomes a denomination indicates a class as well as an occupation.

And as Mr Everyman despises persons with smaller incomes, and adores persons with bigger ones, he becomes a snob in his attitude to the relatively poor and a flunkey in his attitude to the relatively rich. This double vulgarity is supposed to be characteristic of the middle class, standing as it does between the proletariat and the plutocracy; but it is equally prevalent and virulent at every level of income. The skilled mechanic scorns the unspecified laborer and defers to his employer: the plutocrat, insolent to the tradesman, defers to royalty more abjectly than his butler. In all classes there are a few natural republicans and communists whose good manners are the same for all classes; but they are none the less obliged to segregate themselves from people richer or poorer than themselves, because these have necessarily different habits and different rates of expenditure.

Provided their incomes are either equal or large enough to be superfluous as far as personal habits and expenses are concerned, people of the most widely different occupations can associate without embarrassment. Foxhunters and flyfishers meet astronomers and philosophers at dinner parties in country houses on equal terms. When I was young a peer could not possibly visit a shopkeeper; but the daughters of superpedigreed peers now dance at the balls of mammoth shopkeepers and seek husbands there. For in the long run money will take us anywhere, and lack of it will tame the haughtiest peer.

Nevertheless, the class divisions created by differences of income soon produce effects independent of income differences and often contrary to them. My father's tailor, a much richer man than my father with first-hand knowledge of his impecuniosity, treated him as his social superior because both of them held that a shopkeeper is socially inferior to a merchant; and my father, when he went into business, did so as a merchant selling his goods wholesale. When I was a small boy, and wore out my clothes, my father bought a few yards of cloth and took them to a poorer tailor who sat crosslegged on his board in his tiny shop and was quite obviously no gentleman. And this ancient practice had established the notion that a gentleman could not associate in private with the man who stitched his coat and trousers. It persisted long after leading tailors in Savile Row in London and Dawson Street in Dublin had become commercial princes and their names household words in the most fashionable circles. The great-grandson of a duke might be an impoverished commoner, unable to pay his opulent cheesemonger;

but the cheesemonger, however rich, did not presume to dispute his social precedence.

I can remember the time when the standard wage of a clerk in London was fifteen shillings a week whilst that of a skilled mechanic was two pounds; yet people brought up their sons to be clerks instead of masons, carpenters, or fitters, because the black coat, the starched collar, and the pen, were more respectable than the fustian jacket, the corduroy trousers, the chisel, the saw, and the hammer. The clerk, pitiably poorer than the mechanic, was at least richer than the ploughman with his thirteen shillings, or the farmer's "boy" in Oxfordshire with eight shillings and two or three children. I recall these now incredible British figures for the instruction of those who dismiss all changes as Utopian on the general ground that human nature (meaning human conduct, which is infinitely changeable) cannot be changed.

I look back on the oddest class conventions. Sixty years ago, before knockers disappeared from house doors, and wrenching them off at night was a sport of young bloods, I, ranking myself as a gentleman, demanded admission with a volley of raps in a pattern that I could design for myself. It resembled a burst of machine gun fire. But a common person was permitted a single knock only, unless he were a postman, in which case he gave two knocks, peremptory and violent in virtue of his office. As pre-electric bells could not be manipulated in this way, a gentleman's house had two bell pulls, one for visitors and one for tradesmen. To give a knock or ring a bell improper to one's rank was unthinkable. Inevitably we began by associating a single knock with poverty, quite reasonably, and ended, quite unreasonably, by respecting the person who knocked like a machine gun, and despising the single knockist even when the latter was the richer of the two.

These conditioned reflexes, as our scientists now call them, are harder to get rid of than class distinctions due solely to the incompatibility of the rich man's way of living with the poor man's. They will disappear when the basic share of the national income which we call the minimum wage rises to the point at which an extra ten thousand a year can add nothing to the food, dress, lodging, and education of its possessor that is not equally within the reach of Mr Everyman, nor exempt him from doing his daily share of the nation's work any more than it does at present from military service.

While class distinctions founded on differences of income exist, as they must for a considerable time to come, nothing is more stupid and cruel than to attempt to remedy them by ignoring them. Our leading public schools, founded for the instruction of the poor, have become preserves of the rich; and our more thoughtless reformers propose to redress this malversation by infiltrating the schools of the rich with scholarship winners from the elementary schools; so that Eton and Harrow would have, say, ten to fifteen per cent of boys from families with precarious incomes of from two to four pounds a week, and eighty-five to ninety per cent of boys from families with settled incomes of from thirty to a thousand a week. A worse arrangement could hardly be imagined. The two-pound boy and the thirty-pound boy are, for better or worse, quite different animals. Both are extremely undesirable, and should be ruthlessly levelled; but mixing them prematurely is not the way to do it. One of the advantages of the Etonian school at present is that above a certain level snobbery is not tolerated. The thousand a week boy may not give himself any airs at the expense of the thirty-pounder or of the son of a poor clergyman who is forced by his traditions to regard a public school education as an absolutely first necessity, and is enabled to get it by a scholarship. If the boy's father is a Master of Arts he is as respectable as if his father were a Marquess. At school the life is the same for both: the food is the same; the lodging is the same; the table habits are the same; the clothes are the same; the accent is the same; the manners and tone are the same; the politics, religion, prejudices, pecuniary interests are the same. The boys are young gentlemen; and the two-pound boys at the elementary school are cads. The cads call the young gentlemen toffs. A cad unfortunate enough to be thrust into a community of toffs must either transform himself into a gentleman without the habits and accent to support that pretension, or else be as unhappy and out-of-place as a toff would be in an elementary school overcrowded with children from the slums.

The remedy then is not to force the cads and toffs violently into the same schools, but to alter the distribution of the national income in such a manner that the Etonian standard of subsistence and culture will come within the reach of the slum dwellers, who will thereupon abandon their slums and bring up their children as expensively as Etonians are brought up. As Eton already has to keep within the means of the four-figure parents, and treats the sons of the six-figure parents no better, it may be left to go its old way until it finds itself no longer a preserve of pampered plutocratic and pedigree cubs destined to exploit or command huge flocks of cads, but an ordinary school in which the boys have to be trained to earn their bread by social service in common with all their fellow citizens in a world in which there are no cads and in which the present parasitism of the unproductive rich is held to be disgraceful instead of being honored and courted. Eton will then have to assimilate itself to other schools or maintain its uniqueness by specializing in some neglected department of scholarship, science, fine art, or even good manners. Until then, however, its exclusiveness had better be cultivated in separate schools for the poor and the rich with jealously different tie colors. The cads must be taught to be ashamed of their slums and their poverty, but intensely proud of their dignity as workers, and fiercely contemptuous of the parasitic rich. The toffs should be encouraged in their refusal to accept squalid poverty and social ostracism as their lot on any terms, or to abate a jot of their heroic traditions or of the pretensions of their school to be a nursery of potential rulers. Etonian toffs and Polytechnic cads should contact each other only in street fights, the organization of which might be regarded as a legitimate part of their physical exercise, or in the examination halls or laboratories in which their capacities and pretensions will be tested impartially.

Let no-one imagine, however, that the disappearance of class divisions founded on differences of income will produce a united front in which we shall all obey Christ's exhortation to his disciples to love one another. When there are no more untouchables, and we are all intermarriageable, society will be more wholesome; but it will not be quieter nor less incorrigibly quarrelsome. Equality of income and complete touchability and marriageability exist at present at different levels in the trades, the professions, the ranks, and the classes. Yet at every level there are different religious persuasions, political parties, sets, cliques, tastes, and capacities, many of them capable of producing civil wars of the utmost virulence. At present we have a multitude of proletarians who are too preoccupied with their struggle for existence and their long hours of labor to meddle in politics or religion. And at the top we have people who, having no economic anxieties, no work to do, and seven meals a day, are too fatheaded to be capable of religious or political controversy. When both these disablements are removed the numbers of our controversialists will be hugely reinforced: all society will become polemical and partisan. The lion may lie down with the lamb, or at least cease eating it; but when will the royalist lie down with the republican, the Quaker with the Ritualist, the Deist with the Atheist, the Roman Catholic with the Anglo-Catholic or either of them with the Protestant, the Bergsonian with the Darwinian, the Communist with the Anarchist, the Empire-builder with the Commonwealth idealist, the Jain with the Brahmin, the Moslem with the Hindu, the Shintoist with the Buddhist, the Nudist with the Prudist, etc., etc., etc., etc.? The controversies between them are not extinct: they are only forgotten for the moment in the supreme emergency of the Marxist class war: with its struggle between Capital and Labor, between private property and public property. When that struggle is decided and finished they will all revive with a score of new ones to add to the hurly-burly.

Unimaginative people disparage Socialism because it will, they fear, reduce life to a dead level. Never was an apprehension less plausible. Millions of well-fed bumptious citizens with plenty of leisure for argument will provide all the excitement the most restless spirits can desire. Within whatever bounds our incorrigible British quarrelsomeness may be kept we shall still segregate into parties, creeds, and sets. Differences of temperament and capacity will produce segregation when differences in rank and income are forgotten as they now are between children in a family. Even in families segregation comes with adolescence. I have known eminent men who had brothers. I asked one of them about his brother. He said, "Oh, we are very good friends. Of course J couldnt stand his company for two days; but as we never see one another we get on all right." Everyone must have observed how often near relatives, even when inveterately clannish, keep clear of one another. A son or daughter may fall naturally into a group in which their father or mother would be an unhappy intruder. Conversely the parents' circle may be one in which their children, or some of them, are so hopelessly misclassed that their success in life depends on their extricating themselves from it completely. Abraham Mendelssohn found himself unfortunate in being the father of a famous composer and the son of a famous theologian. Dickens's father could hardly have been at home with Maclise, Stanfield, Macready, and the bevy of celebrities of which his son was the centre. Dickens's daughter told me that she could imagine nothing more dreadful than the lot of a man of genius in an entirely commonplace household. Children who, inheriting their father's name and adopting his profession, are expected to inherit his genius (think of Mozart's son and Wagner's!) would do well to change their names and keep the relationship a dead secret, lest they should be dismissed as failures instead of being respected as quite competent mediocrities.

In families nothing worse occurs usually beyond a friendly agreement to differ: the disagreements are not pushed to the length of civil war. But civil wars in which the nearest relatives may find themselves fighting on opposite sides are as possible under Socialism as under Capitalism. Consider for instance the fact that some people are energetic and others relatively lazy. There are people who breakfast in bed and get up at eleven o'clock and people who start work at six. There are people who would rather work ten hours a day and retire at forty. Others would be quite satisfied to retire at sixty after working four hours a day. These last will be subdivided into people who want to work three days for long hours with three days' leisure every week, and others who want a six-day working week as half-timers. Artistic people like myself, loathing office routine and factory work, will demand the very shortest possible working day as robots at brainless machine-minding jobs so that they may have the longest possible daily leisure in which to write books, compose music, paint pictures, or model statues, until their success entitles them to practise these arts professionally and escape from offices and factories, mines and farms, for ever. Others will hate being robots, and clamor for interesting jobs that keep their minds active.

Then there is the income question. Even when all are sufficiently educated to understand the need for equality of income, involving a standard income to which all incomes must be levelled, this will not settle the question of what that income is to be: it will only moot it. And then there will be wigs on the green. Some will say "Let us all live at the rate of £20,000 a year and be made to earn it." Others will say "Let us have plain living and high thinking at a modest thousand a year."

No Government, however socialized, can shirk all these difficulties by letting us do what we please and can. It must fix a national income figure. It must fix the working hours and the age of retirement. Masses of citizens will be infuriated by its decisions; and some will clamor ignorantly for a return to the happy (as they will think) days of the nineteenth century and the imaginary freedom of which it boasted. It will have to agree with the trade unions as to how much the worker is to receive in money which he may spend as he pleases and how much in communized necessities and amenities. Bread and milk can be communized as easily as water and street lighting are at present because everybody consumes them; but a common supply of microscopes, trombones, cyclotrons, and observatory telescopes would be ridiculous. Even food production could not be communized without conflicts between our carnivores and our vegetarians. We are in for lively times, it seems

Some difficulties will be settled, or settle themselves, without bloodshed; but there are others that will be taken very seriously. The restlessly energetic and the easy-going lazy can have their differences adjusted by varying the conditions of their service; but what about the conflict between parents and teachers in the matter of the religious education of children? The parent may be a Catholic and the teacher a Protestant; and Protestant includes Glasite, Plymouth Brother, Jehovah's Witness, and Pillar of Fire, with Presbyterian, Prelatist, neo-Platonist, High, Low, and Broad Church, whilst Catholic includes Roman Catholic, which professes to be supernational. So do all the national catholicisms, Anglican, Greek, and the rest. When all education is compulsory and communized as elementary education is today, and its aim is to make good citizens of little savages, the Government will not tolerate fantastic sectarian teaching at the whim of the individual parent. It must protect the child against such proselytizing, and flatly forbid the inculcation of Jehovah worship and the theory of atonement by blood sacrifice with which our Book of Common Prayer is saturated. Secular education, demanded by the National Secular Society and the Agnostics, has been exploded by the American students of child psychology. American psychologists who have studied the minds of children tell me that a child's first questions, five in number, are What? Where? When? How? Why? Secular science can answer the first three, and partly answer or hope to answer the fourth; but the fifth, the Why? is absolute checkmate to the scientist. When I was young, and Darwinism in its first vogue, scientists were fond of saying that all the books in the British Museum library could have been written by Natural Selection without human consciousness, and would have been word for word the same. This sample of the blazing nonsense of which secularists and scientists are capable is not now even amusing. The child must be taught that it must be a good child; and if when the child asks "Why should I be a good child" the teacher has no more satisfying reply than the agnostic "I don't know," the child will lose all respect for the teacher's authority and have to be told, as Mr Winston Churchill was in his preparatory school, that if it asks disrespectful questions it will be severely whipped. In my infancy I was told that if I was a bad child I should spend eternity after my death burning in a brimstone hell in an agony of thirst, tortured by a magical combustion that would never consume me. This fable served its turn while I was young enough to believe it; but when I was old enough to laugh at it I was left without any credible reason for behaving honorably, and with a habit of deriding all religious teaching as fraudulent, ridiculous, and characteristic of superstitious fools and humbugs. Fortunately by that time I had also evolved a sense of honor which inhibited my worst impulses and dictated my best ones; and I took to pointing out, in my new capacity as a boy atheist, that this natural sense of honor, nowhere mentioned in the Bible, was the real source of honorable behavior and was quite independent of religious instruction. I ranked it, and still do, as a passion.

But before this sense of honor became imperative there was an interval of incredulity during which I was in school a shamelessly unscrupulous liar in my excuses for neglecting my school lessons and leaving my exercises unwritten, the true reason being that I was too busy reading readable books (the school books were utterly unreadable), listening to music, looking at pictures, and roaming over Dalkey Hill: that is, doing the things that really educated me and made me loathe my school prison, where art and beauty had no place, and the teachers, though apparently full of Latin and Greek, and mostly candidates for the pulpit, were, culturally, comparatively ignorant. Now it is easy to say that we should stop telling children lies in the attractive form of fables and legends, and persuading them that if they mock their elders bears will come out of the wood and eat them. Why not tell them the truth to the best of our knowledge, information, and belief as we tell it to the Inland Revenue authorities when we fill up our income tax returns? Well, suppose we find that children at five years old are completely impervious to the scientific truth; that they will mock their elders unless they believe that bears will eat them for it; that they can believe in talking serpents and donkeys, in an ark not much larger than a canal barge containing pairs of every living species, and in prophets living for three days in the belly of a big fish, whilst Calvin's Institutes, Bergson's Treatise on Creative Evolution, and the Communist Manifesto mean nothing to them and have no effect whatever on their conduct! Surely this is what actually takes place. I could read The Pilgrim's Progress with intense interest when I was five years old; but an exposition of the Marxian Dialectic would have been

Greek to me.

Now the Board of Education has to deal with children aged from two to five, to whom the first verses of the gospel of John mean nothing, whereas the first chapter of Genesis is intelligible, entertaining, and entirely credible. They must be educated by fables and legends and allegories and parables or else by the slipper, the cane, the birch, or some sort of painful injury which teaches nothing but dread of detection, and makes the teacher a hostile and hated executioner instead of a guide, philosopher, friend, and auxiliary parent.

In the ten-year-old division the situation is different: the children no longer have any effective belief in tempting serpents, remonstrating asses, and imminent judiciary bears. If they still thoughtlessly assume that such grotesque moralists did exist in the remote past, it will be necessary, if they are to be taught to think honestly and seriously, to tell them frankly on their promotion and initiation to the ten-year-old division that the bear stories were baby-talk suited to their infancy, and that they must now discard them for lessons in scientific natural history and astronomy which disprove them conclusively as records of possible facts.

Promotion to the adolescent stage must be accompanied similarly by initiations and disillusions, thus reviving a tribal institution which, however barbarous its ritual, was a social necessity.

An Education Code regulating such a process will not be enacted without fierce conflicts of opinion. Some of our adults will be five-year-olds in religious matters when they are fifty-year-olds in technical and business matters. I am again reminded of Newton applying his prodigious mathematical faculty to a chronology of the world on the assumption that it was created in the year 4004 B.C., and of Cromwell, great ruler and warrior as he was, wrestling with imaginary covenants between Abraham and Jehovah, both of them to me, who am neither ruler nor warrior, infantile myths and by no means edifying myths at that.

I know that such forecasts of scientifically civilized society, freed from all economic class distinctions, and intermarriageable from end to end, encouraging and reassuring as it will be to the boys of the Nietzschean Brigade who aspire to live dangerously as explorers in all human activities, will be dreadfully disappointing to those who look to Socialism for a millennial paradise. Some sixty years ago or thereabouts I asked a very clever lad (he had just produced a volume of poems) what profession he intended to adopt. He replied quite seriously that professions would soon cease to exist, as a speech from the Socialist leader Henry Mayers Hyndman had convinced him that the revolution would take place in England in 1889, the centenary of the French revolution. I reminded him that in the most perfect Socialist State people would occasionally break their bones and need surgeons to set them, that houses could not be built without craftsmen and master builders nor babies born without midwives: in short, that under Socialism there would be as many crafts, professions, and callings as ever, if not several more.

Though this is as plain as the sun in the heavens it had never occurred to him. He had looked forward to Socialism as a state of things in which nobody will ever be hungry or cold or ill or ignorant or in any sort of trouble. He had been taught to believe in heaven and hell; and instead of examining these beliefs and rejecting them as fabulous he had simply transferred them to Socialism and Capitalism. Instead of a State in which everybody will have to work he had envisaged a moneyless State in which nobody will work.

His case is not uncommon. There is much talk at present of a New Order to follow the war. There may be a new order; but it will still be subject as of old to an eternal tyranny of nature which, though it can be democratized and its burden of labor equitably distributed, can by no means be evaded or abolished. The basic problems which Socialism hopes to solve are precisely those which Feudalism and Capitalism have tried to solve and failed; and many future citizens will regret what they will still call the good old times; for they will understand Socialism no more than they now understand the Capitalism under which they are grumbling or groaning. They will be political five-year-olds to the end of their days. So I am afraid they must be disfranchised and ruled by those who do understand and know the facts, not by those who could not read this book without falling asleep over its first page.

Classes under Socialism? Parties, creeds, trade unions, professional associations, clubs, sects, and cliques, plus the new panels and registers? Yes: plenty of them, possibly on fighting terms, but always on speaking and marrying terms: that is, on equal terms.

CHAPTER IX

THE STATE AND THE CHILDREN

THE statesman must never deal with the State's children as he has to deal with his own. His own children grow up with bewildering rapidity. He has hardly made up his mind as to what to do with his child of five when it has vanished and is replaced by a boy or girl of ten. Before he has learnt how to deal with this newcomer it also has gone and is replaced by an adolescent of thirteen. Presently the adolescent adolesces and becomes an independent person, more a stranger to its parents than their contemporaries. The parents are insensibly led by this experience to regard childhood as a passing phase, to be muddled through as best may be until the grown-up result is achieved, and the cost and responsibility off their hands.

But our children collectively never grow up. Childhood from the State point of view is not a passing phase: it is a permanent institution. So is infancy: so is maturity: so is the second childhood of old age. Their units move up from phase to phase; but there are still as many millions in each phase as before. And each phase must be a planned and organized and richly endowed world for its inhabitants, as a university is. When a child grows out of the five-year-old world there must be a ten-year-old world waiting for it, and after that separate worlds for early and late adolescence.

Now it is clear that these worlds must not be the child prisons which we call schools, and which William Morris called boy farms. These hells are based, not on the need for education, but on the natural and unalterable fact that an attempt by an adult to keep a child amused will exhaust the strongest heavy-weight champion prizefighter long before the child, after half a minute's rest between the rounds, weakens in its importunate, noisy, and physically violent bouts of play, and can be put to bed and got rid of for the night. If this is the experience of the father, who is mostly away from home all day, what must be the strain on the mother, who has not only to keep the children amused, but to care for them in all other respects as well, and prevent them from wrecking the house into the bargain. It is easy to sing "They say there is no other can take the place of mother" or "Home, Home: sweet sweet Home"; but sentimental melodies, though they may satisfy the natural and reciprocal affection between parents and children, do not alter the fact that children in free and healthy activity are unbearable nuisances to adults. They have to be terrorized in the house or let loose to run wild in the streets. Every mother who does not exploit her children as unhappy little slave drudges is glad when law or social fashion compels her to send her children to school. Thus the school is primarily a prison in which children are locked to prevent them from plaguing and exhausting their parents. And the warders and turnkeys, to save themselves from being not merely plagued but driven mad by their prisoners, have to disguise themselves as teachers and make it a caneable offence to move or talk in class except to order. And just as in a prison for criminals the convicts are in a continual conspiracy against their warders, school children are in a continual conspiracy against their teachers. Their first school lesson in citizenship is hostility to the police, which is the negation of citizenship. Their only weapons are lying, and their chief amusement sabotage.

This state of things, though true enough of schools in the lump, is too inhuman to be carried out to its bitter end in practice. Between Squeers and Montessori there are teachers of many sorts. We have schools in which the children are freer and happier than they are at home. But we have nothing like the sort of school which Goethe sketched in Wilhelm Meister; and if we had it would separate itself as one for incipient Goethes rather than for the common run of youth. What the child needs is not only a school and an adult home, but a child world of which it can be a little citizen, with laws, rights, duties and recreations suited to childish abilities and disabilities. Some primitive fictions will have to be imposed on it as religious truth; for it is no use putting Schopenhauer's treatise on Will or Bergson's on Creative Evolution in the hands of a child who is capable of nothing deeper than Aesop's Fables, the Book of Genesis, and The Pilgrim's Progress. When the child passes from the five year into the ten year world it can find there a more scientific and less imaginative view of the old stories. The old books need not be discarded; but the child will change and get more and more, or less and less, out of the books. Works of art, literary or other, need not be expurgated for children. A child of six can read an unexpurgated edition of The Arabian Nights without being touched by the pornographic passages.

Education is not confined to children: in fact liberal education is mostly adult education, and goes on all through life in people who have active minds instead of second hand mental habits. But adult education takes care of itself: all that the State can do is to take care that the materials for it, the libraries and Art galleries and orchestras and open spaces are at hand for it. And for adults there must be freedom of controversy and criticism; for dogmatic instruction is worse than useless as an instrument of liberal education. A citizen who does not know his subject controversially had better not meddle with it politically. The most dangerously ignorant of our rulers are those who, having been dogmatically instructed in our public schools, believe and are satisfied with what they have been told there. The natural man who believes that the earth is flat may be for most practical purposes a safer guide than the scholar who has been taught that it is round, but is ludicrously nonplussed when challenged on the point by a professional flat-earth agitator who knows all the debating points of the controversy.

Children, however, must not be bothered with controversy. A child must be taught dogmatically to dress itself at least twelve years before it is harangued by a nudist lecturer. It must be told that certain words and subjects are taboo in general conversation; that it must not beg pennies except from its parents; that it must come to meals with clean hands in clean clothes; and that it must obey nine out of the ten commandments and several supplementary ones as well without question or argument. It must be taught to do sums before it can understand arithmetic, and learn paradigms and rules by heart before it is interested in language. If when it is told or forbidden to do something it asks for reasons, and the real reasons are far beyond its power of comprehension, it may be necessary to tell it a fairy story or give it the artificial reason that if it does not obey it will go to hell when it dies, or be whipped, or have its pocket money stopped, or that angels will not love it, or that dear mamma will be displeased, or the like; and at this stage the crudest nursemaids and the most bigoted martinet governesses may be more immediately successful than the most profound philosophers specializing in child psychology; but as a reign of terror, however effective, may make its victims nervous wrecks and mental cowards for life, it is intensely desirable that children should be reasoned with to the extent of their capacity as early and as adroitly as possible, and that even when the reasons given are not the real reasons—when it has to be told lies, in short—the lies should be pleasantly encouraging, uplifting, poetic fictions and not damned lies. When I was a child tormenting my elders with endless whats and wheres and whens and hows and whos, the nursemaids said, "Ask no questions and you will be told no lies," which was true, but not edifying. My father, who was to me omniscient and infallible, was my chief victim; and one of the miracles which still puzzles me is the extent to which, under this pressure, he imparted to me so much information on matters in which he must have been as ignorant as myself. The child's final question, which is always Why, is unanswerable, and should perhaps be always answered by a frank "Nobody knows," though stupid scientists put themselves out of court too often by mistaking hows for whys.

We draw the line between junior life and adult life at 21 years of age; but this line has no existence in nature. A sprinter is too old at 19, a statesman too young at 70. A government has to fix age limits for qualifications for practice as a voter, and for retirement or superannuation from public service, because a line must be drawn somewhere; but human life knows nothing of these official stations at which people have to change trains: we go on growing and ageing all the time, gaining mentally and losing physically simultaneously, and passing through phases of obfuscation and perspicacity, failure and success, fortune and misfortune, uncomfortable inefficiency as square pegs in round holes, or easy and happy activity in well fitting ones, making it impossible for the State to segregate its subjects after they have attained their full bodily stature, though they segregate themselves in all directions into classes, castes, cliques, sets, sects, parties, tastes, persuasions, etc. etc.; but the immature must be segregated from the grown-up and educated phase by phase, from two years old to adolescence, if they are to be capable of citizenship when they are fully grown.

But segregation, like all verbal generalizations, is only a bellyful of east wind until its limits are specified. How much segregation is possible or desirable? Too much has difficulties which statesmen have not as yet begun to think of. Take a quaint example.

A man who had made a huge fortune as a shopkeeper bought an estate in Surrey and endowed it as a retreat for working ladies (governesses and the like) who had managed to save some money for their old age, but not enough. A minimum of savings was obligatory, guaranteeing a minimum of character. The estate was a paradise for them. But instead of being perfectly happy there they went mad. The mental hospital was full before the governors guessed the cause. The only company the old ladies had was their own company: old lady company. The governors had to set up lawn-tennis courts, croquet grounds and the like, and invite all the young people in the county to come there for play and practice. They came and chatted and had tea with the old ladies, who immediately recovered their wits and returned to normal sanity. And no doubt this much association with them was as necessary for the education of the young as for the mental health of the old; for even more important than contacts with young people for old people are contacts with adults for children. Children are not childish all through any more than dotards are dotards all through. I have been a child and am a dotard; and I know. The wisdom and knowledge with which a child is born is not confined to digesting its food, changing its teeth, and substituting for mother's milk a diet richer in minerals. These are marvellous accomplishments; but there are mental inheritances no less remarkable. In some respects the wisdom of babes and sucklings, like their digestions, is more trustworthy than it will be when they are grown-up, and even when they have been Cabinet ministers in half a dozen parliaments. And the very old, if the evolutionary process still persists, may be young in the first dawnings of a new faculty. Consequently neither the infant school nor the estate in Surrey is a solution of the social problem for the very young and very old. Some children are older mentally than their parents, and some septuagenarians younger than their grandchildren.

To some extent we provide for this by our mixture of school and family life. The day boy divides his time between the two every twentyfour hours. The boarder has holidays. But neither makeshift is satisfactory. It is not enough to organize the child's working hours: its leisure must also be organized. Our public boarding schools try to do this by the inhuman task work of compulsory games. The late General Baden Powell did far better by inventing the Boy Scouts and Girl Guides, the first serious attempts at the organization of non-adult life as such. Outside the criminal law I can imagine nothing more cruel and mischievous than to force a boy who has the tastes of a naturalist, poet, painter, musician or mathematician to slave at cricket and football when he should be roaming or sketching in the country, or reading or playing an instrument, or listening to the wireless orchestra.

Then there is the question of privacy. There are people who cannot bear to be alone, sometimes because it terrifies them, more often because company is their only pastime. Others are misanthropic; or they can say "My mind to me a kingdom is": they enjoy solitude, and reduce human intercourse to the utmost possible. Between these extremes there is every possible degree of sociability, almost everybody needing some part of the day in a solitary room or place to themselves.

By the way, the organization of child life must not be made the sport of doctrinaires who imagine they are democrats because they are mad on the subject of self-government through votes for everybody. A State controlled by children and unpoliced by adults would soon outdo Nero or Tsar Paul in fantastic cruelty, and fight like Maoris for the fun of it. The atrocities committed by adults with the support of adult plebiscites are bad enough; but what children might do if left to please and discipline themselves I had rather not try to imagine. Children must be made obedient to adults, not because adults are physically stronger but because they know better. And the adults must govern, not always by the strong hand, which is useful only for crude coercion, but by really knowing better and having the awe-inspiring authority and courage of their convictions.

Now this deference to superior knowledge and character is not a slavish abjection to be cast off on attaining adult status, and replaced by sturdy assertions of political democracy and equality. Children learn from their games and lessons that they vary widely in their specific abilities, and cannot hope to excel in all of them. The incipient Newton, able to develop his mathematical master's instruction into a new calculus, may be a duffer at cricket; and even the demon bowler in cricket may be unable to stroke a racing outrigger from Putney to Mortlake. Nevertheless Newton may be able to draw up the rules of cricket much better than the bowler who takes most wickets; and the bowler who cannot handle an oar better than the nearest ferryman may coach a racing crew better than their stroke rower. Understanding and judgment: in short, wisdom, are the qualities of a good ruler; and Nature, prodigal as she is, does not waste this gift on everybody, seeing that society needs few rulers and many carpenters and masons, bakers and weavers, craftsmen and technicians of all sorts, including mothers and fathers, midwives and nursemaids. Nature provides enough born rulers to give democracy a sufficient choice if nobody is disqualified by poverty, ignorance, and neglect; and democracy is the exercise of this limited choice of rulers by the ruled. Unless children are trained to understand this they will grow up bad citizens, as they mostly do at present.

I included just now mothers and fathers among the necessary

technicians in human society, however primitive. They come even
before husbands and wives; for parents may exist before marriage
is instituted. Parentage is a very important profession; but no test
of fitness for it is ever imposed in the interest of the children.
Tribes may limit it by exogamy or endogamy. Civilized nations
may limit it by marriage laws, by tables of consanguinity, by private
conventions as to class and income, and by making gross illtreatment
and neglect of children a criminal offence. In certain rare cases like
those of the poet Shelley and Annie Besant the State may take the
children out of their parents' hands and make them wards in
Chancery lest they should be brought up as atheists; and this disqualification of parents may be compared with striking a doctor
off the register, or a solicitor off the rolls, or disbarring a K.C., or
silencing or unfrocking a priest. In China the State may step in
and dissolve a marriage whether the parties consent or not if it is
undesirable from the point of view of the community. But these
are regarded as emergency measures, not thought of as affecting
the general assumption that marriage must be promiscuous and yet
as indissoluble as our nature can bear. Marriage laws differ in detail
from Scotland to Japan, with monogamy at one extreme and unlimited Kulin polygamy at the other, yet none of the varieties raises
the question whether the brides and bridegrooms are fitted to produce children capable of citizenship, and have them educated accordingly. In this respect there is only one sort of marriage, though there
are several different sets of local marriage laws.

Also there are different sorts of desirable unions, including at one
extreme marriages leading to a lifelong domestic partnership, and,
at the other, moments of intercourse between incompatibles who
could not endure living together. Not that the incompatibles are
always the illtempered, the exclusively selfish, the lunatics, the
drunkards: in short, the unamiable. Newton did not marry: neither
did Kant. Queen Elizabeth and Saint Clare died old maids. But as
sires and dams for eugenic purposes they were certainly not negligible: indeed a case can be made out for their like as a natural
aristocracy, the very last people to be sterilized by law or custom.
There should be a legitimate place in society for their homeless offspring.

Then there is the question of miscegenation and the color bar.
Sometimes it has no sterilizing effect; for it has been said that a
Chinaman's wife never leaves him no matter what her nation or
color may be, and that some of the finest children in the world are

produced by the marriages of Chinese laundrymen to Irish colyeens. This is hardly scientific evidence; but there is some apparent ground for the belief that in tropical and subtropical climates where black and brown skinned people multiply and replenish the earth, pink people (whites, they call themselves) die out, though half-breeds do very well. In Hawaii it is now difficult to find a thoroughbred aboriginal Sandwich Islander: they are nearly all half-breeds except the Japanese, who do not miscegenate. In New Zealand the descendants of our specially respectable settlers there are only a million and a half strong after 100 years of occupation. They should be at least tens of millions. In South Africa the Cape Government has had to appeal for white immigration to keep up the British section of the population. It is strongly denied that this is caused by birth control.

Here the need for interbreeding goes far beyond the social possibility of mixed marriages. Even in Hawaii, Jamaica, and New Zealand, where human concupiscence has overleaped the color bar to a considerable extent, there is no legitimate place for children, however promising, whose parents are domestically incompatible. It is conceivable that some future government may have to rescue half-bred children from the stigma of bastardy and make them wards in Chancery. When poverty is eliminated from our public problems by Socialism such changes will be easier. For instance, when it was proposed that Queen Elizabeth should marry Ivan the Terrible, the case was not prejudiced by difference of income or class. They might have bred excellent children; but either they would have separated pretty promptly or else Ivan would now be known as Ivan the Terrified.

I am not suggesting here that the States of the future will or should tolerate what is called Free Love. They will tolerate hardly Free Anything that they can regulate with advantage to the general welfare. What I am pointing out is that when child life is recognized as a permanent part of the collective life as well as a transitory phase in the life of the individual, and is legally constituted, graded, and educated under public auspices at the public cost, many of the onerous conditions which we now attach to parentage will become irrelevant and unnecessary; and we shall breed from temporary marriages, however brief, as well as from permanent domestic unions. I am myself the fruit of an unsuitable marriage between two quite amiable people who finally separated in the friendliest fashion and saw no more of oneanother after spending years together in the same house without sharing oneanother's tastes, activities, or in-

terests. They and their three children never quarrelled: though not
an emotional household it was not an unkindly one. Its atmosphere
of good music and free thought was healthy; but as an example of
parental competence to guide, educate and develop children it was
so laughably absurd that I have been trying ever since to get something done about it.

CHAPTER X

SCHOOLMADE MONSTERS

UP to a certain age children are as nervous and cowardly as mice,
dreading darkness and ghosts, dogs and cows, and imaginary
dangers of all sorts from robbers to rattlesnakes. In this phase they
can be spoilt for life, as spaniels can, by a domestic reign of terror,
whether the terror is of physical cruelty or of a supernatural hell,
or of both combined.

If not so spoiled they later on become pugnacious, ashamed of
cowardice, and thoughtlessly cruel and mischievous in mere bravado.
They love authority for its own sake; witness or inflict with pleasure
the punishments that intimidate them; make ridiculous rules of
conduct, dress, and deportment which they enforce violently and
mercilessly; slave as fags and rule as prefects; and make it possible for housemasters in boarding schools to leave the most onerous
part of their work to their pupils with the certainty that the
result will be, not destructive anarchy, but ruthless and irresistible
tyranny.

This phase has political importance because, though it is not an
adult phase, it can by systematic cultivation and abortion be prolonged for the entire lifetime. This is done by the more expensive
public schools in England with surprising success, considering that
it is quite unnatural. In Germany under the Hohenzollerns it was
practised even more intensely; and since the fall of the Hohenzollerns, has been carried to still greater lengths by the Nazis. Take
a boy in this phase whose parents are rich. Graft on to him a
tradition that trade and manual labor are degrading; that service
in the commissioned ranks of the army or in diplomacy are the only
occupations worthy of a gentleman, and hunting and shooting,
riding and racing, his only recreations; accustom him to regard

religion as a matter of church going in his best clothes on Sunday mixed up with ordering God to confound the politics and frustrate the knavish tricks of his enemies, and with devotion to an idolized sovereign or Leader who is the living symbol of his country; and you get not only the familiar non-adult plutocrat whose ideas rule this distressful country, but a national God with imperial instincts and a completely prejudiced conviction that the expensive public school is the supreme triumph of divine education; so that under its rule truth, honesty and justice are spontaneous and automatic, and comparatively benighted foreigners better off than they could possibly be under their own rule. This is what such schools as Eton and Harrow, with their preparatories, do in England to the children of her ruling plutocrats; and as the same thing occurs in all the plutocratic States, we get as many rival patriotisms as there are languages and nations, making the peace in our time for which we pray impossible.

This is partly a degenerate survival from the feudal system, in which class stratification was a necessary moral basis. It exists wherever a feudal system has flourished and retains its property, privileges, titles, riches and prestige whilst gladly surrendering its onerous political duties to middle-class prefects. But the popular notion that at its present pitch it is a venerable tradition from the ages of faith and chivalry is a delusion. Not until the nineteenth century, when the feudal aristocracy finally handed over its rulership to, and associated and intermarried with, the purse-proud snob tradesmen enriched by the industrial revolution, were the children of the rich sent to school, not to get scholarship, culture, and such knowledge as they were capable of, but solely to be hallmarked as members of "the upper class." It was the fifty years following the Reform Act of 1832 that produced the curious monster we know now as the Old School Tie, who excels at cricket, tennis, and golf; has class manners and a class accent; knows nothing of the world he is living in or knows it all wrong; and is equipped mentally with the ideas of a seventeenth-century squire.

When I describe the Old School Tie as a nineteenth-century monster, which he literally is, I must not be taken to imply that the opposite product of the industrial revolution, the proletarian, is not, in his way, also a monster. It is true that as he works for his living he may be a productive and serviceable monster, not a predatory and parasitical one. But he is a perverted and distorted creature all the same. I am not a friend of the poor and an enemy of the rich as ignorant people expect a Socialist to be. When I was a child the nursemaid who took me out to exercise me just as she might have taken a dog, took me into the slums where she had friends instead of into handsomer and more salubrious places. Naturally I hated the slums and the dwellers therein. I still want to have the slums demolished and the dwellers exterminated, and am writing this book with this end in view in my second childhood. And I have in my time elicited thunders of applause from slum audiences by expressing these sentiments. But as I grew out of the hands of the nursemaid and associated more with ladies and gentlemen, I did not find them any more bearable morally. In their dreary snobbery and carefully guarded ignorance of the slum life on which they were battening and into which I had been clandestinely introduced I could find no comradeship: they also, I finally concluded, must be exterminated. Only the fictions of fine art gave me any satisfaction; and it became my chosen job to bring these fictions to life, and meanwhile to live as a Bohemian, as a rebel, as an enemy, not of mankind, but of the perversions of mankind produced by private property plus the industrial revolution. The precept "Love oneanother" was impossible with human society divided into detestably unlovable classes. It cannot be too thoroughly understood that Socialism is not charity nor loving-kindness, nor sympathy with the poor, nor popular philanthropy with its something-for-nothing almsgiving and mendicity, but the economist's hatred of waste and disorder, the aesthete's hatred of ugliness and dirt, the lawyer's hatred of injustice, the doctor's hatred of disease, the saint's hatred of the seven deadly sins: in short, a combination of the most intense hatreds against institutions which give economists a strong pecuniary interest in wasteful and anarchic capitalism, artists in venality and pornography, lawyers in injustice, doctors in disease, and saints in catering for the seven deadly sins or flattering them instead of denouncing them.

This being understood, let us return to the cult of the Etonian rival of the Loch Ness monster, the Old School Tie. He is a mischievous anachronism now that he has lost his ancient Christian Catholicism and substituted an unholy commercial Alsatia for the Holy Roman Empire.

When feudalism was in its heyday Western Europe had one supernational God, one heaven for all mankind, and one hell, the hell of Dante, into which all souls, rich or poor, gentle or simple in life, would be cast after death if they were too wicked. Nowadays the British gentleman believes in an insular English God, the German Junker in a god as Nordic as Wotan, the French in a materialistic but thoroughly French No-God, whilst none of them believes in any sort of hell. Wars have become fanatical crusades waged with millions of soldiers, millions of money, and millionfold-multiplied means of destruction and slaughter. The wars of the Roses exterminated only the old feudal nobility, and gave its powers to a new self-ennobled plutocracy. But modern war, which has just produced the suicidal outrage of the conscription of women for military service, threatens to exterminate the human race and destroy civilization to the point at which its powers of destruction are exhausted, and decent people die of discouragement, which is a very fatal disease.

Now these and many cognate nuisances are the result of an educational system which, instead of guiding the natural change from childhood to adolescence and maturity, arrests juvenile development at its most mischievous stage, and forces the experienced statesman to treat the country as an orphanage in which the age limit is fourteen, and the orphans as its mentally defective inmates.

Of course this system, like all other out-of-date systems, does not enjoy complete integrity in practice: the facts are too strong for it. When the schools are invaded by the successful men of business and the professions they are forced to develop, however reluctantly and contemptuously at first, a scientific side and then a business side; and these new sides encroach on the classic routine until it too becomes only a side and a losing one. Rugby, for instance, is not what it was a hundred years ago; and Oundle was turned upside down and inside out by Sanderson, who was not himself an Old School Tie. But the older schooling still prevails enough to make sure that the class enriched by our property system is the one which commands the ruling majority in Parliament, in the Upper Division of the Civil Service, in diplomacy, and, except when there is a world war on, in the commissioned ranks of the fighting services.

The worst of it is that our sincere educationists are unanimous in pressing everybody to be kept at school until they are eighteen, and prepared for three years at the university if they have a taste that way. This will satisfy the parents who wish their children to be ladies and gentlemen with the manners and speech and class prejudices proper to that condition. But the object of a sane State is to make good citizens of its children: that is, to make them productive or serviceable members of the community. The two objects are opposite and incompatible; for there is no advantage in wearing an old school tie if you have to share the social burden of labor and service. If there are no schools available except schools for the poor in which a slave mentality is inculcated, and schools for the rich in which children are trained for a life of leisure, luxury, and privilege, or at best a monopoly of commercial, professional, and political opportunity which is politely called leadership, then the hasty conclusion is that children had better be kept out of school at all costs, and Eton and its like razed to the ground, and their foundations sown with salt.

But untutored ignorance does not make for good citizenship: any system of instruction and training is better than none at all. Our system must go on until we provide a better one. Meanwhile, however, it is clearly no remedy for our present bad citizenship to impose Etonian education on the multitudinous proletariat, including its impecunious middle class section, by scholarships entitling the holders to "places" at the expensive schools, with extension of the age for compulsory schooling to eighteen, and the rest of the "ladders to the university." To abolish schools altogether and make teaching a crime, as Butler's Erewhonians abolished machinery and imprisoned the explorer because they found a watch in his pocket, would only drive education underground as it did in Tsarist Russia, where women, for teaching peasants to read, were imprisoned for twenty years, not quite unreasonably; for peasants who could read encouraged the others to burn country houses. Our Etonian system must die a natural death through the expropriation of its present plutocratic patrons, and the competition of a new organization of non-adult life.

That new system is beyond my powers of planning. It will, I fancy, develop from the middle-class schools in which the pupils are mostly day boys and day girls dividing their daily lives between the school and the home. I was a day boy in a school at which there were both day boys and boarders. The day boys, being more numerous, despised the boarders and spoke of them as the skinnies. The boarders were equally contemptuous and opprobrious.

Now in Ireland a day boy was really only a half-day boy: he did not return to school in the afternoon. The school was not inspected nor kept up to the mark in any way by the education authorities: in fact there was no mark to be kept up to. Lessons were set me which I had to learn on pain of punishment not cruel enough to effect its purpose with boys who like me were free enough at home to have something more interesting to do than poring over unreadable schoolbooks; but I was not taught manners nor loyalties, nor held to any standards of dress or care of my person. Discipline was confined to silence and sitting still, which did not prevent me from carrying on furtive conversations or fights with the boy sitting next, who might be a friend or a foe. I hated school, and learnt there nothing of what it professed to teach. When I escaped from it, and at the age of fifteen was condemned to five years penal servitude in another sort of prison called an office, I knew at the end of my sentence much more of the world than a university graduate from Eton plus Oxford or Harrow plus Cambridge; but I was frightfully undertrained civically and socially. Even my table manners and company manners I got from a most useful volume called The Manners and Tone of Good Society, an admirable text-book which is, I hope, still current and up to date. With this equipment I was able to hold my own to the extent of my parents' straitened means (I had no means of my own, as I preferred penni-less unemployability to any more prison); but all the work of edu-cating, disciplining and forming myself, which should have been done for me when I was a child I had to do for myself as an adult. But for the aesthetic education I had gathered at home through my mother's musical activities, and the rare chance that Nature had en-dowed me with a talent of the Shakesperean kind that began to be lucrative before my parents died, I might have ended as a tramp.

My educational history, except for the literary gift and the musi-cal home, is common to the main body of proletarian upstarts and genteel younger son downstarts who, being at least literate, have to conduct the business and politics of this country and its colonies. The wonder is not that they make a sorry mess of it, and land us in senseless killing matches which half demoralize them and half drill them into the strictest military Communism, but that there is anything left of civilization at all under their management.

Still, the day-boy system, unlike the Etonian, is variable and im-provable. The division of a child's life between home and school can be changed; and as the changes take the child more and more from home into school life successive points are reached at which the school takes the place of the family, and the teachers of the parents. At its humblest beginnings the verminous child is deloused and its teeth attended to. The hungry child gets milk at school, and then meals. If its feet are wet it gets boots; and if boots why not socks, shifts, and finally a uniform? Unlimited "home work," which poisons a child's leisure when it is not left undone, is replaced by limited but compulsory "prep." Play, equipped with apparatus, regulated, and policed, takes the place of mischievous adventures in the streets. School welfare work develops until children are secured against poverty, exploitation, domestic tyranny or neglect, and so on bit by bit, until the school, instead of being an infectious penitentiary into which children are driven to have the three Rs whacked into them, becomes a colony in which parents can see enough of their children and children of their parents to sustain family ties without perpetuating their very serious deficiencies, and provides an organized child life that does not now exist at all except in embryo in the Boy Scouts, Girl Guides, boys' and girls' clubs, Comsomols, Ballillas, Leagues of Youth and cognate bodies and movements which are sprouting everywhere. When these coalesce with the schools into a general system of child colonies conducted by a parallel development of Boards of Education into governments and constitutions for children it will be possible at last to have a selfsupporting civilization of citizens instead of, as at present, a slavery imposed haphazard by physical force on savages.

Let it not be forgotten that in such a civilization the families engendered by the children when they grow up will co-operate with the schools, and retain the natural affection of their own children, without the reservations at present inevitable. It will, I hope, be no longer possible for anyone to say, as I have had to say, that though I never quarrelled with my very amiable parents I cannot deny that they were quite unqualified for the training of their progeny.

In such civilization there will be both more freedom and less. The State will proselytize as ruthlessly as parents are able to do at present, and far more powerfully; for citizenship, like all forms of corporate life, is impossible without a common fundamental religion; and this had better be inculcated by a democratic State with a strong interest in tolerance and free-thought than by parents divided into hundreds of sects, each persuaded that it has a monopoly of salvation and that any sceptical criticism of its tenets is impious and should be proscribed as heresy. Children brought up in such sects produce such incidents as the Thirty Years War about Transubstantiation just as they produce world wars when they are brought up in nations each of which regards itself as The Chosen Race or *Herrenvolk* appointed by God to own and rule all the others.

They call this piety and patriotism. But they all have to agree that in everyday private life thou shalt not steal, and that any teaching to the contrary is not to be tolerated for a moment. No defender of the family against the State goes so far as to allow children to be brought up as Thugs or thieves; nor does any advocate of the totalitarian State propose to suppress freedom of thought and speech as it was suppressed in the Holy Roman Empire; for neither extreme is practicable nor desirable; but it is certain that we cannot organize childhood without organizing and prescribing its religion and its politics to an extent which seems appalling to those who dread government as children dread the police. And so, however we tackle the problem, let us hear no more nonsense about individual Liberty with a large L in matters as to which complete liberty is socially impossible, and the necessary authority can be kept short of tyranny much more surely and effectively when it is exercised by public bodies subject to public criticism than by irresponsible private tyrants in private houses, or in expensive schools which, though called public schools, are really plutocratic class schools, setting the fashion for all education. When child life is seriously organized, the struggle of the teachers will be, not to prevent the pupils from thinking otherwise than as the Government dictates, but to induce them to think a little for themselves into the bargain.

CHAPTER XI

FINANCIAL MYSTERIES: BANKING

NOWADAYS, as businesses become bigger and bigger, and require more and more capital to start with, professional financiers, whose business it is to collect capital for commerce instead of directly operating it themselves, are masters of the situation. The old-fashioned employer has become an employee who would be safer, better off, and infinitely more selfrespecting as a civil servant than as the hired manager of a private company. For the State and municipal services there is no difficulty in finding competent recruits willing to work for less than half or a third of the salaries they would have to demand in private employment, where they would be not only less secure but obliged to be far more socially pretentious as well as conventional in their attire and their political and religious observances than a civil servant, borough engineer, or town clerk.

The obsolescence of the old private employer class with its monopoly of reading, writing and arithmetic as against an illiterate proletarian multitude, and its replacement by hired officials largely drawn from a compulsorily educated proletariat with scholarships open to the clever ones, does not wholly account for the supremacy of the financiers. Finance and money are much more puzzling than direct commercial profiteering for one's own hand with one's own little capital. They produce crazy schemes to which the Everyman family lends a greedy ear, as they all promise plenty of money for nothing. The Currency Crank is a nuisance in every movement for social reform; and the apostles of Social Credit once actually persuaded a Canadian legislature to budget on its imaginary riches. They are supported by the mystery of banking, which seems to create millions of money out of nothing, and by the fact, of which everyone has daily experience, that scraps of paper are accepted in discharge of debts of thousands of golden pounds. In these phenomena there is much more substantial evidence for the existence of the philosopher's stone, with its power of transmuting base metals into precious ones, than the old alchemists were ever able to produce. We may cease to believe in the philosopher's stone, and be convinced by the experience of the Alberta exchequer that there is something wrong with Social Credit; but as long as banking remains a private business, and rich people enjoy enormous unearned incomes without lifting their little fingers to earn it, there will be crazy schemes in the air under one name or another; and the Everyman family will run after them just as they ran after the South Sea Bubble.

What, then, is the mystery of banking?

Centuries ago the Lombard goldsmiths made the discovery which is commemorated in London today by the title of Lombard Street, a first rate city address. In their days people who had a good deal of spare money, and were expected to protect it against robbers by their own hands and weapons behind the bars and bolts and stanchions of their own houses, brought their spare money to the goldsmiths for specially fortified safe keeping, expecting naturally to have to pay for that accommodation. But as these rich people drew out only what they required for the moment, leaving "a balance" to their credit, the goldsmith very soon found himself in permanent possession of much more money than he needed to pay out to the owners for their daily needs. By lending this surplus out at interest he could make more profit than by exercising his craft as a gold smith. So he gave up goldsmithing and became a money lender.

Later on he made another discovery. He found that if he printed bushels of promissory notes for £100, £10, £5, £1 or what not, his customers would find them much more convenient than bags of gold and silver when they had large sums to carry away or pay in or exchange with oneanother, and felt sure all the time that they represented the gold in his safes. The notes would pass from one hand to another for a long time before they came back to him to be accepted by himself as so much gold. And as they never all came in on the same day, and there was always a mass of them floating round, he found that here too he need keep only a percentage in his till of the gold they represented, and could lend the rest out at interest. Here was a second Golconda for him. He had not only discovered the mystery of banking but invented paper money. He had found the philosopher's stone.

But in the Ages of Faith alchemists who found the philosopher's stone, or even looked for it, were burnt as sorcerers; and business men who made a profession of lending money were called usurers and cursed and damned up hill and down dale by the Church. So the goldsmiths said nothing about the use they were making of the balances. They left their customers to believe that all the coins lodged with them were safely locked up inviolate in impregnable safes. And they called themselves neither alchemists nor usurers but bankers, under which name they were not only tolerated but highly respected. Jews, who had been driven by persecution out of every occupation except that of money making, found their feet in the banking business. They were not more rapacious than the Gentiles: rather the contrary if anything; but they were more practised in the handling of money.

The bankers soon found that clients short of money were as profitable as those who had more than they needed. Such clients had to beg for overdrafts to carry on or extend their businesses. At the same time the clients who had large balances were being tempted to draw them out and invest them in stocks, shares, or land. The bankers therefore not only offered to keep their money for them for nothing, but to pay them interest on as much of their balances as they would agree not to draw out without notice. But they never paid as much interest to the depositors as they charged to the overdrawn. As I write, the bankers are paying about one per cent on deposits whilst charging four and a half on secured overdrafts. They lend the money of prudent Peter to passionate Paul at a profit. When Peter is in a momentary difficulty they lend him his own money on the same terms.

Now that banking has spread so enormously that the modern bankers have millions of clients for every hundred that the medieval goldsmith could hope for, it is found that all the bankers need keep for their clients' daily needs is about three shillings from every pound of their deposits. With the surplus they finance empires in the throes of world war, or poultry farmers short of chicken food. All is fish, big or little, that comes to their net.

It is a lucrative and most useful business; but there is a snag in it. The clients do not understand it. They believe that their money is safe in the banker's strong rooms. Sometimes, to make sure that it is all there, they go to the bank and draw it all out. The cashier hands them a bag of gold labelled with their name. They count it, and hand it back to be kept for them as before. They do not suspect that the same bag of gold, with a new label, and the contents adjusted to the account, serves for many simple minded customers, and is a totally delusive security. But the customer who goes through this ceremony, mostly an anxious farmer or a suspicious poor woman, represents a huge number of depositors who, though they have such confidence in their bankers that they never put it to a practical test, neverthe- less believe that their money is safe and untouched in the bank vaults all the time.

Under normal circumstances this delusion is quite comfortable for the bankers. But if a rumor starts that the bank is not solvent all these deluded people rush to draw their money out. There is, as we say, "a run on the bank". Every panic stricken customer demands his full balance of pounds sterling. The banker has kept only a few shillings: enough to meet ordinary demands but not for a simultane- ous withdrawal of all the balances. The first comers in the rush get paid. The bank desperately borrows every farthing it can raise in any direction; but unless the other bankers come to the rescue on pretty hard terms, it must at last close its doors and confess that it has no more ready money. As we say, it breaks; and its unlucky customers lose their savings.

One is tempted to say "Serve them right." Instead of rushing to draw their balances they should have rushed to put every penny they could lay hands on into the bank, and restricted their drafts on it to the lowest bearable figure. They should have agreed to a mora- torium and a rationing of drafts. In short, they should have done the reverse of what they actually did do. They would have done so if they had been carefully taught the meaning of banking, and how it was that the bank in its palatial buildings had been able to do so much for them for nothing. They should have been taught it at school to qualify them as citizens. Instead, they were at best taught to read the obscene satires of Juvenal in their original dead language.

It may be asked why should not the bank managers, before allowing people to open accounts, explain to them, orally or by pamphlet, exactly why all citizens who have more money than their pockets can accommodate can have it kept for them at call in a substantial building with strong rooms and a staff of responsible persons at their service, paying their bills, lending them money, stockbroking for them, acting as trustees and executors, with other services and civilities apparently for nothing or next to nothing, though the bank is all the time paying its shareholders handsome dividends. Well, the result of such an explanation would be that the simpletons would never consent to let the bank play with their money: they would take it home and put it in an old stocking. And the managers who had explained would be sacked for giving away the show.

Another reason for not explaining is that the managers do not necessarily understand their business. They are not theorists: they are practitioners and routineers. The bankers themselves often know no more of the theory than the managers and less of the practice. Those who fully comprehend what they are doing know that banking could be quite easily nationalized by a Banks Purchase Act like the Land Purchase Act which got rid of the old Irish landlords. If a run on the national bank started, the Government could at once declare a state of national emergency and ration drafts just as it now rations eggs in war time. The simpletons would have to behave sensibly instead of ruining themselves and the bank in an ignorant panic. They would have Government security for every farthing of their deposits, and be able to borrow from the bank at cost price to extend their businesses, whereas now they can borrow nothing less than scores of thousands at discounts of twenty per cent or more. But as the enormous present profits of banking would then cease, and its correspondingly enormous benefits be communized, the bankers take good care that banking shall remain a mystery.

Government security sounds comfortably reassuring; but its value rests on the honesty and comprehension of the Government. The power of a Government to do good is greater than that of any private company; but so also is its power to do mischief. National banking under a British Treasury manned by simpletons and supported by a parliament of simpletons would be far more disastrous than the most selfish private banking. For consider the predicament of the simpleton newly elected as such to Parliament under a democratic franchise of One Simpleton One Vote. He (or she) would be accustomed to paper money without understanding it. He would be accustomed to pay a shilling for three halfpence worth of tobacco without knowing that he was thereby paying tenpence halfpenny in taxes. Money would be completely dissociated in his mind from the goods to which it is a title deed, and without which a banknote is worth only the paper it is printed on. Financially he would think always in terms of money and never of goods. If the Treasury wanted money it would seem to him the easiest thing in the world for them to print and issue a bale of banknotes and pay all national debts with them. The Social-Democratic German government did this after the Four Years War when Germany was being plundered to the last pfennig by the victorious Allies. The result was that the price of a twopenny halfpenny postage stamp rose to four thousand million paper pounds, with all other goods dear in proportion and rising from hour to hour. Pensioners and others living on fixed incomes and investments were reduced to beggary; old debts and debentures were paid off with less than the price of a crumb of bread; laborers became millionaires and millionaires became bus conductors, all this being part of a social upset so destructive that the Germans would have suffered less if they had simply handed over their country to their enemies and said "You have conquered us: now be good enough to govern us until we have recovered from our defeat."

Our English simpletons, having lost all the money they had in Germany in this way, now know well that "Inflation" is an evil to be avoided at all costs. Unfortunately they do not know what the word means: as it passes from mouth to mouth and from pen to pen it is connected with high prices for everything and with nothing else. What does inflation really mean? How does it produce catastrophes compared to which the worst that blitzing bombs can do seems hardly worth mentioning?

When the goldsmith-turned-banker issued promissory notes instead of bags of gold to his customers their value depended on his possessing the gold they represented, or at least of his being sure to possess it when they came back to him and he had to redeem their promise. And this value depended on the fact that gold was prized so infinitely that all persons possessing it could exchange it for bread and butter, bricks and mortar, wool and linen, coal and firewood, or anything else purchasable they needed or desired. And this value again depended on the quantity of such goods available; for a person who would not pay a penny for a glass of pipe water in a modern city would pay all the gold in the world (if he had it) for a mouthful if he were perishing of thirst in a desert. Strawberries cost guineas in midwinter and tuppence a basket in July. But when civilization abolishes famines, and ensures a constant supply of human subsistence at fairly stable prices, a goldsmith (or anyone else) can estimate accurately enough for practical purposes what his gold will be worth when his promissory notes come home to roost.

Now if the goldsmith is a rogue or a gambler, or is going through a routine without understanding exactly what he is doing, he may try to enrich himself by issuing promissory notes for more gold than he possesses or is likely to possess by the time they are presented for payment. That is inflation; and its penalty in the case of an individual goldsmith is fraudulent bankruptcy. But when a Government does it and floods the country with promissory notes (paper money) which it has neither gold nor goods enough to liquidate, a hungry man with his pocket full of five-pound notes, offering sixpence for a roll of bread and a pat of butter at a restaurant, is met by the waiter with a shake of the head and the words "Nothing doing." The hungry man offers a shilling with the same result. Half a crown, ten shillings, a pound, five pounds, finally four thousand million pounds for a roll without any butter: a figure actually reached in the great German inflation after the Four Years War. As well as I remember Germany owed me about 200,000 marks, and paid me handsomely with a note for a million marks, worth a few pence as a museum curiosity. Mr Lloyd George called this "making Germany pay"; but as a matter of fact the German government, by the trick of inflation, made me pay.

In a solvent world, however, inflation cures itself. When it reduced German currency to absurdity nobody would deal in it: people bargained not for marks but for American dollars, which were honestly sterling. The German government had to scrap its inflated notes and substitute a new currency with goods behind it. But the calamity was none the lighter for that. The people it had ruined were not unruined by the fact that it was too bad to last, and that the United States were solvent.

It may seem that the German statesmen must have been either extraordinarily stupid or madly dishonest to make the calamity inevitable. But the same thing occurred in Russia under the exceptionally clever, politically well read, and heroically public spirited Bolshevik statesmen, led by Lenin and Stalin, now recognized as beyond question the ablest rulers our age has produced. There was inflation in England, though it did not go so far. In France the government, having borrowed money in all directions during the war in tenpenny francs, quite openly and shamelessly altered the value of the franc to twopence, thus cheating its creditors of four fifths of their due. And nobody was scandalized: all that happened was that when English and American tourists found that they could buy five times as many francs for their pounds and dollars as before, they rushed to France to spend their holidays there cheaply.

That gross ignorance of finance is general in all classes is shewn by such events as the scare that arose when Mr Winston Churchill was Chancellor of the Exchequer lest he should use the money that had been lodged in the Post Office Savings Bank. The people who had accounts there evidently believed that the identical coins they had handed in across the post office counters were carefully labelled with their names and locked in a separate compartment to be handed back to them on demand at any moment. Runs on banks had already exposed this abundantly. The serious part of the business was that when our elder statesmen set to work to reassure these poor people it at once became apparent that they knew little more about the matter, if anything, than the panickers. Later on, when it was proposed to repeal the Gold Standard, which obliged the Bank of England to redeem its notes in gold on presentation, the Government rallied the country to maintain the standard at the forthcoming election as the palladium of British solvency. This seemed sane enough; but before the election it was discovered that nearly all the available gold in the world was locked up in American vaults. The Government had to turn about and assure the electorate that paper money is quite as good as gold coin provided there are goods at its back, and the Government is honest. But again our elder statesmen could not explain, as they did not comprehend the question; and the Governor of the Bank of England confessed that he did not understand money, which was not surprising, as money apart from goods and treated as a separate problem is simple nonsense and cannot be understood by anybody.

It was in fact neither brains nor honesty that were lacking but elementary knowledge of the subject, which is nevertheless simpler than the bookmaking or bridge playing at which so many quite commonplace people are experts. Even the few who understand Einstein's general theory of relativity should not be made Lords of the Treasury until they prove that they know the history of banking and the nature of paper money.

But I am still very far from the end of my tale of the illusions of political ignorance.

CHAPTER XII

ILLUSIONS OF THE MONEY MARKET

It is part of the business of a bank manager to lend money to persons of whose honesty and solvency and prospects of success he has formed a favorable opinion; and this opinion is called credit. Both bankers and borrowers soon slip into a habit of speaking and thinking of credit as if it were the actual solid goods, the bricks and mortar, bread and butter, collars and cuffs or what not, to which the money lent is a title deed, such title deeds (I cannot repeat this too often) being quite worthless unless the goods are in existence and on sale. We hear of people living on credit and building houses on credit, which is utter nonsense, and of bankers creating credit and even creating money, which is dangerous nonsense, though it works well enough as long as the goods are there and the bankers' judgment sound. A finance minister with these delusions is a standing threat of national calamity.

But there is a more dangerous delusion prevalent. There is a money market outside the banks called the Stock Exchange. Its business is the exchange of yearly incomes for lump sums of ready money. This peculiar trade is conducted by brokers who buy incomes and jobbers who sell them. The broker says in effect to the jobber "My client has more money than he needs to spend. He has become possessed of (say) a thousand pounds saved out of the harvest of the present and former years. It is ready for immediate consumption. He will sell it for a future income. You represent the peoples who have incomes to sell. What is the best you can do for my client?" The jobber asks does he want it gilt-edged: that is, guaranteed by the Government; or does he prefer an industrial income, which may grow to any amount, but also may cease altogether. For the price of an assured income will not be the same as that of a risky one. The jobber will say to the broker "If you want an income of £1000 a year guaranteed as the interest on a Government Loan, you must put down, say £33,000; but if you will take chances with an industrial I can let you have it for £20,000, or even £10,000 at double the risk." To put it another way, an income can be bought safely for a sum equal to 33 years of it, or, riskily, for 20 years of it or 10, or less. Or, to put it in the usual way, ready money can be invested at 3 per cent, or 5 per cent, or 10 per cent, or any figure per cent as the case may be.

Now throughout the commercial centuries a rate of 5 per cent on good security prevailed so often in the money market that it produced the illusion that an income of a thousand pounds a year can always be changed into twenty thousand by a stockbroker. A person with a thousand a year is said to be "worth" twenty thousand; and one with fifty thousand a year a millionaire. The national wealth has actually been estimated by statisticians not otherwise insane as the national income multiplied by twenty.

Here some stockbroker will interrupt me by declaring that whatever I may say to the contrary he can as a matter of fact sell a thousand a year of my income for £20,000 and let me have the money, less his brokerage, within a fortnight. Consequently, for the purposes of his business, the multiplication by twenty is practically sound. But his business is limited to the money market: that is, to the ten per cent or thereabouts of the population who have either settled incomes to sell or spare money to buy them with. Apply the multiplication trick to the entire nation, and its absurdity will promptly bring you up against the immutable fact that by no financial magic or any other sort of magic can you consume the harvest of umpteen hundred and sixty in the year umpteen hundred and forty. It simply does not exist. Yet when a proletarian clamor for taxes on capital arises, as it now does over every annual or supplementary Budget, our capitalist statesmen and journalists, instead of making the simple and smashing reply that there is nothing to tax, as the capital was consumed long ago and is no more taxable than the snows of yesteryear, immediately give dozens of reasons for not taxing it, all founded on the assumption that it still exists, shewing that they are as ignorant of the nature of capital and as dominated by the illusions of the Stock Exchange as the proposers of the taxes.

Let us see what capital is, how it works, and what would happen if a Chancellor of the Exchequer budgeted on the assumption that every £5 note in the kingdom represents £100 in goods available for immediate consumption.

Capital is spare or "saved" money. Our industries have been built up, not directly by the Government, but by making about ten per cent of the population so rich that they had more money than they could spend, leaving the remaining ninety per cent so poor that they not only could not afford to save a shilling but actually had their lives shortened and a monstrous quota of their infants killed for want of enough to spend. When the poor complained, our capitalist bishops could think of nothing better to tell them than that it was their own fault that they did not practise thrift, by which the bishops meant "saving" money when their children were crying for bread. Naturally the people set the bishops down as abominably heartless hypocrites; but they were quite wrong in this: the bishops were kindly and sincere enough; but they just did not know what they were talking about, and had been taught at their universities that Capitalism must inevitably and automatically produce perfect prosperity and social harmony if only everyone would buy in the cheapest market and sell in the dearest.

Bishops know nowadays that a world in which out of every hundred people ninety have to be too poor in order that ten may be too rich is neither prosperous nor harmonious nor Christian. Not only bishops but archbishops and deans now proclaim from pulpit and platform the gospel of Christ Communist; but as they are not yet quite clear as to the nature and method of Capitalism (Christ did not know it by that name) I shall try to make the business easier for them.

Take the case of a workman with an allotment. He discovers that he can get nothing out of it until he digs it; and he cannot dig it without a spade. Therefore he must save enough out of his wages to buy a spade. He—or rather his wife—manages to put by a penny a week (or sixpence or a shilling or what they can afford) until they can buy a spade; and with it the workman makes his allotment produce vegetables enough for his table and perhaps a few over which he can sell. The vegetables are the income which he derives from his capital, as we call the sum he saved to buy the spade. So far it is a perfectly honest, reasonable, and socially beneficial transaction. But there is no room in it for idleness. The spade by itself cannot produce anything. Only when it is wielded by a digger will it produce a single potato; and digging is pretty hard work. Also, though the digger possesses the spade he does not still possess the money the spade cost. That has been eaten up by its makers and the ironmonger, and is gone for ever. Now let us imagine a tax collector calling at the allotment for a tax on its capital.

COLLECTOR. You are working with a capital of six shillings [the price of the spade]. We are at war; and capital is now taxed ten shillings in the pound. The Hun is at the gate. You must hand me over three shillings to pay for the war.

ALLOTMENT HOLDER. But I havnt got any of the six shillings: I paid them all for the spade.

COLLECTOR. Then you must hand over half the spade.

ALLOTMENT HOLDER. Rot! you cant do anything with half a spade.

COLLECTOR. True; so I will take the whole spade; and you will in due course apply to the Special Commissioners of income tax for a refund of three shillings.

ALLOTMENT HOLDER. But damn it, man: you cant get my three shillings change out of the spade unless you dig with it; and meanwhile my allotment goes to waste because I shall have no spade to dig it with.

COLLECTOR. This had not occurred to the Chancellor of the Exchequer or the House of Commons when they passed the Appropriation Bill. Therefore you had better save three shillings more. I will give you a month to do it in, and will call for it then.

ALLOTMENT HOLDER. The hell you will! Your silly people dont know their own silly business: they only know how to rob the poor. I will vote against them at the next election.

COLLECTOR. You can vote as you please: this is a free country. But you will have to pay all the same. Good morning: see you this day month.

I do not defend the language of the allotment holder; but still less can I defend the ignorance and folly of the Ministry imposing the tax and the agitators who demanded it.

This, however, is not the end of the situation. Suppose the Chancellor of the Exchequer did actually take the spade. He could do nothing with it unless he took the allotment too. With both he could cultivate the bit of land to much greater advantage than the allotment holder could, as he could throw it in with all the other allotments and provide it with costly machinery and scientific management by agricultural chemists and accountants and statisticians, besides employing the allotment holder on it at higher wages for fewer working hours than he could ever have hoped for as its proprietor. In short, he could socialize agriculture and nationalize land. Only, as I shall presently shew, this cannot be done by a few strokes of the pen in an Appropriation Act. But before I come to that, let me deal with another and very dangerous possibility.

Though the allotment holder's spade can produce nothing without labor the labor need not be that of the holder of the allotment. Suppose the allotment proves so productive that the holder finds that he can have all the vegetables he needs from it and yet have enough left over to provide for another man and his family! Some laborer who has no allotment will offer to do his digging for him for a share of the produce. The bargain makes the holder an idle parasite on his allotment instead of an industrious cultivator of it.

Or suppose he "strikes oil" on his allotment, or discovers gold or diamonds in it when he is digging for carrots! That happens in South Africa. What happens in this country is that the growth of a city or the making of a new road or the bequest of a new public park makes the site of a cabbage patch worth a king's ransom. In that case the laborer to whom the allotment holder has leased his cabbage patch finds that he can sublet it at a rent so much greater than he has to pay to the first holder (now called the ground landlord) that he can live idly in much greater luxury. And if the value of the site still rises his tenant can repeat the operation, and his tenant's tenant follow suit until the limit of the land value is reached, each subletting adding a parasitic family living on an unearned income. Cabbage patches developed into offices in great cities have a dozen families plundering them at present in this fashion on the strength of a few shillings spent and consumed centuries ago in the purchase of a spade and a hatchet.

I became a Socialist sixty years ago because I had curiosity enough to find out how it was that some people got money for nothing whilst others slaved for thirteen shillings a week or less and died in the workhouse after working hard since they were children. For it was still true and inevitable that not one of the cabbage patches, whether it was still an allotment cultivated by its first holder or the site of a bank, insurance company, commercial Trust, multiple shop, or the like, could produce a haporth of carrots or a penny of rent unless men and women were working on it six days a week.

Thus the appropriation of an allotment, or the pre-emption of a ranch by a pioneer settler, will finally split human society into parasites and producers, workers and drones, masters and slaves, as surely as the grant of an estate by William the Conqueror to one of his barons. And whether the capital contributed by the holders be six shillings for a spade or six millions for a colossal industrial plant or a fleet of transatlantic liners, once the plant and ships are constructed and the six millions spent on the subsistence of the workers whose labor has constructed them, those millions are consumed irrecoverably, and their appearance as figures in the balance sheets is only a memorandum having no substance in fact. In that respect it is pure illusion. The notion that capitalists live on air and can be taxed on it is mere lunacy: we all live on labor and not on property; and the pure milk of the true economic gospel is to be found in the scriptures of Ruskin, who, being himself a proprietor with a social conscience, published his private accounts to shew that every penny he had spent on himself had been earned by his work, and the rest given to his country. Cecil Rhodes barred idlers from benefit under his will.

Thus the world lives from hand to mouth and not on stale bread left by its grandfathers. Some of the contrivances by which they made labor more productive are still in use: roads, bridges, canals, railways, aqueducts, harbors, lighthouses, mines, windmills, watermills, factory buildings, and even machinery, from spinning wheels and handlooms to observatory telescopes; and all these still make life easier for us than it would be without them; but without labor daily repeated they would be quite useless, and fall into ruin and decay for want of repair and mending. They make it possible for everyone to work for fewer hours each day and gain more by the same effort: that is to say, to produce not only more material goods but more leisure. A wisely governed community will see to it that both the goods and leisure are enjoyed equally by everybody. A plutocratically governed community will give all the leisure and all the goods to a favored few whilst making the rest work longer and harder than ever for a smaller and smaller proportion of what their toil produces.

As the latter is our plan, are we governed by idiots and plundered by villains? And are the enslaved masses dastards and imbeciles to submit to it? Not a bit of it: they are simply ignorant of political science. The Government has only to do nothing in the matter (*laisser faire*) except enforce voluntary contracts and keep the peace, and the mischief will occur automatically. The allotment holder will never have to say "I want to be an idler and make another fellow do my work as well as his own". The other fellow will come and offer to do it because he has no other means of living. Tolstoy said that the rich will do anything for the poor except get off their backs; but they cannot get off their backs. Tolstoy tried to do it as a private man; and the attempt ended in his writing an autobiographical play in which he confesses himself an intolerable nuisance and mischief-maker, leaving the last act for someone else to write because it had to end with his suicide. Only the State can do what he tried to do single-handed.

We have had glimmerings of good sense in this direction. Take the case of our inventors and authors. Just as the allotment holder takes an acre of barren clay and by his labor makes it produce vegetables, the inventor takes a blank sheet of paper and changes it into a blue print which tells how to make a calculating machine or a turbine; and the author takes another blank sheet and changes it into a poem, a play, a story, or a treatise. Still, just as the allotment will not go on producing vegetables unless someone goes on digging it, so the calculating machine or turbine will produce nothing without somebody operating it, nor the poems and plays and stories and treatises produce any recreation or edification or instruction or enjoyment unless they are continually printed and circulated or performed. But as the inventors and authors do none of this daily labor they must be given some hold on its profits; for they are indispensable to civilization and culture; and if they are to be kept alive they must be paid for their creative work even if they would rather do it for nothing than not do it at all.

At first it seemed simple to make the blue print the property of the inventor, the book the property of the author, and the musical score the property of the composer, just as the allotment is made the property of its digger. But this proved to be a new form of property, so very peculiar that our judges could not for a long time be persuaded that it could exist at all. Allotments were simple: when their diggers produced a potato it could be used only once by one consumer. When it was eaten there was an end of it; and a new potato had to be produced by renewed labor to replace it. But a blue print is none the worse for being used by the machine-maker: he may make a million machines from it, and it is still valid and unconsumed. The same is true of musical scores and books. The oftener they are read or preached or performed or printed the more famous they become: the appetite for them grows by what it feeds on; and they are as good after millions have enjoyed them as when the ink on them was still wet.

Also, though no one could get a potato out of an allotment without obtaining permission from the owner to enter on it and dig, everyone could use blue prints, musical scores, and books without paying the inventor or composer or author a rap.

Clearly something had to be done about it; and this meant that somebody had to think about it more carefully than allotments are yet thought about. The simplest solution was to forbid anyone to multiply copies of a book and sell them, or to perform plays and charge for admission, without first obtaining the author's permission, on which he could place what price he pleased, thus putting them on the footing of allotments as property: not property for personal use but "real" property: that is, property for rent and profit. This seemed more reasonable than property in land; for the landowner did not make the land: it was the gift of nature, whereas the author, though his genius was also the gift of nature, had labored for many months to write his book. The Bible declared the word of God on the subject to be "The land shall not be sold for ever: for the land is mine; for ye are strangers and sojourners with me." Thus socialistically the twentyfifth chapter of Leviticus, verse 23.

It was hard for a navvy or a blacksmith to believe that making scratches with a pen on a scrap of paper was work on which a man could grow as hungry as at wielding shovels and picks and sledgehammers; and for a long time authors had to live by selling their manuscripts to publishers and players. But publication made the book available to everyone to copy; and when a play was performed a shorthand expert could be sent to report it word by word as it was spoken on the stage and thus obtain a copy for publication or for use in another theatre without paying the author. To this the publishers and managers objected very strongly; for they too wanted an exclusive right to print or perform the book or play they had bought from the author; and this he could not sell to them because he did not possess it. So though the authors were too few, too poor, too feckless in business and politics to obtain anything for themselves from Parliament, the publishers, being men of business, obtained it for them and bought it from them for prices which still left most of them struggling with "toil, envy, want: the patron and the jail," until they formed professional associations (trade unions under a more genteel name) and began to exploit their new sort of property more sensibly.

But where did the glimmering of sense come in on the part of the legislators who created copyright? Well, it seems to have occurred to them that if the new property were perpetual and heritable like property in land, not only would I (for example) be making a sufficient living by writing Pygmalions but if I turned out to be "not for an age but for all time" my descendants five hundred years hence would be doing the same without ever putting pen to paper, as pure parasites on the labor of printers, publishers, actors, managers, and booksellers. Most of them could not even claim to be descendants of the Prophet (Shavin Shereefs), as my copyrights would have been sold by my posterity (we are a somewhat improvident clan) and have passed into the hands of persons incapable of producing a single line of literature.

Accordingly, our legislators took a very obvious protection against this mischievous absurdity. They limited the duration of the copyright to the author's lifetime plus a period sufficient to provide for his widow and educate his non-adult children if he should leave any. At present the period is for life plus 50 years in most European countries by international arrangement, subject to certain local modifications which need not be specified here. In the United States the period is 28 years; but as it is renewable for another 28 the period is virtually 56, near enough to the European 50.

The astonishing part of the business is that it has not yet occurred to our legislators that the objection to perpetual heritable property rights in literature applies equally to property in land and industrial concerns. Instead, there is actually an agitation to make copyright perpetual on the ground that it is not fair that a person whose grandfather's father pre-empted a cabbage patch on the site of Chicago should be a millionaire whilst the great-grandchildren of Dickens may be as poor as church mice. The way to remove the anomaly is surely to municipalize the site of Chicago and limit the duration of leases there, rather than make the progeny of authors as arrant parasites as the progeny of pioneer backwoodsmen.

And there is another anomaly to be removed. What of the inventors? Their case had to be dealt with as well as that of the authors. It was even more pressing; for civilized life is changed much more sensationally by inventions than by books. They have made distances which were in my childhood prohibitive almost negligible: in fact they have abolished them in the instance of the electric cable and the telephone. Shakespear made comparatively no social changes: Watt and Stephenson made the industrial revolution. One would have thought that if any difference were to be made between the inventors and the authors, the inventors would be given the better terms. Yet the author's copyright lasts for his life and 50 years, and the inventor's patent fourteen years from its registration, and this only by a renewal after 7 years.

Such anomalies shew that our legislators are groping their way in the dark from one abuse to the next without foresight, hindsight, or present comprehensive vision. Moses, dead these 35 centuries, was politically minded enough to prescribe a limitation of property rights by a jubilee at the end of every fifty years, when they were to be thrown into a common pool; but as the social machinery necessary for such a change was not then practicable the jubilee never came off, and would have wrecked civilization (such as it was) if it had. But at least Moses had the sagacity to see that something of the sort would become necessary, just as Gladstone, when railways were legalized, foreseeing that the shareholders and their descendants must not own them for ever, provided for their sale to the community as scrap iron at the end of a certain period. But as when the appointed time came the Government was antiSocialist, and not equipped to take the railways and carry them on, Gladstone's provision was set aside by our judges as completely as the Mosaic jubilee.

It is plain through all this that the mischief of "real" property lies in its perpetual inheritance. By the nineteenth century it had resulted in a misdistribution of the national income so outrageous that it could be neither defended nor ignored. Babies were millionaires and workers worn out by a lifetime of toil were paupers. Lapdogs were overfed on mutton cutlets and warmed on drawingroom hearthrugs whilst children were being stunted and famished for want of sufficient food and fuel. When the nation urgently needed more and better housing, clothing, education, and meals, the labor that could have produced them was employed on "fancy goods" (mostly entirely unnecessary rubbish) and ministering parasitically to the parasites. Though the evil was not understood it was so glaring that a serious attack on it was begun.

In spite of the precedent of the copyrights and patents the first attack was not on the duration of property rights. The Government, pressed for money to carry on the great departments of national business that cannot be left to private capitalism because no commercial profits can be made out of them, began to confiscate the incomes of the rich with a vengeance. When I was in my teens income tax was twopence in the pound. It is now nineteen and sixpence on incomes exceeding twenty thousand, which means not only their nationalization but the destitution of their numerous parasites and the bankruptcy of their owners. It is now explicitly and officially admitted that such incomes are unearned by their recipients. In short, as it is no longer denied by economists that such recipients, as "drones in the hive," inflict precisely the same injury on society as thieves do, we, instead of putting a stop to the thieving, have, like Wotan in Wagner's Ring, taken as the rule of our economic policy "What a thief stole steal thou from the thief."

Finally, still not understanding the matter, we attacked inheritance by instituting "death duties" (estate duties) and assessing them on the purely imaginary capital values of the Stock Exchange.

All this, now in full operation under pressure of a war waged at a rising cost of twelve million pounds a day, is wrecking the capitalist system on which civilization is still largely dependent. It seems simple to take the millionaires by the scruffs of their necks and ruin them; but as we cannot do it without ruining Bond Street and Bournemouth as well, besides having to find jobs for their butlers and housekeepers, their cooks and housemaids, we are finding ourselves in a devil of a mess instead of in an earthly paradise. Take my own case, for example. Thirty years ago I spent some months of my spare time writing a play called Pygmalion, for which, thanks to the Copyright Acts, I have been enormously overpaid in comparison with the actors and scenepainters and stage staffs who were doing all the work. Thanks to the invention of the cinematograph (which, by the way, I did not invent) I lately received a further windfall of £29,000, on account of my film rights. The financial result was that I had to pay £50,000 to the Chancellor of the Exchequer within two years. And the result of that catastrophe is that I am now using my copyrights not to have my plays filmed and thereby give employment and enjoyment to my fellow citizens, but to forbid and suppress them in order to reduce my income to a point at which it will be possible for me to live on it. And though the war is calling on everyone to work hard to the utmost that nature can bear to avert defeat by German Nazidom, workmen in all directions are refusing to work overtime lest they should earn enough to become subject to income tax.

A friend of mine, lately deceased, was in very comfortable circumstances when he was unlucky enough to inherit a vast estate and the title of Marquess. He immediately became indebted to the Exchequer for a sum equal to thirteen years' income from the estate by way of death duties, though there was no possibility of getting more out of it than its current year's harvest. My friend said to the Chancellor, "Obviously I cannot pay you in money; but I can give you land [6000 acres or 60,000: I forget which]." The Chancellor, though in principle an ardent land nationalizer, and a minister in a Labor Government, had to refuse the offer, not being in a position to cultivate and manage even one acre of national land. How they settled it, if they ever did, I cannot tell: all I know is that when I had to pay my £50,000 I did not offer some of my copyrights instead; for as we have no national theatre or picture house, nor any national studio, the Chancellor could do nothing with a copyright.

I shall now be asked why, if taxation of capital is insolvent and impossible, it has lasted so long in practice in the form of death duties. The answer is that it has never really existed, and would have broken down at once if it had been levied on all the capitalists every year (which is what its advocates intend) instead of in individual cases at long intervals. If the Chancellor demands thirteen years' income of an estate within one year, but does so only every 33 years: that is, once in a generation, it is clearly possible for the owner to provide for it by saving and insurance; and as this is what was actually done, all went smoothly until in 1914 the Four Years War began, when the carnage in Flanders was so mortal that the life of a company officer at the front was estimated to last six weeks instead of 33 years. When three successors were killed within six months the family estate had to pay death duties three times within a single year on its imaginary capital values, its complete confiscation leaving its heirs still in debt to the Crown: a poor reward for the supreme sacrifice of patriotism. In such cases the death duties had to be remitted. They have never been practicable and never can be practicable except when they are payable only at intervals considerably longer than the number of years income demanded within one year.

Confiscation of unearned incomes is practicable only to the extent to which socialistic enterprise provides employment or State pension for all their parasites. Wars do this by employing them as soldiers, munition workers, and in the industries by which soldiers and munition workers, whose work is destructive and homicidal, have to be supported by productive workers. Thus the Four Years War obliged the Government to build national factories and control private ones, dictating their products, ascertaining their costs of production, and limiting their profits very drastically. But when that war was over all this employment ceased. The national factories were scrapped and the control dropped. There would have been riots if the demobilized soldiers had not been bought off by doles instead of being organized and set to work socialistically to earn a decent subsistence. This they could not do for themselves without land, or direction. The dole imposed on us a new horde of parasites living in abject poverty.

Poor parasites are much worse than rich ones: they can neither save capital, nor give employment, nor set an example of handsome living like the rich ones.

In 1939 the situation was again saved for awhile by the resumption of the war; but it will recur and finally ruin us unless we train rulers who can realize that mere confiscation of unearned income by taxation, with abolition of inheritance by death duties, is not enough, as land and industry must be kept working from day to day, from minute to minute, cultivated, managed, labored without a moment's intermission, or the nation will starve, though the Chancellor of the Exchequer may be sitting on a boxful of share certificates and title deeds. The new Bolshevik Government of Russia in 1917 found this out by trial-and-error. They were not crazy enough to estimate their national resources by multiplying the national income by twenty: they simply beggared the Russian capitalists, landlords, and profiteers on Socialist principles by the direct method of simple violent expropriation. The immediate results were so disastrous that it is a wonder to this day that Bolshevism survived the catastrophe. The Soviet leaders, having read no later Socialist gospel than that of Karl Marx, and being therefore pre-Fabian, did not realize that Socialist statesmen must not nationalize a penny of capital nor an acre of land until the nation is provided with a civil service ready to use that capital and cultivate that land without a day's delay. When Lenin saw what happens when private enterprise is wrecked "on principle" before the political machinery to continue its work is ready, he had to restore sufficient private trading and farming, called The New Economic Policy (it should have been called the old one), to carry on until the Government was equipped to take them over.

It may now be taken as proved up to the hilt that neither Christian principles nor Marxian principles nor the business experience of bankers and stock brokers can steer a modern State safely into genuine democracy. But it is not impossible to ascertain by examination and conversation whether the examinee understands financial economics fundamentally enough to be made a Chancellor of the Exchequer or Lord of the Treasury without risk of our being led into marshes and bogged there by Will o' the Wisps called capital values, land values, social credit, savings, thrift, and all the other disguises of Something for Nothing. The Treasury offices should bear on their front, not LIBERTY, EQUALITY, FRATERNITY, but NOTHING FOR NOTHING AND DAMNED LITTLE FOR A HALFPENNY.

CHAPTER XIII

SENSE AND NONSENSE ABOUT COMPENSATION

As we shed our illusions one by one, or perhaps ten by ten, it becomes evident at every step that civilization, formerly dependent on private property and private enterprise, has outgrown both, and is bursting them into rags in all directions. This, being a matter of pressing facts and not of opinion, has to be faced by citizens of all parties. Those who think they can deal with it by saying "I dont hold with Socialism" are as useless as Socialists who imagine that abolition of private property will set everything right automatically. They both find themselves forced continually to get rid of private property and inheritance molehill by molehill and sometimes mountain by mountain under emergency after emergency without in the least knowing how to do it.

On one point they differ angrily. Those who do not hold with Socialism insist that the expropriated should receive what they call compensation, meaning that they should get back their confiscated property in another form. The others maintain vehemently that they should receive no consideration at all and be left to work or starve as they deserve. They argue that as private property is in effect theft, those who profit by it should be punished instead of compensated. Virtuous indignation is a much relished form of self-indulgence in England, and no doubt elsewhere. But it does not alter the fact that ladies and gentlemen thrown mercilessly on the streets to starve have not really the alternative of working. They do not know how to work and have not been broken-in to it. Some of them are too old and some too young. They have many dependents, among whom the poor relations are as helpless as themselves, and the workers may find their occupation gone. A lady's maid applying for a job as a ragpicker would be refused as "not the sort we want" as surely as her ruined mistress would; and if the expropriation were extensive much fewer ladies would be employing ladies' maids. Besides, the State cannot, like a private employer, get rid of employees by simply discharging them. They come back as paupers, or, more politely, as "destitute persons," entitled to relief under the Statute of Elizabeth and all its modern extensions. The notion that they are in any way culpable is ignorant and silly. They can no more help being proprietors than the rest can help being proletarians. If there were any crime in the matter, it is the proletarians who should be punished for being poor and not the proprietors for being rich. No Compensation is simply deliberate cruelty to animals. There is far too little compensation today. When our handloom weavers were ruined by the power looms in factories they were driven to Luddite rioting for lack of compensation, which it would have been cheaper to give them.

Sensible and humane people will admit this without argument; but they will also ask what good compensation will do if the proprietors are compensated: that is, left as rich as they were before. This very pertinent question shews that compensation is the wrong word. Proprietors as a class will not and cannot be compensated; but their expropriation can be adjusted so as to prevent the proprietor of any particular patch of property having to bear more than his or her fair share of its change from private to public ownership. This can be done easily, and is in fact being done continually, by purchasing the patch at its market price and paying for it by taxation falling on the whole body of property holders. The result is not compensation: it is adjustment, and should be so called.

I am myself a landlord, and, what is worse, an absentee landlord. Since I inherited my property some thirty years ago I once spent a few hours in its neighborhood without entering or identifying a single house on it. Yet I pocket a modest income from it, earned by the labor of its inhabitants, who have never seen me nor received any service from me. A grosser malversation can hardly be imagined; but it is not my fault: I have to accept it as the law of the land; for there is no alternative open to me. I am strongly in favor of this little estate of mine being municipalized; but I expect to be paid as much for it as I could obtain by private sale to a private purchaser. For why should I be left destitute by an unadjusted seizure of my scrap of the town when the landlords of my next-door neighbors are left not only enjoying their rents as before, but finally raising them by the value of the improvements effected through my extinction?

Surely the just course is to pay me the price of my land and send the tax collector to take from me my quota of the price, at the same time making all my fellow landlords contribute their quotas of it. At every such transaction a piece of land passes from private to public ownership; the municipality is richer by the use or rent of it; the landlords as a class are poorer by the price of it; and the ratepayers are richer by the same amount. Our classical political economists proved that rates fall finally on rent; consequently when rates fall rents can be raised; but this is true only when the tenant-ratepayer is rack-rented: that is, paying a rent so high that if it were raised by a shilling he would give up his holding. But this occurs only in the case of extremely poor weekly tenants. To the extent to which the rent falls short of this, as most rents do, the tenant enjoys a share of the economic rent; but he has no power to raise the rent next door, nor can leaseholders, though they can sublet at a profit if they are very substantially underrented. But these avenues to evasion are mainly theoretical only; and most of them are negligible. And as the landlords are all the time being taxed on their incomes so that their candles are being burnt at both ends, municipalization adjusted by purchase has only to be carried out to the end to make all urban land public property, with the landlords, left landless, extinct as a class, and their heirs brought up to work for their living like other people.

Simple as this seems, it needs some elementary economic and political reasoning for its comprehension. Nobody who does not comprehend it can safely be trusted to deal with schemes of municipalization and nationalization. It deals with a key position, and is therefore the test for a key qualification.

Though the transfer of urban land and the goodwill of local business from private to public ownership can be effected very largely by this method, there are cases in which it would not act mercifully to the landlords. Some of the great private estates cover whole towns, or sections of capital cities larger and enormously more highly rented than many provincial towns. To go to one of our territorial peers and say "We are going to municipalize such and such a house on your estate; but you shall not feel the loss, as we shall pay you its market price, and levy it on all the other land-lords in the parish as well as on yourself" would be a mockery if he could reply "Thank you for nothing: I own the whole parish and shall have to find the whole price." As long as we could fairly retort that he could well afford it we could go ahead without re-morse; but there would come a point at which he could not afford it without a cruel change in his circumstances: that is, having to live as, through no fault of his own, he was never taught to live and does not know how to live, beside having to cut off his pro-vision for aged relatives or servants who have tended him faithfully for years in the past. The personal privation is comparatively neg-ligible; for a ducal ground landlord does not eat more than his

gardener nor wear out his clothes as fast; and in his travels sometimes has to rough it very uncomfortably. But he has all sorts of
entanglements and engagements which would make his sudden complete expropriation a calamity to many others. He is entitled, like the
authors, to a notice of such an event long enough to see himself
and his widow comfortably out of the world, and his children
educated for their definitely foreseen future. This can be done, in
reason, by a terminable annuity or a pension for the lives concerned.
Our experience of the younger sons cast out as penniless gentlemen by our present arrangements does not encourage us to have any
more of them hanging about in the future. The poverty of people
who do not know how to live poorly is much more painful than
the poverty of a casual laborer who gets as much as he has ever
been used to, and has not to keep up false social pretences by living
beyond his income—or no income.

If the future is to be a socialistic future the case of people with
unearned incomes will be further affected by the fact that work
will be compulsory for everybody. It always has been for most
people; for not only has the proletariat had to work or starve, but
even the feudal nobility has been subject to morally compulsory
service in the army, the church, or diplomacy. It is only in the
middle class that there is not only no sense of social obligation to
work when one can afford not to but a strong convention that such
"independence" (meaning complete dependence on the labor of
others) is the hallmark of gentility. Gentlefolk must not be seen
carrying parcels.

Now the social obligation to work is not in the least abrogated
by the possession of plenty of money. So far this is legally recognized
only in the case of military service. The man with twenty thousand
a year unearned income has to go into the trenches equally with the
ne'er-do-weel who takes the King's shilling because he does not
know where to turn for his next meal. And military service now
includes all sorts of work under the heading of war work, and
under war pressure has made them equally compulsory. Obviously
this compulsion is as salutary in peace as in war; so the day may not
be far distant when the rich will have to put in the same working
day as their proletarian neighbors. In that case what advantage will
an unearned income confer without its present leisure? We could
say to the millionaire compelled to work alongside his fellow citizens
in field, factory, mine, ship, or office as he is now compelled to serve
in the army "If you and the other millionaires will surrender your

unearned incomes we can cut down your work day by x hours, and everybody else's as well."

Every advance in social organization will make this a better bargain for the renters when they are no longer allowed to be parasites. Even now idle lives are not happy: their victims have to bore and torment each other by a senseless routine of fashion which is not even invented by themselves but imposed on them by the luxury trades which prey on them, the best of it being the country life in which every month is devoted to the hunting and slaying of some animal or bird. This is rather a dog's life than a civilized man's, however healthier it may be than the life of the London season. Trade Unionism and Labor legislation have done something to mitigate the poverty and slavery of the poor; but there is no thought for the miseries of the rich, who are assumed to be living in a state of continual enjoyment, poor devils!

CHAPTER XIV

THE VICE OF GAMBLING AND THE VIRTUE OF INSURANCE

INSURANCE, though founded on facts that are inexplicable, and risks that are calculable only by professional mathematicians called actuaries, is nevertheless more congenial as a study than the simpler subjects of banking and capital. This is because for every competent politician in our country there must be at least a hundred thousand gamblers who make bets every week with turf bookmakers. The bookmaker's business is to bet against any horse entered for a race with anybody who thinks it will win and wants to bet that it will. As only one horse can win, and all the rest must lose, this business would be enormously lucrative if all the bets were for even money. But the competition among bookmakers leads them to attract customers by offering "odds", temptingly "long", against horses unlikely to win: whilst giving no odds at all on the most likely horse, called the favorite. The well-known cry, puzzling to novices, of "two to one bar one" means that the bookmaker will bet at odds of two to one against any horse in the race except the favorite. Mostly, however, he will bet at odds of ten to one or more against an "outsider". In that case, if, as sometimes happens, the outsider wins, the bookmaker may lose on his bet against it all that he gained on his bets against the favorites. On the scale between the possible extremes of gain and loss he may come out anywhere according to the number of horses in the race, the number of bets made on each of them, and the accuracy of his judgment in guessing the odds he may safely offer. Usually he gains when an outsider wins, because mostly there is more money laid on favorites and fancies than on outsiders; but the contrary is possible; for there may be several outsiders as well as several favorites; and, as outsiders win quite often, to tempt customers by offering too long odds against them is gambling; and a bookmaker must never gamble, though he lives by gambling. There are practically always enough variable factors in the game to tax the bookmaker's financial ability to the utmost. He must budget so as to come out at worst still solvent. A bookmaker who gambles will ruin himself as certainly as a licensed victualler (publican) who drinks, or a picture dealer who cannot bear to part with a good picture.

The question at once arises, how is it possible to budget for solvency in dealing with matters of chance? The answer is that when dealt with in sufficient numbers matters of chance become matters of certainty, which is one of the reasons why a million persons organized as a State can do things that cannot be dared by private individuals. The discovery of this fact nevertheless was made in the course of ordinary private business.

In ancient days, when travelling was dangerous, and people before starting on a journey overseas solemnly made their wills and said their prayers as if they were going to die, trade with foreign countries was a risky business, especially when the merchant, instead of staying at home and consigning his goods to a foreign firm, had to accompany them to their destination and sell them there. To do this he had to make a bargain with a ship owner or a ship captain.

Now ship captains, who live on the sea, are not subject to the terrors it inspires in the landsman. To them the sea is safer than the land; for shipwrecks are less frequent than diseases and disasters on shore. And ship captains make money by carrying passengers as well as cargo. Imagine then a business talk between a merchant greedy for foreign trade but desperately afraid of being shipwrecked or eaten by savages, and a skipper greedy for cargo and passengers. The captain assures the merchant that his goods will be perfectly safe, and himself equally so if he accompanies them. But the merchant, with his head full of the adventures of Jonah, St Paul,

Odysseus, and Robinson Crusoe, dares not venture. Their conversation will be like this:

CAPTAIN. Come! I will bet you umpteen pounds that if you sail with me you will be alive and well this day year.

MERCHANT. But if I take the bet I shall be betting you that sum that I shall die within the year.

CAPTAIN. Why not if you lose the bet, as you certainly will?

MERCHANT. But if I am drowned you will be drowned too; and then what becomes of our bet?

CAPTAIN. True. But I will find you a landsman who will make the bet with your wife and family.

MERCHANT. That alters the case of course; but what about my cargo?

CAPTAIN. Pooh! The bet can be on the cargo as well. Or two bets: one on your life, the other on the cargo. Both will be safe, I assure you. Nothing will happen; and you will see all the wonders that are to be seen abroad.

MERCHANT. But if I and my goods get through safely I shall have to pay you the value of my life and of the goods into the bargain. If I am not drowned I shall be ruined.

CAPTAIN. That also is very true. But there is not so much for me in it as you think. If you are drowned I shall be drowned first; for I must be the last man to leave the sinking ship. Still, let me persuade you to venture. I will make the bet ten to one. Will that tempt you?

MERCHANT. Oh, in that case—

The captain has discovered insurance just as the goldsmiths discovered banking.

It is a lucrative business; and, if the insurer's judgment and information are sound, a safe one. But it is not so simple as bookmaking on the turf, because in a race, as all the horses but one must lose and the bookmaker gain, in a shipwreck all the passengers may win and the insurer be ruined. Apparently he must therefore own, not one ship only, but several, so that, as many more ships come safely to port than sink, he will win on half a dozen ships and lose on one only. But in fact the marine insurer need no more own ships than the bookmaker need own horses. He can insure the cargoes and lives in a thousand ships owned by other people without his having ever owned or even seen as much as a canoe. The more ships he insures the safer are his profits; for half a dozen ships may perish in the same typhoon or be swallowed by the same tidal wave; but out of a thousand ships most by far will survive. When the risks are increased by war the odds on the bets can be lowered.

When foreign trade develops to a point at which marine insurers can employ more capital than individual gamesters can supply, corporations like the British Lloyds are formed to supply the demand. These corporations soon perceive that there are many more risks in the world than the risk of shipwreck. Men who never travel nor ever send a parcel across the seas, may lose life or limb by accident, or have their houses burnt or robbed. Insurance companies spring up in all directions; and the business extends and develops until there is not a risk that cannot be insured. Lloyds will bet not only against shipwreck but against almost any risk that is not specifically covered by the joint stock companies, provided it is an insurable risk: that is, a safe one.

This provision is a contradiction in terms; for how can a safe transaction involve a risk or a risk be run safely?

The answer takes us into a region of mystery in which the facts are unreasonable by any method of ratiocination yet discovered. The stock example is the simplest form of gambling, which is tossing a coin and betting on which side of it will be uppermost when it falls and comes to rest. Heads or tails they call it in England, head or harp in Ireland. Every time the coin is tossed, each side has an equal chance with the other of winning. If head wins it is just as likely to win the next time and the next and so on to the thousandth; so that on reasonable grounds a thousand heads in succession are possible, or a thousand tails; for the fact that head wins at any toss does not raise the faintest reasonable probability that tails will win next time. Yet the facts defy this reasoning. Anyone who possesses a halfpenny and cares to toss it a hundred times may find the same side turning up several times in succession; but the total result will be fifty-fifty or as near thereto as does not matter. I happen to have in my pocket ten pennies; and I have just spilt them on the floor ten times. Result: fortynine heads and fiftyone tails, though five-five occurred only twice in the ten throws, and heads won three times in succession to begin with. Thus though as between any two tosses the result is completely uncertain, in ten throws it may be six-four or seven-three often enough to make betting a gamble; but in a hundred the result will certainly be close enough to fifty-fifty to leave two gamblers, one crying heads and the other tails every time, exactly or very nearly where they were when they started, no richer and no poorer, unless the stakes are so high that only players out of their senses would hazard them.

An insurance company, sanely directed, and making scores of thousands of bets, is not gambling at all; it knows with sufficient accuracy at what age its clients will die, how many of their houses will be burnt every year, how often their houses will be broken into by burglars, to what extent their money will be embezzled by their cashiers, how much compensation they will have to pay to persons injured in their employment, how many accidents will occur to their motor cars and themselves, how much they will suffer from illness or unemployment, and what births and deaths will cost them: in short, what will happen to every thousand or ten thousand or a million people even when the company cannot tell what will happen to any individual among them.

In my boyhood I was equipped for an idle life by being taught to play whist, because there were rich people who, having nothing better to do, escaped from the curse of boredom (then called *ennui*) by playing whist every day. Later on they played bezique instead. Now they play bridge. Every gentleman's club has its card room. Card games are games of chance; for though the players may seem to exercise some skill and judgment in choosing which card to play, practice soon establishes rules by which the stupidest player can learn how to choose correctly: that is, not to choose at all but to obey the rules. Accordingly people who play every day for sixpences or shillings find at the end of the year that they have neither gained nor lost sums of any importance to them, and have killed time pleasantly instead of being bored to death. They have not really been gambling any more than the insurance companies.

At last it is discovered that insurers not only need not own ships or horses or houses or any of the things they insure, but that they need not exist. Their places can be taken by machines. On the turf the bookmaker, flamboyantly dressed and brazenly eloquent, is superseded by the Totalizator (Tote for short) in which the gamblers deposit the sums they are prepared to stake on the horses they fancy. After the race all the money staked on the winner is divided among its backers. The machine keeps the rest. On board pleasure ships young ladies with more money than they know what to do with drop shillings into gambling machines so constructed that they occasionally return the shilling ten or twentyfold. These are the latest successors of the roulette table, the "little horses," the dice casters, and all other contraptions which sell chances of getting money for nothing. Like the Tote and the sweepstake, they do not gamble: they risk absolutely nothing, though their customers have no certainty except that in the lump they must lose, every gain to Jack and Jill being a loss to Tom and Susan.

How does all this concern the statesman? In this way. Gambling, or the attempt to get money without earning it, is a vice which is economically (that is, fundamentally) ruinous. In extreme cases it is a madness which persons of the highest intelligence are unable to resist: they will stake all they possess though they know that the chances are against them. When they have beggared themselves in half an hour or half a minute, they sit wondering at the folly of the people who are doing the same thing, and at their own folly in having done it themselves.

Now a State, being able to make a million bets whilst an individual citizen can afford only one, can tempt him or her to gamble without itself running the slightest risk of losing financially; for, as aforesaid, what will happen in a million cases is certain, though no one can foresee what will happen in any one case. Consequently governments, being continually in pressing need of money through the magnitude of their expenses and the popular dislike of taxation, are strongly tempted to replenish the Treasury by tempting their citizens to gamble with them.

No crime against society could be more wickedly mischievous. No public duty is more imperative than the duty of creating a strong public conscience against it, making it a point of bare civic honesty not to spend without earning nor consume without producing, and a point of high civic honor to earn more than you spend, to produce more than you consume, and thus leave the world better off than you found it. No other real title to gentility is conceivable nowadays.

Unfortunately our system of making land and capital private property not only makes it impossible for either the State or the Church to inculcate these fundamental precepts but actually drives them to preach just the opposite. The system may urge the energetic employer to work hard and develop his business to the utmost; but his final object is to become a member of the landed gentry or the plutocracy, living on the labor of others and enabling his children to do the same without ever having worked at all. The reward of success in life is to become a parasite and found a race of parasites. Parasitism is the linchpin of the Capitalist apple-cart: the main Incentive without which, we are taught, human society would fall to pieces. The boldest of our archbishops, the most democratic of our finance ministers, dares not thunder forth that parasitism, for peers and punters alike, is a virus that will rot the most powerful civilization, and that the contrary doctrine is diabolical. Our most eminent churchmen do now preach very plainly and urgently against making selfishness the motive power of civilization; but they have not yet ventured to follow Ruskin and Proudhon in insisting definitely that a citizen who is neither producing goods nor performing services is in effect either a beggar or a thief. The utmost point yet reached in England is the ruling out of State lotteries and the outlawing of the Irish sweepstakes.

But here again the matter is not simple enough to be disposed of by counsels of Socialist perfection in the abstract. There are periods in every long lifetime during which one must consume without producing. Every baby is a shamelessly voracious parasite. And to turn the baby into a highly trained producer or public servant, and make its adult life worth living, its parasitism must be prolonged well into its teens. Then again old people cannot produce. Certain tribes who lay an excessive stress on Manchester School economics get over this difficulty easily by killing their aged parents or turning them out to starve. This is not necessary in modern civilization. It is quite possible to organize society in such a manner as to enable every ablebodied and ableminded person to produce enough not only to pay their way but to repay the cost of twenty years education and training, making it a first-rate investment for the community, besides providing for the longest interval between disablement by old age and natural death. To arrange this is one of the first duties of the modern statesman.

Now childhood and old age are certainties. What about accidents and illnesses, which for the individual citizen are not certainties but chances? Well, we have seen that what are chances for the individual are certainties for the State. The individual citizen can share its certainty only by gambling with it. To insure myself against accident or illness I must make a bet with the State that these mishaps will befall me; and the State must accept the bet, the odds being fixed by the State actuaries mathematically. I shall at once be asked Why with the State? Why not with a private insurance company? Clearly because the State can do what no private company can do. It can compel every citizen to insure, however improvident or confident in his good luck he may happen to be, and thus, by making a greater number of bets, combine the greatest profit with the greatest certainty, and put the profit into the public treasury for the general good. It can effect an immense saving of labor by substituting a single organization for dozens of competing ones. Finally it can insure at cost price, and, by including that price in the general rate of taxation, pay for all accidents and illnesses directly and simply without the enormous clerical labor of collecting specific contributions or having to deal in any way with the mass of citizens who lose their bets by having no accidents nor illnesses at any given moment.

The oddity of the situation is that the State, to make insurance certain and abolish gambling, has to compel everyone to gamble, becoming a Supertote and stakeholder for the entire population.

As ship insurance led to life insurance, life insurance to fire insurance and so on to insurance against employer's liability, death duties, and unemployment, the list of insurable risks will be added to, and insurance policies will become more comprehensive from decade to decade, until no risks that can worry a reasonably reckless citizen are left uncovered. And when the business of insurance is taken on by the State and lumped into the general taxation account, every citizen will be born with an unwritten policy of insurance against all the common risks, and be spared the painful virtues of providence, prudence, and self-denial that are now so oppressive and demoralizing, thus greatly lightening the burden of middle-class morality. The citizens will be protected whether they like it or not, just as their children are now educated and their houses now guarded by the police whether they like it or not, even when they have no children to be educated nor houses to be guarded. The gain in freedom from petty cares will be immense. Our minds will no longer be crammed and our time wasted by uncertainty as to whether there will be any dinners for the family next week or any money left to pay for our funerals when we die.

There is nothing impossible or even unreasonably difficult in all this. Yet as I write, a modest and well thought-out plan of national insurance by Sir William Beveridge, whose eminence as an authority on political science nobody questions, is being fiercely opposed, not only by the private insurance companies which it would supersede, but by people whom it would benefit; and its advocates mostly do not understand it and do not know how to defend it. If the schooling of our legislators had included a grounding in the principles of insurance the Beveridge scheme would pass into law and be set in operation within a month. As it is, if some mutilated remains of it survive after years of ignorant squabbling we shall be lucky, unless, indeed, some war panic drives it through Parliament without discussion or amendment in a few hours. However that may be, it is clear that nobody who does not understand insurance and comprehend in some degree its enormous possibilities is qualified to meddle in national business. And nobody can get that far without at least an acquaintance with the mathematics of probability, not to the extent of making its calculations and filling examination papers with typical equations, but enough to know when they can be trusted, and when they are cooked. For when their imaginary numbers correspond to exact quantities of hard coins unalterably stamped with heads and tails, they are safe within certain limits; for here we have solid certainty and two simple possibilities that can be made practical certainties by an hour's trial (say one constant and one variable that does not really vary); but when the calculation is one of no constant and several very capricious variables guesswork, personal bias, and pecuniary interests, come in so strongly that those who began by ignorantly imagining that statistics cannot lie end by imagining, equally ignorantly, that they never do anything else.

CHAPTER XV

THE ILLUSIONS OF WAR FINANCE

WARS, they say, have never stopped for want of money. They need not. Once civilization has got as far as organization and division of labor permanent war becomes possible. When Adam and Eve were driven out of the Garden and had to fend for themselves they had to feed and clothe and house not only themselves but their children; otherwise the race would have perished with them. It is thus a condition of human survival that every human couple should be able to support by its labor at least three unproductive, greedy, mischievous brats as well as themselves. There are plenty of instances of couples who have brought up ten or fifteen children, and been rewarded by their governments for this patriotic service. Such feats may cost hard labor for many years; but a thousand couples, civilized and organized, with their labor divided and aided by machinery, can support not only their families, but sufficient police forces, armies, and even some idle and extravagant drones too, without unbearable difficulty.

Billions of couples could maintain millions of soldiers fully equipped for millions of years without becoming bankrupt. That is why wars need never cease for want of money.

To realize this possibility requires careful management, because there is always a limit to the number of men a community can afford to put into the field of battle and into the industries which equip them. Modern nations cannot exist without victuals, clothes, fuel, and shelter. Take all the men out of these civil industries; and not only war but human life becomes impossible. The problem of how many can be spared for the army and the munition factories, if not accurately solved, may mean defeat by starvation. This is simple enough in theory; but where capital rules, the practical calculations become complicated. Capital is, as Marx shewed, insatiable in its quest for cheap labor; for, other things being equal, the cheaper the labor the bigger the dividends. If labor costs ten shillings per day per head at home, and there are places abroad where it costs ten shillings a week, capital will stream abroad to that place unless the Government is wise enough and strong enough to keep it at home and see that it is employed where it is most needed. But a Government of capitalists will not do this: on the contrary, it will easily be persuaded by Cobdenite fanatics that not only can the most profit be obtained by foreign trade but that when all nations become dependent on it they will starve if they make war on oneanother, thus making Free Trade a guarantee of universal peace, and, as such, something that we cannot have too much of. By 1851, the British Government had become completely convinced of this, and celebrated their conviction by the first of the great Exhibitions in that year: an Exhibition being an assembly of samples of all the goods produced by all the nations to promote free trade in them.

The consequences were anything but millennial. When England's first need was to demolish the slums in which her people were rotting, and nourish her children well enough to stop the frightful infant mortality in them, the needed capital was sent away to South America, Malaya, Egypt, the Congo, India, and wherever else native labor was cheaper: that is, where all the natives could live on less than the natives of the British Isles, poor as these were. Sixty years ago the London dockers struck for "the dockers' tanner" (sixpence an hour); and the London match girls struck for something better than five shillings a week and for precautions against "fossy jaw," as they called necrosis of the jaw from phosphorus poisoning. Today I find that my box of matches has been made in India; and the cotton trade of Lancashire, once the source of many fortunes, is desperately trying to compete with Japanese labor costing a penny an hour. With our natural resources in coal and iron we still make machinery for export; and we still cling to the ridiculous paradox that the more we export and the less we import in exchange for it the better off we are; but the end of it is that we have become dependent on other nations for the bread we eat, and that a successful blockade would starve us; for we cannot eat our coal and iron: a hard fact overlooked by Cobden. Blockading becomes the object of modern war strategy everywhere. War of man against man with rifle and bayonet is rare now; and lancers, hussars, and dragoons drive tanks and know horses only as creatures to back for the Derby. War is war on shipping waged from the depths of the sea by submarines and from the air by armed planes, a sunken convoy being worth a dozen mechanized stalemates in the field.

Meanwhile, on the money front, "foreign securities," meaning paper title deeds to unearned imports, are compulsorily sold to our allies for helping us with the blockade. In this way a creditor nation at war may easily become a debtor nation in a few days without knowing what is happening if its statesmen are not very competent in financial business. What has happened in the British Isles is that they have reduced themselves to dependence on other countries and on their colonies for their food, making foreign trade a matter of life or death, and then stuck a ramrod into the machinery of foreign trade by engaging in world wars. In the Four Years War we came within an ace of being starved out by the German submarine; and as I write we are in the same predicament again. We are tightening our belts and being rationed in an agony of quite wellfounded dread that this time the German submarines may get the better of our destroyers and battleships.

Nevertheless it remains true that England, by scientific collective farming and public control of foreign trade and of the export of capital, can not only feed herself, but maintain to the crack or doom the continual warfare she is always waging somewhere or other, as far as finance is concerned. A thoroughly socialized country can afford a war much better than an unsocialized one, though it is much less likely to provoke one. Still, as it may have to make war on war and on barbarism and crime, especially modern national barbarism, the question of war finance must not be shelved on the ground that the present war will be the last war, and that victory (assumed by the combatants on both sides to be quite certain) will produce a new order in which war will be unknown and impossible. Whatever else it may do it will certainly not do that.

When a war has to be financed, a statesman must bear a few fundamental facts in mind. Though a war can be financed by raising loans in the money market it cannot be waged on credit. The soldier cannot fight on promissory notes: he must have his bully beef and his ammunition on the nail. Loans may be negotiated and orders given; but as the goods must be delivered and distributed to the combatants day by day, they must also be produced day by day or the war cannot go on. War is a matter of ready money and ready manufacture: the postponement of consumption and anticipation of production which is bought and sold in the money market is not possible for the soldier, who is consuming and expending all the time at a terrific rate.

How then is it that the cost of a war can be "funded" (added to the National Debt) as it always now is more or less? The reply is that the postponements and anticipations in which the money market deals are natural impossibilities which do not occur at all: they are only Stock Exchange illusions. Between individuals the illusions work well enough. Smith has expectations which he wants to sell for ready money. Jones has more goods, mostly perishable, than he needs for immediate consumption, and would like to secure his future by exchanging them for Smith's expectations. They effect the exchange; and the transaction may be described as a postponement of consumption by Jones and an anticipation of production by Smith; but from the point of view of the State there has been neither postponement nor anticipation: all that has happened is that Smith has consumed certain existing goods instead of Jones and Jones abstained instead of Smith, the quantity and availability of the goods remaining unaffected. The goods expected by Jones do not yet exist and will not exist until they are created in the future by productive labor. It is on the credit of this future productive labor that Jones's existing store of spare goods has been obtained by Smith.

But the soldier's labor is not productive: on the contrary it is destructive, incendiary, devastating, homicidal. Glory, victory, patriotism, liberty, posterity, heroism, are fine words; but they butter no parsnips. The prodigious consumption in war must be accompanied by an equally prodigious production, not in the future but now, on the spot, in advance of the consumption; for until the goods are produced the troops cannot eat them, wear them, and shoot them off, leaving nothing tangible behind but cripples, corpses, rags, smithereens, and ruin. The world cannot go into debt for a war: it must pay as it goes without an hour's delay.

But though the world cannot go into debt States can. They can borrow not only from oneanother but from their own people, calling the operation War Savings, which is utter nonsense, as war eats up savings at the present rate of fifteen millions a day. But the consequent illusion that wars can be fought on credit is soon reduced to absurdity by inevitable events. Under the American Lease and Lend arrangements England and Russia are borrowing their war stores from the United States. In the Four Years War, most of the Allies borrowed its cost from England, and England borrowed it from the United States. But when it came to repaying the loan or the interest on it the debtors defaulted in all directions. France repudiated four-fifths of her debt by simply devaluing her currency. England's debtors defaulted without apology: they could not pay and did not. England, having assumed responsibility for their borrowings, defaulted also, to the indignant surprise of the Americans, who ought to have known better. It is already admitted that the Lease and Lend borrowings can never be repaid in hard cash, and must, except for purely metaphysical satisfactions, be regarded as gratuitous contributions to the war chest. The interest on the money borrowed from our own people will no doubt be paid punctually; but the money to pay it with will have to be made by the labor of its lenders and confiscated by taxation of income. There is nothing to be hoped for from the defeated enemy in the way of plunder; for nothing short of exhaustion and bankruptcy will force a well-armed Power to yield. The good Samaritan, far from being able to rob the man who had fallen among thieves, had to give him twopence to pay his hotel bill with, which is precisely what the Allies will have to do for Germany when they have defeated her. After the Four Years War England tried to make Germany pay. We demanded gold: the Germans had none, unless we would lend it to them. We demanded ships and steel; and the first payment nearly ruined our own shipbuilders and steel smelters. Hastily forbidding the Germans to send us another ship or another ton of steel, and being asked what, in that case, they could send us instead, we replied, fatuously, potash, whereupon the whole absurdity exploded in general derision and we began to complain that Germany, having lost the war, had won the peace. Our boasted determination to make Germany pay,

THE ILLUSIONS OF WAR FINANCE

so useful at elections, was succeeded by an agonizing dread lest
she should prove capable of doing so and thereby inflicting
on us a ruinous crisis of industrial depression and unemployment such as she herself suffered after her victory over France
in 1871.

There is no end to the follies which even the cleverest financiers
commit when they let the business habits of the banks and the
money market come between them and the vital facts of life. The
gentlemanly Whig historian Macaulay went so far as to contend that
an increase in National Debt indicates an increase in national prosperity, though the proletarian Cobbett, hard down on facts, saw "the
Funding System" clearly as the chief agent in the process described
by the poet Oliver Goldsmith in the prophetic lines

> Ill fares the land, to hastening ills a prey,
> Where wealth accumulates, and men decay.

In truth the National Debt, as the business world sees it, is a
National Delusion. After the Four Years War the payment of interest on it rose to about a million a day, which would have staggered Macaulay had he lived to enjoy it. But it did not make any
considerable difference to the masses. The nation's creditors were
the nation's capitalists: the nation's capitalists were taxed and surtaxed on their incomes. The interest on the debt was levied by income tax and surtax. The capitalists were receiving their interest;
but they were also paying it. All that was happening was a redistri-
bution of income among them in the direction of equalization, which
was to the good, and was effected by graduation of the tax. I was a
holder of War Loan Stock. I was taxed at a higher rate than my
fellow capitalists who had smaller incomes. But then I had to pay at
a lower rate than others who had bigger incomes. Whether I lost
on the swings what I gained on the roundabouts I do not know: I
never took the trouble to calculate. But the masses who were exempt
from income tax neither paid nor received a farthing in the business.
And as the Government, by its power of confiscation and consequent
advantage of gilt-edged credit, had been able to raise the money at
the lowest possible rate of interest, whereas its private competitors
would have had to tempt us by at least double that rate, the nation
had its war cheaper than its commercially produced luxuries. It
actually cost less to bombard the Rhineland cities than to rebuild
them. This is one of the many paradoxes of the capitalist system,
which we endure because we never argue paradoxically on hard

facts, but always straightforwardly on assumptions which are partly romantic and partly mere commercial habits.

Since the resumption of the war in 1939 astonishing contributions to the War Loan in its varied forms have been made by proletarians living on weekly wages. They earned the money by their labor, and are looking forward to enjoying the interest on it. But as they will have to earn the interest by their labor exactly as they earned the capital (all blown to smithereens), they will still be chasing the carrots their riders are holding in front of their noses. The surtaxed capitalists will be equally unaware that their interest is coming out of their own pockets. Finally the owners of the land will skin both workers and capitalists alive by raised rents. I can remember when the weekly rents paid by our wage slaves varied from two or three shillings to five or six. Now they vary from fourteen to twentytwo. For permission to live and work on the soil of England I have paid its owners tens of thousands of pounds over and above the interest on the cost of the buildings they have provided; and I grudge it none the less in that I have been able to extort a very little of it for nothing from my own tenants. Thus the matter is complicated in detail solely by the debts we incur to oneanother; for in the lump there can be no debts, because the lump lives in the natural world; and the natural world lives from hand to mouth. However it may stock its wheat and freeze its meat, no year of it can ever live on the harvest of a past or future year; and when there are people claiming or appearing to do so, something is rotten in the State.

In this matter as in others the Machiavellian statesman may have to exploit and even to create the illusions that reconcile citizens to the slavery of military service and the burden of war taxation; but financial confusion and catastrophe await any nation in which the statesmen share these illusions!

CHAPTER XVI

ON WAR AND ITS GREAT MEN

WAR is not one of the complicated economic, financial, or judicial public institutions that are in a mess because they are mismanaged by political amateurs who do not understand them. Everybody understands war only too well; for it is a primitive blood sport that gratifies human pugnacity. Successful players at it earn fame enough to satisfy the maddest human ambition. I enjoy civil celebrity; but as I have never killed anybody in a violent manner I am hopelessly outshone by warriors who have hundreds of thousands of violent deaths to their credit. Napoleon was a contemporary of Kant, Goethe, Mozart, and Beethoven. Compare their tombs, and you will get an aesthetic measure of how much more we admire a great soldier than a great philosopher, poet, or composer. Adolf Hitler, when, having decimated Poland and demolished half Warsaw, he drove the British army out of France into the sea and the Red Army out of the Baltic provinces and back to the Don, was lord of half Europe whilst Einstein was an exile, with a much smaller income than a baseball champion. We speak of war gods, but not of mathe-matician gods, poet or painter gods, or inventor gods. Nobody has ever called me a god: I am at best a sage. We worship all the conquerors, but have only one Prince of Peace, who was horribly put to death, and, if he lived today in these islands, would have some difficulty in getting exempted from military service as a conscien-tious objector, if indeed he did not catch the war infection and head the rush to enlist.

There is then no secret about all this, no misunderstanding. Though war is now so diabolical that modern belligerents have to protest that they are fighting in self-defence, and that every war is a war to end war and to save civilization, we go on killing one another and glorifying our successful commanders as before.

Such devilment is a trump card in the hands of pessimists; but it is only another specimen of the time lag by which ancient moral valuations and the education proper to them become ingrained habits, and persist long after the facts have changed and reduced them to mischievous superstitions. The vogue of Napoleon and Alexander may trace its origin to the primitive tribes where no reputable woman will marry a man unless he can produce trophies proving that he has slain at least four adult male foemen in single combat; but neither Napoleon nor Alexander produced a scalp or scrotum to prove that he had ever killed an enemy in battle. They never brought home a slain mammoth or sabre-toothed tiger, nor even a wild boar, to their wives to cook for the family dinner. In-deed Napoleon, brave as he shewed himself in his early Italian cam-paigns, reproached himself for having behaved with downright poltroonery on his way to Elba disguised as a postilion; and in a political crisis he was so nervous that he lost his head and would probably have had it chopped off had he not been saved by the presence of mind of one of his brothers. Alexander got drunk and murdered his best friend; but this is not why we admire him. But by ordering the deaths of a prodigious number of people the two achieved the utmost eminence attainable in human history. The great soldier-slayers are made despots, and, when they die, leave this form of government to be practised by men not great, and sometimes conspicuously the reverse. Then there is trouble. Inadequate despots at their worst have to be assassinated by their own courtiers, like Nero and Tsar Paul. In any case it soon becomes apparent that Conqueror despotism is disastrous in the intervals between the occurrence of great soldiers, and that for these long intervals some alternative must be found, as the world must be governed whether there are geniuses to govern it or not. When none are available, and it must be governed by dunderheads, these dunderheads must themselves be governed by a set of rules based on history, experience, and regard for the common welfare. Such sets of rules are what we call Constitutions.

When conquest becomes the road to glory and power, nations forget public welfare and strive for military hegemony, calling it the Balance of Power, but meaning an overbalance in their favor. Each sovereign State, when it feels strong enough, claims to be the headquarters of a Chosen Race, under whose government all other States would be better off than under their own. In Germany this is explicitly discussed, reasoned, proclaimed, preached, and finally put to the test of war. In England it is assumed in silence as a truth so selfevident as to call for no discussion among sane people. Under great rulers the pretension holds good: under their little successors it produces world wars and makes super-State Constitutions necessary. The League of Nations is the latest attempt at such a constitution; but the framers of its Covenant were careful to break its back by the impossible condition that all its decisions should be unanimous. Also that the Committee of Intellectual Cooperation thrust on it later by a private sociologist should have no funds, no publicity, and consequently no attention. So the Powers went on making war as if the League and its committee did not exist. Mussolini fired on Corfu at the start just as England declared war on Germany at the finish, neither of them dreaming of submitting their cases to the League, which might just as well not have existed for all it could do to prevent a second world war. But the League, whether renamed International Council or what not, will have to be revived with sensible and practicable covenants; for civilization no less than its component States must have a constitution or be dominated by dunderheads, do-nothings, incapable hereditary monarchs, ambitious conquerors, popular speakers and broadcasters, financial and commercial gangs, successful revolutionists who are no rulers or stick-in-the-mud rulers who are no revolutionists: in short, by amateur actors of all sorts clever enough to make themselves the idols of the mob of political ignoramuses who are idolized as Democracy.

Meanwhile the League, through its most anomalous and yet most useful organ the International Labor Office (the only feature that was ever real about it), holds the fort as best it can.

Military discipline is instructive. More than fifty years ago I was marching in a procession which numbered at least a thousand men. It was broken up and scattered in hopeless confusion and terror by twenty pale nervous policemen armed with nothing more deadly than their clubs. Not one of the thousand knew what to do or what any of the others would do; so they all ran away, except those who were overtaken and knocked on the head. I did not run away: I walked away; and as I was respectably dressed and seemed unconcerned nothing happened to me except that one elderly man who recognized me as one of the orators who had exhorted the thousand to march to victory before the procession started, rushed up to me and cried, "Tell us what to do. Give us a lead," making me acutely conscious of my disgraceful exposure as an impotent windbag. I could only tell him that there was nothing to be done but to make our several ways to the place of meeting as best we could.

Now this man was visibly less frightened than some of the twenty policemen. He wanted to fight them more than they wanted to fight him. But each of the twenty policemen knew what the other nineteen were going to do, and had the law on his side. He had a uniform, a helmet, and a weapon, and could depend on the cooperation of nineteen uniformed, helmeted, weaponed comrades. It was a triumph of expected behavior over mistrust and anarchy. Since then I have had nothing but a sardonic smile for Shelley's "Ye are many: they are few." It made an end for me of the democratic delusion that the world is or ever can be ruled by majorities of unorganized individuals. Even the organized are at the command of the minority who can make decisions, who know what to do, and can do it. And these are as likely to be ambitious scoundrels as men of good will. Real democracy must find some means of distinguish-

ing between them and of disfranchising citizens ignorant enough
to admire scoundrels and prefer being ruled by them. Morris's
warning that "no man is good enough to be another man's master"
(having a mastermind himself, he knew what he was talking about)
is hopelessly irreconcilable with the democratic delusion that anybody is good enough to be everybody's master. As we must be
ruled we must have rulers. What we call liberty depends on our
power to choose our rulers (there are always enough to leave us a
choice), and on the knowledge and wisdom with which we exercise
that choice.

When I am asked on what ground I hold that there are always
enough born rulers to give us a choice I can reply only that there
is a force in nature which used to be called Providence. It arranges
these things. We can give no scientific account of it as yet; but the
practical politician has to accept it as a fact in spite of the air of
superstition it has acquired from its ecclesiastic associations.

Discipline is as necessary and as potent in industry as in war: not
until a man ceases to be a man and becomes a factory hand can he
produce anything. War is itself an industry with the function of
killing, sinking, burning, and destroying to order, for which purposes modern mechanization has greatly increased its range and
efficiency. It is this peculiar and terrifying function that brings
us back to a very old question. What justifies a citizen in killing
his neighbor, whether as a private person for private ends, or on
a jury, or as a field-marshal? Killing is sometimes too simple a
matter to argue about: a farmer must kill rabbits and squirrels or
they will kill him. Sometimes it is very complicated: for instance I
have said that, outside the criminal law which disposes of people
who are obviously as mischievous as rabbits, the best reason for
killing a neighbor is his possession of three shillings when you have
only half a crown. Now this is a highly arguable proposition. If your
object in killing him is to appropriate to yourself his three shillings,
or even the odd sixpence that is between you, then you are committing a vulgar crime and are not fit to live in civilized society. A
jury will presently give effect to that view by handing you over to
the public executioner. But if as a sociologist you have realized that
the first condition of the stability of a civilized State and the first
condition of justice, production in its proper order, good breeding,
good feeling, and good manners, is equality of income; if you
believe consequently that the State should take both your half-
crown and his three shillings and hand you back two and ninepence

apiece, and he is prepared to resist this operation to the death, then you have a strong case for killing him if you cannot disarm him.

This final argument of thy life or mine is as effective for evil as for good. Dick Turpin demanding your money or your life, and Adolf Hitler demanding your territory or your life, cannot be defeated by moral remonstrances: you must either hand over your money to Turpin or carry a pistol and be quicker on the draw with it. And to hold your own against Hitler you must have bigger battalions than he, or better weapons, or both. Compared to Turpin he is at the disadvantage that he must secure the consent of millions of his neighbors to place their consciences at his disposal and kill everyone whom he wants to have killed even at the risk of their own lives. And you beat Turpin finally not by carrying a pistol but by organizing a police force so ubiquitous and efficient that he despairs of evading it. And for this you also must induce a body of your neighbors to place their power to kill at your disposal.

Killing by deputy makes killing easier. Hitler, since he was a humble corporal, has never killed anybody. Other people have done his killing for him. Torquemada never burnt a Jew. Cromwell did not cut off King Charles's head, nor King James turn the rack on Guy Fawkes. They induced other people to do it for them.

This means that there is a limit to war in the person of the conscientious objector. The most completely disciplined official draws a line somewhere. A prison warder will flog a man for half a crown; and there is never any difficulty in finding a hangman willing to operate for a modest fee and the privilege of selling pieces of used rope to private collectors of such curiosities. But the warder is not necessarily an unscrupulous and cruel wretch who will do anything for a few shillings or even for fun. All flogging schoolmasters are not sadists, though I am sorry to have to add that the biographies of those contemporaries of mine who have passed through our gentlemanly private preparatory schools prove that some of them certainly are. But no body of men can be induced to do another man's killing for him unless he can convince them that they may honorably do so. The percentage of blackguards and sadists who enjoy cruelty for its own sake have to pretend that they are patriots and ministers of justice to secure the toleration of their fellow citizens.

The mechanization of modern war greatly reduces the power of the human conscience to keep its abuses in check. It would be hard to induce a youth of ordinary goodnature to take a woman with a baby in her arms and tear the two to pieces with a Mills bomb in full view of the explosion. But the same youth, thousands of feet up in a war plane, preoccupied with the management of his machine and the accuracy of his aim, will release a bomb that will blow a whole street of family homes into smithereens, burning, blinding, mutilating scores of mothers and babies, without seeing anything of his handiwork except the glow of a conflagration which is as pretty as a display of fireworks. The hospital surgeon sees what the pilot has done; but it is the pilot and not the surgeon who releases the bomb.

The infantry soldier does not even see the fireworks. I have stood on a modern battlefield watching a group of soldiers waging war. I pitied their extreme boredom. They had a camouflaged cannon, and were feeding it with shells. Each shell had to have a fuse screwed into it before it was passed to the men who pushed it into the breech of the cannon. Then a man pulled a string; and the shell went off into the air with a tremendous Bang-Whizzzz. Where it went to, what it did when it got there, whether it exploded or not, was unknown to these weary men picking up shells, screwing in fuses, closing the breech and pulling the string over and over again without the horror of seeing any result from their monotonous toil. I could not work up the smallest interest in the business after the first shot even when I tried to remind myself that another group of men, similarly employed on the German side, might at any moment send a shell into my midriff equally joylessly. I recalled the battles described by Homer which had delighted my boyhood, and wondered sardonically what Homer would have said to this battle in which I was under fire, and which our war correspondents would have to make as thrilling on paper as the fights on the plains of Troy in which the gods and goddesses themselves took part. A duller entertainment I cannot conceive. But it rubbed into me the utter divorce of the warrior from the effects of his soulless labor. He has no sight or knowledge of what he is doing: he only hands on a shell or pulls a string. And a Beethoven or a baby dies six miles off. All he feels is a longing for his spell of duty to be over and his ration of bully beef ready for him. I did not even see yellow as Goethe did at Valmy, Wagner in Dresden, and a chauffeur of mine at King's Cross during a raid. The notion that these heavily bored men were being heroic, or cruel, or anything in the least romantic or sensational, was laughable.

Only the dogfights of the planes bring back modern war to the heroic duels of Ajax and Diomedes, Hector and Achilles, but with the quaint difference that the victor must fly away without "consolidating his position" or obtaining a surrender or military decision of any kind. Battles used to last one day, and end in victory or defeat. They now last for months without decisive result, the offensives beginning with alarming successes and then petering out, and the whole sanguinary business being presently overridden by blockade, exhaustion, starvation, revolution, or some other event remote from the field of battle, where the armies "fertilize the field that each pretends to gain."

It must not be assumed, though it sometimes is, that soldiers are all for war and civilians against it. The contrary would be nearer the truth. It is by soldiers that we are told that if we could see one day of war we 'should never want to see another. Experienced soldiers who are capable of anything better than soldiering come to loathe war as heartily as Paderewski came to loathe the piano. Marlborough was as successful a general as Napoleon. Wellington defeated Napoleon. Bismarck defeated France and Austria and created the German Reich by "blood and iron." All three ended by desiring peace at almost any price. Napoleon seems to be an exception; but he was forced to go on feeding the French people with military glory because they could understand nothing else that he could do. Our Lord Protector Cromwell, when he found that he could defeat every general within his reach, did not try to found a world empire with himself as its despot: he exhausted every possibility of parliamentary government before its uselessness for anything but obstruction and speechifying forced him to govern by martial law with a staff of majors general to deputize for him whenever he had to say, like Napoleon when he heard of Trafalgar, "I cannot be everywhere." It is the civilians and the women who keep up the romantic prestige of war, not the soldiers.

I am afraid it is still true that when a chief of State is chosen by the people instead of by heredity or an admittedly divine right, he must impress his electors by doing horrible things. Heaps of human skulls in the market place, virgins buried alive beneath the posts of his hut, human sacrifices executed by priests clotting their hair with human blood, seem to civilized ladies and gentlemen to be detestable crudities; but these refined people worship Jesus and take comparatively no account of Socrates and Mahomet, for no discoverable reason except that Jesus was horribly tortured, and Socrates humanely drugged, whilst Mahomet died unsensationally in his bed.

When neglect of sanitation brought frightful plagues on great cities chroniclers held them up as displays of the majesty and greatness of Almighty God; and now, even in ultra-modern Russia, the present war was sanctified by a Te Deum in the very cathedral which had been used as an anti-religious museum. We sacrifice every freedom to war: freedom of speech, of the Press, of our lives and all our liberties save only our freedom to fight. We abolish even our freedom not to fight. When war becomes such a ruinous nuisance that the great Powers will combine to impose peace on the rest, the lesser States will fight them for the right to fight, and convert the war to end war into a war to end peace.

We may take it then without further instances that war cannot be abolished and must therefore be supranationally controlled and converted into a police force for the frustration of attempts to make it a means of gratifying imperial and other anti-social instincts, whether national or personal. For war is not necessarily a culmination of human depravity: it is now a romantic superstition rooted in courage and generosity—chivalry in short—rather than in the aboriginal savage ferocity on which it was grafted. These virtues are not obsolete: very far from it. Employment must be found and organized for them. In business, in science, in politics, in exploration and research of all kinds there is now infinitely greater scope for the restless courage of the young and the considered enterprise of the mature than in mere homicide and destruction. H. G. Wells is pioneering the path of wisdom when he urges that heroic enterprises must be provided for our young men, as without such opportunities they will either make political mischief or waste themselves in fruitless sports. The axiom that Satan will find mischief still for idle hands to do applies to idle virtues and capacities as well.

It would be a mistake, however, to suppose that armies are made up of aspiring young heroes driven to seek in soldiering a satisfaction for energies thwarted in all other directions. They are composed very largely of physically hardy men who are so helpless mentally that they need a constant direction and tutelage that they can find nowhere except in the army. They are the tools by which the conquerors become Great Men. And they find officers who, though better nourished and trained, are in the same predicament. We have to reckon not only with war in the abstract and with idolized conquerors, but with the living men of war as a species. For just as there are human varieties which we call the black man, the colored man, the yellow man, and the white man (more correctly described in yellow China as the pink man), we have in civilized society the military man, the economic man, the religious man, the scientific man, all needing separate acquaintance and study by the statesman. To lump them for all purposes as common humanity is to make trouble.

As we are on the subject of war, let us take the military man first.

CHAPTER XVII

THE MILITARY MAN

THE Military Man claims for the pursuit of his passion and the exercise of his talent exemption from civil morality. Marshal Ney, "the bravest of the brave," was a nobody off the battle field. War was as necessary to him as water to a fish. He followed Napoleon as long as Napoleon had an army; deserted him when he lost it; and joined him again the moment he recovered his army: a career of devoted pugnacity which led to his being shot, not too magnanimously, by the Allies for his second desertion. Then there was Napoleon himself, to whom winning battles was such child's play that he came to regard himself as invincible. Millions perished to gratify his ambition and exercise his talent before the European nations combined strongly enough, and found a commander able enough, to extirpate him. What one man of his type can do is astonishing. As I write, Adolf Hitler is in full Napoleonic career: men are dying in millions, cities crashing in ruins, and an empire distintegrating because of him. And like Napoleon, he is idolized for it: our contemporaries die for their upstart Führer as Frenchmen used to die for their upstart Emperor. All the Napoleons and Hitlers from Alexander and Attila to this day have been classed by their fellowcountrymen not as the villains of historical melodrama, but as its heroes. Their civilian worshippers give them votes enough to enable them to control parliament as long as they are successful; and parliament gives them soldiers by ordaining compulsory military service for all ablebodied citizens.

Now compulsory military service is the most complete slavery known to civilized mankind. Why does mankind force itself to submit to it, and glory in it? And first of all, why did war exist long before modern compulsory military service? To what extent is the natural man a fighter, a robber, a slayer: in one word, a soldier, in spite of Mark Twain's quite sound ruling that "the average man is a coward"?

One can only guess at how it began. What we know is that in every hundred men there are some who can think and plan and wait for the results for years ahead, even beyond their own lifetimes for the sake of the world's future, and others who can think and plan and wait no farther than from hand to mouth, being practically unconscious of their own future—much less that of the world. They are often recklessly brave because they cannot see beyond the nearest enemy nor lust beyond the day's appetite. They do not apprehend danger because they do not apprehend anything beyond the ends of their noses. In early days such men had to live by hunting animals and eating them, by robbing strangers and enslaving or killing them. They specialized as hunters and shooters and soldiers and fighters, ripe for organization as warriors by anyone with the requisite brains and energy and taste for the job. Thus we got the Military Man. For commander he prefers the country gentleman who produces nothing but the spoils of hunting, shooting, and fishing, and who considers service in the army or in militant diplomacy as the only professions worthy of his rank, and trade or manual labor as beneath him.

Now if the race is to survive every woman must have her man and every man his woman: two to the unit. But though the woman has to bear all the labor of childbirth and to nourish and protect the human infant during its long nonage, her man is to her more than a mere fertilizer. He must be a fighter who can protect her against rape, and her helpless children against robbery by strange fighters. He must catch and kill the animals she has to cook for the family and flay for fur clothing. Consequently before selecting him as her mate she demands proof of his ability to kill strangers. In the west he must shew her the scalps of those he has slain. In the east a scalp is not evidence: it might be that of a woman. It must be an organ of an adult man. The Danakil women of Abyssinia are reported to demand from their warriors four such trophies if they are black, but to accept one if pink. It is therefore not, as Italian soldiers have imagined, mere senseless ferocity which leads the native tribesmen to mutilate their slain enemies: the trophies are the primitive equivalents of the Victoria Cross, the *croix de guerre,* and the rest of the hallmarks which stamp civilized men as warriors of proved prowess for the defence of hearth and home.

Meanwhile what are the thinkers and planners at long range doing? They are discovering the fundamental art of agriculture and thus making peaceful civilization possible. They see the advantage of waiting a year for the harvest and many years for the growth of fruit trees and timber trees. They tame the ox instead of eating it, and harness it to the plough. They kill vermin to exterminate it, not to eat it; and they soon find out that the worst species of vermin is the human sort whose motto is "Thou shalt starve e'er I starve" whilst their own is "We must stop killing and robbing and eating one another or we shall all starve."

This natural division of human society into barbarians and civilized citizens, into Napoleon-Hitlers and Conscientious Objectors, into Shakespeare's Henry V and Wagner's Parsifal, into cannibals and vegetarians, is confused by their intermarriage; so that pure specimens are rare; but it remains marked still. Heredity, as Mendel shewed, does not operate by making the union of a white parent with a black one produce grey children exclusively: it produces also entirely black and white children in certain proportions. The black inherit the traditions of the white and the white those of the black. And the external pressures on them are strong both ways. Women are forced by their circumstances to be peaceful, economical, and provident for the sake of their children: that is, of the race; but they are equally forced to admire and encourage pugnacity in men, their bodyguards. Being provident they are acquisitive, jealously pugnacious in defence of their belongings, and vindictive.

Besides, the traditions which begin with crude barbarism conflicting with the beginnings of civilization do not remain crude. A wonderful and fascinating glamor of poetry and romance grows up to glorify the risks and braveries and battles and victories and even the love affairs of the fighters. "When Adam delved and Eve span where was then the gentle man?" Cain the slayer has become, if not the gentle man, certainly the gentleman. Idealized by romancers and troubadours as the perfect gentle knight whose strength was as the strength of ten because his heart was pure, he turned Don Quixote's head. He also turned mine. When I was a small boy and an arrant coward I represented myself by fantastic lying as an invincible fighter. When I was taken to the theatre to see a costume play I was interested as much in the swords of the actors as in the play. When I looked forward, as all boys do, to what I should buy when I was grown up and had plenty of money I had not a moment's doubt that my first and most cherished purchase would be a revolver. If anyone had prophesied that I should grow up and have plenty of money and reach my eightyeighth year without having ever bought a firearm, I could not have believed him. The literature that stirred my blood with the thunder of the captains and the shouting in the Bible, and the combat of Christian with Apollyon and Greatheart with the giants in The Pilgrim's Progress, could still stir me in Gilbert Chesterton's war song of Lepanto. Gilbert grew up to be a man of enormous size; but at his biggest he still played with a bayonet like a boy. In 1914, in my fiftyninth year, I was astonished and scandalized to find traces of war excitement still stirring in me.

Lovers and practitioners of literature know better than anyone else how barbarism, surviving in a disguise of chivalrous heroism, has ended in an idolatry of famous warriors quite as fanatical as that of the glorious company of the apostles or the noble army of martyrs. The wisest of the French kings, grandfather to the wisest king of England, is remembered not by his aim at a France in which every man should have a chicken in his pot, but by Macaulay's ballad of the battle of Ivry in which God figures as the Lord of Hosts. The monarch or statesman who wishes to head off a popular movement can still do it infallibly by drawing a war across its path. However loudly a reformer may sing the praise of Jesus as the Prince of Peace, the firing of a single cannon-shot will change the hymn to "The Son of God goes forth to war." People will do nothing for peace and freedom except fight for them (or against them) even if they have to sacrifice both in the process. Glory was not invented by Napoleon: it was readymade for him by all the bards and all the romancers: he had only to appropriate it as an aureole and exploit it to the utmost of his capacity for winning battles, and other generals' capacity for losing them, to make himself emperor of most of Europe for a dozen years. Conquerors can defy all constitutional laws until they are defeated. Popular pugnacity, idolatry, and glory worship are their impregnable bulwarks.

But the worship of glory, though it accounts for the mentality of the staffs of commissioned officers which a conqueror never lacks, hardly fits in with the illiteracy of the rank and file who have to do the bayonet and bullet work, the "common soldiers," the infantry and cavalry of whom even poets laureate can say nothing more glorious than "Theirs not to reason why: theirs but to do and die," and of whose sergeants Wellington complained that it was impossible to find one sober or to get an order executed after eight o'clock at night. Yet without these heroes Blenheim, Waterloo, Balaclava, Wagram, and Austerlitz would be nameless. What was the attraction of soldiering for them?

Well, it was more of a necessity than an attraction. Civilization confers benefits on mankind; but it also imposes activities and efforts of which we are not all equally capable: indeed of which some of us are not capable at all. Work has to be planned: decisions have to be made: temptations have to be resisted: complicated processes have to be understood. The capacity to meet these demands varies from individual to individual, and also from class to class when there are wide differences of education and income. Those who can find out what to do in organized business are scarce. Those who can find out how to do it are scarcer still. Men who are hopelessly at a loss until they are told what to do and shewn how to do it are very common in any proletarian population. For them the choice is between docility and starvation. They would be absolutely at the mercy of the planners and deciders were it not that their bodily strength and senseless courage make them as indispensable to their employers as their employers to them.

Even the extreme cases of this fecklessness are numerous in large modern populations. Put them as low as five per cent: still, a population of forty millions, half of them women, provides a conqueror with a million never-do-wells who can find the tutelage they need, with assured food, clothing, lodging, selfrespect, and status, in the army and nowhere else. In uniform their conduct is often exemplary and their bravery proved by their full share of Victoria Crosses. Demobilized, they are presently in the dock for yielding to childish temptations or being driven by helpless want to sign worthless cheques or spend money that does not belong to them.

Beside these poor fellows, for whom the State should provide tutelage as it should secure freedom from it to stronger natures, we have a mass of persons of ordinary capacity who are not politicians. They accept society as they find it, and will take any legal and respectable employment if it is made worth their while. Cromwell got his Ironsides not only from the fanatical Republicans and Levellers, but from the respectable men who were satisfied with the wages he offered and with his assurances that in his army they would be in godly company where drunkenness and foul-mouthed conversation would not be tolerated. Our modern conscribed Ironsides are denied this modicum of decency, and apparently do not desire it;

for they could easily impose it on oneanother. The modern proletarian is to that extent a blackguard.

In short, conquerors and glory merchants have never been at a loss for soldiers so far. They have enlisted even geniuses of the highest order: Coleridge and John Bunyan voluntarily entered the army as common soldiers; and Bunyan served not on his own side, but on that of the Royalists who afterwards kept him in prison for twelve years for not belonging to the Church of England.

Finally the military barbarian enjoys such prestige, and the military genius such power, that the civilized man has to defend himself by making war on war and becoming himself a barbarian in the process. Experienced conquerors like Marlborough and Wellington may hate war; but romantic agitators extol it unrebuked as a necessary school of manly virtue, and are supported by such facts as that it is hard to shake civilization out of its deepest ruts by anything less terrible. It has taken two world wars to force us to set our clocks and arrange our working and sleeping hours by the changes of winter, spring and summer, obvious and simple as that step has proved. How many Armageddons a reform of our spelling and arithmetic will cost, I cannot guess. Yet the economic case for a British alphabet capable of spelling my name with two letters instead of four is enormously more pressing than the meteorological case for adjusting our watches to the two hours difference between midsummer and midwinter daylight.

Therefore let no statesman dream that he can rule out war from the possibilities against which he has to provide until it abolishes itself by its own cost and cruelty. There is no escape from it at present. To "resist not evil" as the disciples of Tolstoy and Mahatma Gandhi would have us is to invite aggression and conquest. To arm to the teeth is to provoke a race of armaments and wars of self-defence. The prudent statesman cannot in any case do without the military man. He must even provide for the special education of a certain proportion of the population as military men: that is, as romantic barbarians. But he must know what he is doing and take care to retain political control of them. And this he can do only by being both abler and wiser than they. Just as the best available operating surgeon may be the worst possible judge of whether an operation is necessary or not, the most brilliant conqueror may be a very bad judge of whether a war is necessary or not: he is certain to be a biased judge in any case.

It sometimes happens that the born soldier is abler and wiser than the statesman. His government may be better than any existing civil government, and his power needed to break down superstitions which the civil government is not strong enough to get rid of. Napoleon could not have made himself emperor had the Directorate he kicked out been intelligent, efficient, and honest. If the Allies had not abused their victory over Germany after 1918 instead of restoring her to health and sanity as carefully as they restored injured German prisoners of war, Adolf Hitler's rise to power would have been impossible. Before a country can need a military Savior it must reduce itself, or be reduced by bad internal government, to a condition by which it must be ruined if somebody does not save it; and we and our allies were stupid and cowardly enough to reduce Germany to that condition and give Adolf Hitler his opportunity. For seizing that opportunity he deserved from his country all the gratitude he got; but his victory went to his head, and made him believe that he also (like Napoleon) is an invincible Man of Destiny, the destiny being to save the whole world by conquering it.

Now it is not enough to conquer the world: the conquered must be conciliated by finding themselves better off under the conqueror than they were before he imposed his rule on them. Julius Caesar was wise enough to understand this. When he, like Napoleon, found that winning battles was child's play to him, and also that he could govern people much better than they were governing themselves, he took care to make the people he conquered, as far as he could, glad that he had conquered them, and very reluctant to have their old rulers back again. Stalin understands this. Even Napoleon understood it far enough to announce himself always as Liberator, and be accepted for a moment by Beethoven as a hero. It is futile for a government threatened by a conqueror to call on the people to resist him to the death in defence of Democracy, Liberty, King and Country, and all the rest of the verbiage of the patriotic recruiting platform if the country is in fact so badly governed that any change is welcome, and any promising pretender sure of a following. Had the Bourbon monarchy in France been efficient enough to give its soldiers their pay punctually instead of settling Marie Antoinette's gambling debts with it the insurrections which began the French Revolution would have been crushed by the French army, and its reforms carried out under Louis XVI quite constitutionally, in which case Napoleon would have been Heaven knows what: perhaps discharged from the army for outstaying his leave, perhaps an elderly marshal in the royal service, which was his own guess. It does not matter now; but the lesson of his career and that of his twentieth-century imitators remains: to wit, that incompetent governments with obsolete ideologies, however democratic they may be in form, go down before up-to-date conquerors. And when the conqueror's victory goes to his head and makes him a pathological phenomenon instead of a political one (an event which may be regarded as in the course of nature; for unlimited political power corrupts as surely as prussic acid poisons), there is the devil to pay: a debt which we are just now (1944) paying through the nose.

CHAPTER XVIII

THE ECONOMIC MAN

ALL men are Economic Men from their conception to their death, whereas the other categories are minorities, and sometimes very small ones.

A meal, a beverage, a bed under a roof, and necessary clothing come first with us all; for without them we perish. Up to that point therefore we are all economic problems for the statesman. But nine out of ten of us can be bought off for £2 a week per family, which even the most selfish Capitalism can and must afford so as not to kill the goose that lay the golden eggs before there is time to replace it with a younger and more auriferous goose. Man is at his most economic when hungry, cold, and naked. When you feed, clothe, and house him, however miserably, he ceases to be wholly economic, and becomes a creature with aspirations and scruples, with a conscience, with "views," with passions and prejudices that are all immaterial and irrational: that is, metaphysical.

Keir Hardie, the founder of the Independent Labor Party, once addressed a string of very wretched men who were waiting to scramble for a casual job at the London docks at dawn on a cold winter morning. They were the worst-paid male manual workers in London; and their poverty was being rubbed into them mercilessly by heavy rain. Accordingly, Keir Hardie talked Socialist economics to them as their most urgent political interest. He then, as a candidate for the local parliamentary seat, invited questions. Thereupon a man, blotted against the dock wall for some half shelter from the downpour, stepped out and said he had listened to the speaker's able address, but had been surprised to find that it contained no politics. What they wanted to know, he said, were the speaker's views as to the disestablishment of the Church in Wales.

On the off-chance of being picked by the foreman for the job of unloading a ship for sixpence an hour at the risk of accidents which occurred every twenty minutes according to the records of the London Hospital, this economic man had become a metaphysical man. He was not a Welshman; and the establishment or disestablishment of the Welsh Church would not have made a farthing difference to him. And he was a typical voter. For all practical purposes the citizen who is not made desperate by starvation is almost insanely metaphysical. He drove Ferdinand Lassalle to despair by his "damned wantlessness." We need to make the Economic Man much more economic, not to go on pretending that he is only a fiction of the capitalist economists. He has already raised his highest terms from £2 a week to £4; and it is possible to raise them finally to the largest dividend of the entire produce of the nation's labor that will leave enough for new capital and nothing for any idler or waster. That is the Communist ideal, between which and poverty there are many degrees that will satisfy philanthropists and Trade Unionists who still believe in private property and the sufficiency of the profit incentive.

It is clear, then, that the quality mankind lacks to make the Economic Man correspond to the actual human animal, and to make the Capitalist system work as beautifully in fact as it did a hundred years ago on paper, is economic insatiability. How rare it is is shewn by the fact that a very moderate degree of ability enables individuals to become rich if only they devote all their energies to making money. This the ordinary person will not do. A street hawker must keep hawking until he has gained a shilling for a bed in a dosshouse and a couple of meals. He must hawk that much or starve. Give him a half-crown early in the day, and instead of going on hawking until dark as usual, and perhaps quadrupling his day's income, he will instantly quit the kerb and take himself off with his basket to live at leisure for the rest of the day and tomorrow as well.

A skilled worker on piece-work in a factory finds from time to time that an improvement in methods enables him to earn twice as much every week as he is accustomed to live on. Instead of raising his standard of life by a hundred per cent he knocks off work at the

factory for three days in the week. He is insatiable, not for wages
or for work, but for leisure and freedom. His employer, however
generous, is consequently forced to stop this "absenteeism" by cutting the piecework rate, whereupon the workers strike, and there is
no end of trouble and loss to both parties until the workers consent
to accept a share of the improvement in production small enough to
leave them obliged to come to the factory every day as before.

One might infer from all this that our ten per cent of rich property-
owners who are born supersatiated with both money and leisure
exercise no economic pressure on the statesman; but a statesman
acting on this inference would soon find that though poverty is dole-
fully satiable, prosperity is practically insatiable. In east London revolt against poverty can be bought off for £4 a week at most and less
than a pound at least. Further west peace is not to be had so cheaply.
A young married couple in Mayfair, even when childless, think they
need at least nine domestic servants; that their sons cannot be educated for less than £300 a year each and double that to finish at the
university; that their teeth cannot be examined or their eyes tested
for less than three guineas, with all their other occasions priced on
the same scale.

Karl Marx shewed that Capital in pursuit of Surplus Value (unearned income) is utterly insatiable and utterly unscrupulous. How is
this fact to be reconciled with the equally certain fact that capitalists
are human animals and that the human animal is neither insatiable
nor unscrupulous? Why does human animal No. 1 submit to life in
a single overcrowded room in a slum, and human animal No. 2,
luxuriously housed in a spacious mansion in a fashionable London
square, build a palatial shooting lodge in the Highlands, a castle in
the Lowlands, a seaside country house to bathe from, a princely
pied à terre on the Riviera, and a first-class steam yacht to take the
air on the open sea? Ask No. 1 why he does not build castles: he
replies that he cannot afford them: he is too poor. Ask him why he
does not refuse to accept starvation wages: he says that the alternative is starvation without any wages. Ask him why he does not revolt: he will say that the police wont let him and that the police have
army and navy, artillery and Air Force, at their backs; besides, even
if there were no police, he wouldnt know how to revolt or to feed
himself while he was doing it.

Catechize No. 2, and he will probably resent your impertinences
and order his servants to shew you out and not to admit you again.
But he may be enough of a philosopher to have asked himself why

he acts as he does; and in that case he may be disposed to discuss his conduct with you, and even to admit your right, if you have reasonable credentials, to call him to account for it. You ask him why, being able to live in only one house at a time, he builds or buys four or five. As likely as not he will tell you that as a matter of fact he lives mostly in hotels and sleeping cars, and keeps up four or five houses with their staffs of troublesome servants (waiting mostly on each other) because society is organized in such a way that he must do it "to keep up his position," and because he finds himself esteemed and confirmed in his self-respect in proportion to his expenditure on superfluities. He may add, "I cannot sack all these people who are dependent on me. They would starve, knowing no other service but the service of the rich, to which they have been brought up. In defence of that service they would fight to the death, just as they now vote for it." There are several Number Twos who would add, "I am myself a man of simple needs and tastes that money cannot gratify; and I hate this whole damned business of fashionable society and wish I had been born in Russia; so get out and dont bother me. Talk to the Government and the democracy about it, since only they can change it all."

Do not be put off: press your question by demanding why when he has spent every penny that society obliges him to spend he tries to increase his superfluous income by investing continually in stocks and shares. He retorts by asking you what else he is to do with it. If he does not lend it out at interest his bankers will. If in desperation you fall back on "Sell all that thou hast and give it to the poor," his answer is that if he sells his stocks and shares he will only be substituting some other shareholder for himself, and that even if he could find a means of giving the price to "the submerged tenth" of a modern proletarian population the dividend would not buy them a single meal apiece, and the only effect of the transaction would be to add himself to the number of the destitute. It is a demonstrable truth that in a capitalist system the wisest practicable economic advice to the rich is "Invest all thou canst spare at the highest rate of interest compatible with reasonable security." Thus in the end the rich man is perforce the Economic Man in spite of his own human nature; and the statesman is obliged to deal with him as such in the lump though he knows that in nature there is no such animal.

All the same there is a snag in the business. If capital is pecuniarily insatiable and men are not, the two will sooner or later be landed in a scandalous contradiction. For it is an inevitable consequence of human satiability that every increase in the quantity of any desirable article reduces its market price; and this applies to capital (spare money) as surely as to food or clothing. To keep up the price of fish many have to be thrown back into the sea. Tons of wheat and coffee harvests have to be burnt to keep the rest saleable. Overproduction is the curse of Capitalism, and commercial competition its mainspring; yet commercial competition makes overproduction inevitable. When a hundred people want a hundred pairs of new boots, and ten competing shopkeepers, each hoping to secure the entire sale, order a hundred pairs from the boot factories, who will accordingly manufacture a thousand pairs, nine hundred of these will be left unsaleable on the shop shelves. Until nine hundred people wear out their boots and buy up the superfluous pairs the shops give no further orders to the factories; and the factories have to discharge their workers and add them to the unemployed. Hence we get the cycles of overproduction followed by unemployment and trade depression, the booms and slumps, the crises and recoveries, which are characteristic of the capitalist system and are dreaded economic nuisances.

When the slump comes the factories cannot at once discharge all their workers, stop their machines, lock up their buildings and offices, and leave their engines to rust and their capital to "eat its head off." They must keep producing unsaleable goods to keep their factories alive; and as they cannot sell the goods at home they are driven to seek new markets abroad. And as the separate nations compete forcibly for such markets a strong economic interest in wars of conquest arises among industrialists whose operations are too big to be stopped without ruinous damage. And this interest extends from the manufacturers to their bankers and financiers, whose fortunes stand or fall with theirs.

Now the financial gentry, though their interests are bound up with those of the manufacturers, do not themselves deal directly with manufactured goods: most of them have never in their lives been inside a factory or workshop nor down a mine. They live by selling capital: that is, spare money. And capital, like any other sort of desired goods, is dear or cheap according to the quantity on sale in the money market. Just as there is a point at which fish must be thrown back into the sea, and coffee and wheat burnt to keep up their prices, so there is a point at which only a destruction of capital can check the fall of its price to nothing, or even to a negative figure at which we should have to pay bankers and strongroom builders for keeping our spare money for us instead of lending it very lucratively.

To illustrate how this works I must begin by pointing out a very important difference between land and capital.

Land increases in market value in direct ratio to industrial development and increase of population. Capital does just the reverse. When I was young I could buy a secure income of £1000 a year for £20,000. I could not get £20,000 by working; for five or six pounds a week was all I could earn; but I presently became the proprietor of copyrights which proved lucrative and enabled me to reap the fruits of other peoples' labor to the extent of £20,000 more than I was accustomed to live on. Few people were in that position; and my spare money, my capital, had a scarcity value of five per cent per annum. But the invention and multiplication of machines, and the elimination of the waste of competition by the amalgamation of competing business firms and companies without any equivalent increase in the cost of labor, kept increasing the unearned spare money on sale until its price fell to three and even to two-and-a-half per cent. When I laid hands on another £20,000, I could get only £500 a year for it instead of £1000 without running risks. The Government was able to pay off all the people to whom it was paying five per cent by borrowing the money at two-and-a-half. In fact it was hardly necessary to go to that trouble, as its possibility compelled most of the holders of the five per cent stock to accept the new rate instead of the old.

This did not suit the financiers at all. It did not suit me. The usual measures were taken to limit the accumulation of spare money by destroying the goods that the money represented. Wheat was burnt, coffee was burnt, and netted fish were thrown back into the sea whilst the proletariat were badly short of the food they could not afford to buy. But these childish peckings at the downward movement of the value of spare money could not arrest it. Burning bags of coffee was silly: what was needed was destruction on a scale that only governments with thousands of millions of money and millions of soldiers at their command could hope to achieve. It seemed the work of Providence when the South African war broke out, and I was able once more to obtain £1000 a year for £20,000.

But King Edward the Seventh insisted on having peace for his coronation, and stopped the war on terms that left South Africa practically victorious. No matter. For our masters the financiers it was enough that the price of spare money was up again to five per cent.

A period of great industrial activity followed, with the inevitable result that spare money accumulated again, and a colliery to which I had lent money on mortgage at six per cent paid me off and left me looking in vain for five per cent on the lump of spare money thus thrown back on my hands. I could hardly expect that Providence would restore the value of my money again.

But it did.

The Four Years War came just in the nick of time; and I lent the Government at five per cent £20,000 for which I should have been lucky to get three per cent the year before. My patriotism was applauded in the Press.

Twenty years after the armistice I was in the soup again. Spare money was a drug in the market. Burnt offerings of wheat and coffee were offered up on an unprecedented scale. Herrings were jettisoned by the hundred thousand. My bankers would pay me so trifling an interest on my deposit account that negative interest loomed on the horizon. Then the armistice crashed; and the war with Germany was resumed and was presently complicated by a war with Italy at a cost which presently reached fifteen million pounds a day. The Government invited me to lend it my spare money at two per cent. I shook my head, waiting for five, perhaps for ten. So it confiscated my riches by a tax of nineteen and sixpence in the pound.

Can I ascribe these coincidences to mathematical chances? Eminent mathematicians of my acquaintance have gone to Monte Carlo, where, having proved that certain results of spinning the ball on a roulette table could occur only once every thousand years, they saw them occur three times in seven weeks. Still, three coincidences of war with gilt-edged securities at two-and-a-half per cent was more than I could swallow. I could not fall back on Providence; for a Providence that has to burn down the house to roast the pig is an incredible Improvidence. When a miraculous coincidence recurs regularly under the same circumstances one begins to suspect that it is no miracle, but simple cause and effect, purpose and design. Somebody is working the oracle.

Who, I cannot find out. War used to be good for me financially: I have been too old for military service and have lost only one near and elderly relative by it. Others have made enormous fortunes by it, selling old ships for ten times their pre-war value, besides enjoying swollen rents and dividends without lifting a finger. Do not tell me that war profits nobody: I know better. If money were all I cared about I should be as militarist as Adolf Hitler or Benito Mussolini.

This being so, I am assumed to have had my share in starting the war. Now I have never written a line to start a war. Far from caring for nothing but money, I should be a much richer man if I had given to my business a hundredth fraction of the time, attention, and interest I have given to my profession and to public questions. War is more distressing for me than for the Jingos because I feel the losses on both sides, whereas they seem to feel they have made a good bargain when the slaughter of one Englishman is followed by the slaughter of two Germans or Italians. I can never forget that the loss to Europe, and consequently to us all as Europeans, is the same whether the slaughtered man's name is John or Fritz or Beppo. I have not the consolations and exultations of English patriotism; for I am an Irishman who on native patriotic principles should rejoice in England's defeats. I loathe war, and feel no difference in point of atrocity between the blitzings of London and those of Naples and Cologne. They both sicken me.

Now I am not at all singular in this. All the capitalists I know hate war as much as I do. To imagine that any of us would deliberately throw a lighted match into a powder magazine to raise the rate of interest by two or three per cent is to fly in the face of human nature and plain fact. The notion that all the financiers, all the Jews, all the bankers, all the shareholders of the munition firms, the bully beef and woollen cloth firms, the boot firms, the shipbuilders, and the rest of the industrialists who profit by war, to say nothing of the unemployed proletarians, who are never as well fed, clothed and housed as they are in the army, are infernal scoundrels, is manifestly false. As to the Governments offering war to the electorate as a health tonic and a necessary ingredient in the sustenance of a virile national character in the pseudo-Nietzschean manner, they are perhaps honester than the pseudo-Christian governments; but in England governments take care to profess their Christian belief that God is on their side, and that their wars are forced on them to make future wars impossible.

And yet war still follows two-and-a-half per cent as surely as night follows day. The truth is that the need of Capital for death and destruction sets in motion the human force of natural pugnacity, professionalized in the Military Man. With him we have already dealt.

CHAPTER XIX

THE EDUCATED

Mr H. G. Wells never misses an opportunity to remind us that species which fail to adapt themselves to the natural conditions in which they have to live, and to change their habits as these conditions change, are doomed. The alternative is to adapt the conditions to our habits, including our faiths and hopes. Both these activities are practicable to an extent to which we dare set no limit, in spite of the people who keep saying that we cannot change human nature, nor the climate, nor move mountains. Not only are they changeable, but if left alone they change themselves so much faster than we change our minds that our haphazard governments are never able to keep our institutions up to date.

The most staggering of our failures to change our institutions synchronically with the changes in the social and natural facts is our school system. Long ago, when all our books were written in Latin, unless we could understand Latin we could not read books at all, nor write them. Without Latin we were illiterate. Today Latin is a dead language in which no books are written. A person understanding no other language would be hopelessly illiterate and virtually deaf and dumb. Yet our school system ignores this change and still proceeds on the assumption that Latin is the language of literature and culture. The result is that our governing class, which has gone through the mill of preparatory school, public school, and university, is as illiterate as it is possible for any civilized class now to be, and maintains a contempt and dislike for intellectual, artistic, and scientific pursuits of which only the grossest ignorance is capable. And here again we find that though there is no such animal in existence as the totally illiterate Educated Man, yet as a social force people who have been through the schools must be counted as illiterate and anti-cultural by the statesman.

Dr Inge has told us wisely that if we formulated our ideal of education we might say that we should be taught all that concerns us to know in order that we may become all that concerns us to be. It is a national tragedy that, scholarship apart, his own public school and university education taught him nothing that concerned him to know, and thereby grievously hindered and delayed his becoming all that it concerned him to be, which was much more than Dean of a cathedral too large for its congregation.

It is not the ignorance of the uneducated that threatens us most, though it has become very dangerous now that Votes for Everybody, masquerading as Democracy, has been established on the assumption that everybody is politically omniscient. Ignorance can be instructed: it is easy to write on a clean slate. But the slates in our schools are not clean: they are scrawled all over not only with sham Latin verses, but with fabulous history, barbarous superstitions, obsolete codes and slogans, and the accumulated nonsense and rubbish of centuries; for these slates are never cleaned; and anyone attempting to clean them is punished, or, if out of reach, is denounced as an enemy of God and Man. From the slates of Eton and Harrow, Rugby and Winchester, our rulers learnt that Deists like Voltaire, Rousseau, and Tom Paine were villainous atheists, and that Washington, Brigham Young, Marx, and Lenin were subversive monsters. Also that the battles of Trafalgar and Waterloo, which substituted Louis XVIII for Napoleon as a fitter ruler of France, were triumphs of civilization and British good sense. These are only a few notorious samples of the rubbish on which the minds of our school children are nursed. In rare cases it provokes a fierce resistance in such strong minds as that of Voltaire, educated by the Jesuits and yet now world-famous as the implacable enemy of the French Church; and its political corruption and absurd anachronism has been denounced and torn to pieces by so many pens that I shall pass it by as already sufficiently exposed, and deal here with aspects of the question which are in more danger of being overlooked. But it is so effective in most cases that an old school tie may still be regarded as the badge of a seventeenth century squire.

Education is inextricably entangled in the problem of childhood. I have already pointed out that statesmen must not deal with the children of the nation as parents must deal with their own, because the children of the nation never grow up and the children of the parents do. Now the parents cannot learn their business as such until they have brought up more children than they will now consent to bring into the world, spoiling the first two or three in the process by either too much interference or too little. This gives the statesman an advantage over the parent. When dealing with children of any given age in the lump, he has the experience of all relevant human history to guide him, whereas the parents begin without any experience at all, and find their problems changing from year to year. School teachers have the same advantage: for instance, Eton knows how to handle boys between 13 and 18 much more scientifically than their mothers can.

This explains the saying of William Morris of Kelmscott quoted on page 49. Great among the greatest Victorians as poet, craftsman, and practical man of business, and one of the few who remained uncorrupted by Victorian false prosperity to the end, he said, speaking as a parent and a Communist, "The question of who are the best people to take charge of children is a very difficult one; but it is quite certain that the parents are the very worst." And the well-to-do classes to which he belonged so far agreed with him that their children are not brought up by their parents, but by nurses, domestic servants, governesses, and school teachers. Before schooling was made compulsory, the poor had to bring up their own children; and a few of them did it wonderfully well; but in the lump they put their children out to work for miserable wages before they were half grown; resisted fiercely the factory legislation that forbad this exploitation; and were glad to get them off their hands and leave them to the elementary teacher for half the day when this was imposed on them by the State. A provincial mayor effected a startling reduction in infant mortality by giving a pound sterling to every mother in his city who could shew him a baby still alive on the first anniversary of its birth.

Confronted with these facts our sentimental hearthstone vaporing about parental care and the sacredness of the family as the inviolable unit of human society is only an excuse for doing nothing. Elementary civilization is impossible without a moral code like the Ten Commandments, a technique of language, writing, and arithmetic, and a legal code of compulsory behavior completely abolishing individual liberty and free will within its scope. Unless people can be depended on to behave in an expected manner they cannot live in society, and must be either corrected or, if incorrigible, killed. Their life must be mostly dictated and institutional, and their activities determined and predicable. And somebody must teach the codes to the children. They must be imposed on the child dogmatically until it is old enough to understand them. They can be imposed in various ways, by merciless whippings of children and cruel punishments of adults as well as by less savage and mischievous methods; but they must be imposed somehow, or the human world will be an Alsatian madhouse. The necessity is fundamental; and the statesman who imagines that a formula of Liberty, Equality, Fraternity, will solve all his problems will discover. if he is capable of learning from experience, that liberty must give way to equality and that fraternity may mean either the fraternity of Cain and Abel or the friendship of David and Jonathan. Children, if they are to grow up as citizens, must learn a good deal that their parents could not teach them even if they had the necessary time. The statesman must make provision for this teaching or he will presently find himself faced with the impossible task of maintaining civilization with savages instead of citizens.

But if civilization is to be maintained by everybody doing what everybody else does, what is to become of progress, of change, of evolution, of invention, of free will, free thought, free speech, personal rights, and everything that distinguishes living men from automatic stick-in-the-muds? The question comes home to me because in many respects which seem to me of vital importance I want the world to stop doing what everybody is doing and do something else, even to the extent of making some present activities criminal. And history shews that if nobody is allowed to advocate and initiate such changes, civilization will fossilize and perish. So without law and order, convention and etiquet, there can be no civilization; yet when these are established there must be privilege for sedition, blasphemy, heresy, eccentricity, innovation, variety and change, or civilization will crash again by failing to adapt itself to scientific discovery and mental growth. Governments have to persecute and tolerate simultaneously: they have to determine continually what and when to persecute and what and when to tolerate. They must never make either persecution or toleration a principle. British mistrust of principle and logic is rooted in the wisdom of this rule.

The moral of this is to disqualify uncultured persons, ignorant of the lessons of history, from meddling in cultural matters. When we have (and we probably shall have) separate Cabinets and even separate parliaments for cultural questions, industrial questions, agricultural questions, and the rest, there will still be a bias towards persecution, because persecution is not only always necessary but immediately and obviously reasonable, whereas toleration, though equally necessary, is immediately and apparently unreasonable and dangerous. The case for it is finally a mystical one, and is thought out only by the few persons who, like myself, are, as authors, journalists, sociologists, and propagandists of one sort or another, pioneering in advance of the majority, and demanding for their literary activities an exemption from the common law as complete as that claimed by the physiologists for medical research. Under such headings as

Freedom of the Press, Free Thought, Free Speech, Freedom of Conscience, we claim exemption in matters of opinion from the laws against sedition, blasphemy, obscenity, and are actually allowed a large impunity for ridicule, caricature, political invective, and vulgar personal abuse. Advertizing enjoys impunity also for lying on matters of fact, with the object of obtaining money on false pretences. This, the most obviously outrageous of such claims, is the only one that is completely conceded; for though prosecutions for seditious, blasphemous, and obscene libel occur often enough to keep their possibility alive and dreaded, prosecutions for obtaining money by lying advertisements are unheard of today. Anybody may make a fortune in the manner of Mr Ponderevo in the famous Wells novel called Tono Bungay.

This last extremity of toleration is quite indefensible, and can be accounted for only by the unofficial control of the State by the commercial plutocracy; but there is a case for a large licence in matters of opinion for writing, printing, and preaching. All progress means change of opinion even if it is only technical opinion; and new opinions often appear first as jokes and fancies, then as blasphemies and treasons, then as questions open to discussion, and finally as established truths. In England and America respectable women used to be publicly flogged for joining the Society of Friends (becoming Quakeresses); yet now membership of that body is regarded as promising a high degree of intelligence and probity. Twenty years ago Russian Bolshevism was reprobated in England, as it still is in Nazi Germany, as an infamy to be stamped out by every civilized nation. Today the Bolshevist Constitution is discussed as a model for all advanced communities; and England and Russia have sworn a friendship and alliance, defensive and offensive, for the next twenty years. Some of my plays were for many years under the ban of the censorship as disgracefully unfit for public performance by reason of their obscenity and blasphemy; and all of them were classed as seditious and paradoxical. They are now disparaged as old-fashioned and prudish by the young lions of dramatic literature. Why was I not muzzled effectually instead of being, though a bit injured in pocket and reputation, for the most part tolerated and left comparatively free? Doubtless the plutocratic anarchism that protects the advertisements had something to do with it (quite a lot of money has been made commercially out of my books and plays); but so many reformers have been burnt at the stake or hanged, castrated, and quartered for opinions that nobody now dreams of questioning, that persecution of opinion is blacklisted in our newspapers as a dangerously shortsighted policy. But in practice it is never possible to carry tolerance very far, because the sanctity of established morality, having become a thoughtless reflex, will not allow people to admit that morality is a matter of opinion at all until changes in their circumstances damage them so vitally that they must either change their minds or perish.

We must then make up our minds to persecution up to an uncertain point as being a necessary function of government. It is unhesitating when a country advanced in civilization has to govern a less advanced one. Thus British Government ruthlessly persecutes suttee, Thuggee and the car of Juggernaut in India, and Voodoo in Africa and the West Indies. Our Liberal friends of India, with their wits in Macaulay's history of the seventeenth century, sometimes talk as if our duty to India is to cease all persecutions and establish freedom of thought, speech, worship and education there. In truth, the persecutions are our only excuse for being in India at all. Probably we do not persecute half enough either at home or abroad. Our toleration of idleness and parasitism is indefensible. It is true that current persecution of Jews as such in Germany, and of Africans, Chinese, Japanese as such in the British Empire and the United States, has given the practice a bad name. There is nothing sensible to be said for robbing and murdering or exiling a German citizen because his grandfather worshipped in a synagogue, or for forbidding a black African to learn a skilled trade (one of our worst and stupidest crimes). But it is always difficult to draw a constitutional line between persecution and moral anarchy. A statesman may read Mill's Essay on Liberty or Croce's History as The Story of Liberty ten times over without having his mind made up for him as to whether this or that activity should be tolerated or declared a felony.

And now, what has all this to do with child-education? Almost everything, I should say; for as the child must be taught a morality as a religion the question at once arises whether it is to be taught the morality and religion of its school teacher or of its parents; and if the parents are Plymouth Brethren or Jehovah's Witnesses, and the teacher a Darwinian agnostic, a conflict will arise as to whether the State should step in and impose on the parents a staff of teachers in the selection of whom they have had no choice. In the nineteenth century a figment called secular education was advocated by the atheists and agnostics and Darwinians, which meant teaching no morality or religion at all in the schools; but as children must be taught to behave themselves in school this was impossible, and in practice meant only substituting fear of the cane for the fear of God. Another expedient was to have Bible classes from which the parents could withdraw their children if they liked, and in which no sectarian comments by the teachers were allowed. As most parents were only too willing to have the education of their children taken off their hands they accepted these compromises and expedients with indifference. Many of them, including some strongly anticlerical ones, sent their girls to convent schools because the nuns were the only teachers who taught gentle manners, however little else they taught. As to the capitalist States, they left people living in houses valued at as much as £30 a year to bring up their children as they pleased, and concerned themselves with the education of the poorer children only to the extent of having them taught enough to enable them to read written and printed directions and notices and timetables and the like, and to count money: qualifications which had become indispensable in modern industry. As to turning them out as fully cultivated citizens such a thing was not dreamed of.

Now in the more socialized States of the future all this trifling will be forgotten. The State will insist on what we call forming the child's character as a citizen, and, if the parents inculcate subversive doctrines, will take it out of its parents' hands as resolutely as it did in the case of Shelley's children and Annie Besant's. The conflict between the two authorities would be serious if any considerable number of parents knew or cared enough about the matter to proselytize their children thoroughly; but most of them ask nothing more than that their children shall attend the nearest church or chapel in their best clothes, and describe themselves as members of the family sect. This simplifies the case for the parents, and for the State also as long as elementary education means nothing more than teaching children to read, write, and cipher. But when it comes to teaching citizenship, as we now see it must if civilization is to be real and not merely an organization of gangsterism as it largely is at present, our schools must inculcate political principles, manners, morals, and religion. The need for religion is quite independent of belief in the tribal god whom Blake called Old Nobodaddy, or of any god at all. In Russia, the League of the Godless is a religious order. In India the Jains have built temples of extraordinary magnificence for a creed from which God is expressly excluded as a force beyond human comprehension which we must not presume to name. There are British sects in which the belief in God is so thorough and logical that parents must not discuss religion with their children: they must leave them wholly in the hands of God. A well known friend of mine who was a convinced atheist and militant freethinker was the son of devout Glasite (in England Sandemanian) parents, and the grandson of a leader of that little sect. But his attempt to bring up his own son as an anti-clerical and atheist was completely defeated when the boy went to a public school, where he distinguished himself by a brilliant success on the most conventional lines. For the boy had an "inner light" of his own different both from the inner light of his atheist father and that of his Glasite grandparents. His father was disappointed just as his grandfather had been. This inner light has to be reckoned with; for we beget many ugly ducklings, all of whom do not turn out to be swans.

Now what is this inner light?

Scientifically it is still a mystery; but for the purposes of a Ministry of Education it is the personal view the citizen takes of the facts known to him or her. It is therefore of cardinal importance that the citizen should know the facts as far as they are known or knowable. It seems to follow that parents, parsons, teachers, and propagandists of every sort must be prevented at all costs from telling children lies instead of teaching them science.

Yet all these authorities tell lies to children as the most sacred truths. When my father, after conscientiously fulfilling his parental duty by expatiating to me on the supreme excellence and authority of the Bible as a source of enlightenment and instruction, was tempted by his love of anti-climax to add that it is "the damndest parcel of lies ever invented," he was not uttering a blasphemous falsehood: he was only exaggerating a fact for the sake of a chuckle. For the Bible does contain a good many lies which ought never to be told to children, and which are yet inculcated by all the Christian Churches as divine truths. Who can defend teaching children, or adults either, that there are such beings as witches, and that it is our duty to kill them? Or that the universe was made and is ruled by a tribal deity who was so shocked by the wickedness of the human race he had himself created that he sent a flood to drown it, but was persuaded to spare one family because its patriarch put him into goodhumor by roasting a joint of beef under his nose? Or that a later deity, equally shocked by his own handiwork, sent his innocent son into the world to be horribly tortured and slain to expiate our crimes, and that those of us who believe this will go to heaven no matter what sins we commit, and those who do not will be damned.

everlastingly however virtuously they have lived? What civilization could any State build on these savage superstitions of vindictive theism and blood sacrifice? And who would now be obsessed by them if they had not been inculcated during infancy? Surely the Russian Government, the German Government, the Voltairean French Government are right in decreeing that children in their jurisdiction shall be protected against such inculcation, and better informed. Should not the British Government in the present crisis warn the Church of England that it will be disestablished and disendowed if it does not at once stop declaring in the eighteenth of its Thirtynine Articles that the majority of the human race, including our Russian allies, are to be held accursed?

What shall we tell naughty children? They are all naughty occasionally, sometimes in a crisis of nerves, sometimes more rationally because they do not see why they should not do as they like. It is easy for a Ministry of Education to rule that the parent or teacher or nurse must not tell the child lies nor beat it nor drug it. But suppose its mother says, "I find that the best and only means of discharging a crisis of nerves is a smacking. Can you suggest anything better?" Suppose the teacher says, "When a child asks why it should not do as it pleases I cannot ask it to read Hobbes's Leviathan or Herbert Spencer's Data of Ethics: I have to tell it that there is such a place as hell and that it will be sent there if it does not do what it is told. This is a lie; but the child believes it and understands it and behaves itself. If I may not tell it this lie, what lie am I to tell it? seeing that the truth is beyond infantile comprehension." My own nursemaid kept me in order by threatening that if I persisted in disobeying her "the cock would come down the chimney." To me the cock was an avenging deity. And I doubt whether the most enlightened Ministry of Education could have managed me at that age more effectually than the nursemaid. Mahomet, one of the wisest men who have ever had this problem to tackle, could not govern the Arabs, nor wean them from the worship of sacred stones, without inventing a hell which was not only terrifying but disgusting, and substituting for the stones a God (Allah) who was certainly a great improvement on Jehovah, but in whose existence we can no longer believe as naïvely as Mahomet did. Dante elaborated the picture for the Christian Churches. Many people still believe quite seriously in hell; and though a considerable number of influential persons scoff at it, the results are not reassuring: those who no longer fear anything beyond the grave are sometimes dangerously unscrupulous on this side of it.

In the Middle Ages men committed crimes; but they made very substantial efforts to expiate them. Our criminals within the law are left to their consciences (when they have any); and though they subscribe to charities to mitigate the poverty and disease their selfishness creates, they leave us neither the cathedrals nor the great charities and schools we owe to William the Conqueror and his like.

It seems then that the State must tell its citizens lies of some sort to keep them in order, and that the lies must vary according to their ages; for a boy or girl of ten will not be afraid of the cock coming down the chimney.

As my own education operated by a succession of eye-openers each involving the repudiation of some previously held belief, and consequently of my conviction of my father's infallibility, to say nothing of my own, I do not see why, when child life is organized into age groups as it has always been in our schools with their First Latin Juniors and Sixth Forms and the like, the promotion of a child from one group to an older one should not be marked by a ceremony of disillusion, in which the novices should be informed that they may now scrap the childish part of their religious instruction as poppycock no longer suitable to their advancing years. As long ago as the first century A.D. Paul wrote of the "putting off of childish things" as a normal incident of growth; and as this must occur to all children anyhow more or less, it had better be done frankly and systematically so that we may get rid of our present tophamper of people with incalculable mixtures of childish superstitions which they have not put off with the mature conclusions of their adult experience and observation. When we deliberately tell the child a lie to establish a conditioned reflex of good conduct in its childish mind, we should in common decency disabuse it of that lie when it is old enough to understand more of the little we know of the truth of the matter. The alternative is to dictate the child's conduct in every detail, and associate disobedience in its mind with physical torture: a process sometimes called breaking its spirit. This method, though it is still practised extensively in private life, and officially in public schools, is objectionable for several reasons. It is no more desirable to break a child's spirit by punishment than to break its limbs. It is cruel, and destructive of all friendly relations between children and their parents and teachers when it is carried out deliberately in cold blood. It is too easily employed by the callous, the stupid, the ill-tempered, the sadistic, in whose power no child should be left, whereas it is impossible for the kindly and thoughtful: a situation

exactly the reverse of the desirable one. It can only enforce obedience, which is entirely different from voluntary morality, and ceases
when the child reaches twenty, superior to its middle aged father or
teacher as a fist fighter, and dangerous if morally uneducated. Being
merely deterrent and intimidatory its efficacy depends on certainty
of detection, which is impossible of attainment. It does its utmost to
destroy its victims' natural selfrespect and sense of honor, on which
after all, civilized life depends; and though such destruction is not
completely possible yet it can go far enough to make it a point of
honor with its victim to defy it. No high civilization is possible
until it is got rid of.

Later on we shall see that the renunciation of punishment and
its metaphysical coefficient expiation, will not abrogate the right of
civilized society to restrain and control mental defectives who cannot
go straight without tutelage, and "weed the garden" by killing
human nuisances as ruthlessly as it kills cobras and man-eating tigers.
Political traitors and murderers are not the only people who in the
future will have to justify their existence by their social conduct.

Discarding then the plan of civilizing by dictation and corporal
punishment we are left with the alternative of education by fables
and parables based on hypotheses which, though as scientific as we
can make them, are yet at best provisional. And this brings the
ministers of education up against the question of how much realism
infants can stand, how much children, how much adolescents, how
much adults in youth, middle age, elderliness and old age, and how
little when we are at war and the news from the front is alarming.
How far can they discard their traditions and habits (conditioned
reflexes)? For the individual has to go through in a single lifetime
what western civilization has gone through in fifty generations: an
Age of Faith and an Age of Iconoclasm and disillusion. And Iconoclasm and disillusion produce disgust and pessimism unless the
shattered hope and broken faith are replaced by a better and more
credible hope and an equally confident faith.

Altogether a pretty job for our Boards of Education. But they
need not be overwhelmed by it. There is enough hope and faith in
Socialism to justify us in the scandal of iconoclasm and of admitting
that Proudhon was right when he defined property ("real property")
as theft, and that Ruskin was right when he said that we must be
either beneficial workers or thieves or beggars. Marxism is not an
infallible gospel for all future ages; but it has turned up trumps in
Russia, and is quite sound enough to go on with for the present.

Though Darwinism has "banished mind from the universe," and neo-Darwinism banished life from it, and now avers that it is just a predetermined laboratory of Robots trying to become conscious of their own machinery by cutting bits out of the brains of dogs and counting the drops of their saliva, yet Creative Evolution comes surging in irresistibly, with its infinite possibilities bringing greater hopes than the fabled medieval paradise could inspire. That is enough to carry us through a few more generations; and enough is enough.

Only, we must not forget that though the old fables are dead for some of us they are not yet dead for everybody. I recall something that happened to me one night when I attended a great meeting of the Salvation Army in the Albert Hall to commemorate Mrs. Booth, the wife of the Army's founder. I had been invited because I had written a play with a Salvation lass as the heroine, and, in a letter to the Press, corrected an ignorant ribald who had libelled the excellent Salvation bands. I was placed in the very centre and focus of the great amphitheatre. I could sing not altogether discordantly and unskilfully; and as there is no better fun than community singing, and the Army hymn tunes were delightfully exciting and quite free from the dullness that has given "sacred music" a bad name, I led the singing in my crowded box with tremendous gusto. A tribute to my performance came from a young Salvation lass, who, her eyes streaming with tears, grasped both my hands and cried "Ah! *we* know, dont we?"

What could I say? Those who believe that the truth is never out of season will no doubt insist that I could and should have said, "My good girl, you are quite mistaken. All this about climbing up the golden stairs to heaven that I have been singing about with such *élan* is superstitious rubbish. There is no such heaven and no golden stairs. May I recommend you to study the works of Mr Charles Bradlaugh and Colonel Ingersoll. I share their scepticism. Good evening."

But I could not say this, and did not want to say it. Instead, though I could not fill my eyes with tears, I did my best to make them beam like hers as I returned the grasp of her hands, and, with my heart apparently too full for speech, left her convinced that "we knew" and that I believed everything she believed and hoped for everything she hoped for.

Anyone who blames me for this sympathetic hypocrisy is unfit to be a Minister of Education.

CHAPTER XX

THE HALF EDUCATED

IF we class the holders of university degrees as educated, we must find another heading for those whose parents cannot afford such luxuries, and who have to leave school early in their teens and begin earning their living or part of it as junior clerks, shop assistants, and other white collar and black coat employees to whom not only elementary education but middle class manners, habits, and appearances are necessary. Let us call them the half educated. They are recruited continually from above by the grandchildren of the downstart younger sons of the landed gentry, educated as dayboys in cheap private schools, and from below by upstarts from the laboring classes whose aptitudes are literary and arithmetical rather than manual, and whose mothers long to see them dressed and respected (comparatively) as ladies and gentlemen. I myself began as a downstart with social pretensions which I had no means of supporting, and am therefore acutely conscious of downstart snobbery and impecuniosity. I escaped from it into professional celebrity by the rare accident of being gifted with a lucrative artistic talent. The upstarts escape when they, too, happen to possess lucrative talents, especially the talent for business. But the main body of the half educated, having no lucrative talent exceptional enough to enrich them, have to stay as they are, poor, pretentious, unorganizable because they are on speaking terms neither with the laborers nor the leisured, and consequently so restricted in their matrimonial opportunities that they are not only half educated but half bred.

Yet it is they who run most of the business of the country; and among whose sons are Shakespear and Dickens, Bunyan and Blake, Hogarth and Turner, Purcell and Elgar, and a dynasty of leading actors from Burbage to Barry Sullivan, to say nothing of their famous merchants, soldiers, lawyers, and churchmen. Looking abroad we notice that Spinoza and Rousseau, rather than slave as clerks, teachers, or literary hacks, earned their bread more sensibly by grinding lenses and copying music. Thus in the half educated middle class the career seems open to the talents, though it would be truer to say that genius is finally irresistible in all classes, however poverty and ignorance may starve it and delay it. Still, the middle class dayboy can always dream of becoming, if not a Shakespear or

President of the Royal Academy, a citizen of credit and renown like John Gilpin. And John Gilpin's errand boy may become John Gilpin's shopman or a postman. Middle class children brought up in a not unbearably overcrowded house with books and a piano and a few pictures in it, and taught to read and write easily, can pick up all the knowledge they are capable of and care for, a process which, as it goes on all their lives, and is not restricted to school-hours (which often simply interrupt it), leaves them much better educated than the average Bachelors of Arts. Their half education is the better half. They would employ professional tutors if they could afford to pay for them and find efficient ones and not schoolmasters without vocation or good manners.

The remedy is not to send them to Eton and Oxford, Harrow and Cambridge, and make Old School Ties of them, with the ideas and traditions of Sir Leicester Dedlock substituted for those of John Gilpin. Both were worthy and wellmeaning men; but both are out of date. For though commercial John stands against feudal Sir Leicester as Guelf against Ghibelline, his day schools ape the boarding schools of the country gentlemen.

May I, as a conspicuous specimen of the half educated, say a word about my own schooling?

My school was conducted on the assumption that knowledge of Latin is still the be-all and the end-all of education. This was a matter of course: I was given no reason why I should learn Latin instead of some living language. There was, in fact, no reason, as there were plenty of translations of all the classics that have any survival value. The method of teaching was barbarous: I was ordered to learn the declensions and conjugations and instalments of the vocabulary by rote on pain of being caned or "kept in" after school hours if I failed to reel off my paradigms without prompting. When I could do this, which was easy enough to a child accustomed to pick up new words and memorize them, Caesar's commentaries and Virgil's famous epic were thrust into my hands, and without a word of explanation as to what these old commentaries had to do with me, or why I should concern myself laboriously about an ancient Trojan called Eneas, I was ordered to enter the lists against Dryden and extemporize translations of these works, failing in which I should, as before, be caned or kept in. And all the time, even when I was not being punished, I was suffering imprisonment, the worst of punishments, for half the day, condemned to sit still, silent and attentive all the time, except for half an hour of relaxation in the playground, during which I yelled and ran about like a mad creature in a reaction against prolonged unnatural restraint. And there seemed no end to this. To stumble through the lines of Caesar and Virgil led to nothing but Greek paradigms and a demand for a translation of Homer's Iliad, which I had already devoured for myself in the stately English of Lord Derby, which I preferred to Pope's pretty rhymes.

Why, if I was to have a dead language forced on me, they should not have begun with Greek instead of the culturally inferior Roman I was not told, perhaps because the reason was too silly, being that the school had not yet advanced from the Norman conquest to the Renascence. I escaped from my classical school just as Homer was threatening, but not before I was confronted with algebra without a word of the explanation that would have made it interesting to me. I left school, like Shakespear and Dickens, with little Latin and less Greek; and even that little I had been taught before I went there by my clergyman-uncle. What I did learn at school I should have been better without, as it was only what a convict learns from his fellow prisoners and from fear and suffering, though I must not pretend that, apart from the imprisonment, these were severe enough to make a song about.

I must add that as I was a day boy and never a boarder, and under no sort of control from my amiable and most uncoercive parents in my free time, which included some long intervals between one school and another, my relations with other boys were those of gangsters, rather worse in fact, because gangsters presumably work for plunder, whereas we made mischief for its own sake in mere bravado. Just as we had been in a conspiracy against our schoolmasters we were in a conspiracy against the police, into whose hands I should probably have fallen had I been in the streets instead of, as it happened, mostly a solitary wanderer in enchanting scenery to the magic of which I was very susceptible. All the same, when I visited a Russian penal settlement in 1931, and was asked to address some edifying remarks to a crowd of juvenile delinquents (boy thieves mostly), I felt obliged to tell them that though I was a very distinguished and "successful" person, I should have been taken up by the police in my boyhood but that by chance I had not been found out.

I was equally distinguished, respectable, and even venerable when one day, wandering along the seashore in Scotland, I found myself the target of a barrage of stones, heavy or sharp enough to injure me seriously if they had found their mark on my head. I had come within range of a fishing village, or possibly a mining village, where the children were at play. Their notion of play was to throw stones at a strange elderly gentleman with a beard, defying him meanwhile with war cries describing him opprobriously as a Beaver.

Being considerably frightened, and too old to run away fast enough, not to mention that flight would have encouraged my assailants and greatly increased their enjoyment, I concluded that there was nothing for it but to frighten them more than they were frightening me. They had three things to fear: the police, the straps with which their parents corrected their behavior, and the possibility of my seizing and clouting one of them who might be any of them. Accordingly I strode towards them under fire with a resolutely vengeful air. They dispersed and fled, leaving me fortunately scathless, but quite convinced that some other alternative to imprisonment in school than letting children loose to amuse themselves in their own way must be found if civilization was to survive.

It may be said that these children were poor, wild, and savage. But at about the same time the medical students of London, much older, educated to the point of being able to write prescriptions in Latin, metropolitan in culture, and in training for a specially benevolent and scientific profession, had amused themselves by attacking an American temperance reformer in the crowded streets, blinding him in one eye and injuring his spine. He died soon after. Secondary education had not civilized the students: it had barbarized them.

Now if the Scottish laddies who lapidated me had been organized as Boy Scouts, they would never have dreamt of treating me as Saint Stephen was treated 2000 years ago. The Boy Scouts and the Girl Guides are our first attempt to organize child life as such; and it is noteworthy that they were founded not by educational reformers but by a soldier. Philanthropists who idolize children as little angels, and dominies, who demonize them as diabolical little wretches who must have their wills broken and their original sin castigated out of them, are as mischievous as democrats who idolize adult suffrage as the foundation of all wise government.

The problem of how far children or adults need guidance and coercion, and how far they should be left free to think and act for themselves is always a difficult one. It is cruel to leave a child to find out for himself what it must do and must not do, what it must learn and not learn to fit itself for civilized life. Breaking-in children as gamekeepers, sportsmen, shepherds, and trainers of performing animals break-in their dogs may make them efficient agents and bigoted defenders of civilization as it stands (first rate Conservatives in short) but it spoils them as agents and defenders of evolution. The respectable citizen who has been broken-in to the belief that WHATEVER IS, IS RIGHT, is as great a nuisance as the abandoned Bohemian who has been provoked into assuming that WHATEVER IS, IS WRONG. There is no golden rule by which the eligible degree between those two extremes can be determined. Evolution means change; and change upsets law and order: the two must be balanced. Henrik Ibsen, when pressed to join this or that political party, always said "I belong to no party: I have within me both the Right and the Left. I am pleased to find my new views influencing Liberals, Conservatives, Socialists, and especially workmen and women; but I will not label myself Liberal or Conservative or Labor or Suffragist. Party rules are not golden rules: there are no golden rules."

I find myself in the position of Ibsen. His objection to adopt a party label is shared by those who have room in their heads for more than one political subject, and who take the trouble to find out how their views would work out in practice. My method of examining any proposition is to take its two extremes, both of them impracticable; make a scale between them; and try to determine at what point on the scale it can best be put in practice. A mother who has to determine the temperature of her baby's bath has two fixed limits to work between. The baby must not be boiled and must not be frozen. Within those limits she must proceed by trial and error. She dips her elbow in the water, and soon finds out that below 70 degrees Fahrenheit the water is too cold and above 100 it is too hot. Within these contracted limits bathing the baby is possible and effective. A statesman who has to provide baths for millions of children or soldiers has to face the same problem.

But the statesman has more complicated problems to solve: for instance, the Cobdenite problem of Free Trade versus Protection. At the Protectionist extreme a nation should make everything for itself and be entirely selfsupporting and independent of international trade no matter how much more labor our goods may cost to produce at home than abroad. At the Free Trade extreme we should produce nothing that can be produced more cheaply abroad, specializing in the production of the goods that can be produced more cheaply at home than elsewhere. Both these extremes are impracticable. Take my own case; for I can speak on that with some authority. I can write plays better than I can do anything else. On Cobdenite principles, I should do nothing all day but write plays or dictate them. Every other sort of labor should be done for me; and every moment during which I was occupied in any other way should be regarded as an unpatriotic waste of my time. Yet I spend some of my day doing the work of a gardener's laborer or a woodman to keep myself sane and sound just as our eminent statesmen play golf, cut down trees, lay bricks, or paint pictures. I have to attend to the business of my profession as well as to its direct exercise. If I were to specialize completely my plays would deteriorate; and I should die before my time. Slaters and riveters who have nails and every other accessory handed to them so that they do nothing except that bit of the work which employs their peculiar skill would go mad if they did nothing else. Women in factories where machinery and "scientific management" (sometimes called rationalization) has reduced their labor to a single operation repeated continuously and performed with the utmost economy of time and effort, have to give it up because they soon begin to dream of it and be haunted by it until their lives become unbearable, and its relatively high earnings no longer tempt them to be robots doing only one thing.

Nations are like individuals in this respect. To save themselves from ceasing to be human beings and becoming shortlived robots falling asleep in less than a minute if they attempt to read a book, or dying in mental hospitals, they must do many things as bungling amateurs as well as some things as skilled professionals. And their statesmen must be neither whole-hog freetraders nor diehard protectionists, nor indeed Ists of any sort, but what Mr Lancelot Hogben calls Scientific Humanists, knowing just how much trade to protect and how much to set free. Their mothers must neither boil the baby nor freeze it, but know within thirty degrees or less what the thermometer should mark in the bath. And their playwrights should not only write plays very well, but play the piano very badly as I do.

When school education as distinguished from natural education was first practised it was assumed that a child destined to be a scholar should be allowed to do nothing but study, and be kept hard at it all the time, the penalty for idleness or inattention being merciless flogging. It was assumed also that every child, no matter what its tastes, aptitudes, or capacity may be, is a potential theologian, philosopher, and Latin poet and orator of the first rank. Later on, when Greek was added to Latin, and later still and very reluctantly, mathematics, the child was called on to be Homer, Plato,

Pythagoras, Aristotle, Cicero, Virgil, Newton, Leibniz, and Einstein all rolled into one.

To carry these assumptions out on living children thoroughly soon reduces itself to absurdity: it is found that all work and no play makes Jack a dull boy, and that you cannot make a silk purse out of a sow's ear except in a plastic factory. Accordingly we divide school education into elementary and secondary, technical and liberal, and give games and physical exercises a place in the curriculum. Yet in the preparatory and privileged schools of the plutocracy and their middle-class imitations we still treat every pupil as a potential Admirable Crichton. Dickens, in Dombey and Son, made us weep over the death of poor little overworked Dombey at his preparatory school; but it would have done us no harm to think a bit harder about the tragedy of Toots at the same institution, which only made us laugh. Toots was an unfortunate boy who, being rich, had his mind destroyed by a senseless attempt to make him a classical scholar and Latin poet: a destiny infinitely remote from his aptitudes and capacity. I cannot too often repeat that teaching children subjects that do not interest them either directly, or at least as necessary steps to the fulfilment of their hopes and desires, not only makes them unhappy but injures them both physically and mentally. A German crammer told me that three out of five of the crammed never recover from the operation. Thus when a pupil has no natural impulse to learn, and yet must not be left in ignorance, we must supply an indirect motive.

For instance, a child may be strongly repelled by the multiplication and pence table, which nevertheless has to be drummed into it at all costs. But let a child be convinced that not only can it never hope to be given pocket-money until it knows its tables, but that the mastery of them will result in the possession of its first shilling, and it will go through its task without being hurt by it. An adventurous boy with a craze for exploration or for the sea may have no mathematical turn; but he will tackle enough mathematics to qualify him as a navigator as willingly as our air pilots tackle the Morse code, not in itself a very attractive study.

How much, then, should our future citizens be taught? That "A little learning is a dangerous thing" is true; but the proposed remedy "Therefore drink deeply at the Pierian spring" is not advisable in more than a percentage of the cases. A monarchy in which every citizen was trained for kingship, an army in which every infantry soldier had to be qualified to act as field-marshal, an observatory in which the porters and cleaners were required to be proficient in higher mathematics, or the like, would soon convince us that people who are too clever for their jobs are as troublesome and inefficient as people who are too stupid for them. By all means throw the extremes of learning open to everyone so that no talent or capacity shall be thrown away for lack of training and opportunity. Statesmen must know the importance of this, and see to it that whoever wills and can shall have ways open for them to the utmost instruction.

But the statesman has not only to make all knowledge accessible to those who seek it, but to impose some knowledge on those who do all they can to escape it. He has to set his scale from complete illiteracy at the bottom to the whole encyclopedia at the top, and determine the point at which compulsory education shall stop and voluntary education and voluntary ignorance begin. Civilized people must be able to read and write, were it only to read printed public notices and write reports, instructions, messages, and cheques. They must know their tables and be able to count money. They must know something of mensuration and calculation. They must know why civilized people must be disciplined, why laws and etiquet are necessary, what they may do in everyday life and what they must not do. They must understand banking and know how to use ready reckoners, clock faces, maps, railway guides, and books of reference. To qualify them for special berths they may have to use logarithms, the binomial theorem, and the calculus: but for general purposes these may be classed as accomplishments and done without. There is in hard fact an irreducible minimum of knowledge without which men cannot live in civilized society; consequently its acquisition must take precedence of their liberties and eccentricities. We all wish to be free from government interference; but we soon find that without it we shall be either savages or the slaves of ruffians. In vain do we claim, as free Britons, a right to unlimited ignorance and unlimited idleness. Such liberty has landed most of us in bondage to which a decent chattel slavery would be preferable.

All this means that secondary education may be voluntary. But it does not mean that it should be free from government control. Secondary schools must be provided even when no one is obliged to attend them. They cannot be left to private enterprise: Fagin's private school for pickpockets cannot be tolerated: all schools must justify their activities from the commonwealth point of view. If, as this book proposes, our rulers are to be elected from graduated panels of qualified persons by registers of qualified voters, the certifi-

cates of such qualifications must be issued by some examining body
which will itself accept school certificates on obvious points; and
it is clear that if certificates from State schools are to be accepted
without question by the panel makers those from private schools
will pass only when searching government inspection has guaranteed that privilege for them.

In this there would be no very startling novelty: it would be only
a revival of the old and very sensibly meant benefit of clergy. At
present private persons seeking private employment find that certificates of matriculation help them to obtain employment as clerks
in important firms. University degrees, worthless as they are (sometimes actually detrimental) as evidence of practical ability or knowledge of the business world, are indispensable in certain directions.
The direct public services are now accessible only by examination
except in the very highest ranks (Cabinet ministers and reigning
sovereigns may be illiterate ignoramuses); and the extension of the
qualification system to all political activities, including those of both
elected and elective, is not a novelty, but a development which is
being forced on us by the appalling results of trying to achieve
democracy by giving votes to everybody who can pencil a cross on
a ballot paper. What happens when adult suffrage is grafted on to
the Party System invented by Sunderland can be studied in the
history of the Spanish Republic after the revolution of 1931, as told
by Salvador Madariaga, a mentally qualified philosophic historian
with a modern post-Marxist outlook, informed by personal contacts
with and participations in the events he describes and judges. The
moral is that of all matter-of-fact history: to wit that it is the half
educated, and not the helpless ignoramuses and incapables who,
given a nation to govern, can do nothing but kill oneanother until
they can afford no more slaughter and the people will submit to any
tyranny that promises peace.

The missing half of their education is the political half.

CHAPTER XXI

THE CORRUPTLY EDUCATED

TODAY education suffers political corruption as it never did in the
Ages of Faith, when there was in Europe one God and one creed,

dissent from which was silenced by burning heretics alive. Everybody was educated as a Catholic Christian or as a Catholic Mahometan, with the Bible or the Koran as the unchangeable and unquestionable foundation of all moral law. This view is by no means dead. I vividly remember a meeting in the Midland Hotel in London, at which leading Churchmen and politicians of all faiths and parties were assembled to confer with the heads of the big business companies to discuss, and if possible agree upon, their moral and religious principles. Ruskin had already appealed to the consciences of these business magnates by calling them captains of industry, and defining entirely honest merchants as persons who were prepared to die rather than cheat their customers, this being his general test of honesty in all occupations and professions.

At the meeting there were no Protestant bishops (at that time some Church of England bishops were capable of feeling offended by being asked to meet tradesmen); but the Catholic cardinal attended and spoke; and a peer of the realm, interested and active in allotments, represented the House of Lords. I was present as a prominent Socialist and public speaker. I spoke; the cardinal spoke; the peer spoke: in fact every public speaker present spoke, preaching the nobility of commerce in the way afterwards followed by the Rotarians; but the captains of industry were dumb until they were called on explicitly from the chair to profess their principles. They rose, not too willingly, and said briefly that they had only one principle in business, which was the principle of their Lord and Savior Jesus Christ: to do unto others as they themselves would be done by.

This shut us up completely. The discussion was taken out of the reign of Queen Victoria and replaced in that of Charlemagne. I rose and silently stole away; so did the others. The rule in competitive private business, which is to aim at the biggest profit regardless of the ruin of rival profiteers or the starvation of the proletariat, is virtually compulsory on employers, however philanthropic: they are forced to keep it and their articles of religious faith in separate thought-tight compartments. Indeed there was no thinking in the matter at all, except by the Ruskinist intellectuals. The piety of the captains of industry was only an old habit, acquired in the Ages of Faith, and surviving quaintly as a Sunday reflex to anything that sounded like preaching. It had nothing to do with their business really. As far back as the seventeenth century a first-rate economic document entitled The Life and Death of Mr Badman, by John Buyan, gives a penetrating description of the modern business man whose religion it is to buy in the cheapest market and sell in the dearest. Bunyan's comment is, "What is this but trading without conscience?"

But Mr Badman could not leave it at that. Finding that if he was to preserve his respectability he must trade on respectable principles, and in fact get a new conscience which could approve of his profiteering, thereby entitling him to call himself Mr Goodman, he soon found what he wanted in the teachings of the French Physiocrats, and the famous treatise of Adam Smith, shewing that the wealth of nations depends on freedom of trade from clerical and feudal control. The Church of England itself helped him by the hand of the Reverend Thomas Malthus, who contended that overpopulation and not trading without conscience is the cause of proletarian poverty. Thus trading without conscience disguised itself as freedom of conscience; and Free Trade became the battle-cry of Mr Badman, and was established, educationally in the universities and politically in Parliamnt, as fundamental in economic morality.

This revolution in economic morality, fitting neatly into the great Protestant revolution called The Reformation and The Renascence, culminated in the nineteenth century in a counter revolution against all Badman morality, with Ibsen and Nietzsche as its prophets, La Rochefoucauld and Oscar Wilde as its wits, and Karl Marx tearing off Mr Goodman's mask and renaming him Mr Bourgeois. I was myself a champion of both Ibsen and Marx, concluding that the way of Mr Badman-Goodman-Bourgeois is the road to ruin, and that the way of escape is intellectually through Freethought, and economically through the substitution of public for private property: in short, through Communism.

Meanwhile, however, it became clearer and clearer that if these changes of outlook were to be established on the secure foundation of popular consent and sincere approval, they must be inculcated in the schools as fundamental in education. Napoleon failed because he could not make Bonapartists of all the children in Europe. The Bismarck-Hohenzollern empire failed because, in spite of its resolute imposition of the necessary idolatry on the German schools and universities, it could not impose it on the rest of the world. Hitler outdid the Hohenzollerns in his childmoulding of Germans into Hitlerists; but his doctrine tried to combine Socialism with anti-Bolshevism, and both with an irrelevant extermination of Jews as such, subjugation of Latin races as inferior to Teutonic races, and finally a world supremacy of pure Germans, pure Germans being a species as imaginary as fairies.

Still, Napoleon, Bismarck, the Kaiser, Mussolini, and Hitler were quite right in their perception of the fact that no systems of government can stand for long unless they get hold of the children and can bend the sapling in the way they wish the tree to grow. They must all not only grow their chosen flowers but weed the garden and destroy the vermin ruthlessly to the utmost of their power: the definitions of flower and weed and vermin being in their own hands. Honest government is impossible without honest schools; for honest schools are illegal under dishonest governments. Honest education is dangerous to tyranny and privilege; and systems like the Capitalist system, kept in vogue by popular ignorance, Churches which depend on it for priestly authority, privileged classes which identify civilization with the maintenance of their privileges, and ambitious conquerors and dictators who have to instil royalist idolatry and romantic hero-worship, all use both ignorance and education as underpinnings for general faith in themselves as rulers. Such corruption is at present universal. Democratic education cannot be tolerated under Capitalism because it inevitably leads to Communism, against which Capitalism has to defend itself by systematic propagation of capitalist doctrine and vilification of Communist teachers so as to make us all proselytes of the Manchester School with an inculcated phobia against any State interference with private profiteering or concern with national welfare. Not only is the trend towards Communism treated as a social danger to be stemmed at all costs: government itself is assumed to be an evil to be minimized as far as possible and to have its powers not only constitutionally limited but broken, even at the cost of revolution and regicide, until the real power passes to private capital and finance, and its official representatives are either disarmed royal scapegoats or armed protectors of private property. All this propaganda has to be disguised as education, and the schools, founded for the enlightenment of the poor and the encouragement of scholarship, are made inaccessible to proletarians by fees beyond their means, and at the same time kept in the atmosphere of feudalism with all its duties abolished and its privileges retained: in short, of simple plutocracy. Finally, education in practice comes to mean mental and moral obfuscation.

Now this is all very well from the capitalist point of view; but Capitalism cannot develop its possibilities without genuine technical education. It must confine its obfuscation to the cultural side. Its accountants may be political idiots; but they must know that two and two make four and not five. Its carpenters must know that twelve feet are longer than twelve inches; and its ship captains know that the world is not flat, even when they have been taught that Jesus was omniscient when he said that in the day of his coming the stars would drop on the earth as specks of soot fall on a pancake.

Thus we have technicians of the utmost eminence politically and religiously obfuscated to a degree that should disqualify them from taking any part in public affairs. They use the words Communism and Communist to denote everything and everybody vile, and thus make infamous all proposals that rate the welfare of human society above the luxury of the propertied classes. They label Lenin and Stalin as bloodthirsty scoundrels and guttersnipes just as their fathers labelled Hegel, Tyndall, and Bishop Colenso as destroyers of religion. Honor, privileges, and authority are heaped on rich and "well connected" persons who have hardly brains or skill enough to knit socks. Although the country is up to the waist in Communism because there are so many vitally necessary public services out of which capitalists can make no profit, they assume that Communism is as impossible as it is wicked, and throw about such words as Proletariat, Bolshevist, Dictator, Liberty, Democracy, Law and Order, without connecting them with the facts of human life that are staring them in the face all the time: in short, without knowing what on earth they are talking about.

And here again I must remind you that they are not all hypocrites and confidence-trick-swindlers deliberately and cunningly lying for their own ends. They are mostly quite decent folk just parroting the noises they have heard round them all their lives and see printed in their newspapers every day.

Though we can contemplate the political corruption of education, and indeed most of our social evils, without despairing of human nature, we must none the less understand it and stop it. The famous utterance of Jesus on the cross "Forgive them; for they know not what they do," was no remedy for the crucifixion. Whether the Jews understood what they were doing or not, they did it; and it was their Roman ruler's business to prohibit it instead of bowing to the people's will and becoming the accomplice of their bigotry.

But prohibition is not the whole and sole business of governments. They have to establish and perpetuate as well, by education and legislation, especially by education. Consequently we have to face the fact that when the private or "vested" interests which really control and exercise government at present find that if people are allowed to understand banking and rent and insurance they will demand nationalization of all three, and later of land and provision of capital, and will refuse to continue paying rents, premiums, and interest to private monopolists, or leaving their bank balances in private hands without government security for their safety, they will take care that any schoolmaster who explains these subjects shall be sacked and replaced by one who inculcates instead a sense of the sacredness of private property and private contract, and reiterates that our noblest birthright is freedom to do what we please on this basis in money matters, with all the other tenets and slogans of the Capitalist Utopia and its paper paradise.

Against this State proselytism it is waste of time to raise the old Whig hue and cry of freedom. No government can operate without a creed and a set of commandments, nor will refrain from proselytizing its children accordingly and persecuting heresy. Our notion that only Nazis, Fascists, and Bolshevists do this, and that Britons never, never would tolerate it is silly: our laws are and always must be based on orthodoxy, and enforced as such, just as much as Russian, Italian, or German laws. Though proletarian orthodoxy will differ from capitalist orthodoxy, it will be inculcated in the schools and enforced in the courts just as our present capitalist orthodoxy is at Eton and the Old Bailey. And its legislation will not take the Whig direction of less government interference. Under democratic rule citizens will be ruthlessly liquidated for transactions which under our plutocratic rule lead to seats in Parliament, titles, and peerages.

However, orthodoxy does not cover the whole field of human conduct. There is and always will be a Nomansland ahead in which morals are disputable and changeable. We have accepted the ten commandments as the law of God; and by our statute law any person baptized into that faith and lapsing from it after confirmation is subject to ruinous penalties. Yet all our pictures and statues, our dolls and teddy bears and Noah's arks, are flat breaches of the second commandment. We make it a patriotic duty to kill when we are at war, and enforce all the consequences of "real" property in spite of Proudhon's irrefutable demonstration that such property is theft.

The practical conclusion is that though we must teach and enforce a code of morals, and make every child learn its catechism as well as the multiplication and pence tables, yet we must keep all our moral measures open to discussion. The devil's advocate must always be allowed to plead his case against the wisdom and spirit of our laws, though not to resist their execution until he has persuaded us to repeal them.

This is the correct academic attitude; but as opportunities for discussing laws are limited, and the desire for their repeal or alteration is often quite irrational, it may happen that the only way to change the law is for so many people to break it that it becomes a dead letter, in which case it repeals itself, and should be formally repealed by the government lest it should be revived later on for tyrannical purposes.

Under these puzzling circumstances the best we can do educationally is to let children know, as soon as they are capable of such knowledge, that laws and creeds are mutable and not eternal, and must change as our mental and spiritual powers evolve, but are meanwhile necessary instruments of civilized discipline, and indispensable factors in what we call gentlemen's agreements, without which social life is impossible.

When changing we must be careful not to empty the baby out with the bath in mere reaction against the past. In Russia, for instance, the reaction against the illiteracy and tyranny of capitalist-dominated Tsardom was so intemperate that when it was placed in power by the revolution of 1917, it went too far. Education was decreed for all at the public expense; but authority and discipline in schools were regarded as treasonable. Middle class Bohemianism, mistaken for proletarian emancipation, was at first the order of the day. Teachers were strictly forbidden, as they still rightly are, to hurt children as a teaching method; yet the urgent need for a common doctrine in education, and a religious faith in the omniscience of its prophet, was such that the Soviet Government aimed at making every little Russian a complete Marxist philosopher as madly as Eton aims at making every English boy a complete Latin poet, theologian, and higher mathematician. This inhuman process, restricted at Eton to the plutocratic, professional, and baronial classes by its cost, was imposed in Russia on the entire population. It is not surprising to learn that for years past now discipline has been re-established in the Russian schools, and that though what we call secondary education is provided at the public expense for those proved capable of it, literary scholarship has to be paid for by those who think it worth the money. To teach either Latin versification or the Marxist dialectic to children who should be learning arts and crafts is as wasteful and mischievous as teaching trades or crafts to pupils who are keen on mathematics, history, or languages, but have hardly enough manual dexterity to sharpen their pencils or lace their shoes securely. The educationists who think that everything should be taught to everybody are as bad as the "practical" people at the opposite end who think it sufficient to teach people the technical routine of the trades or professions by which they will have to earn their livings. Such education may produce efficient robots: it will not produce citizens.

Yet there is something, after all, in the notion that everybody should be taught everything. We have to consider tastes as well as capacities; for we should be savages if we knew nothing beyond the things we can do well. Many have strong intellectual tastes and no creative intellectual capacity: they read every philosophical treatise they can lay hands on without being able to produce a single original syllogism, whilst others who can neither read nor write are powerful practical reasoners. Crowds pay to see football matches and prize fights without ever kicking a ball or wielding a boxing-glove. Others delight in music without being able to play any instrument or sing a note in tune. They know all about their favorite arts and sports, whilst the most famous performers know nothing but how to do it. I once addressed a public meeting at which another of the speakers ranked as the greatest living British composer. He surprised the audience by saying, "Shaw knows a great deal more about music than I do." To a young musician who asked him for lessons in harmony and counterpoint he replied that he knew nothing about these things. I earn my bread by writing plays for people who could not, to save their souls, write a line of dramatic dialogue, though many of them know ten times as much as I do of the world's dramatic literature. We have to cultivate the tastes of millions of spectators, listeners, connoisseurs, critics, and dilettanti: in short, amateurs, as well as the capacities of the handfuls of born practitioners.

Is there, then, an irreducible minimum of aesthetic education as there is of elementary education? Granted that it is waste of time to teach music to a deaf child or painting to a blind one, how far should we treat every child who can hear as a potential Handel, who can see as a potential Raphael, and who can speak and write as a potential Homer or Shakespear, in view of the fact that such prodigies occur in the world perhaps once in many generations? We are tempted to reply "Not at all" but are checked on considering that the value of the prodigies when they do occur is so enormous, and lasts for so many centuries, that everybody should at least be given a chance of attaining creative eminence. For poverty, ignorance,

drudgery, hunger, and squalor will extinguish talent and hinder
genius; and such extinction goes on all the time wherever nine-
tenths of the population are proletarians. "Owen Meredith" (the
first Earl of Lytton) proclaimed that "Genius is master of Man:
Genius does what it must; and talent does what it can"; and certainly, in spite of slavery, serfdom, and proletarianism, ancient
Greece produced Phidias and Praxiteles, Eschylus and Sophocles,
Aristophanes and Euripides; Italy produced Michael Angelo and
Raphael, Titian and Tintoretto; England produced Shakespear, Germany Goethe, Norway Ibsen, and Ireland my astonishing self, to say
nothing of the great composers who have carried music to heavenly
summits. But none of them came from the illiterate poor. Get rid
of the curse of poverty and the possibility of fruitful genius will
be multiplied tenfold.

Still, the notion of educating every Jack and Jill to be a genius
remains too silly to be discussed. Genius will find its own way if it
starts fair, and need not be meddled with by the academic authorities
once that start is secured for it.

But though education must not meddle with Beethoven or
Michael Angelo or with Shakespear, this does not mean that it must
not meddle with music, painting, and literature. There was a time
when, had the national income been equally distributed, the whole
life of every ablebodied adult would have been spent in producing
the wherewithal to live. But now, with machines for muscles, and
knowledge of how to obtain nitrogen from the air, oxygen and
hydrogen from water, and power from the winds and waves and
tides, it needs only a sensible political organization to enable us
all to live more comfortably with five half holidays and two whole
ones every week than most of us, working all the hours we can
spare from eating and sleeping, have ever lived before. Such resources, however, can be distributed in various ways. Ninety per
cent of the population can do a hundred per cent of the work with
no leisure, in order that the remaining ten per cent shall have a
hundred per cent of the available leisure. But leisure without aesthetic
education is ruinous. For what do we do when we find ourselves
with uncultivated unfurnished minds and plenty of unearned money?
We know of no pleasures but eating, drinking, drugging, sexual intercourse, fighting, hunting, killing, gambling, adorning our bodies
with fantastic dresses, and exercising authority and exacting deference and worship for their own sakes. The late Henry Salt, a famous
Shelleyan humanitarian who began his adult life as an Eton master,

entitled his autobiography Seventy Years among Savages.

Of course this was an overstatement, as all statements must be if they are to receive any attention. The leisured people are drones in the hive; but they are living human beings, and as such are driven by their vital urges to seek power over their circumstances and knowledge of their nature even in the absence of external incentives to any pursuit but that of pleasure. To the best of them that pursuit is tedious, boresome, and unsuccessful. Yet here again the statesman must act on Salt's estimate; for though it may be impossible to find a single complete savage among the monopolists of leisure, it is nevertheless true that their class vote is a savage vote and their institutions barbarous. In detail the leisured have their musical sets, their amateur acting sets, and their literary sets as well as their sporting sets and political sets; but in the lump they hate intellect, despise art as epicene instead of valuing it on that account, and initiate their children into the mystery of sport by daubing their faces with the blood of the hunted foxes. They are for empire not for commonwealth, for war not for peace, for sensational mischief rather than humdrum welfare, for privilege not for equality: in short, for savagery against civilization. And the workers, in their holidays and half holidays, ape them even more savagely, being not only without aesthetic education but living ugly lives in ugly quarters. The noun aesthete, to the very little extent to which it is now used or even known, is a term of derisive contempt; and the notion that leisure will destroy a nation which is not a nation of aesthetes seems too ridiculous to be discussed. Nevertheless it is a sound proposition, and so important that I must defer its fuller consideration until I deal with public health in the context of Science.

Under rulers misguided enough to believe that the highest good on earth or in heaven is a life of opulent unearned leisure people are not taught what their rulers do not want them to know, and do not themselves know. But there are ignorances which, being against all interests, plutocratic and proletarian alike, are purely stupid. Our children are taught how to put on their clothes and button them without assistance, and how to use knives and forks; but they are never taught how to feed themselves. Adults who have been through all the schools and taken their degrees believe that they cannot live without eating flesh and drinking alcohol. They go into pharmacies and buy and swallow tablets of the most dangerous drugs with as little misgiving as they bought and swallowed sweets at the confectioners when they were children. They learn of the existence of these drugs from their doctors, who prescribe them as recklessly as they prescribe fish, flesh, fowl, wine, and champagne jelly. It is nearly fifty years since I was assured by a conclave of doctors that if I did not eat meat I should die of starvation; and doctors still take the same line professionally as if all the vegetarians, including myself, had died of starvation in the meantime. I recall a symposium of eminent physicians who gravely decided that alcohol in the form of distilled or fermented drinks is an indispensable factor in human diet.

Instruction in sex is as important as instruction in food; yet not only are our adolescents not taught the physiology of sex, but never warned that the strongest sexual attraction may exist between persons so incompatible in tastes and capacities that they could not endure living together for a week much less a lifetime, and therefore should not marry oneanother even though their offspring, which is what Nature aims at, might be eugenically first rate and their sexual union therefore highly desirable from the public point of view. They are not even warned against venereal disease, and, when they contract it, can only raise the old cry, "Why was I not told?"

Such facts are suppressed at first lest immoral conclusions might be drawn from them. When the motive of the suppression is forgotten it persists as a habit and a taboo. Taboos are enforced ruthlessly without being understood, and finally provoke a revolt against them as such, though it is a scientific fact that some of the primitive impulses which existed before the invention of language remain unspeakable and should be gratified in silence. Shelley's Epipsvchidion is a wonderful effort by a supreme master of language to utter the unspeakable; but the result is a rhapsody of nonsense that has no contact with natural history.

The statesman, confronted by hard-headed people who demand that children should be taught facts and not fancies, and others who demand that children should be put off with fancies and have all the facts carefully concealed from them, soon finds (if he is capable of learning from experience) that truths must be reserved for people capable of digesting them, and that this capacity varies not only from individual to individual but from age to age. Also that when fabulous storks and cabbages are substituted for facts the sillier the fables are the more easily will they be discarded when the truth can be discussed without taking the children out of their depths.

I have written much elsewhere, notably in my prefaces to Misalliance and Heartbreak House, touching our schools, and need not repeat it here. Schools in my time were prisons, as they still are, with instruments of torture and executioners all complete. Prisons and torture should be as completely dissociated from the normal daily life of children as they are from the normal daily life of adults. Child life should be so organized in its successive age groups as to create a strong collective opinion among children that there are certain things everyone must learn and know. Public opinion, far from being non-existent among children, is so tyrannical that it needs restraint rather than release. Learning should bring, not book prizes and medals, but privileges and liberties, status and earnings; for in this way only can children be educated as citizens. Competitive examinations should be abolished, as they give the competitors an interest in oneanother's ignorance and failure, and associate success with the notion of doing the other fellow down. Competition should be between teams, as this incites members to share their knowledge and help oneanother.

I have included earnings among the incentives; for the habit of earning money and providing for needs by earning should begin early. Children should have regular pocket-money, and not be thrown on the world with no practice in fending for themselves out of an earned income. All this means that children should live in an organized society with rights and constitutions, and be brought up neither as household pets nor as chattel slaves. They must be policed as adults are. Some of them should be liquidated as congenital and incurable idiots or criminals; and they should all respect the police and be taught that unless they fit themselves to live in civilized society they cannot be allowed to live at all; but they should not regard their parents and teachers as police officers, judges, and executioners. Homes, families, and schools should not be workhouses and prisons as well. Children should be educated to live more abundantly, not apprenticed to a life sentence of penal servitude.

Education is not concerned with childhood alone. I am in my 88th year, and have still much to learn even within my own very limited capacity.

CHAPTER XXII

THE AESTHETIC MAN

ALMROTH WRIGHT, the founder of the aesthetic theory of sanitation, in full Sir Almroth Wright, K.B.E., and of great distinction as a bacteriologist, physician, and philologist, remarked quite casually at a discussion following a lecture of mine, "I believe the effect of sanitation is aesthetic," and, having thus opened an epoch in hygiene, sat down and thought no more about it. But I thought a good deal about it. I could no more persuade him that he had made a notable discovery than Halley could persuade Newton that his device of fluxions (the calculus) did him credit and would be of enormous value to mathematicians. There was nothing for it but to steal his thunder, not for the first time. It is useful to know a man who has discovered the philosopher's stone but does not know the value of gold.

Three hundred and sixty years ago or thereabouts Shakespear warned us against people without music in their souls. "Let no such man be trusted" he said emphatically, declaring them fit only for treasons, stratagems and spoils. This daring but profoundly scientific pronouncement is startling at first. A late Chancery judge of the highest character, on being handed the vocal score of an opera in a case in which I was concerned, put it down with the remark that it meant nothing to him. Dr Inge, greatest of all the Deans of St Paul's, is so "unmusical" that his only recorded comment on cathedral music expresses a doubt whether the Almighty enjoys "this perpetual serenading." Men of the first quality have been tone deaf and color blind. But their cases prove nothing except that they disliked some particular sort of music. William Morris, one of the greatest and wisest word musicians of the nineteenth century, hated the modern grand piano and would not have one in his house. Mozart hated the flute. Bad jazz, played on good instruments deliberately degraded and burlesqued by mechanical contraptions, provokes musical people to switch off the wireless. The most maddening noise I ever heard was from a first-rate organ in a Cape Town cinema played with all its stops out all the time. Shakespear is not contradicted by such instances. Dr Inge is specially susceptible to the Gospel of St John, the English authorized version of which enchants by its verbal music. Morris, when he was dying, was moved to tears by old music that was not banged at him from steel-framed concert grands, but played as it was intended to be played. I can testify that he could sing perfectly in tune. Samuel Butler disliked Beethoven (so did Chopin) but had a craze for Handel. Besides, art is not so cheap that a love for all its forms can be obtained without some aesthetic education. A complete public school and university training may leave its graduates so barbarously ignorant that when war comes they are found in all directions trying to close public art galleries and museums, beginning with the British Museum, and to use them as military stations and stores and offices. Yet even these Philistines are often highly susceptible to the poetry of nature and the colors and sounds with which it is associated; for the unhappiest art-starved school prison, though it may hang no pictures and allow no musical instruments, cannot shut out the sky, the ripening crops in the fields, the trees changing color in autumn, the scent of flowers, the songs of birds, and the Eolian chords of the winds. Nor can the slum schools which imprison children for nine years and turn them out unable to speak English properly or to read and write except as a task, cut them off from the bands, the street pianos, the mouth-organs, and singsong. I should class persons insensible to all these aesthetic impressions as dangerous defectives, as Shakespear did.

Was Shakespear right when he made his extraordinary pronouncement? Was Plato right when, using the word music in the largest aesthetic sense without technical limitations, he valued music as an essential branch of republican education? It certainly makes a startling difference. Take the case of John Ruskin. He was a graduate of Oxford University and a professor of aesthetics there until he shook the dust of the place off his feet when it tolerated vivisection as a method of research. Why was he so different from the typical Oxford graduates and professors of his time? Why was his literary power so prodigiously better than theirs? Why did he see at a glance through the pseudo-scientific imposture that took them in so easily, and the economic imposture which made Gladstone declare that the social system of landlord, farmer, and agricultural laborer was the natural, sound, and eternal basis of society whilst Ruskin was denouncing it with invectives which make the Jeremiads of Karl Marx read like the pale reproaches of a Sunday school teacher? The explanation is that his parents, instead of packing him off to preparatory school and afterwards to Eton or Harrow, Rugby or Winchester, to get rid of him, kept him at home; made him learn the authorized version of the Bible verse by verse; and steeped him in the glories of European art and scenery instead of in the traditions of the public-schools.

I am no doubt biased in this matter; for I attribute my own eminence, such as it is, to the fact that I am much better educated than
the public school and university products, by whose reckoning I am
wholly uneducated. By this is meant that though I began with an
extensive knowledge of music, English, German, and Italian, from
the sixteenth century to the nineteenth, not by reading books about
it but by listening to it and singing it; though I knew the nine symphonies of Beethoven and the three greatest of Mozart's as well as I
knew Pop Goes The Weazel; though I had looked at pictures and
engravings of pictures until I could recognize the handiwork of the
greatest painters at a glance, yet I could not read the Satires of Juvenal
in the original Latin, my imprisonment for years in a school where
nothing was counted as educational except Latin and Greek having
left me unable to read the most conventional Latin epitaph without
guessing, or to write a single Ciceronian sentence. I possess Dryden's
translation of the Satires and have dipped into them enough to know
that it is impossible to read more than a page or two of such a mass
of ignorance, vulgarity, bad manners, and filth; and though, thanks
mainly to Gilbert Murray, I know as much as anyone need know of
the ancient Greek drama, and have learnt all that is now to be learnt
from Homer and Virgil from Lord Derby, Morris, Dryden, and Salt,
yet I consider myself lucky in having had my mind first well
stocked in my nonage by Michael Angelo and Handel, Beethoven
and Mozart, Shakespear and Dickens and their like, and not by
Latin versemongers and cricketers.

Take the case of history as an indispensable part of the education
of a citizen. Have you ever reflected on the impossibility of learning
history from a collection of its bare facts in the order in which they
actually occurred? You might as well try to gather a knowledge of
London from the pages of the telephone directory. French history
was not one of my school subjects; but by reading with great entertainment the historical novels of Dumas *père* I had a vivid conspectus
of France from the sixteenth to the eighteenth century, from Chicot
to Cagliostro, from the conquest of the nobility by the monarchy
under Richelieu to the French Revolution. Like Marlborough, I had
already learnt all I knew of English history, from King John to the
final suicide of the English feudal aristocracy and its supersession by
the capitalists on Bosworth Field, from the chronicle plays of Shakespear. Adding to these congenial authorities the Waverley novels of
Water Scott I came out with a taste for history and an acquaintance

with its personages and events which made the philosophy of history
real for me when I was fully grown. Macaulay did not repel me as a
historian (of sorts) nor Hegel and Marx bore and bewilder me. At
last I became a historian myself. I wrote a play entitled In Good
King Charles's Golden Days. For the actual occurrence of the incidents in it I cannot produce a scrap of evidence, being quite convinced that they never occurred; yet anyone reading this play or
witnessing a performance of it will not only be pleasantly amused,
but will come out with a knowledge of the dynamics of Charles's
reign: that is, of the political and personal forces at work in it, that
ten years of digging up mere facts in the British Museum or the
Record Office could not give. And whereas most of us leave school
resolved never to open a schoolbook again or even think of these
instruments of torture, I should starve if the effect of my books and
plays were not to make the sort of people I write for buy another of
them and yet another until there are no more to read.

That I can write as I do without having to think about my style is
due to my having been as a child steeped in the Bible, The Pilgrim's
Progress, and Cassell's Illustrated Shakespear. I was taught to hold
the Bible in such reverence that when one day, as I was buying a
pennyworth of sweets in a little shop in Dublin, the shopkeeper tore
a leaf out of a dismembered Bible to wrap them in, I was horrified,
and half expected to see him struck by lightning. All the same I took
the sweets and ate them; for to my Protestant mind the shopkeeper,
as a Roman Catholic, would go to hell as such Bible or no Bible, and
was no gentleman anyhow. Besides, I liked eating sweets. I was too
infantile then to reach my more mature conclusion that the reason I
could read and remember the Bible stories and not read school books
was that the Bible stories were translated when English literary art
was at the summit of its majesty, the translators having believed
that they were Englishing the very words of God himself.

Even the wretched defrauded children who are not allowed to
read novels or poems are allowed to read Bunyan and the Bible as a
pious duty. But for this blessed exception it would probably be
found necessary to exterminate them.

The statesman must therefore take care not to be imposed on by
the customary classification of education as either religious or secular.
The education that sticks after school is aesthetic education. Such
terms as scientific education and secular education are thoughtless
nonsense: science transcends all pigeon-holes; and secular education
means teaching with a cane instead of a creed. The classification

proper for statesmen is into aesthetic and technical education; but to avoid being enslaved by these headings the statesman had perhaps better have a look at the works of the Italian philosopher Benedetto Croce, who abhors classification.

To have access to aesthetic education, which must be voluntary, it is necessary to begin with technical education, which must be compulsory. The books that taught me were sealed to me before I learnt to read and could not buy books without money and a knowledge of how to count it. In some branches apparatus can be dispensed with. One can be educated by pictures without knowing the names of cobalt and gamboge, and appreciate Wagner without knowing the difference between B flat and a bull's foot; but literature is accessible only through the alphabet, and purchaseable only through the multiplication and pence table. Mathematics, which is also a realm of enchantment, must begin with simple arithmetic, and should be carried far enough to enable the student to use a ready reckoner and a table of logarithms. This includes, not necessarily any skill in solving equations, but at least a knowledge of what algebra is. In school I was set to perform certain algebraic operations, but left in such complete ignorance of their nature that I guessed for myself that $a + b$ was shorthand for Eggs and Bacon. Consequently I rejected equations as utter nonsense for the next twenty or thirty years (those eminent mathematicians Bertrand Russell and the late Karl Pearson could testify to this) until one day J. L. Joynes, amazed at my ignorance, told me that a and b meant neither bacon and eggs nor brandy and Bibles. But, being the son of a famous Eton master and educated accordingly, he failed to explain what they did mean; and not until I had in the course of my literary work to take the matter into serious consideration did I find out for myself.

It is evident that my schooling was a complete failure, and that the aesthetic education I received out of school was my salvation. My excuse for describing it here as a matter of public importance is that it is typical of the economic class to which I belonged, which may be defined roughly as the impecunious younger-son hangers-on of the propertied class: the gentlemen without the incomes of gentlemen. They cannot afford to send their sons to the public schools and universities, and would lose caste if they sent them to the ungentlemanly proletarian schools. They must therefore send them to cheap private adventure day schools, where they are not really taught at all, but are set school tasks (called "lessons") and subsequently catechized to ascertain whether they have memorized them, failing which they are punished, though seldom severely enough (that would be too much trouble for the executioners and too repugnant except to born Sadists) to overcome their preference for doing something more agreeable to their tastes and appetites. The teachers are unskilled and untrained as such; and the classes are too large. I can remember sitting in a row of about fifty boys in alphabetical order called a history class. Each day we were set a chapter in The Students' Hume. The teacher would go through the chapter and through the alphabet, asking questions about the facts and dates mentioned in it. As my name began with the letter S, I could calculate within ten lines or so what question would fall to me. I can still remember that in the chapter about the Peninsular War the answer to the question that always came was "The retreat from Burgos." From the ten lines hastily read on my way to the classroom I was even able to afford a prompt to the boy next to me if he had not been equally studious.

Now though I cannot deny that on these occasions I not only gave my enemy the teacher an excuse for pretending to believe that I had exhumed the whole history of the Peninsular War, but learnt that there had been a retreat from Burgos, it can hardly be claimed that I was learning history, whereas when I was at home reading Quentin Durward, A Tale of Two Cities, or The Three Musketeers, I was learning it very agreeably. And inasmuch as attendance at school kept me away from such books for half the day, I must affirm that my schooling not only failed to teach me what it professed to be teaching, but prevented me from being educated to an extent which infuriates me when I think of all I might have learnt at home by myself.

The statesman should, I maintain, rank fine art with, if not above, religion, science, education, and fighting power as a political agency. Yet we have not even a ministry of the fine arts; and our promiscuous democracy confronts our rulers with the votes of an electorate taught to regard fine art as sinful so far as it is taught anything at all about it. The situation is saved only by the impossibility of life without art. Fortunately, those who have never looked at pictures have looked at sunsets and landscapes and seen them as Turner and Constable did. Even the Calvinistic zealots who try to drive every enjoyment out of life except that of money making, cannot keep music, oratory, and literature out of their Sunday rituals. And such zealots are in a minority. People to whom the fine arts are accessible without reproach if they have money to pay for them, indulge in them to their hearts' content. Grand pianos are *de rigueur* even in drawing rooms where they are never opened: mothers sing or paint in watercolors: novels are knocking about all over the house. Even in country houses where the only amusements are killing birds, beasts, and fishes, each month having its ordained slaughter, and children have their faces smeared with the blood of the newly slain fox at their first hunt, there is natural beauty, and the joy of riding across country, which is more aesthetic than most amateur dancing. Even in shooting, the pleasure is not in the slaughter but in the artistic skill of the operation.

But though there is no such thing, even among people who spend most of their lives in countinghouses, at table, and in bed, as a completely Philistine class, there is a widely spread impression that fine art is self-indulgent, unproductive, unnecessary, effeminate, unpolitical, unscientific, and highly suspicious morally. To the agricultural population fine art as such is a form of debauchery and nothing else; for though, thanks to the wireless, farm laborers and gardeners no longer believe, as they did within my recollection, that songs and ballads are guilty secrets to which bawdy verses are quite appropriate, and the ability to sing Gently, Johnny, my Jingalo or The Seeds of Love need not now be concealed like an illicit love affair, yet, I fancy, this change is still too largely regarded as an enlarged toleration of immorality rather than as a recognition of the holiness of music.

The source of this misconception is plain enough. The appropriation of land by private owners has created a proletariat and forced it to labor for a sordid subsistence without leisure, culture, pocket-money, or the sort of clothes that can be worn without shame at artistic entertainments or in public picture galleries. In this condition, though people must have pleasures of some sort to make life bearable, they know of none that they can afford except intoxicating drinks and tobacco, both of them used to produce anaesthesia enough to drown the sorrow of poverty, betting on horses and dog races so as to maintain a continual hope of unearned riches, and above all, sexual intercourse, which they have been taught to hide as original sin. In such a state of things, association of pleasure with drunkenness, gambling, and fornication, and with nothing else, produces a conditioned reflex which makes the poor proletarian identify enjoyment with vice and sin, and art, being enjoyable, with smut and wickedness. Inevitably the poor proletarian educates his child as he trains his dog, by the whip, and punishes aestheticism as corruption, thereby making aesthetic education impossible.

The remedy is, of course, leisure and money. The soldier who, when I was pointed out to him as a teetotaller, said I was a damned liar because no man with a shilling in his pocket could pass a public-house without going in and having a drink, was a product of poverty and unremitting toil as inevitably as John Ruskin was a product of leisure and money. A Poor Law which puts food, lodging, and clothing first, and leisure and pocket-money nowhere, is socially half blind. The Frenchman who said he could do without the necessities of life if only he had its luxuries was wiser than the framers of the statute of Elizabeth or the Gradgrinds of 1832.

When the statesman has learnt that liberal education is aesthetic and aesthetic education propaganda he must not forget that art is as powerful for evil as for good. Nietzsche defined nations as people who read the same newspapers. He might have gone further and defined Roman Catholics as people who see the same pictures and images. What he would have said of the invention of the cinema, which brings the same dramas to action and speech over the whole inhabited world, and has made Hollywood an international city aesthetically spreading its doctrine as no established Church has ever succeeded in doing, making Roman Catholicism, Anglican Catholicism, Greek Catholicism, Moslem Catholicism and the rest seem petty failures beside the real Catholicism of "the pictures," I shall not guess.

The political levity which leaves this gigantic propaganda engine and its stupendous profits in the hands of casual gangs of American speculators is now faced with a dangerous new popular morality of Individualistic Anarchy tempered by socks on the jaw administered to villains armed with automatic pistols by good-looking young men engaged in the sexual pursuit of young women beautified by having their eyebrows plucked out and replaced by artificial ones more artistically designed and situated. It is something more than a coincidence that when votes are given to people whose heads are stuffed with this nonsense, the old wars between tribes and nations and churches and dynasties grow suddenly into world wars in which socks on the jaw are represented by the bursting of shells filled with high explosive, and the automatic pistols by Juggernaut tanks.

Now all this means that the statesman has to deal not only with the hard facts of the actual world, of which neither he nor the people he governs can have any very extensive up-to-date knowledge, but with a fairyland created and nursed by the fictions of poets and romancers, illustrated and decorated by draftsmen and designers, emotioned by painters and musicians, voiced by orators, and simulated in the theatres and cinemas to such an extent that its fantastic codes of honor and dishonor, of love and hate, praise and blame, patriotism and treason, manliness and womanliness, and conduct generally, take the place of observation and reasoning, and make democracy a fantasy acted by people in a dream. It is what makes such madness as world wars and such cruelties as criminal codes possible. It is what enables political and military adventurers to become worshipped as Messiahs, and to lead millions of men to risk starvation, wounds, and death in the attempt to establish their country as the Kingdom of God on Earth with some dressed up little mortal on the throne as the Christ of the second coming.

In this state of things the professional artist is not respected as such, though he may be petted and privileged; for by calling himself an artist he gives away the show. The scientist who professes Omniscience, and the militarist who professes irresistible Omnipotence, is taken seriously in spite of the glaring folly of such pretensions; but the artist who is seen or known to be operating the illusions with his pen, his brush, his orchestral score, though he may achieve enduring fame, is never enthroned, obeyed, and followed to the death by whole nations like the adventurers who keep up the illusions and exploit them. Compare the careers of Phidias and Pisistratus or Richard Wagner and Adolf Hitler, and you will feel the difference. The honest artist does not pretend that his fictions are facts; but he may claim as I do that it is only through fiction that facts can be made instructive or even intelligible. But that is not the same as pretending that they are not fictions. To work deliberately on the popular beliefs they create is one of the tricks of political rascality; but it is also a necessary art of honest statesmanship; for fools must be governed according to their folly and not to a wisdom they do not possess. To practise this art, therefore, one must be realist enough to see through more of the romantic illusions and know more of the hard facts than Mr Everyman. That is why Napoleons are as scarce as Washingtons and Stalins.

When I was first in company with Anatole France he asked who I was. Answering for myself I said, "I am, like you, a man of genius." This was, according to his French code, so immodest that it startled him into riposting with "Ah well: a whore (*courtisane*) has the right to call herself a pleasure merchant." I was not offended; for it is true that all artists make their livings as pleasure merchants and not as seers and philosophers; and the similarity of the case of the *courtisane* was not new to the author of Mrs Warren's Profession.

But why did he not say "a confectioner has the right to call himself a pleasure merchant," which would have been equally true? Or a jeweller? Or a trader in any of the hundreds of articles in our shops that are not necessities of life and have an aesthetic value only? They are even more to the point; for as a matter of fact the *courtisane* with brains enough to argue the point never makes Anatole France's excuse: her plea before Mrs Grundy is, "It is I and my like to whom you owe the purity of your unmarried daughters." She contends that sexual satisfaction is not a luxury but a necessity which defies the restrictive conditions which Mrs Grundy attaches to it.

I myself cannot bear to admit that I am a mere pleasure merchant. I use the pleasure given by my art as a playwright to induce people to read my plays or see them performed, and thereby enable me to live by them; but I am uncomfortably aware of the fact that needy and shallow playwrights have to exploit the viler pleasures given by indecency, scurrility, profanity, immorality, and falsehood solely for the sake of the money they draw. Even the best play must be enough of a potboiler to attract an audience, however small and select. Our greatest dramatic poet, Shakespear, had to practise his art "as you like it" to enable himself to retire as a country gentleman with a coat of arms. And persons born with a vocation for acting find themselves impelled to exercise it for its own sake even when the pay is less than that of a laborer and the penalties include ignominy and outlawry as a rogue and vagabond.

Thus the statesman finds himself up against the problem "What am I to do with these pleasure merchants?" Cromwell's decision was to class theatres as the gates of hell, and refuse to tolerate plays or players on any terms; but as he and his fellow Puritans loved music and sang hymns he presently found himself tolerating the new art of opera and opera singing, not foreseeing that one day it would be said that "an operatic tenor is not a man: he is a disease," and that the castles he was blowing up would be rebuilt by prima donnas. His soldiers smashed statues and burnt church organs only to hasten the birth of the Wagnerian orchestra. The Moslems whitewashed the frescoes of St Sophia in obedience to the Second Commandment, and presently found themselves enchanted by the magical windows in the mosque of the Sultan Zulieman. Napoleon, to make a presentable emperor of himself, had to go to an actor to learn how to do it. A Dean of St Paul's refused to allow the ass on which Christ rode into Jerusalem to be depicted in his cathedral; but in that fane there is now a statue of a horse with a less venerated rider. It is in fact impossible to suppress fine art or disable or exterminate its agents: it has been tried over and over in all sorts of circumstances and has never succeeded. Civilized statesmen are forced to recognize that the hunger for art is as inevitable as the hunger for bread. It would be quite logical to argue that as hunger leads to thieving and murder, the habit of eating must be put down, or at least allowed only under the most miserable conditions as by the Poor Law of 1832; but the grandchildren of the Manchester School now have to admit that food must be doled to everyone, idle or industrious, honest or dishonest; and the most sordid Philistines are finding that men deprived of art have to drink alcohol to make their lives endurable.

Art, however, is nowadays much more than an appetite which civilized humanity inherits from primitive savagery and may have to be dropped like some other such inheritances. It has become an instrument of culture, a method of schooling, a form of science, an indispensable adjunct of religion. The playwright, for instance, is not only a "chastener of morals by ridicule" and "a purger of the soul through pity and terror" (these are the time-honored classical definitions) but a biologist, philosopher, and prophet as well. Authors in particular have always been allowed to be philosophers and prophets when their inspiration carried them beyond mere trade in pleasure. The authors of the Bible enjoyed supreme scientific and historical authority until a rift opened between the priests and the Baconian men of science which widened from century to century until science and art marshalled themselves into hostile camps and went to wordy war with one another. It was a civil war (very uncivilly conducted); for art, science, and religion are really identical and inseparable in their foundations; and I, who in my teens would believe nothing that a priest taught, and everything that the professed scientists taught, soon found that professional science had come to a dead end in Materialism and Rationalism, and that until they were put back in their proper places further advance was possible only over their dead bodies. I began, as all serious artist-authors had to in the eighteen-eighties, by writing novels (the theatre being mentally dust and ashes) and actually produced five jejune samples in that *genre*. The first two I wrote on lines of the science of that time, the hero of the second being a complete Rationalist practising electrical engineering as a profession. Then, finding I could get, no further in this direction, I quite deliberately and consciously abandoned it, and made the hero of my next novel a totally unreasonable musical composer, like Beethoven. This is noteworthy, not as a Shavian personal incident, but because it was happening to the world as well, or going to happen to it.

The movement involved, not an abandonment of science, but an extension of it. It found Darwin's Natural Selection being mistaken everywhere for Evolution, as it still is by people who understand neither Natural Selection nor Evolution. It really rescued Evolution from Neo-Darwinism (Darwinism gone mad) and revived Evolution as a living creative force.

I did not at first follow up my change of line, which occurred in 1881, because I then had my attention diverted to economic science by Henry George, and was presently swept into militant Marxism for the next ten years. When I gave up novel-writing, and after an interval occupied by Marxist propaganda and critical journalism, undertook the resurrection of the drama, the old biological problems still called for new solutions. In an elaborate lecture on Darwin I disposed of the problem of evil which bothered St Augustine and pleased the Darwinists because it was a thick stick to beat God with. I got rid of the Darwinist muddle of inherited and acquired habits by pointing out that as to an evolutionist all habits are acquired the controversy was about nothing, all that was necessary to clear it up being a deeper study of inheritance in the light of embryology. This was thirtyseven years ago; and the professional scientists have not yet got as far as I, the professional artist, got in 1906. Yet the scientific material I was using was all discovered by them, not by me.

When the childish follies of our statesmen culminated in the orgy of slaughter and destruction, death and damnation, which called itself the war to end war, but is now, in the middle of another war, called the Four Years War, I wrote not only one play but a cycle of five entitled Back To Methuselah. In this, six years before Pavlov's treatise on Conditioned Reflexes was translated into English, I took up the subject of reflexes and carried it so far as to forecast a more highly evolved people amusing themselves in their childhood by manufacturing and playing with dolls who could spout romantic poetry and formulate Athanasian creeds, seeming to be as alive as our own statesmen, poets, politicians, and theologians when they were really only "shuddering through a series of reflexes." This was going farther than Weismann, who was a reflexo-maniac, or than Pavlov dared; but as I worded it all in common vernacular speech, and set it in a framework of aggressively vitalist creative evolution, it missed fire in the laboratories.

I, an artist-philosopher, mistrust laboratory methods because what happens in a laboratory is contrived and dictated. The evidence is manufactured: the cases are what newspaper reporters of police cases call frame-ups. If the evidence is unexpected or unaccountable it is remanufactured until it proves what the laboratory controller wants to prove. But the artist's workshop is the whole universe as far as he can comprehend it; and he can neither contrive nor dictate what happens there: he can only observe and interpret events that are beyond his control. A laboratory may be a fool's paradise or a pessimist's inferno: it is made to order either way. Its door may be shut against metaphysics, including consciousness, purpose, mind, evolution, creation, choice (free will), and anything else that is staring us in the face all over the real world. It may assume that because there is no discovered chemical difference between a living body and a dead one, only a difference in behavior, there is no difference. It may rule out all the facts that are incompatible with physicist determinism as metaphysical delusions. In short, it may reduce itself to absurdity in the name of science with a large S. Fine art is allowed no such licence.

But let no statesman or elector imagine that an artist cannot be as dangerous a fool as a laboratory researcher. The painting, the statue, the symphony, the fable, whether narrative or dramatic, is as completely contrived, selected, dictated, and controlled by the artist as the laboratory experiment by the scientist. It is equally subject to his prejudices, his ignorances, his blunders, and much more to his corruption by the public taste on the ground that "They who live to please must please to live." Idolatry of artists is as dangerous as idolatry of scientists. Their knowledge is small, their hypotheses provisional, their ignorance boundless, their vision limited, their mental apparatus very defective. Shakespear raised a biological problem when he set up "a divinity that shapes our ends, rough-hew them how we will." It was certainly not solved by Darwin; but then it was not solved by Shakespear. Goethe led the way to the evolutionary solution, but got no farther than a guess. Scientific advances mostly begin with guesses, jests, paradoxes, fictions, superstitions, quackeries, accidents, and apparent irrelevancies of all sorts. None of them is beneath a statesman's notice or above his criticism. Though he must consult many specialists he must bear in mind that they are all fallible. Molière took an opinion on the effectiveness of his comedies; but it was the opinion, not of the French Academy, but of his cook. He knew better than to classify the cook as illiterate and the Academy as infallibly literate. Classification, as Croce rightly insists, may mislead anyone who has not thought carefully about its limits. Descartes, now claimed as the father of the neo-Darwin-Weismann-Pavlov School of Determinist physics, might as justly be classed as the Archmetaphysicist on the strength of his famous "I think, therefore I am."

Any statesman simple enough to rely on such nomenclatory pigeon-holes may keep his papers in order; but he will soon get his mind very much out of order. It is convenient to file thinkers under different heads as Men of Science, Religious Men, Artists, Philosophers, Sociologists, Politicians and so forth just as it is convenient to file them as painters, sculptors, carpenters, plumbers, masons, ritualists, Quakers, Conservatives, Liberals, careerists, doctrinaires, Christian Scientists, allopaths, homeopaths, or humbugs. In such classifications Descartes would appear utterly remote from Mrs Eddy; yet Mrs Eddy's "I think I am ill; therefore I am ill" is as near to Cartesianism as the letter E is to the letter D. Men may be classified intellectually and morally as blunderers and liars; but people who conclude that blunderers are always blundering and liars always lying are political nuisances. Newton blundered ridiculously: Columbus mistook America for China: Titus Oates must have told the truth quite often or he could not have lived. The statesman's catalogues and files must have more cross references than entries; and if his conclusions and convictions come to him like thieves in the night he must not let himself be prejudiced against them on that account. Did not so accurately introspective a teacher as Jesus warn Christians that their salvation might come to them like that?

It is generally admitted that even good men have their weaknesses: what is less recognized is that rascals have their points of honor. Artists who will starve rather than violate their artistic consciences, heretics who will go to the stake or be thrown to the lions rather than call a communion table an altar or burn a pinch of incense before an image of the goddess Diana, may be unscrupulous blackguards in money matters and in their dealings with women. Complete intellectual integrity is as impossible as complete moral integrity. The strictest rationalist on one subject may on others be a recklessly prejudiced guesser: the most exact mathematicians overdraw their bank accounts in sheer carelessness. Doctors who prescribe scientific diets smoke and drink and eat to an extent that knows no rule but self-indulgence. I am very tidy in my bedroom, and so untidy in my study that though I have installed elaborate filing systems I lose hours looking for mislaid papers. You can classify me by my age, my height, my native language, the color of my eyes, the length and breadth of my head, for these facts are ascertainable and manageable; but when critics and biographers try to classify me as an author I smile. I fit none of their pigeon-holes.

Yet we cannot do without pigeon-holes, statesmen least of all; for statesmen have to legislate, to organize the nation's work, and to select fit persons to administer laws and plans. Though every individual is unique and different, separate laws cannot be made for every individual; therefore the individual must fit himself to the law instead of having it fitted to him. Yet if national organization is to be efficient it must not be conducted by square pegs in round holes: to avoid this both the pegs and the holes must be classified. For private purposes a classification of human beings as women and men is useless: a woman choosing a husband, or a husband a wife, must discriminate between such various temperaments as those of the egotists and the unselfish, the managerial and the docile, the termagant and the angel in the house, the mean and the prodigal, the worrying and the careless, the placable and the vindictive, the secretive and the communicative, the good companion and the bore, and the other extremes and shades which make marriages so different; but the statesman cannot go into all this: he must regulate the lives of the people on the assumption that for certain purposes, and up to a certain point for all purposes, women are all alike and men are all alike though in fact none of them are quite alike. He must draw lines between the classifications, and persecute or kill people on one side of the line and encourage and promote those on the other. And when he comes to the artist classification he, seeing that artists are the most effective propagandists, must make up his mind as to what doctrines to forbid and what to tolerate.

For instance, if the Church of England is to remain "established" as it is at present, statesmen may have to revise the Book of Common Prayer, which is saturated with the doctrines of the atonement by blood sacrifice, the parthenogenic birth and the supernatural divinity of Jesus and his identification with the old tribal idol Jehovah, the eternal survival of all individual human beings in a material heaven or hell as described by Mahomet and Dante, the acceptance of the Bible as an infallible and up-to-date encyclopedia, and other doctrines which the ablest of the clergy and of their congregations find incredible or unreasonable or socially mischievous and sometimes all three.

This puts the cleverer clergy in a difficulty which statesmen have to face equally. Both of them have not only to ascertain the truths of science but to govern and direct millions of people who are neither cognisant of the more subtle and recondite of such truths nor capable of taking them in when they are explained to them. Take the leading case of Galileo. It is usually written of as a persecution of a great observer and fearless reasoner by a pack of superstitious, narrow-minded, ignorant priests. This is mere Protestant scurrility: Copernicus had convinced the Vatican and the ablest of the Italian priests that, as the artist Leonardo had already guessed, the earth is a moon of the sun, not the centre of the universe. But they had to govern their simple illiterate flocks, not by the incomprehensible and apparently paradoxical views of Copernicus and Galileo, but by imposing childish Bible stories on them as infallible truths from the hand of God himself. Among these stories was one of Joshua making the sun stand still until he had finished and won one of his battles. If Galileo were to tell the people that Joshua should have stopped the earth instead of the sun, and that the story must have been invented by somebody so unlike God as to be grossly ignorant of astronomy, their faith would be shattered; and Christendom would collapse in an orgy of selfish lawlessness. Therefore they said to Galileo in effect, "We know as well as you that the earth moves round the sun and not the sun round the earth; but we must not say so; and you must not say so." Galileo, being a sensible man, saw their point and assured the people that he had made an unfortunate mistake and that the Church was always right. And the people, who knew that the sun moved because they saw it move from the eastern to the western horizon every day, and knew that the earth was flat because when they dropped an orange it lay still where it fell instead of rolling off as a pea does off a saucepan lid, were satisfied, and would have crowded to see Galileo burnt if he had persisted in what they took to be blasphemous nonsense.

Sure enough, when the truth got about, what the priests feared did largely happen. The quest of salvation gave way to the quest of commercial profits; and Manchester supplanted Rome as the head-quarters of civilization. But the people still know as little of the minds of Adam Smith and David Ricardo as the Italian people of the minds of Thomas Aquinas and Aristotle; and the statesmen in both countries who have to rule them, though they need no longer pretend to believe that the earth is flat and that the sun moves round it, are still obliged to spout romantic balderdash made popular by works of art produced by poets, playwrights, novelists and historians. "History" said Mr Henry Ford "is the bunk." Much of it certainly is; yet our political orators have to talk in terms of it, and, when in power, to persecute realists (Marxists for instance) as heretics for telling the truth just as the Copernican priests and Popes did. But Marxist artists are inspired to produce communist Utopias, paint pictures glorifying labor, and compose symphonies expressing revolutionary enthusiasms. These in their turn will produce a public state of mind to which political careerists will have to pander, and which practical rulers must exploit if they are to keep the people in hand. As to the genuine leaders, who can obtain a hold only by changing public opinion, they too must use the fine arts to tempt people to listen to them and be persuaded by them.

We see then, that it is the duty of the statesman to persecute anti-social conduct, and that the artist's conduct is the most infectious of conducts and can be dangerously anti-social. How is the statesman to discharge this duty? How is he to checkmate pernicious art whilst encouraging salutary art? In industry he checkmates the anti-social employer by Factory Acts, sending into the factories and workshops inspectors who order the employers to do certain things and not to do others. Any employer who cannot make his factory pay on these conditions must find some other occupation better suited to his incapacities. In short, the employer is moralized by Act of Parliament. Can we moralize the artist similarly?

Our inexperienced and ignorant electors and their representatives think this very difficult task quite easy. Just inspect the works of art, and if they are improper send for the police. The magistrate can have them burnt. Many pornographic books and pictures have been destroyed in this way; and some classics have shared their fate. Sometimes the writers of the books have been burnt too.

Now this rough-and-ready method, which has done so much to humanize our factories and to deblackguardize all the arts, and is simple enough when there is nothing but crude blackguardism in question, breaks down very mischievously when it is confronted with those higher works of art, the most important of all, which, as instruments of evolution, dare to criticize public opinion and existing institutions. I was myself officially classed for many years as a pernicious blackguard, and injured in reputation and pocket, because I used my art to expose the real roots of prostitution, and, later on, shewed how a prostitute and a thief, both of them professed enemies of morality and scoffers at religion, got caught and converted by their consciences—theologically speaking, by the Holy Ghost—and "saved."

I was not the only victim. Shelley, Ibsen, Tolstoy, Maeterlinck, and Brieux shared my fate whilst playwrights whose plays did not rise above the level of reports of the proceedings in the police and divorce courts were effectively protected by certificates of propriety from the censor costing only two guineas per play. This absurdity was produced by the fact that when the problem of moralizing the aesthete arises, the first expedient that suggests itself—I resist the temptation to say the first thought that comes into a fool's head—is to appoint a censor to examine all works of art and decide whether they shall be made public or even permitted to exist. The arguments for a censorship are irresistible: it is plain to silly people that all that need be done is to find a censor who combines all the wisdom, learning, and concern for human welfare of the Vatican, the Judicial Committee of the House of Lords, the episcopates of all the Churches, with the omniscience of the Holy Trinity, and put fine art under his thumb. The statesman, unable to find such a paragon, and educated to class artists, especially theatre artists, as Bohemian undesirables, satisfies the demand by giving the job to a petty official with a salary of two or three hundred a year or less. The petty official, finding his mental powers unequal to his judicial duties, makes a list of words that must not be used, and subjects that, being controversial, must not be discussed by frivolous persons such as all artists are assumed to be. Obvious subjects are religion, sex, and politics. Thus an unofficial American Roman Catholic censor, much dreaded in Hollywood, being confronted with a certain play written by myself and entitled St Joan, found the word halo in it and ordered its excision as religious. The heroine happening to remark that soldiers are often fond of babies, that, too, had to come out, because babies are sex. And so on, until there was nothing intelligible left of the play, which, though sexless, is full of religion and politics. As this clerical censorship in the United States can do nothing to enforce its judgments except to exhort all American Roman Catholics (twenty millions) to stay away from entertainments of which it disapproves, and as the Roman Catholics in the States number less than a seventh of the population and commit quite as often as Protestants the sins which their Church forbids, I can afford to snap my fingers at it; but in the British Isles plays can be suppressed locally by chief constables of police and nationally by the Lord Chamberlain on the advice of "King's readers" with modest salaries. At their hands I suffered

damage as aforesaid for many years in respect of plays by me which
are now set free by enlightened Lord Chamberlains who have overridden the follies of their readers. Their predecessor, under whom I
suffered, is remembered by his two quoted utterances "I am not an
agricultural laborer" and "Who is Tolstoy?"

The first play that got me into trouble called attention to the fact
that prostitution, supposed to be the fault of the vicious propensities
of sexually abandoned women and their male clients, was really an
economic phenomenon produced by an underpayment of honest
women so degrading, and an overpayment of whores so luxurious,
that a poor woman of any attractiveness actually owed it to her selfrespect to sell herself in the streets rather than toil miserably in a
sweater's den sixteen hours a day for twopence an hour, or risk
phosphorus poisoning in a match factory for five shillings a week, or
the like. How badly this revelation was needed was proved years
after when the international organization of prostitution by capitalist exploiters, known as the White Slavery, became such a tyranny
that the Government was forced to take some action. And all it could
think of was an Act to have male brothel keepers flogged, with the
result that a valuable monopoly was conferred on procuresses: in
fact on my Mrs Warren. If my play had not been suppressed by the
censorship the matter might have been better understood, and the
remedy not so mischievously futile.

As I knew very well that it is useless to denounce a wrong remedy
without finding the right one, and that the only remedy for privileged slander is to live it down, I did not howl vainly about my
personal grievance. I pointed out that the London music halls, which
had been sinks of silly smut, had been cleaned up and changed into
decent variety theatres by compelling the managers to obtain a
licence from the London County Council from year to year to carry
on their operations, leaving them free to perform what they pleased
for twelve months at the risk of being driven out of their business at
the end if their proceedings had been scandalous enough to convince
the majority of a numerous and sufficiently representative public
authority that they were not good enough for their job. As usual, I
might have saved my breath to cool my porridge. The only response
was the old cry for clerks at a few hundred a year to exercise faculties beyond the pretensions of the greatest saints and prophets, and
powers it has cost two revolutions to deny to English kings. In Eire
at present these powers are wielded by a public-spirited and well-
intentioned gentleman, whose reported view is that as eighty per

cent of the Irish cinema audiences are children, no film unsuited to children should be exhibited. Divorce having been abolished in Eire, playwrights must mention it only to condemn it, and must treat marriages as indissoluble without mentioning that they have to be annulled all the more frequently. This is only a sample of the official list of restrictions and prohibitions which make serious drama impossible in Eire except in so far as it is cleverly disingenuous. Unofficially the censor advocates a historical drama dealing with the ancient history of Ireland from his own point of view (he was one of the heroes of the 1916 rising). As that history, though romantically charming, and capable of producing good effects on the minds of children, is, I should guess, at least ninetynine per cent fabulous, it fails to provide for that element of truth to nature and critical comic relief without which romance ends in disillusion and cynicism. Don Quixote without Sancho Panza could only have driven us as mad as he was himself.

Those of us who suffer from democracy on the brain are flanked by an anarchical Left objecting to any governmental control of art, and a Right wing holding that everything should be controlled by authorities elected by the votes of everybody. The Right wing agrees that the theatres should be controlled by the municipality. But its notion of that control is the existing censorship with its absurdity complicated by impossibility. I have known people not otherwise noticeably mad to propose that all books and plays, before being licensed for publication or performance, should be read by all the members of the municipal authority, and the question of granting the licence be decided by vote in full council. It has not occurred to them that the reading of the plays and books would occupy all the time of the members to the entire neglect of all other public business, and even then soon fall so far into arrear that publication and performance would jam and stop dead. And the minds of the municipal councillors would be damaged by excessive reading, mostly of trash.

Moreover it must not be supposed that the abandonment of all these expedients would leave the drama free. It would simply hand it over to the police. In the United States of America, where there is no State censorship, the police sometimes arrest an entire company for performing plays which are considered objectionable by some piously officious or impenetrably conservative chief constable, or against which a hue and cry has been raised in the press, as in the case of Ibsen's Ghosts. This is why our theatre managers unanimously support the censorship of the Lord Chamberlain. His licence, costing only two guineas, insures them against police interference: at least they think it does. At all events it gives them an official expert opinion in a matter which they are often quite unqualified to judge for themselves. They can be prosecuted under the criminal law for obscene libel, blasphemous libel, seditious libel, or for keeping a disorderly house. As the consequences may be much more serious than those of a refusal of a licence they very wisely prefer the lesser risk.

Now the author shares all these risks except that of keeping a disorderly house. There is no censorship of books; but whoever writes or publishes an unusual one risks having it burnt by order of a police magistrate. Whoever sells it risks imprisonment and a ruinous fine. For merely buying the book, possessing it, and reading it, or listening to its being read, the penalty may be penal servitude for an unlimited period. People used to be transported for reading Paine's Age of Reason or Shelley's Queen Mab. A prosecution of a teacher for agreeing with Charles Darwin's book on Natural Selection took place in the United States quite recently on the ground that the book, being contrary to the Holy Scriptures, is blasphemous; and there is nothing to prevent a similar prosecution in England at any moment. During the Four Years War a question was raised very logically as to whether the New Testament, inopportunely quoted by a bishop, was not a seditious libel. As long as such prosecutions are legally possible no prevalence of desuetude can guarantee an author against their resurrection if he has anything new to say. Accordingly, not only are theatre managers as men of business strongly and very sensibly in favor of censorship, but authors, even when they have something new to say, are less afraid of the censor than of the chief constable, the public prosecutor, and the common informer. I should cling to the censorship myself if I believed, as many of my colleagues do, that its certificate of propriety is a valid defence against prosecution.

Thus the problem of keeping fine art clean and wholesome, far from being a simple one to be solved by paying somebody a modest salary to deal with it, is really insoluble; for the job is beyond human capacity. The willingness of somebody to take it on—and there are always dozens of eager applicants for it—is conclusive proof of the gross incapacity of that somebody for the only part of it that really matters. For indecency and vulgarity the fundamental remedy is the culture of audiences and readers, and the protests of critics. Jeremy Collier cured the profaneness and immorality of Restoration drama without any official authority. But the censorship, established not to

THE AESTHETIC MAN 199

clean up the stage, but to muzzle Henry Fielding, one of the greatest
of British authors, made the theatre the most stagnant cultural institution in the country.

Are we then to place theatre managers in a privileged position,
"beyond good and evil" as Nietzsche put it, so that they may violate
social morality with impunity? Both the scientific professions and
mercantile occupations make the same claim much more impudently
(always, of course, in the name of liberty) and have even had it
allowed for a while; but no British government will trust the exploiters of fine art so far. And to go to the other extreme and place
its control in the hands of petty officials is to sin against the Holy
Ghost. Apparently there is nothing to be done but leave it to the
police, as in America and France, until both playgoers and playwrights are cultivated to a point at which they will do their own
censoring in the light of their own culture.

There is, however, an alternative which works fairly well in established practice. Theatres are licensed by the local municipal authority
from year to year on condition that they are sanitated, fireproofed,
provided with doors enough to empty them quickly without disaster
in case of panic, and, in the case of new theatres, isolated. But a
theatre may be quite satisfactory in these respects and yet be conducted very immorally. Even when the plays performed are of the
most desolating blamelessness they may have to be divided into acts
with long intervals between for drinking at the refreshment bars,
with the foyers so crowded with alluringly dressed prostitutes that
the place is not really a temple of dramatic art but a White Slave
market and drink shop: technically a disorderly house.

Against this misuse neither the regulations of the sanitary authority nor the powers of the Lord Chamberlain can prevail. It is not the
building that is at fault, but its management. The manager is guilty
of what the General Medical Council calls infamous professional
conduct.

Clearly the case for licensing the manager is as strong as for
licensing the innocent building. Such a licence need not involve an
examination, like a doctor's diploma or a barrister's call. Any respectable person can, by paying a small annual fee, obtain a licence
to keep a gun, or a wireless set, or a dog, or a tavern, or to sell in the
streets as a hawker. There is no reason why he or she should not be
able to obtain a licence to keep a theatre on the same terms, provided it can be cancelled on proof of misuse, and it be made a
punishable offence to keep a theatre without it. Such licensing is a

familiar device. Its substitution for the present censorships would relieve the Lord Chamberlain from an odious duty which should not be
connected with the King's household (Henry the Eighth being now a
long time dead) and would make it impossible to suppress works of
art by forbidding their performance, publication, or exhibition,
whilst making someone responsible for their character and for the
general decency of his conduct as a purveyor of artistic entertainment. The liability to prosecution for obscene, blasphemous, or seditious libel in respect of each particular work of art would still
remain; but such proceedings should be in the power of the public
prosecutor only, and not that of the common informer, nor even of
a chief constable, though he could report and recommend in the
matter, just as the common informer could complain.

I hope I have made it clear that we are not in the dilemma of
control by individual censors or no control at all. The choice is
between a well considered collective control and a thoughtless one
that defeats its own most vital ends.

CHAPTER XXIII

THE MAN OF SCIENCE

THE department of science with which governments are most concerned is biology, the science of life. It includes physiology and
psychology, and is the basis of public health legislation and private
medical practice. It has gone far beyond the Churches in its viola-
tions of individual liberty and integrity. The Christian Church takes
an infant from its mother's arms, sprinkles a few drops of water on
it, and dedicates it as a soldier and servant of God: a ceremony that
has never harmed any infant and has beneficially edified many god-
fathers and godmothers. The State, by the advice of the biologists,
takes the infant from its mother's arms and poisons its blood to
exercise its natural power of resisting and overcoming poison. It
lays hands on soldiers, nurses, and other adult persons supposed to
be specially liable to infection, and repeats the operation with various
specific poisons guaranteed to produce specific immunities. A well-
known soldier friend of mine told me he had undergone forty inoculations and been none the worse. His blood had been healthy enough

to make short work of all the poisons.

Not everyone is so lucky. Every inoculation has effects which vary from a few hours malaise with perhaps a faint or two, or disablement for about a week, to temporary paralysis following inoculation against diphtheria, permanent illhealth, and at worst death from the horribly disfiguring disease called generalized vaccinia following inoculation against smallpox.

Now we have here the danger of a tyranny which was not thought of by the authors of Magna Carta, of the Habeas Corpus Act, of the Petition of Rights, or the American Declaration of Independence and Constitution. I would make the Government a present of all my rights under these famous documents rather than be compelled, whether as infant or adult, to have my person violated and my blood poisoned on the advice of a trade union of doctors with a pecuniary interest in the operation, or an array of figures compiled by self-styled men of science with childish notions of statistics and critical evidence. Men have submitted to castration to secure lucrative employment as superintendents of seraglios or singers in opera houses and churches; and Chinese parents have had the feet of their female children painfully bound and lamed because it was the fashion under the Manchu dynasty; but compulsion of everybody willynilly to dangerous blood poisoning repeated for every virus discoverable by the new electron microscope, to sterilization, to extirpation of the uvula and tonsils, to birth delivery by the Caesarian operation, to excision of several folds of the bowel and of the entire appendix, to treatment of syphilis and malaria by doses of mercury and arsenic, iodine and quinine, all of which have been advocated by eminent physicians and surgeons, and some of them legally enforced today, and this without protest or even mention from the loudest champions of individual liberty of thought, speech, worship, and trade (especially trade), marks the rise of an abjectly credulous worship of everything calling itself Science which goes beyond any tyranny recorded of the religious creeds of Rome, Mexico, or Druidic Britain. I have often said that there is in nature a law of the Conservation of Human Credulity (like Joule's law of the Conservation of Energy) so inexorable that it is impossible to dispel one delusion without creating another equivalent one; but as I witness the atrocities and stupidities of professional science, and the extent to which its claim to be exempt from all moral obligation in its pursuit of knowledge is conceded by our statesmen, I am tempted to throw Joule over, and regard credulity and idolatry as plagues in which action and reaction are not equal, and to conclude that as the domain of genuine science is unlimited, so also is the domain of delusion. The omniscience, infallibility, and incorruptible truthfulness formerly reserved for an ideal variously called God, Allah, Brahma, etc., is transferred to every Tom, Dick, or Harriet who has cut up a dog or a guinea pig in a laboratory, and written a book or a paper describing how the unfortunate animal responded.

Let me describe a flagrant and famous example of this infatuation. For the moment the Pontifex Maximus in biological science is Ivan Petrovich Pavlov, lately deceased, in celebration of whom I have just heard a broadcast eulogy which would have been excessive if Pavlov had been all the greatest benefactors of mankind rolled into one, with all the gods and their prophets and all the philosophers and discoverers thrown in. He was in fact the prince of pseudo-scientific simpletons. What did he do to impose on us so outrageously?

He devoted 25 years of his life to the study of Conditioned Reflexes, and gave the result to the world in 23 lectures translated into English by his colleague Dr Anrep and published here in 1927. The book is entitled Conditioned Reflexes: an Investigation of the Physiological Activity of the Cerebral Cortex. This is an imposing title; but all it means is Our Habits: How We Acquire Them and How Our Brains Operate Them. There have been some complaints of the style of the book as difficult. This is unjust: there is not an ambiguous sentence in it: both its sense and its nonsense are quite lucidly expressed in language which is, like Dr Johnson's, pretentious and unvernacular but never obscure. Its translator must not condescend to write that there are milestones on the Dover road; but an announcement that a communicatory channel between the metropolis and the seaport is indicated by a series of equidistant petrifacts is equally clear if you know the language; and it looks much more dignified and learned.

What, exactly, is a conditioned reflex? I became intellectually conscious of one some fifty years ago, when there was opened at Chelsea a Naval Exhibition. It contained facsimiles of Nelson's last flagship and of the first class passengers' quarters in a modern Peninsular and Oriental Liner. I gazed without discomposure on the cockpit in which Nelson kissed Hardy and died. But in the passage between the P. and O. cabins I suddenly felt seasick, and had to beat a hasty retreat into the gardens.

This was a perfect example of a conditioned reflex. I had often been made seasick by the rolling and pitching of a ship. The rolling and pitching had been accompanied by the sight of the passengers' quarters and the smell of paint and oakum. The connection between them had been so firmly established in me that even when I stood on the firm earth these sights and smells made me squeamish.

At first this experience of mine seems merely funny. But on further consideration it becomes not only scientifically interesting but appalling. If a reflex can persist when it has become completely detached from its original cause, it can itself produce a new reflex which can become similarly detached and produce yet another new reflex, and so on *ad infinitum*. What if all human activity be nothing but the operation of innumerable reflexes with all rational connection between them and the original facts hopelessly lost? May not this explain why the human race is at present (1944) concentrating all its energies on destroying itself? Is not such a possibility frightful enough to make a scientific investigation of conditioned reflexes a matter of the most urgent importance?

It is Pavlov's great merit that he must have had some sense of this importance; for he devoted his life to its investigation.

Unfortunately he was handicapped by two powerful conditioned reflexes in himself which he failed to recognize as such and allow for. One was the nineteenth century reaction against an old tribal idol called Jehovah, who demands blood sacrifices and dominates the Bible from Noah to Samuel, and then gives way to the more civilized gods of Koheleth (Ecclesiastes) and Micah, finally softened by Jesus into "Our Father which art in heaven." Unfortunately the disciples of Jesus went back on Micah by making the Crucifixion a blood sacrifice and thus reviving Jehovah as the final infallible authority on scientific questions (that is, on all questions), to be worshipped as such on pain of severe punishment on earth and eternal torment after death. The revolt of modern common sense against this atavistic idolatry is called Iconoclasm (an VIII century movement), scepticism, atheism, materialism, agnosticism, rationalism, secularism and many other names. It is now so strong that it denies not only the existence and authority of Jehovah but of any metaphysical factors in life whatsoever, including purpose, intuition, inspiration, and all the religious and artistic impulses. It boycotts volition, conscience, and even consciousness as unaccounted for by Science. In short, it seeks to abolish life and mind, substituting for them a conception of all motion and action, bodily and mental, as a senseless accidental turmoil of physical collisions. Such a divorce from the facts makes it not only useless to the statesman but extremely dangerous.

In Pavlov's case this reduction of Science to absurdity was arrived at not by reasoning but by an entirely unreasonable association of ideas: that is, by a series of "conditioned reflexes" of precisely the same nature as that which led my stomach to imagine that the firm earth of Chelsea Botanic Gardens was the Bay of Biscay in a gale. When reading him one must bear in mind that his use of the word "therefore," like most of his assertions of "obvious relations" between this and that, indicates, not a logical sequence, but only an association of ideas, or, as he would say, a conditioned reflex. But do not forget that a reflex may be a good guess, just as a perfect verbal syllogism may be only an absurd pun. You have to be careful with Pavlov. When he is thinking-out a theory of reflexes he is worth reading. When he is trying to fit his theory into his experiments he entangles himself in such nonsense that you may be tempted to pitch the book to the other side of the room and take up a detective story. He all but admits this in his final lecture whilst desperately defending the experiments, and urging his successors to continue them as the only genuinely scientific method of investigation.

For here you have come up against the second specific reflex which damns him as an investigator. Let us study its history for a moment.

Those who have studied the orientation of the monoliths of Stonehenge know that the first scientists were priests who impressed their congregations by their apparently prophetic knowledge of the solstices and the stars and the right times to sow and reap. But to impress people incapable of grasping scientific achievements priests had to propitiate their terrible gods by human sacrifices (Jephtha's daughter and Iphigenia for instance), and later on, with more profit to themselves, by the slaughter of birds and animals. For these dedicated butcheries they invented the altar; and to make the altar august and awful they invented the temple with its holy of holies. To give to their precepts and laws the authority of divine revelation they invented the oracle and the holy scriptures. As Augurs, they practised the crude magic of cutting birds open and reading the future in their entrails. Thus, being at the same time men of science, priests, magicians, astrologers, and political rulers, they at last got science so mixed up with religion, priestcraft, popular superstition, and politics in the same porridge that the task of extricating science from it still baffles our subtlest analytical powers.

The conditioned reflexes produced by the mixture are innumerable and untraceable. Many of them cancel one another out; for some are too cruel for civilized people to tolerate, and from being what Pavlov calls excitatory have become inhibitory. But some of the worst and some of the most ridiculous still flourish. They were at work in Pavlov's laboratory far more authoritatively than in the cabin of the peasant who on Holy Eve poured molten lead into cold water and played at divining the future by the fantastic shapes the crumbs of lead took as they solidified. The modern communion table, like the heathen altar, still commemorates a blood sacrifice; but instead of sacrificing human flesh and blood we symbolize them by bread and wine eaten and drunk by the celebrant or the worshippers or by both.

Thus the ancient god whom Noah bribed by a meal of roast meat got blended with the cannibals' god who was eaten by his worshippers to acquire his qualities, just as they ate their vanquished enemies in war to acquire their strength and bravery and skill with weapons. Sir James Frazer, who has just died, devoted his life to tracing these crisscrossed rites and their reflexes in a monumental book called The Golden Bough, extending to many volumes. I read the first chapter or so forty years ago, when the first volume was new, but soon got oppressed by the sameness of its instances of human delusion, and have not opened it since. Lest I should make this book of my own unreadable I shall confine myself here to the reflexes which connect science with the sacrifice of living animals.

The most striking recent instance is the action of the British medical profession when it was shaken by the impact of American osteopathy. An American doctor named Still had discovered that certain ailments were connected with displacements in the spine, and that he could cure them by correcting these displacements. He called himself an osteopath, and founded a manipulative technique which, like Kellgren massage and other manipulative systems, needed about two years training to acquire. In England, where the highest surgical degrees can be obtained by postulants who have never performed a surgical operation, Still's addition to the things a doctor ought to know and be able to practise was very ill received, especially as the established period of training already occupied five years and cost much money. But the resistance to it was not only a trade union resistance: it was also undertaken as a scientific resistance. In spite of an overwhelming mass of clinical evidence in its favor it was held that it could not be scientifically demonstrated and proved unless a dog in a laboratory had its spine dislocated with the usual results, and then cured by correcting the displacement by Still's method. The osteopaths accordingly went solemnly through this ritual, whereupon it was reluctantly admitted that osteopathy had become so far scientific.

Obviously this senseless sacrifice of a dog on the laboratory altar had nothing to do with science: it was simply obedience to a conditioned reflex acquired before the Pyramids were built, and "reinforced" (Pavlov's word) again and again through so many centuries that it had become inveterate. There is no other explanation of Pavlov's choice of a ridiculous and revoltingly cruel routine of research when so many sensible and humane methods were open to him, and of his insistence on its continuation in the very pages in which he confesses its failures.

What he actually did was to devote twenty-five years of his life to experiments on dogs to find out, as data for his biological theory, whether their mouths watered, and if so how much (counted in drops of saliva) when they had certain sensations such as the sight or smell of food, the hearing of words or noises, the feeling of certain touches, or the sight of certain persons and objects. He set metronomes ticking at them, buzzers buzzing at them, musical tones sounding at them, heat glowing at them. He tickled marked places on their bodies, and then fed them, with the result that they came to associate these sensations so invariably with food that soon their mouths watered when without any offer of food they were simply buzzed at, ticked at, played at, glowed at, or tickled. The natural mouthwatering at the sight or smell of food he called an unconditioned reflex. The watering provoked by some sensation which had become connected in the dog's experience with food, like my nausea at the Chelsea Exhibition, he called a conditioned reflex.

All the experiments involved tapping the salivary ducts by boring holes in the dog's cheek and establishing a permanent fistula there, as the very delicate apparatus needed to measure the saliva could not be attached to the dog's tongue, its natural channel.

From these observations Pavlov drew inferences for which he claimed a thoroughly scientific character. He had committed himself to the condition that the sequences of salivation and insalivation observed by him must be consistent, inevitable, invariable, and necessary if they were to be accepted as scientific evidence. They failed to fulfil this condition. The sequences as often as not—indeed more often than not—contradicted his theory flatly. Sometimes their actual order exactly reversed the theoretical order. Far from being consistent, inevitable, invariable, necessary, they were often capricious and contradictory. Pavlov was honest enough to admit their failure in his final lecture, though his conclusion is that there must have been either something wrong with the laboratory apparatus or "temperamental" with the dogs; for he urges his successors to persevere with his method until they contrive better apparatus and discover a sort of dog with sufficient consideration for his theory to react in the desired manner.

As it may seem incredible that so clever a scientist could be so absurd, I hasten to add that his naturally keen intelligence did not reach imbecility in a single jump. He deceived himself step by step by a method which welcomed every failure as a new discovery and an addition to his theory. Thus when he stimulated the dog, and the dog did not salivate, he did not conclude that either his theory or his method must be wrong. He thought he had discovered that reflexes have negative phases as well as positive ones, and can be classed as Excitatory or Inhibitive. This, if not an original discovery, had some common facts to back it; for though the mention of jam may make a child's mouth water, and it will eat the jam greedily at first, yet if you give the child a whole pot of jam and a spoon, and invite it to eat it all up, it will presently leave the pot unfinished, refusing to swallow another mouthful. Its unconditioned reflex to jam has become negative and inhibitive. Pavlov could have learnt this from the nearest nursemaid without the expense and trouble of buying a dog and making a hole in its cheek; but his Druidic reflex forced him to reject the testimony of nursemaids unless consecrated by the ritual of dog sacrifice.

When the sequences occurred in the reverse order to the expected one, Pavlov announced the discovery of a new phenomenon: the Paradoxical Phase. And here also he was fortified by the fact that when a man wants to get up and work he puts on his clothes in their accustomed order, and when his work has tired him out and he wants to go to bed and sleep (the negative phase) he takes off his clothes in the reverse order (the paradoxical phase).

Pavlov then tried to make his dogs produce the paradoxical phase at his will. He failed. He immediately announced the failure as the discovery of an ultra-paradoxical phase.

Now it is clear that an experimenter who can interpret results either positively or negatively, logically or paradoxically, paradoxically or ultra-paradoxically, can make them prove anything he likes.

Give me that much latitude and I can prove, by spectrum analysis, that the moon is made of green cheese. Perhaps I will some day, and be proclaimed by the British Broadcasting Corporation the greatest scientist of all time.

Pavlov did not confine his researches to the reflexes. He wanted also to discover and localize the different spots in the brain which operated the reflexes when the dog was stimulated in different ways or in different places on its skin.

To effect this the most obvious method was to cut out portions of the dog's brain and see how it got on without them. In the nineteenth century experimenters with the same object burnt out portions of monkeys' brains; but Pavlov preferred his salivation method as being more exactly measurable. It was exact enough as far as counting the drops of saliva went; but here again the results were not consistent, not invariable, not inevitable. But Pavlov's reasoning method was proof against this discouragement. When he traced the reflex to a particular spot in the brain, and presently found that some neighboring spot would do just as well, he announced a new discovery: Irradiation. He was no doubt familiar with the fact that if you let a drop of ink fall on a piece of blotting paper it does not concentrate itself on the spot on which it falls, but spreads all round. Evidently an impact on the brain did the same. The apparent failure of the experiment was therefore accounted for by the two words Concentration and Irradiation.

Sometimes, however, when he tested a connexion between a spot in the dog's brain and its front paw, he found that the same spot responded equally to the dog's hind paw, or, conversely, that the front paw set quite another spot going. Another failure? Not at all. He knew that a wire charged with electricity can induce a parallel current in a neighboring wire. Evidently the message from the dog's skin to its brain has the same property: there are induced messages as well as original ones. Not another failure: only another discovery.

Pavlov's conclusions were now impregnable. Every experimental observation fitted them like a glove. No control experiment could upset them: no contradiction could remain unreconciled: no house of cards or castle in the air could be better put together. It sounds so like genuine physical objective science that people who are no better reasoners than Pavlov, and want to believe in him, cannot see that the story of his dogs in his book is a crackle of blazing nonsense from beginning to end.

It imposed, and still imposes, on people of first-rate ability. When it appeared, my friend and fellow sage H. G. Wells was so impressed that he announced that if he saw Pavlov and myself drowning, and only one lifebuoy were within his reach, he would have to throw it to Pavlov and leave me to drown. He had met Pavlov in Russia and been charmed by him to the extent of maintaining that he was a tender humanitarian in his methods, loving his dogs and being loved by them, whereas I, never having met him, had gone so far on the evidence of his experiments as to call him a scoundrel, meaning a person who repudiates common morality in the pursuit of his personal or professional interests. As a matter of fact anyone except a professional scientist doing the things to his dogs (bought for the purpose) that Pavlov did would be not only prosecuted for cruelty to animals but held up in court as a monster. Here is Pavlov's own account of the matter in his nineteenth lecture (pp. 320–22).

"The only method so far available for such a study consists in observing the effects of partial destruction or complete extirpation of different parts of the cortex. This method naturally suffers from fundamental disadvantages, since it involves the roughest forms of mechanical interference and the crude dismembering of an organ of a most exquisite structure and function. Imagine that we have to penetrate into the activity of an incomparably simpler machine fashioned by human hands, and that for this purpose, not knowing its different parts, instead of carefully dismantling the machine we take a saw and cut away one or another fraction of it, hoping to obtain an exact knowledge of its mechanical working! The method usually applied to the study of the hemispheres or other parts of the central nervous system is essentially as primitive as this. Hammer and chisel, the saw and the drill; these are the instruments which must be used to open up the strong protective skull. Then we tear through the several layers of enveloping protective membranes, rupturing many blood vessels, and finally we injure or destroy whole lumps of the delicate nervous tissue in different mechanical ways— concussion, pressure and incision. But such is the marvellous functional resistance and the peculiar vitality of the living substance, that, in spite of all these gross manipulations, within the lapse of only a single day it is sometimes impossible without special and exact investigations to observe anything abnormal in animals submitted to cerebral operations. Accordingly, even by these primitive methods, some insight into the functions of the cortex can be gained. But the obvious usefulness of these crude methods should on no account satisfy the physiologist. He should strive to apply new advances of technical science and to seek ever new and more appropriate methods for the study of the exquisite mechanism of the hemispheres. Naturally the methods available for the investigation of the cortex at present, by means of extirpation of different parts, can but lead to entangled pathological states, and even the most guarded deductions with regard to the constitution of the cortex cannot therefore be ensured against a high probability of error. Indeed, since the special function of the cortex is to establish new nervous connections and so to ensure a perfect functional correlation between the organism and its environment, every disturbance of any part of it will be reflected upon the whole mechanism. Besides this direct influence of the operative procedure, which may reasonably be expected with time to diminish spontaneously, there is another very serious complication of the operation which appears later on—namely, the development of a scar at the place of cerebral lesion which now becomes a source of irritation and leads to further destruction of the surrounding parts. On the one hand the scar, owing to its mechanical irritation of the surrounding normal parts of the brain, sets up recurrent outbursts of nervous excitation; on the other hand, owing to pressure, distortion and rupture, it progressively disintegrates the hemispheres. I have been unfortunate in attempting to improve the operative technique, having made, as I now think, a big mistake. In order to obviate haemorrhage during the operation I used to remove in the dogs, long before the operation on the brain, the temporal muscles which cover the skull; this resulted in a partial atrophy of the bones of the skull, so that these could now be opened, often without the loss of a single drop of blood. But the dura mater in these cases also undergoes considerable atrophy, becomes dry and brittle, so that in most cases it is impossible to make use of it to close up the cerebral wound completely. As a result the wound was left after the operation in direct communication with the more external tissues, which led to the formation of a very hard scar ultimately penetrating and growing into the cerebral tissue. Almost every animal that was operated upon suffered from attacks of convulsions which on some occasions occurred so soon as five to six weeks after the operation. A few animals died during the first attack, but more usually the convulsions were not severe in the early stages and occurred at infrequent intervals. In the course of several months they recurred more frequently and increased in force, finally either proving fatal or else leading to a new and very profound disturbance of the cortical activity. Therapeutic measures in the form of repeated anaesthesia or extirpation of the scar were found to be unreliable, though sometimes they were unquestionably effective."

On page 353 we learn that "the dogs lived from one to six months after operation: death occurred in all cases on account of severe attacks of convulsions." On other pages we read of dogs living for three or four years with their brains mutilated. On page 284, "one and the same injurious influence causes severe and prolonged disorders in some dogs; in others the disorders are only slight and fleeting; while yet other dogs remain practically unaffected."

It must be agreed that the case against the experiments has here been stated with masterly clearness and extraordinary candor by Pavlov himself. He admits not only their crudity and their cruelty, but their uselessness. And yet the conditioned reflex which has associated science with blood sacrifice is so strong in him that his final appeal to his successors is not only to carry on his research but to persist in his futile and revolting method.

Note that Pavlov never mentions pity. He excludes it on the ground that it is psychological and therefore unknown to physiology; that it is subjective and not objective; that it is metaphysical and not material; and as he will not admit that psychology is science or that subjective or metaphysical considerations are scientific, such unconditioned reflexes (natural feelings) as pity, mercy, compassion, kindness, are out of the question and should be discarded by legislators as sentimental trash. But as the attempt to blind himself to this extent is contrary to his nature and beyond his powers as a human being, he has no sooner postulated it as a condition of his integrity as a physiologist than we find him describing certain reflexes as self-preservative, investigatory, freedom seeking ("it is clear that the freedom reflex is one of the most important," p. 12): that is, as psychological, subjective, and metaphysical. And he does not notice this. His whole attention is engaged elsewhere. He does not see that even the alimentary reflex, which is standard in all his experiments and observations, is a vital and not merely a mechanical reflex. Only once does he allow himself to be sentimental. He speaks of "the twentyfive years in which numerous fellow workers on whom I now look back with tender affection have united in this work their hearts and hands." Why should his unfortunate dogs have had no share in this surprising lapse from objective physiology into vulgar subjective emotion?

The political administrator cannot deal with Pavlov's faulty reasoning, his bogus correlations and corollaries, his counting the ratios of three or four observed facts as percentages, because there is no law penalizing these dangerous aberrations, nor against his pretension that laboratory-made science is the whole of science. It is nothing to the magistrate (officially) that the experimenter confesses that his laboratory methods are crude, illadvised, futile, and in their intention impracticable. That does not make them illegal. But their cruelty does. The existing law is clear on the point that if you keep a dog you must not illtreat it; and as Pavlov not only illtreated his dogs horribly but assumed that as a scientist he could do so with impunity, he brought the police up against the very troublesome public question of how far they should tolerate, and even enforce, practices which both common law and common sense class as criminal and detestable. For the case of the Pavlovists is by no means unique. The slaughter of sentient creatures for food, the hunting of them for sport, the poisoning of them as vermin, the trapping and killing of them for fur, oil, hides and tallow, involve much cruelty which nevertheless nobody dreams of prosecuting. War and the punishment of criminals are atrociously cruel; but they are licensed as acts of justice and patriotism. The Pavlovian vivisectionist, when reproached for cruelty, always retorts that it does not become men of pleasure who cruelly hunt foxes and stags to death without anaesthetics, merely for the fun of it, to reproach men of science for cruelty to dogs in the pursuit of knowledge.

I am no sportsman; and if I had the power I should say to the stag hunter "Your cruelty is neither necessary nor unavoidable; and you must find some other way of amusing yourself." For there are obviously other ways. The vivisector, if I said the same to him, would plead that for him there are no other ways. I should reply "Then you must find some." If he asked how, I should say "Use your brains and shake off your Druidic superstitions. There are probably fifty lawful and decent ways discoverable by human thinkers. You are not a thinker: you are only a mentally lazy fathead doing what was done last time, like all fatheads." He would no doubt retort that he could not argue with a sentimental aesthete whose mind is hopelessly unscientific; and all the vivisectionists would agree with him; but the statesman must not let public questions be settled by epithets (he sometimes does, I am sorry to say), and must be as critical of the sect of scientists as of any other denomination.

The scientist may here remind me that this summary dismissal of cruel sports does not cover the cruelty of the criminal courts, the fear of which is a necessary factor in our civilization. It is true that governments have to restrain anti-social behavior by attaching deterrent consequences to it, and that these consequences will not deter unless they are unpleasant enough to be dreaded. But the vivisector's victim has not been guilty of anti-social behavior, nor can its torture deter other animals from such behavior.

The fear of government may be the beginning of civilization just as the fear of God is the beginning of wisdom. In practice both are fear of consequences; but we shall see later on that these consequences must not involve physical mutilation and torture. For the moment, however, my subject is the Man of Science; and I have not yet dealt with the practitioners of the art of healing, who are much more numerous than the laboratory researchers, and who enjoy extraordinary privileges and widespread faith in their knowledge as men of science. Vivisectors are not popular and never will be; but "the doctor" is everywhere regarded as the friend of man and foundation of Science. As such he must have a chapter all to himself.

CHAPTER XXIV

THE MEDICAL MAN

The privileges of a doctor, whether employed by the State or in private practice, are so extraordinary and so dangerous that they raise some of the knottiest problems the statesman has to face. They become more and more troublesome as medical services pass more and more into responsible public hands and out of irresponsible professional associations (virtually trade unions) of private ones. In most callings incompetence is followed and exposed by failure. A craftsman who makes a mess of his jobs soon finds that he cannot make a living by them, and has to find some employment within his capacity or starve. But the most disastrous duffer who sets up as a healer, registered or unregistered, will find that out of his first twenty patients nineteen will get well in spite of his treatment; and the patients will give him credit for the nineteen recoveries and tell their friends what a wonderful doctor he is. As to the one patient who dies, well, we must all die some day; and nobody expects a doctor to make his patients immortal.

Why do the nineteen convalescents get well if their doctors do them more harm than good? Because the Life Force, or Life Urge, or *Élan Vital*, or Breath of Life, or whatever you choose to call it, not only keeps us alive, but maintains a repair department which gets to work the moment a living person is attacked by an infection or disabled by a lesion of any kind. It mends broken bones and diseased organs, and cleans up the foulest infections, often in spite of everything the most foolish doctors and the most unscrupulous curemongers can do to baffle it. When, as in most cases, the doctor is not foolish, and has clinical instinct enough to help the Life Force instead of hindering it, the results are still more satisfactory and convincing; but anyhow the doctors, the nurses, and the apothecaries get all the credit, and the Life Force none. The Life Force, instead of creating faith in itself, creates faith in doctors and drugs, whether they are helping or hindering.

Whoever doubts this has only to study the clinical history of doctoring. Shakespear wrote a potboiling play, still very popular, which he frankly called As You Like It lest it should be supposed that he was holding the mirror up to nature in it. He took the story from a novel written by a doctor named Thomas Lodge. In the days when I was a literary unemployable I made an index to the works of Lodge, including his medical treatises. His notions of plague sanitation were surprisingly sensible as far as they went; but his *materia medica*, the drugs he made his unfortunate patients swallow, are beyond decent description. He regarded a disease as a case of possession by devils who could be driven out by introducing the most filthily disgusting substances into the human habitation they had invaded. He believed also that if gold or precious stones were ground up and administered as powders, their preciousness would be unendurable to those devils who were evil enough to love filth and loathe lovely things. I do not know whether Shakespear read Lodge's medical books as well as his novel called Rosalynde. If he did, it accounts for his anticipation of the most modern science by making Macbeth cry "Throw physic to the dogs" on the ground that disease is mental in its origin. But the British people were not as wise as Shakespear; and they believed in Thomas Lodge's doctoring as devoutly as they now believe in Harley Street.

Turn now to the deathbed of Charles II a century later, attended by the most eminent doctors within reach. Read Macaulay's description of what they made him swallow in the belief that they were curing him instead of helping to kill him. Another century brings history almost to the bedside of a great grandfather of mine. What his doctors put into his mouth I do not know; but descriptions have come down to me of his roarings as they fired him, and of the cuppings and leeches with which they bled him. His doctors were the most eminent in the Irish capital. And nothing could shake their authority; for whatever they did to their patients Nature cured them in most cases no matter what they prescribed. And they were honest enough, as Godfearing men, to admit the existence of a *vis medicatrix naturae* of which science could give no account, and which was taken by both doctors and patients to represent God's will. In this they were far in advance of the biologists of my own time, who in their reaction against the authority of the Church and the Bible, will not admit that Nature has any hand in the matter, nor indeed that there is any such agency in existence. Until the middle of the nineteenth century they allowed the relatives of their patients to say "God's will be done"; but when Darwin abolished God (quite unintentionally) they claimed all the credit for themselves, including such divine attributes as Omniscience, clinical Omnipresence, and Infallibility.

With the growth of real knowledge, lay scepticism, and aesthetic fastidiousness, the disgusting part of Lodge's *materia medica* and the old firings and bleedings became impossible; but the new prophylactic inoculations, which infect the living blood with pathogenic germs instead of draining it off to nourish leeches, and the immobilizations which treat human beings with broken limbs as if they were tables and chairs with broken legs, and degrade the vital operations of surgery to mechanical jobs of plumbing and carpentry, are possibly more lethal than the old doctorcraft of Sydenham and Abernethy, and the surgery of Ambroise Paré. Still, when one is sick, there is nothing for it but to call in the doctor and do what he dictates; and when the *vis medicatrix* does his work for him the generations which no longer believe in God transfer all their credulity to medical practice, and are as benighted as before. The consecrated wafer from the communion table may be wholesomer than the pill from the apothecary's shop. The conversion of the believer in Bible miracles to a believer in "the miracles of science" may easily be a change for the worse.

The most staggering political instance of this occurred in the nineteenth century, when our governing classes changed their belief in the efficacy of baptism for a more fanatical belief in the efficacy of vaccination, and made it compulsory by law. The truth is that it failed to fulfil its promises, and received its death wound from two appalling epidemics of smallpox (1871 and 1881) when vaccination and revaccination were compulsory, long after its equally dreaded rivals, typhus and cholera, had been abolished by aesthetic sanitation. The home made statistics on which it was based were easily pulled to pieces by its opponents; but compulsion was not withdrawn until a monstrous persecution, ruthlessly enforced by deluded magistrates, provoked a rebellion against it to which Parliament had to yield, very reluctantly, by making it subject to conscientious objection. Yet the medical broadcasters and writers of leading articles still keep repeating like parrots that vaccination abolished smallpox, though vaccinia is now killing more children than smallpox.

As I write, the newspapers are featuring an agitation for and against a new regulation to check the alarming spread of venereal disease which always follows the troops during a war. The regulation obliges infected persons to report their condition to the authorities and present themselves for prescribed treatment. One would expect that the first inquiry by our legislators would be as to the efficacy of this treatment. But no: they concern themselves wholly with the inroad on individual liberty made by the compulsion. Now it happens that there is the gravest doubt as to whether the prescribed treatment of venereal disease is not mischievously mistaken. It began as a survival from the practice of the alchemists, who attributed magical properties to metals, especially to mercury. Mercury is a deadly bone-rotting slow poison; but it suppresses the first symptoms of syphilis (the great pox) and apparently cures it. It therefore became the established medical practice to treat syphilis by administering mercury. I can remember when it was the only treatment known. But in some cases the patient remains contagious, and the disease breaks out again years later in the aggravated forms called secondary and tertiary syphilis. Mercury became unpopular just as vaccination became unpopular; and there was general relief when it was announced that an infallible substitute had been found in the salts of iodine. But this poison, which some patients could not endure on any terms, proved also a disappointment; and at last a combination of drugs called Salvarsan was introduced as a new sovereign remedy, guaranteed infallible and harmless. It was generally believed to be a substitute for mercury. The truth was that it combined mercury with arsenic, a very potent poison. Many hundreds of experiments have been made to arrive at a combination of these poisons which will really cure the disease as well as suppress it; and the latest combination is the one to be prescribed under the new regulation. A new series of drugs is said to be producing magic cures of gonorrhea; but it is puzzling the doctors because it apparently effects a complete cure whilst leaving the patient still infectious, and the gonococcus (the characteristic microbe) still alive and active.

There is nothing new in this. One of the most mischievous diseases is malaria. Its symptoms are suppressed by quinine, which has been prescribed for it for centuries past; but it does not cure it, as the attacks recur year after year. Grave doubts have arisen as to whether the suppression of the symptoms may not be the suppression of the nature cure. When, as in the case of syphilis, the suppressive agent is a malignant poison, it is strongly held in certain quarters that the terrible secondary and tertiary recurrences of the worst symptoms are not the disease at all, but the specific effect of the poisons with which it has been treated. The Naturopaths, as they call themselves, who hold this view, allege that in their hospitals, if the general care of the patient's well-being is duly attended to, syphilis "cures itself" and neither recurs nor leaves the patient infectious. But on the other hand it is asserted with equal conviction that syphilis never cures itself, but can be treated with drugs which, though as poisonous as the disease in allopathic doses, in homeopathic dilutions provoke the Life Force to rally victoriously to the attack on it. How can a statesman allow himself to be guided by the advice of doctors when they differ so irreconcilably?

Scepticism as to the utility of drugs is shared by the surgeons. They use drugs only to produce temporary insensibility to pain (anaesthesia), an art now carried to such perfection that operations that formerly had to be performed in minutes may now last a day, and surgeons anaesthetized locally have actually operated on themselves. Operations formerly impossible or desperately difficult and dangerous are now safe and easy. This, as far as operations are necessary and beneficial, is a most blessed mercy; but it makes the vivisection of human beings so practicable that when an organ goes wrong the obvious surgical remedy is to cut it out and let some other organ take on its job. "If thy right hand offend thee cut it off" seems simple and sensible when we can get on well enough with the left. As operations are very lucrative, rich people paying from fifty guineas to several hundreds for them, surgeons are far more certain that there is nothing like the knife than cobblers that there is nothing like leather. I never fully realized the extent to which this has gone until a young surgeon in the Commonwealth Overseas assured me that a few years hence all babies will be delivered by the Caesarian operation instead of by midwifery. It is much quicker and easier— for the surgeon. It is argued that it is also much less injurious to the child, especially the child lugged from the womb by a forceps, and less painful to the anaesthetized mother. And nobody ever mentions the scandalous fact that surgeons receive no specific manual training in the use of their instruments, and have to pick up their craft as best they can in the dissecting room. Within my memory obstetric expertness was picked up by medical students in visits to the child-beds of the poor, with the startling result that though infant mortality is scandalously greater among the poor than among the rich, maternal mortality is sometimes greater among the doctored rich than among the ignorantly midwifed poor. Queen Anne gave birth to seventeen children not one of whom grew up. They would have been safer in the mud-floored cabins of Connemara.

What is the statesman to do in the face of all this evidence? The physicians and surgeons badger him for compulsory powers to inoculate, to drug, and to vivisect, threatening him that if these powers are withheld the human race will be exterminated by microbes and appendicitis. The Peculiar People exhort him to trust in prayer as prescribed in the Bible, and the Naturopaths in the *vis medicatrix naturae*. Between these extremes there are innumerable treatments and hygienic systems clamoring for recognition, for enforcement, and for prohibition of the alternatives.

It is easy to say that the statesman who does not know what to do should do nothing; but he has not really that despairing alternative. The cry that something must be done is too strong for him. He yields haphazard and piecemeal to the professions, the agitations, the sects, just as he yields to big business wherever the pressure is strongest or the cry loudest, and tries this or that recommended measure, positive or prohibitive, and lets it do its best or its worst until it is tested by trial and error. When he seeks to inform himself he is confronted with a riot of violently conflicting opinions and faiths which leave him as ignorant as before and much more confused. A strong mind and commonsense must make the best of a very responsible job.

Certain conclusions seem fairly obvious. There is nothing more insane in our social system than allowing a doctor's income to depend on the illnesses of his patients. There is no need for this. In Sweden the family doctor is paid a fixed fee for the year, whether the family is sick or sound. It is the doctor's interest to keep all its members sound. On a cold day a Swede without an overcoat, if he meets his doctor in the street, is urged to go home and put it on. Happy the doctor whose patients are never ill! No doubt it is in his interest to kill excessively troublesome patients and chronic invalids instead of regarding them as godsends; but though excessively troublesome people and incurables are politically better dead, it is not etiquet for doctors to kill them except in the very painful cases in which morphia has to be used recklessly. Swedes who reside in London find no difficulty in engaging a private doctor on these terms, which are already accepted by our club and panel doctors. The arrangement is not feasible privately in cases involving surgical operations or consultations with specialists; but these are called for not by the patient but by the family doctor, who does not profit pecuniarily by such interferences unless he receives a secret commission from the surgeon or specialist, a practice which has sprung up in the United States and provoked legislation against it. As it is not legal here under the general law against secret commissions, it need not worry us; but it does not remedy the evil of the surgeon's pecuniary interest in operations and the specialist's in illnesses.

It is idle to declare that we have, in the honor of a noble profession, a psychological guarantee against medical corruption. For here again we come up against the fact that a thousand persons may be deeply corrupted by a common interest to which every one of the thousand is personally superior. Doctors do so much charitable work in pure impulsive generosity that it seems cynical to subject them to a criminal code. But the statesman soon finds that generous impulses and professional codes of honor, priceless as they are, are negligible as against the continuous and inexorable pressure of the need for money. The occasional generous impulses act fitfully in all directions: the pecuniary pressure never varies and never lifts. If crime brings promotion to the police officer; if litigation is profitable to the solicitor; if war is the soldier's only avenue to distinction, the surest enhancer of the price of capital, the bringer of lucrative business to many trades, and constant employment at increased wages to the proletariat, then, as surely as night follows day, crimes will be "framed-up"; blackmailing lawsuits will be provoked by Dodsons and Foggs; nations will have to arm to the teeth for fear of one-another's warmongers; and vocational codes of honor will be enforced by professional associations as codes of etiquet for the protection of lucrative abuses.

Here again Nature and sanitation step in and do beneficent work of which the doctor gets the credit even when his measures have been all mischievous. Nature punishes dirt, ugliness, war, malnutrition, underfeeding, overfeeding and the like crude offences against her, not by instant vengeance on the individual offender but by periodical epidemics which infect and strike down all whose blood is not potent enough to resist the contagion of a specially fierce onslaught. The Black Death suggested an attempt to exterminate the human race in a fit of disgust at the stinking filth of the cities. The general name for such attacks was The Plague. We read descriptions of them by Thucydides and Defoe, and sometimes think of them as incidents of the past; but the description of nineteenth century cholera by Dr Axel Munthe is equally terrible; and the Spanish influenza which outdid the battles of the Four Years War in slaughter is within the living memory of most of us. My father escaped alive from an attack of cholera in the last great epidemic; and I escaped similarly when I was infected in the second of the two great smallpox epidemics which reduced vaccination to absurdity in 1871 and 1881. We are still subject to "plague, pestilence, and famine: battle, murder, and sudden death"; and our prayers to be delivered from them supernaturally are still ruthlessly ungranted.

But there is always a substantial majority of people whose blood is healthy and potent enough to defy infection and produce armies of phagocytes, antibodies, antigens and what not to defeat the contagious hosts of pathogenic microbes which are the weapons of the disease in its most ferocious epidemic concentrations. When the rest are all dead or recovered, the epidemic, instead of redoubling its vehemence and carrying its war of extermination to the bitter end, slackens and ceases as miraculously as it began, apparently satisfied for the moment with the friendly warning it has given to clean up our cities and reform our habits, feed our lambs, and flee from the wrath to come.

Nobody blames the doctor for the plague, which is regarded as an act of God; but as it slackens, and cases are less and less fatal, he gets the credit of all the recoveries. If he has inoculated his patients against the disease, those who escape infection attribute their immunity to the inoculation and not to the resistance of their blood to it; and as a huge majority of the deaths will be those of the poor, the illiterate, the ignorant, and the careless who have not been inoculated, imposing statistics will be available suggesting that the inoculation (or any other sort of prophylactic in use) secures immunity. The doctor, formerly called in only when the patient was actually ill, is now called in to administer prophylactics to children and adults who are in sound health. One does not grudge him his fee; for medical incomes in the lump are too precarious; but his wishful belief in lucrative and easy prophylactics throws all his weight on their side as against sanitation, which has rid us of typhus, cholera, and the Black Death whilst inoculations have left smallpox and diphtheria still dreaded.

Of all legalized tyrannies none is more unbearable than those which lay violent hands on us and our children and inject poisons into our veins or thrust them down our throats. When compulsory vaccination was doing its worst, and children died, horribly disfigured, from vaccinia, the doctors denied that vaccination had anything to do with it, and diagnosed the case as syphilis contracted and communicated to the children by the parents. The poor were defenceless against such accusations; but at last a couple managed to sue their accusers for slander. The defence was that vaccinia is indistinguishable from syphilis at its worst, and that the mistake was therefore excusable and inevitable. As vaccinia was killing one baby every week (it now kills more babies than smallpox) the effect of this medical testimony on those who knew of it may be imagined. But to make it and similar cases known, the anti-vacs had to publish a special newspaper and get what circulation they could for it. The newspaper press in general would do nothing in the matter but repeat the falsehood that vaccination has abolished smallpox, and suppress every scrap of evidence to the contrary. Now that vaccination has been succeeded by inoculation against diphtheria, we have the same credulity, the same suppression of the fact that it has been followed by spells of infantile paralysis more or less prolonged, and the same parade of amateur statistics on a background of threats that every child who is not inoculated will die of diphtheria after infecting all the other children until the human race is wiped out of existence by a bacillus which has been found in the throats of people who are quite well. Nobody mentions that the children of parents conscientious and careful enough to have their children "immunized" will come out of any statistical test better than the children of the comparatively careless. Poverty, too, produces startling vital statistics which can be turned to account by the exploiters of any nostrum. If the jewellers had thought of claiming that the possession of a gold watch and chain is an infalible prophylactic against smallpox, their statistics would have been quite as convincing as those of the vaccinists.

The statesman who takes the trouble to spend half a day in learning the history of these official quackeries will probably resolve at first that nothing will induce him to impose any specific treatments by law. He may even be tempted to make their practice criminal. This was actually done in the case of direct inoculation of smallpox, which was in fashion before cowpox inoculation was substituted. A clever and imaginative doctor named Jenner, professionally trained by the famous John Hunter, believed in smallpox inoculation so enthusiastically that he wrote a pamphlet in which he declared that the pockmarked faces which formerly met him everywhere had now almost disappeared through it. One of my grandfathers boasted that though both inoculated and vaccinated, he caught smallpox after all. One day Jenner was consulted by a dairymaid. In the course of their conversation she said "I cannot catch smallpox because I have had cowpox." Jenner, catching at the new idea, saw in his imagination the whole world redeemed from smallpox by harmless inoculation with cowpox. His vision spread like wildfire. Parliament voted £30,000 to Jenner, and nothing to the dairymaid.

When the vaccinated child of a noble family presently died of smallpox Jenner changed his mind about cowpox and substituted horse grease; but the public and Parliament preferred their foster-mother the cow to the horse, and went ahead with cowpox, making inoculation of smallpox a criminal offence. As bacterial examination was then unknown, and, when it became known, no characteristic bacillus either of smallpox or cowpox could be found, Parliament could only prescribe vaccination without defining it. Any sort of ulcer that could be induced in a calf was officially cowpox, and was then propagated from arm to arm of the babies. Later on the bacteriologists declared that inoculation with the disease itself is the correct method; and all the modern anti-toxins are, like homeopathic remedies, "a hair of the dog that bit you." But the law still sticks to the dairymaid and to "calf lymph", which may be produced by smallpox inoculation, in spite of its being felonious. As to Jenner's last favorite the horse, it has come to its own as the vehicle for inoculation against diphtheria.

But no extremity of superstition, persecution, biological sciolism, or venal professionalism will stop the march of science. However

complete the conspiracy of silence about the blunders and failures
of medicine may be, the really scientific doctors and biologists know
about them and cannot rest until they find out what is wrong
with them. When Koch's tuberculin, which was to have abolished
tuberculosis, occasionally produced ulcers which rotted off the
limbs of the patient, Almroth Wright, alarmed in his practice as a
doctor, and having a strong dash of the artist philosopher in him, set
to work to find out why this happened, and soon discovered the
curious rhythm of phases in which the resistance of the blood to
infection alternates between victory and disastrous defeat. When
blood transfusion came into fashion we were not told that though
it sometimes cured it also sometimes killed, nobody knew why. Karl
Landsteiner, who was in the guilty secret, tackled the problem, and
found that there are at least four different sorts of human blood. If
the wrong sort is transfused the patient dies: if the right sort, the
patient is saved. And so, out of the continual process of trial and
error, the triers who have good reasoning faculty as well as mere
curiosity eliminate the errors bit by bit. The statesman must keep
close up to date all the time or his head will be dangerously cob-
webbed with the exploded errors. This is largely the case of our
Cabinets at present. They regard Jenner and Lister as the latest
lights of science, and know nothing of Almroth Wright or of Joseph
Needham (whose famous mother, by the way, like mine, soaked
him in music instead of in neo-Darwinism). To pass from Lister
and Weismann to Scott Haldane and his better known post-Marxian
son J. B. S. Haldane is like passing from the dead and hopeless past
to the living and pregnant future.

Faced with such a mess of real tentative Science with ancient magic
and half-baked modern science changing its conclusions from year to
year, voiced by naturalists who know the physical facts but reason
foolishly about them, and philosophers who reason skilfully but
do not know the facts at first hand, we can hardly be too critical
of hygienic legislation. Yet legislate we must: *laisser-faire* is quite
out of the question. Free trade in gin and cocaine would wipe out
a proletariat so miserable that it cannot face life without dopes.
Sanitation must be enforced or we shall have plague, cholera, and
smallpox back again. Slums must be demolished because they are
ugly and dirty, and replaced by noble thoroughfares and garden
cities on the ground that hygiene, like culture, is essentially aesthetic.
Lousy people and their belongings must be deloused, forcibly if
necessary, when they are rehoused. Buildings handsome but mis-

placed must be moved, as they were first in America, and are now in Russia pushed about without even disturbing the inhabitants.

In all such sanitary and aesthetic reform the statesman is on safe lines. There is no danger of his being confronted by an infuriated mother crying, "You have killed my first child by your inoculation; and you will get at my second only over my dead body." If city householders will not connect their sinks and closets with the main drain the local health authority will still break into their privacy and make the connection whether they like it or not at their expense, thereby making short work of the tradition that an Englishman's house is his castle; but no conscientious objection need be feared, because our aesthetic instinct is so strong that though public opinion tolerates the conscientious objector to military service because he may be a saint, it will not tolerate a dirty fellow on any excuse.

Now as the municipal statesman sends his sanitary Gestapo into an unhealthy private house and prosecutes the tenant for not calling in a plumber to attend to the drainage, he prosecutes a parent for not calling in a doctor to attend to his sick child or for not calling in a baker to feed his hungry child. People are in fact prosecuted and imprisoned for these omissions without benefit of conscientious objection or liberty of the subject. And the justification of these compulsions and penalties is that the statesman knows the truth about nutrition and hygiene. As a matter of fact he knows little about either, because little is as yet known. So when the doctors announce that they have extirpated or greatly reduced the mortality from a disease, and the statistics of the Registrar-General shew that it is as mortal as ever, or that the reduction is no greater or perhaps less than before, the statesman must receive the medical statistics with the thumb to the nose. If a startling reduction in the mortality and prevalence of a disease, loudly claimed as the effect of this or that drug or inoculation, is found to follow notification of the cases and isolation of the patient (this occurred with smallpox in 1885 after the failure of vaccination) then the statesman may enforce notification and isolation. But disinterested vital statistics and their skilled and equally disinterested interpretation must always be his test. He must steel himself against the pretensions of the doctors to have any monopoly of medical science or any greater wisdom in acting on it than the rest of us. He must not value barristers by the number of their clients who have been hanged, doctors by the number of titled and royal persons who have died in their hands, or biologists by the number of dogs they have vivisected. Above all, he must stand out against the claim of medical research to be free from the ordinary moral obligations of humanity, and to exercise powers and privileges now denied to priests and monarchs. He must say to the laboratory researchers who justify cruelty by declaring that they hope to learn something from it "There are some things you must not know: for instance, if you turn boiling water into your wife's bath to ascertain what temperature her body can bear before it disintegrates you will presently add to that knowledge the knowledge of what it feels like to be hanged." He must use legislation to force scientific research into humane methods just as the legislators who imposed the Factory Acts forced industrial enterprise (or shall I call it the art of money-making?) into methods that are at least comparatively humane, and drove the sweaters who were incapable of prospering by such methods out of business. Pavlov might have done some really useful scientific work if he had been up against a State stern enough to assure him that what he did to the least of his dogs would be done even to himself. As to the present privilege of the doctor to poison and the surgeon to mutilate, and, when the results are fatal, to certify that the patient died a natural death, it may be difficult to abolish it; for it is hardly possible to hold a coroner's inquest on every death, and medical practice at the risk of being hanged might prove too unattractive to secure enough recruits; but we might at least make our surgeons pecuniarily independent of unnecessary operations and our physicians of imaginary ailments, substituting strong positive inducements to put the improvement of our vital statistics before every other professional consideration. The doctor's honor and conscience, and the oath of Hippocrates, would then raise his calling to the highest dignity, and be a sufficient guarantee of its good faith and public spirit.

It is conceivable that modern States dominated by Mr and Mrs Anybody elected by Mr and Mrs Everybody may yet play such tricks with compulsory sterilization of people they dislike or dread and compulsory rejuvenation by inoculation from monkeys of people whom they regard as desirable parents, that their subjects will be more uncomfortable than the Spaniards or even the Jews were under Torquemada. He was a mischievously ignorant man; but a little half knowledge might have made him worse instead of better: perhaps almost as mischievous as the General Medical Council is and will remain as long as it is madly entrusted with functions and powers which should be exercised only by the Ministry of Health, a lay authority concerned solely with hygiene, and accessible to professional doctors as experts and assessors only.

But always we need more knowledge; and this means controversial instead of dogmatic education. The schools teach only one side of their subjects; and until their graduates know both sides they had better know nothing, and should be ruthlessly excluded from public authorities. My own education has been gained from discussions: that is why I am so much less cocksure than the dogmatists, and why I find it impossible to take their pretences seriously, though I lend a comparatively hopeful ear to amateurs, artists and athletes who have discovered curative techniques (yogas) by experiments on themselves, naturopaths, and generally all therapists who are boycotted and despised by the registered professionals.

CHAPTER XXV

ARCHITECTURE A WORLD POWER

ARCHITECTURE is a tremendous weapon in the aesthetic armory of the statesman. Six of the Seven Wonders of the World are architectural, and the other a colossal statue. A Wonder is not an invention or discovery, however useful. The wheel, the arch, the safety pin, the sewing machine, the explosion engine, the telephone, the wireless set, the cinema, the televisor, are inventions of stupendous scope; but they are not wonders. A wonder is some work of Man that takes your breath away when you see it. I had my breath taken away literally and physically when I first stepped into the giant choir which is all that remains of the cathedral at Beauvais. Twenty years later, knowing what I had to expect, I stepped into it again; and again it took my breath away. It is decidedly one of the wonders of the world. I was much older when I saw the ruins of the temple of Jupiter at Baalbek; but what staggered me here was not only the apparently superhuman feat of building it, but the fact that the Arabs had thought it worth while to attempt the even more impossible feat of demolishing it, which they had to leave half unachieved. They could have built a city with the labor it cost them; and yet they were unable to finish the job. Nothing could have nerved them to such an effort but the knowledge that they could not kill Jupiter and put Allah in his place so long as that mighty temple stood there to impose its majesty on the whole civilized world. In England our Puritans were similarly nerved to smash every statue they could reach in our cathedrals. The glories of aesthetic inspiration provoke a fury of iconoclasm when the religions and institutions they celebrate come to be hated instead of worshipped. Moses and Mahomet forbad the making of graven images or likenesses of anything in the earth beneath or the waters under the earth. But the aesthetic impulse defied Moses and Mahomet. The Christians, whilst accepting the other commandments as words of God, silently and spontaneously ignored this one. The Moslems whitewashed the mosaics in St Sophia when they captured Constantinople; but they tried to outdo the Christians by building a mosque bigger than St Sophia. When they found that size is not the secret of great building, Sultan Zulieman made them build another mosque, which succeeded where the big one failed, and was and is a gem of its various arts without violating the second commandment.

What has all this ancient history to do with the statesmanship of tomorrow? I find the case very freshly put in a letter to the later Ensor Walters, written by me at sea in the Gulf of Siam on the 4th February 1933. He had been my valued colleague in the old St Pancras vestry, and had attained deserved eminence as a Methodist minister. Here it is.

Dear Ensor Walters,

I am writing this in the Gulf of Siam after inspecting a remarkable collection of religions in Egypt and India. The apparent multiplication of Gods is bewildering at the first glance; but you soon discover that they are all the same God in different aspects and functions and even sexes. There is always one uttermost God who defies personification. This makes Hinduism the most tolerant religion in the world, because its one transcendent God includes all possible Gods, from elephant Gods, bird Gods, and snake Gods, right up to the great Trinity of Brahma, Vishnu and Shiva, which makes room for the Virgin Mary and modern Feminism by making Shiva a woman as well as a man. Christ is there as Krishna, who might also be Dionysos. In fact Hinduism is so elastic and so subtle that the profoundest Methodist and the crudest idolater are equally at home in it.

Islam is very different, being ferociously intolerant. What I may call Manifold Monotheism becomes in the minds of very simple folk an absurdly polytheistic idolatry, just as European peasants not only worship Saints and the Virgin as gods but will fight fanatically for the ugly little black doll who is the Virgin of their own church against the black doll of the next village. When the Arabs carried this idolatry to such extremes that they did without black dolls and worshipped any stone that looked funny, Mahomet rose up at the risk of his life and insulted the stones shockingly, declaring that there is only one God, Allah, the glorious, the great, and pinning himself to the second Commandment that no man shall dare make a graven image of Allah or any of his creatures.

And there was to be no nonsense about toleration. You accepted Allah or you had your throat cut by somebody who did accept him, and who went to Paradise for having sent you to Hell. Mahomet was a great Protestant religious force like George Fox or Wesley. The main difference between the opposition of Islam to Hinduism and the opposition between Protestant and Catholic is that the Catholic persecutes as fiercely as the Protestant when he has the power; but Hinduism cannot persecute, because all the Gods—and what goes deeper, the no Gods—are to be found in its Temples. There is actually a great Hindu sect, the Jains, with Temples of amazing magnificence, which excludes God, not on materialist atheist considerations, but as unspeakable and unknowable, transcending all human comprehension.

So far, it is all simple enough for anyone with religious sense. When you are face to face with the Temples and the worshippers, you find that before Mahomet and the founder of the Jains were cold in their graves, the institutions and rituals they founded began to revert to the more popular types, and all the Gods and no Gods became hopelessly mixed up, exactly as the Apostles backslid when Jesus was killed. In the Jain Temple you find shrines and images, and baths where you must wash all over before you may enter the shrine and adore the image. If you can find an intelligent Priest who is a real Jain theologian, you say "How's this? A God in the Jain Temple!" He explains to you that the image is not a God but a portrait of one of their great Saints; and that the man just out of the bath prostrating himself is not worshipping but expressing his respect for the memory of the late eminent Ensoramji Waltershagpat. But it is like Dean Inge trying to explain away St Paul. It is perfectly plain that the image is a super refined Buddha, and that Jainism and Buddhism have got hopelessly mixed. Jain Buddha is attended by sculptured elephants. You ask what they mean, and are told that they are purely ornamental works of art. Then your eye lights on an image of Ganesh, the Hindu God with the head and trunk of an elephant. On the point of exclaiming *"Que diable fait-il dans cette galère?"*, you remember that you must not put your courteous host in a corner, and politely hold your tongue, but think furiously.

It is always the same. Outside the few who have religious sense, and who are equally at home and equally estranged in all the temples of all the faiths, there is the multitudinous average man. What he demands from the founder of his faith is, first, miracles. If, like Mahomet, you rebuke him and tell him that you are not a conjurer, or, like Jesus, turn on him angrily with "An evil and adulterous generation seeketh after a sign", you will waste breath; for when you have become famous through your preaching, and cured the sick by healing their minds and thereby curing their bodies, your average man will invent miracles enough for you to eclipse Saint Anthony of Padua. Then he will make you his God, which means that he will beg from you, and, when he is properly frightened of you, make sacrifices to propitiate you, even to the extent of killing his daughter (Iphigenia or Miss Jephtha) to please you; but he will soon begin to cheat by substituting a ram for his son (Isaac) and making the sacrifice purely symbolic and imaginary. And so finally it is not through the authentic principles of the founder of his faith that you must get at him if you are to make a decent human being of him. You must govern fools according to their folly. In Jamaica and Rhodesia all the good negroes and their great ministers and leaders are Fundamentalists. If you rubbed Bradlaugh and Ingersoll into them, you would probably not only shock but demoralize them. You find the same thing in our mining villages.

Methodism has made men religious without splendid temples: it houses God very shabbily. Prelacy houses him magnificently: so much so, that the poor cannot feel really at home there. But the value of big building for getting hold of the popular imagination was powerfully impressed on me at Baalbek, Delphi, Eleusis, and Karnak, where Jupiter, Apollo, and the Egyptian Gods had colossal Temples. People stare at these ruins and wonder at the prodigious feats their builders achieved, handling blocks of stone weighing several tons as if they were bricks, and raising them hundreds of feet to the tops of giant pillars as if they had got far beyond our baby steam cranes. But the really impressive thing about them is not the enormous labor and expense lavished on building them, but the still more amazing labor, care, and cost spent on smashing them. You have in that a convincing testimony to the influence they exercised over the imagination of the people. The Arabs, the Protestants of the East, could have built a hundred splendid mosques with the labor that made good their resolution that of the tremendous temple of Jupiter at Baalbek not one stone should be left standing on another, and to leave Apollo homeless at Delphi and Eleusis. What our Puritans did to our Cathedrals was mere schoolboy mischief in comparison. The rage that accumulates in religious hearts when these wonders of architecture become dens of thieves, and substitute sensuous ritual for the search for God, must have risen to earthquake force when it scattered Delphi.

CHAPTER XXVI

THE THEOCRATIC MAN

IT is clear from my letter to Ensor Walters that a freethinking Western can feel as much at home in the temples of the farthest east as in a British or foreign cathedral. The dozens of personifications by which the manifold nature of the Life Force is represented trouble him no more than the three persons of the Trinity, plus the Virgin Mother goddess, to say nothing of a host of minor gods called saints. And how could these have stood against the polytheism of ancient Greece when Zeus and Apollo, Juno and Aphrodite and Athene confronted the world in forms of more than human beauty wrought by such sculptors as Phidias and Praxiteles to impress our imaginations? Generations of painters, from Giotto and Cimabue (whose colossal Virgin is frankly a goddess) to Raphael and Michael Angelo, had to make this huge theocracy apprehensible, visible, susceptible to prayers, candles, and incense, for the multitude of worshippers, with such success that generations of Popes, Emperors, and Prime Ministers have had to connive at all the miracles of Lourdes. "Zum Canossa gehen wir nicht," said Bismarck; but he had to go all the same. So had Mussolini.

The sectarian minister for whom foreign gods are idols, and their worshippers heathen idolaters to be converted to his sect, is a dangerous mischief maker on whom the warning of Jesus against destroying the wheat in the effort to uproot the tares is lost. The statesman must, when he meddles with religion, do so as a complete freethinker. All the aesthetic dramatizations of divinity must be impartially dealt with by him.

But must he therefore tolerate them all? Decidedly not. He has to deal with the education of children, and soon finds that the current personifications of God include abominable idols as well as respectable divinities. The Bible tells us of many gods: Jehovah, Dagon, Moloch, Baal, Chemosh, the noble God of Micah the Morasthite, and the Father, Son, and Holy Ghost of the Christians. Jesus, Mary, and Mahomet have been personally deified. The Jews selected Jehovah as their god: we, with our characteristic thoughtless inconsistency, have retained Jehovah whilst adopting the Christian trinity, thus establishing a convenient Spenlow & Jorkins combination under which we can forgive our enemies or slaughter them just as it suits us. So though no statesman dare tolerate an elementary school which inculcated the worship of Moloch, the worship of Jehovah is not only tolerated but taken tacitly as a matter of course even when the school is "secular" and "undenominational." Now in the light of modern thought and knowledge any comparison between the Jehovah of the Book of Numbers and Dagon or Baal is to the disadvantage of Jehovah. In the Book of Micah he appears completely reformed as a god not only of Israel but of the whole human race, abhorring the blood sacrifices of the Numbers deity and requiring nothing from us but mercy, justice, and the humility that befits our abysmal ignorance. But the old Jehovah with his blood sacrifices breaks out again in the New Testament, where, by his ordinance, the Son is executed horribly to atone for the Father's misdeed in not creating mankind better. By this confusion belief in God has been brought into such shameful discredit that professional science has become rabidly anti-clerical, and will swallow the follies of Weismann and Pavlov rather than have any god back at any price. Jehovah is thus the worst enemy of deism today. The fact that his worship has been legally abolished in Russia and Germany is as creditable to these countries as the omission to abolish it is discreditable to ours.

But what is to take its place? Simple abolition leaves us between pragmatic atheism, which makes no provision for evolution, and sentimental Christianity, which makes its prophet a universal scapegoat, and is not practicable by statesmen; for, however far they may go in its direction by not punishing evildoers, they must very vigorously resist, suppress, and occasionally exterminate them. The statesman has really no choice: he must be pragmatic.

But Pragmatism means making the best of people as they are; and what they are depends on what they believe. The obsolescence of unchanging creeds leaves them incredulous, agnostic, and irreverently pragmatic. Their children have neither the old Mosaic discipline nor any new faith. Moral anarchy becomes rampant. Unscrupulous individualism, unscrupulous nationalism and rationalism, unscrupulous imperialism, unscrupulous corybantics and anacreontics have culminated in monstrous world wars and smash-and-grab revolutions to settle questions that could and should be settled reasonably. Romantic nature, abhorring the vacuum, fills it in Germany with Wotan and the fighting Siegfried instead of the compassionate Parsifal. The Russians tried to fill the void with Marxism, but found that it needed a nation of philosophers, and are now singing Te Deum in the cathedral they had desecrated and refurnished as an anti-religious museum. At this moment the god of all the continents is Mars; and plunder and tribute are called sanctions. The need for a supernational court of justice is desperately pressing; but nothing comes of it because, having become incapable of conceiving a supreme court declaring the justice of God and trusting to its moral force, we all object that it would be useless without a military police and air force capable of killing all belligerents, and bombing out of existence any city in which its authority was defied.

We forget (if we ever learned) that it was just such a militarization of the Christian Church that broke its spiritual power and made it a mere Papal State. The suggestion in my play entitled Geneva of a court of pure justice, without police, prisons, punishments, or any powers except the power of justice over the human mind, is taken no more seriously than Shakespear's midsummer night's dream.

Clearly the statesman of the future must find some credible substitute for Jehovah lest civilization should perish in lazy negation. He may call Jehovah's supplanter by a dozen different names; but he must get rid of certain Jehovian attributions, especially the attribution of infallibility; for the Creator, the Holy Ghost, the Word (properly the Thought), the Cosmic Energy, the *Élan Vital*, the Divine Spark, the Life Force, the Power that makes for Righteousness (call it what you will) is not infallible: it proceeds by trial and error; and its errors are called the Problem of Evil. It is not omnipotent: indeed it has no direct power at all, and can act only through its creations. Its creations are not omniscient: they proceed by guesses; and evil arises when they guess wrong with the best intentions. It has neither body nor parts; but it has, or rather is, what we call a soul or passion, for ever urging us to obtain greater power over our circumstances and greater knowledge and understanding of what we are doing. It is also an appetite for truth (correspondence of beliefs to facts), for beauty, for justice, for mercy, lumped by the Churches as saving virtues, against which, however, we must set such appetites as pride, covetousness, lust, anger, gluttony, envy, and sloth, lumped as the seven deadly sins, but evidently only the excesses and abuses of the self-preservative instincts. Besides, the list is incomplete: for instance, it omits sadistic cruelty, which ranges from physical torture and mayhem (maiming) to sarcasm and teasing, and is specially abhorrent as the most effective weapon of the sinful many against the virtuous few.

Another attribution to be got rid of is that of Omnipotence, or unlimited physical power to interfere directly in human affairs and secure victory for righteousness in spite of human wickedness. Suits at law used to be referred to the justice of God by setting the plaintiff and defendant to fight it out with sword and buckler. Those who could not fight could hire champions to fight for them. They now hire barristers, who argue, cross-examine, and orate instead of fighting. But still victory goes to the cleverest advocate and consequently to the longest purse, as it does in war to the biggest battalions and the ablest generals without regard to the justice of God except for such trouble as the Holy Ghost can make in the consciences of the parties. In my childhood I heard a pious Irish mother say to her adult son, when he warned her that she was in danger of losing her train, that she would catch it "with the help of God." His reply was "Yes; but you will have to look pretty sharp yourself." That is what the statesman must always say to the theocrat.

Now what all this means is that the statesman has to do the work of God with nothing to help him except his knowledge, his ability, and his conscience. And as consciences vary in scope, health, and quality, and are mischievous without knowledge, only persons who have passed the most searching tests we can devise should be eligible for democratic election as supreme rulers. Our plan of votes for everybody, in which the farsighted candidate is defeated by the nearsighted one, the effective doer by the eloquent talker, the reluctant volunteer for a heavy duty by the ambitious climber who seeks authority as a notable addition to self-importance, is an impracticable figment. Our wisest have no chance under it, being misunderstood, disliked, and feared rather than admired and obeyed. Demagogues whose political talent is irresistible learn the arts by which Demos can be gulled, and maintain themselves in power by a combination of the same arts with the strong hand and the Awe struck by their conspicuous superiority to their rivals. A supreme Cabinet of the wisest is not possible in such circumstances; and so we shall be driven to the panel system to select fit operators for the brain work of democracy. If that fails, we shall become part of the Problem of Evil, and be exterminated like the mammoths and mastodons by some new species of greater political capacity. For we have no reason to suppose that we are the Creator's last word.

CHAPTER XXVII

THE COLLECTIVE BIOLOGIST

BIOLOGY is clearly the first concern of the State. Indeed it is the first concern of every living thing; but I am not dealing here with that part of it which can be left to individuals to put into practice. Individuals may be able to keep themselves alive for a while; but keeping a million people alive in a limited space, and for how long, requires public measures that are beyond the power of any individual; and if these measures are to be more than empirical there must be some general theory, some frame of reference, some brain-work, at the back of them. Our leading legislators, doctors, and dramatic poets are all biologists, specializing in what Pope called the proper study of mankind: namely, Man. They must be assisted by professional statisticians (biological mathematicians); for statistics are indispensable, and home-made ones no use.

Now it may be doubted whether biology can rank as a science at all; for its very first task is to define the difference between a living body and a dead one; and in this our physiologists and biochemists have failed so completely that some have been driven to declare that scientifically there is no difference. And indeed no dissection, no analysis, has discovered anything in a living man that is not present also in his corpse. Nevertheless the two behave so differently that those who deny any difference must be dismissed as lunatics.

The earliest really scientific biologists, as far as we know, were the writers whose scriptures are jumbled together in the Book of Genesis. They were not analytical chemists, and knew nothing of gases, salts, cells, hormones, chromosomes, vitamins, gens and antigens, genes and gametes, chloro- and other phyls, soma and phyla, with the names of which our scientists bang us into dumbness. But they knew them in the lump as matter, or, as they called it, "the dust of the ground." Their sculptors could make a shaped image out of it, but not a living body. They knew that when it shaped itself into a moving feeling thinking body something strange must have happened to it. Not knowing what it was, not being such fools as to deny its occurrence on that account, and believing as they did that creation, being apparently miraculous, must be the work of a god, they described the process in the words "the Lord God formed man of the dust of the ground, and breathed into his nostrils the breath of life; and man became a living soul." They observed also that after a time the body ceased to live and decomposed into its original materials. And from this they inferred that man had displeased God and provoked Him to declare and decree that "Dust thou art; and unto dust shalt thou return."

This was not a bad beginning of biology as a science. Its authors were enormously more scientific than their modern successors; for though they dramatized the facts in terms of their deistic cosmogony they were on the basic facts all the time, and not stupefying themselves by trying to measure the universe by making a dog's mouth water or cutting off the tails of generations of white mice. And we are still facing these basic facts which, though we have stripped them of their fabulous dramatization, are now all the more miraculous. Rousseau exhorted us to get rid of our miracles; but the more old fairy tales we get rid of the more miraculous creation becomes.

What are the miraculous facts from which a statesman must start? Some force in nature which he must accept dogmatically because he sees a good deal of what it does but nothing of what it is or why it does it, takes a miscellaneous heap of stuff which may as well be called the dust of the ground as anything else. It shapes it into various forms, all of them fantastic and some of them ridiculously grotesque. It sets these shapes working and willing for a while, some of them for moments, some for years, some for centuries. Some of them grow without travelling; others stop growing and travel! They use up their substance and gather more to replace it, building it into themselves until they are tired of living, whereupon the force deserts them and they return to dust. The length of their lives varies according to their circumstances and education, both of which are controllable by the State. In ill governed countries enormous numbers of children die in their first year. I am still alive to some extent in my eightyeighth.

The business is not so simple as this summary makes it. The miraculous creative force does not create one sort of creature and stick to it. The creatures are so various that they suggest instruments rather than final achievements. Creation is like a carpenter's shop with its array of hammers, saws, chisels, planes, screws, nails, vices, lathes, and the rest, all designed to increase the power of the carpenter over his materials, and all useless unless the carpenter understands their uses and can handle them without cutting his fingers. But the comparison is a misfit at many points. In the workshop of the universe the carpenter is omnipresent, but invisible, inaudible, intangible, inscrutable. He has no fingers to cut, no hands, no muscles, no brain. In the words of the Church of England he is "without body, parts, or passions." He has therefore to make tools that will act without handling of their own accord, endowing them with consciousness, purpose, will, pride in efficiency, and shame when they serve the carpenter badly.

And as the carpenter is always seeking better tools and trying new ones experimentally his tools must have an appetite for improvement, which I call the evolutionary appetite. Also as the tools wear out and must renew themselves they must have a reproductive appetite. As they cannot satisfy these appetites without knowledge they must have an appetite for knowledge which we call shortly curiosity. And as they have to take care of themselves meanwhile they must have an appetite for self-preservation. These appetites being simply primitive facts, so far utterly unaccountable, unreasonable, miraculous, and mystical, the statesman has to make the best of them, and find a name for them. They are called instincts.

The bothersome part of the business is that the instincts are not always agreed: they may conflict very strenuously. Some of them produce courage, others cowardice. Curiosity has driven highly intelligent people to explore the poles at risks and hardships which Mr Cherry-Garrard has described very vividly in his book entitled The Worst Journey in the World. Self-preservation induced most of us to stay at home and let the poles go hang. Dr Edward Wilson, who shared the worst journey with Cherry-Garrard, cared nothing about the poles, but wanted to dissect the eggs of the Emperor penguin, and paid the penalty of his curiosity by being frozen to death. One asks, like Hamlet, what were the penguins to him or he to the penguins that he should die for them? Columbus, to induce men to sail with him to Asia by the west route over the sea, had to employ convicted criminals whose sentences were severe enough to make the risk worth while for the sake of the pardon attached to it. Ruling statesmen everywhere have to intervene in these conflicts armed with all the State powers of reward and punishment, throwing their weight on one side to excite and induce or on the other to discourage and prevent.

This function calls for judgment and decision of a very high order, not coverable by any set of cut and dried commandments or maxims. It is easy to say "Thou shalt not kill"; but the statesman must reply "What! not kill a flea when I catch him in my bed! not kill a million locusts or white ants to save the country from devastation and the human race from extermination! not kill poisoners and traitors and saboteurs! not kill invaders and conquistadores! Why, killing them is a daily necessity in my business."

But there are grimmer facts to be faced. This mysterious creative force works on different planes, producing at its best a creature which makes us exclaim admiringly "What a piece of work is a man!" and at its worst a deadly virus. It creates on every degree of the scale between these extremes; and the appalling aspect of this variability is that at any moment it may slip down as if it had changed its mind or were having a bit of cruel fun. The living man, its masterpiece, not only becomes a heap of maggots when he dies and no longer knows nor cares what happens to him, but while he still lives may find his flesh renewing itself not as human flesh but as the horrible and agonizing proliferation of inferior cells that we call cancer. It may produce bone where it should produce muscle: in Dublin there is the skeleton of a woman whose muscles became so ossified that her arms were as immovable as those of a statue. The soft or fluid tissues and liquids of the normal human organs may be replaced by stones.

In our dreadful need to know why the force plays these impish tricks on us we subscribe or bequeath hundreds of thousands of pounds to Cancer Research Funds and the like, hoping that if the Why must remain inscrutable at least some helpful light may be thrown on the How. But the funds are eaten up by vivisectors who, after innumerable ritual sacrifices called experiments, tell us they have succeeded in producing cancer in a mouse. Not much for our money, this. The force, called the Holy Ghost in the Church of

England, creates disquieting doubts by acting occasionally in a very unholy manner, as if it had no conscience. Its apparent cruelty is used by the vivisectors to persuade us that it does not exist; that what we are witnessing is a chapter of accidents, what we are doing a set of habits called reflexes, and what we are saying a babble which would be exactly the same if consciousness did not exist, there being nothing at work but Natural Selection operating without purpose, yet, by the prodigious mathematical chances possible in unlimited time, producing "conditioned reflexes" which simulate intelligent behavior and deceive the unscientific.

No statesman worth the name could be imposed on by this nineteenth-century rubbish. He has to deal with life and death, health and disease, conscience and consciousness, will and purpose, creation and evolution, as facts; and if the disciples of Weismann and Pavlov assure him that his facts are illusions, he will reply "Very well; but illusions are facts; and facts are what I have to reckon with. Anyhow, as healthy tissue and cancer are living facts and not illusions, will you tell me, if you know or can find out, how one can slip down into the other, and whether and how it can be prevented from doing so; for that is what concerns a minister of public health. And please do not tell me what happens to mutilated dogs and guinea-pigs and starved rats and mice, as I have to deal with what happens to unmutilated citizens who suffer these changes whilst others who eat and drink the same things remain unchanged. I am concerned with what happens naturally in the world, not with what you contrive unnaturally in your laboratories. If you cannot answer my questions be good enough to stop wasting my time and get out."

Even when the doctors and chemists find a remedy the statesman has to consider whether it is economically possible or humanely practicable. Any chemist can tell the Treasury how to make diamonds by crystallizing carbon or to extract gold from sea water. But the cost of the process is more than the resultant diamonds and gold are worth. Any serum therapist can recommend to the health authorities a series of prophylactic inoculations guaranteed to prevent most of the listed diseases. Lawrence of Arabia told me that he had in his military career endured over forty inoculations. And no doubt the fact that he did not die of any of the forty diseases against which he was inoculated will figure as a statistical proof of the efficacy of the prophylactics. But the statesman dares not on such evidence, or indeed on any evidence, impose forty compulsory inoculations on every citizen. Besides, inoculations may go wrong:

I have described how vaccination and tuberculin inoculations have sometimes proved more deadly than smallpox and phthisis, and how Sir Almroth Wright devised a technique by which inoculations can be made safer. But whereas the scientist in his cloistered laboratory thinks only of the effectiveness of the precautions he prescribes, the statesman has to think of their cost when practised on millions of people. A single inoculation needing nothing more than the prick of a lancet or of the needle of a hypodermic syringe, involving no subsequent disablement, can be made compulsory if its merits are well advertized; but if a country doctor can make it harmless only by spending pounds on turning his surgery into an equipped laboratory, and hours examining blood under his microscope and counting microbes in his test tubes to ascertain the phagocytic index of every patient, the precaution must be dismissed by the statesman as economically impossible. To ascertain the indexes of forty millions of people once (to say nothing of Lawrence's forty times) would take too long and cost too much even if doctors were trained in the precautionary technique. Yet without the precaution the inoculation may do mischief often enough to provoke a popular reaction in which objection to all inoculations and immunizations as such becomes a conditioned reflex reinforced by the fear of meddling artificially with the living human blood: "a quite peculiar juice" as Mephistopheles called it. Anything is possible in a matter which nobody yet understands. The Christian sings that God moves in a mysterious way His wonders to perform; and the most fanatically atheistic scientist has no more to tell us about it.

The situation is full of trouble for the statesman. On the one hand the few proletarian Intelligentsia cry "Hands off our bodies and bloods" whilst the many Unintelligentsia run after charms, spells, baptisms, circumcisions, vaccines, and the like as eagerly as they run after racing tips. The doctors, most of them in straitened circumstances through their dependence for a livelihood on the ailments of the poor, favor any practice that makes health as lucrative as disease. When I was on a public health authority we paid half-a-crown for each revaccination; and children who opened the door in response to a ring or knock when their parents were out were sometimes seized and re-vaccinated on the spot, with tempestuous sequels when the parents were anti-vacs. No doubt the doctors were honestly convinced that vaccination is harmless and prevents smallpox; but the half-crown had more to do with that honest conviction than an unbiased scientific study of the subject. Doctors are as prone as other

people to wishful thinking, and do not realize that as all thinking
is wishful thinking, it cannot occur until a wish acts as father to
the thought. Most of us believe what we wish to believe in the teeth
of all evidence. The statesman is finally driven to regard all pecuniarily interested professional evidence with deep suspicion, and even
to pass or repeal Acts of Parliament in flat defiance of it.

Now diseases spread beyond the class in which they begin. A
German monk named Oken discovered in 1808-11 that our bodies
are made up of living cells, which he was intelligent enough to call
Transmutations of the Holy Ghost, which is the Christian name of
the Life Force. The smallest of these cells, invisible even through
the electron microscope, may swarm in the blood. When the Life
Force goes wrong, how or why nobody knows, they change their
shapes and divide into armies with distinctive uniforms, in which
they fight and eat oneanother, whilst their human host suffers dis-
comfort, pain, disablement, disorder of normal functions and their
organs: in short, disease or illness. When the lungs go wrong a
uniform peculiar to them is assumed by the cells, another and
different one when the bowels go wrong, another when the muscu-
lar control of the throat goes wrong and produces involuntary con-
tractions that may kill the patient, and so on. These specialized
cells, called germs, microbes, bacilli, spirochetes, leucocytes, phagocytes, and what not, can escape into the air by the breath, the
spittle, the handkerchief, the excretions, the clothes, and can con-
vey the disease to anyone unlucky enough to come in contact with
them while in a negative phase of defence, and thus unable to prevent them from multiplying millionsfold by splitting in two.

When the physiologists discovered these curious incidents of disease, their first crude conclusion was that the microbes not only
operated and spread the diseases but were actually the diseases themselves, and that if you could kill the microbes you could abolish the
diseases.

Like all crude first conclusions this was easily and eagerly swallowed, and at once became popular and persistent, as it is at present.
But though it accounted roughly for the spread of disease and its
culmination in plagues and epidemics, it broke down over their
completely mysterious cessation. For instance, the ravages of the
Black Death fitted into the theory well enough; but why did the
Black Death not spread until its multiplying microbes had ended
the human race instead of dying out as it did? In the Dublin hospitals as they were in my boyhood, microbes were called animalculae;

but nothing was known of their characteristic uniforms; and the suspicion that they were connected with disease did not go beyond such tales as one told me by my father of a man who, suffering from toothache, kept his mouth open above the fumes of henbane, whereupon a multitude of suffocated animalculae dropped out; and the toothache ceased. Surgeons operated in their oldest coats, and held their smaller instruments conveniently between their lips; for they had to work very quickly before anaesthetics were discovered. And nothing untoward happened most of the time. Operations were usually as successful as they are now with the most careful precautions against microbes. Some of them, notably extirpation of the kidneys or the ovaries, which are now fairly safe, were then regarded as desperate; but the change was effected by oldfashioned surgeons who used unsterilized pipe water, and whose new precautions went no farther than the maintenance of an unchanged temperature in the sick room until the patient was out of danger.

Cases did not always go so smoothly. From time to time the operations in the hospital suddenly became fatal. If a nurse scratched her finger with a pin, she died of septicemia. All the surgical patients died: an operation was an execution. But this ghastly state of things did not last. The "hospital gangrene" as it was called, became milder and milder and presently died out, leaving the hospital unvisited for another spell, just as plagues died out in cities. It is now hardly known. A surgeon named Lister had just brains enough for the crude germ theory; and though his manual dexterity as an operator was below the average, his precautions against microbal infection involved such an access of aesthetic cleanliness that the consequent disappearance of hospital gangrene made him famous. Unfortunately his bactericidal surgery, which he called antiseptic, killed the defensive and recreative cells as well as the aggressive ones, and made his surgery far more incurable than that of his oldfashioned competitors. In 1898 I underwent an operation which left a hole in my left foot which the recreative cells had to fill up for me. But Lister was then in full vogue; and the hole was stuffed daily with iodoform gauze to kill the microbes. It did, with the result that I went on crutches for eighteen months. Then an old pre-Listerian surgeon countermanded the gauze and prescribed lint soaked in pipe water full of microbes and kept damp by a scrap of oiled silk. I was well in a fortnight.

Lister was not content with iodoform gauze. He invented a "donkey engine" which spread a mist of carbolic spray through the operating room, and poisoned the microbes, the patient, and the surgeon simultaneously. He thought that what was needed to abolish disease and make the human race permanently healthy was the substitution of carbolic spray for the atmosphere by a donkey engine at every street corner. The *fin de siècle* stank of carbolic acid.

But the surgeons objected to being suffocated and poisoned, and to have their operations made incurable after costing the private patient from fifty guineas to several hundreds. Lister was not publicly discredited: that would have shattered the faith of the public in his profession; so his donkey engine was silently scrapped and he himself enshrined in the medical Valhalla, symbolized by his statue in Portland Place. His method was dropped, except the aesthetic cleanliness which was incidental to it. Surgeons and nurses wore spotless white overalls. Sir Almroth Wright dealt the *coup de grâce* to antisepticism by polemically knocking out the last remaining Listerian. Like Lessing he not only decapitated Lister but held up the head to shew that there were no brains in it. And he shewed that ordinary water with ten per cent of common salt in it would do everything that Lister with his carbolic spray had undertaken to do and scandalously failed.

To me, with my discarded crutches and the stigma on my instep, this is a story of fifty years ago. Yet by many of my readers it will be received with incredulous astonishment as almost blasphemous. The medicines and remedies they buy in the pharmacies are still advertized and labelled as antiseptic. Jenner and Lister are canonized as therapeutic miracle workers; and the truth about them is a jealously guarded trade secret. But unless the public health authorities are let into such secrets they may do much mischief. They did so at the turn of the century when in their campaign against tuberculosis they plastered railway stations and other public resorts with exhortations to the people never to spit but always to use a handkerchief. They are still doing it. "Coughs and sneezes spread diseases: always use your handkerchief" is urged on us by posters; and in the cinemas films exhort us to capture the billionfold germs from the atmosphere and shelter them in our pockets.

Worse advice could hardly be given. Microbes, though they are products and not causes of disease, are none the less infectious; but they are neither immortal nor invulnerable. An exposure to sunshine for a fraction of a second kills most of them. They flourish and multiply only in damp and darkness. When huge cities like London and Paris discharged their sewage into their open rivers, it was found that the water two miles downstream from the city was purer than

twenty miles upstream. Villages which had used their streams as
open sewers and rubbish dumps were, on being provided with
drainage systems which hid the sewage in damp darkness, presently
smitten with typhoid fever. Evidently there was something wrong
with the Swiss policy of *Tout a l'égout* which raised the hopes of
Voltaire as vaccination raised those of Macaulay. Something wrong
with the drains. Something wrong with the handkerchiefs.

Now what was wrong with the drains was damp darkness; and
that was precisely what was wrong with the handkerchiefs also.
When we blow pathogenic microbes out of our noses on to the
sunlit ground through our fingers they die on the spot and infect nobody. When we collect them into damp handkerchiefs and stuff
them into dark pockets they multiply until they find themselves
comfortably in the laundry, where they infect the clothes of dozens
of households. Local epidemics are mostly traced to laundries when
they are traced at all. If I had drafted the *fin de siècle* posters they
would have run like this. "If you have a cold, and are in the country,
never use a handkerchief. Use your fingers when nobody is looking;
and select the sunniest spot you can find. When you are on city
pavements or indoors use a paper handkerchief and burn it."

Fire, not water, is the surest and safest disinfectant. When a verminous person brings his clothes to the sanitary authority to be
deverminated, they are not steeped in carbolic acid. They are put
into an oven heated to a temperature that no louse can live through.
Lord Samuel, in his suggestive Utopia entitled An Unknown Land,
rightly makes his Utopians use electric furnaces instead of water-
closets. To sterilize water we boil it. Milk, we "Pasteurize" it.

But here again, we fall into Lister's error. Pasteurized milk, to any
healthy palate, is undrinkable; and so is boiled or distilled water.
Fire destroys the creative cell and the pathogenic one indiscriminately; and anyhow, though we may burn an infected handkerchief
we may not burn an infected living human being. Dead bodies can
be cremated. All of them ought to be; for earth burial, a horrible
practice, will some day be prohibited by law, not only because it
is hideously unaesthetic, but because the dead would crowd the
living off the earth if it could be carried out to its end of preserving
our bodies for their resurrection on an imaginary day of judgment
(in sober fact, every day is a day of judgment). But a disinfectant
which destroys what it disinfects, burning down the house to roast
the pig, is not applicable in cases where our task is to preserve both
the house and the pig. Our plan of getting rid of foot-and-mouth

disease by slaughtering its victims is not available in outbreaks of measles, a disease negligible when I had it as a child, but now become deadly. The parents would object, and the slaughterers be lynched.

What we need is a selective disinfectant that will slay the pathogenic cell and spare the creative one. The only one we know is healthy living blood. We inhale millions of microbes every day and are none the worse, because our blood slays them more irresistibly than Samson slew the Philistines. The new electron microscope has revealed defensive hosts of phagocytes which the magnifiers used by Metchnikoff and Sir Almroth Wright could not detect. The statesman who can make our blood healthy by abolishing malnutrition, dirt, and ignorance need not trouble about the microbe scare that has dominated and corrupted hygienic science for a century past.

CHAPTER XXVIII

THE COLLECTIVE STATISTICIAN

In dealing with a disease the first thing a sanitary authority has to ascertain is its prevalence, and whether and how fast it is increasing or decreasing. These figures it must gather from the death certificates of the doctors, who give as the cause of death their diagnosis of the case. Now not only may a diagnosis be erroneous; but doctors do not always give the same name to the same disease. When I had a seat on a Public Health committee, I took the unprecedented step of examining our reports of vital statistics, printed by us at great expense, and never either circulated to the public nor read by any member of the committee except myself. We had to deal with a terribly overcrowded borough in which three gigantic railway terminuses, with their square miles of goods yards, had displaced thousands of our people and crowded them into very insanitary tenements. Typhoid fever was endemic. On looking it up I found the death rates less than I expected, and would have been misled had my eye not been caught as I turned the pages by another figure under the heading Enteric Fever. I happened to know that typhoid and enteric are two names for the same disease. The doctors used them indifferently. Knowing also that a famous physician, Sir

Clifford Allbutt, had said to his students in the course of a clinical lecture "This, gentlemen, is called scarlet fever; but all the cases are different" I wondered how many other names—dysentery for instance—belonged to the typhoid-enteric category. At all events it was clear that such statistics were useless and might be seriously mischievous. I got the typhoid ambiguity removed, and incidentally imposed on the committee as a person of profound learning; and since then doctors have been officially instructed that they must use the same name for the same disease in death certificates, and never fall back on heart failure or dyspnœa (shortness of breath) as a cause of death when they are puzzled. But new names are easily found; and until diagnosis becomes much more scientific, mortality statistics will need very careful sifting by expert statisticians (not by doctors) before legislation can be based on them safely.

Pursuing my examination I was glad to find that there were no deaths from smallpox, which was apparently extinct in the borough. The Jennerians would have held this up as a triumph of vaccination; but I knew better. I looked for typhus and cholera, which in my childhood were dreaded plagues. They were equally extinct; so it was arguable that either vaccination prevented typhus and cholera as well as smallpox or else it had no effect, and some other cause common to all three diseases had been at work. Presently, however, smallpox broke out again; and though the epidemic was trivial and its mortality negligible in comparison with those of the days when vaccination was compulsory and ruthlessly enforced, still it was serious enough to set revaccination raging throughout the borough, and causing much illness and disablement. Now smallpox, like typhoid, has more than one name. It is describable as pustular eczema. If that is too long, varioloids will do. Accordingly, when one of our medical members complained that a patient recently revaccinated by him had been sent to the smallpox hospital, the case was re-diagnosed as pustular eczema or varioloids, and the patient hurriedly transferred to the general hospital. The resultant statistics shewed that not a single revaccinated person had contracted smallpox during the epidemic, which presently wore itself out as unaccountably as it had broken in. I then understood how it was that smallpox had been abolished in the German army by revaccination before the great epidemic of 1871. No army surgeon in Germany dared to diagnose it under its usual name.

Vital statistics are vitiated not only by the fact that diagnosis is very far from being an exact science, much of it being mere nomenclature and nothing else, and not uniform even at that: they are the work, not of skilled statisticians but of amateurs who imagine that simple arithmetic qualifies them to prescribe their nostrums to public health authorities for compulsory national administration. The old vaccination statistics which seemed so convincing a century ago gave cases of smallpox epidemics of which it was gravely recorded that a hundred per cent of the unvaccinated patients had died and a hundred per cent of the vaccinated recovered. This impressed people who imagined that the scene was a city with a hundred thousand inhabitants. It was in fact a hamlet in which there had been two cases. Neither doctors nor magistrates, it seems, were mathematically gifted enough to know that there can be no percentages until the cases run into thousands, and are not of much value until they reach many thousands.

Through my acquaintance with the late Karl Pearson I was early impressed with the necessity of mathematics in biology and indeed in all branches of science. Pearson, always smiling and charming, would not admit that anyone who was not a mathematician could claim any scientific authority whatsoever. I subscribed faithfully to his journal *Biometrika* without understanding any of its equations or more than, say, five per cent of its sentences. But I found that the biometricians, though their technical skill and subtlety seemed wonderful to me, were as credulous, as prejudiced, as thoughtless as to the facts they were measuring and the assumptions from which they started, as Isaac Newton himself. Even their counting was not to be depended on; for they added up facts and opinions indiscriminately, and cooked their calculations by "weighting" them with fancy figures which represented nothing but their personal guesses and tastes.

The public services need therefore a department of statistics and mathematics to which the statesman can submit for skilled examination all the correlations involved in legislative projects and current administrative practice, as well as to prepare such periodical budgets of information as the census and the statistical abstract. Official figures are not infallible, as they have to be collected and assembled by fallible mortals; but as there are degrees of fallibility we can select our statisticians by the method of imagining the possible extremes, and determining the most eligible spot on the scale between them. At the bottom of the scale of authority are the professions or individuals whose incomes are at stake. At the top of it are the persons gifted by the Life Force with a passion for veracity and accuracy in the abstract which can find employment only in an otherwise impartial collection, correction, and correlation of information. A public department of statistics would attract these pernickety persons as Civil Service candidates; and such a department would be at the practicable top of the scale of authority. The statesman should accept no figures from the doctors, the lawyers, the clergy, the bankers, the artists, the artisans, the laborers, or the individual cranks until they were critically examined and correlated, corrected, and endorsed by the department. Had such a test been in operation in the nineteenth century such a cruel blunder as compulsory vaccination would have been impossible. The figures, correlated with those of typhus and cholera, would have shewn that vaccination was actually delaying the conquest of smallpox by sanitation, which did not triumph over Jennerist sciolism until the enforcement of notification and isolation in 1885.

Now the triumph of sanitation was, as Sir Almroth Wright was the first to point out, a triumph of aestheticism. Smallpox, typhus, cholera, tuberculosis and the Black Death follow dirt and ugliness, stink and squalor, meanness and poverty as surely as they vanish before beauty and cleanliness and seemliness and sweet sootless air. What offends and degrades the mind, whether through the senses or the intellect, degrades the body. It is true also that what injures the body may injure the mind; but an injury is not necessarily a degradation: the loss of a limb or an organ disables its victim, but does not change a higher order of life into a lower one, as when healthy human growth becomes cancerous proliferation. Beethoven lost his hearing; but he composed his greatest symphony when he was deaf. Milton's poetry was no worse when he lost his sight. A sane Ministry of Public Health must assume that it is the mind that makes the body and not the body the mind. St. John's gospel in Greek is that in the beginning was the Word. In plain English it is that in the beginning was the Thought, of which the word is only the name.

At this point the Health Ministry becomes an Education Ministry. What we need are not pills and potions, prophylactic inoculations, physical jerks, and the like. The most liberal supplies of chalk and opium will not abolish cholera. We need agreeable surroundings, the satisfaction of physical cravings before they become mental anxieties, poetry, music, pictures, books, and leisure to enjoy them and acquire a taste for them. Without such tastes we have no pleasures but those of gluttony, drunkenness, and the sexual lust which becomes importunate for some years before it is wholesome to indulge it, and is irresistible in the absence of aesthetic counterattractions to sublimate it at best and at worst make it too fastidious for the streets. An overcrowded mass of people who know nothing of the fine arts, and have neither money nor leisure for thinking, or for hunting, shooting, skating, boxing, golfing, cricket, or football, is a hotbed not only of syphilis but of all the other diseases as well. Overcrowding is in fact more deadly than hunger or cold. Today the newspapers announce the building by the State of 30,000 cottages in which no inhabitant will have a separate room. And the Prime Minister simultaneously calls for larger families! When will we begin to understand that One Citizen One Room is far more pressing than One Man One Vote?

CHAPTER XXIX

THE GENETIC STATE

WE have concluded that the statesman need not bother about microbes. But this relief only lands him in a vitally imperative concern with Eugenics, also called Genetics. It has been discovered that by selective breeding and appropriate nurture, strains of plant life can be produced which are immune from diseases which formerly destroyed them. Our stockbreeders have found by trial and error that the secret of improving horses, cattle, swine and poultry to the extent of almost transfiguring them is to take care of their pedigrees. Adolf Hitler, who is not a stockbreeder, has, by using his brains, arrived at the same conclusion as to his own species. But being a Nationalist German he assumes that the destiny of the human species is to be conquered and ruled by its Nordics, who should subjugate the Slavs and the Latins, and incidentally exterminate the Jews, the Poles, and any other strains that may prove implacably recalcitrant.

He has actually induced his fellow Germans to let him organize them for a heroic world war; and they are at this moment fanatically spending their blood and money in millionfold quantities to achieve the necessary conquest. But the experiment, though at first sensationally successful on the field of battle, has not borne out the efficacy of systematic inbreeding from Nordic pedigrees. The Scandinavian and Anglo-American Nordics have proved so recalcitrant that Adolf has been obliged to exclude them as eligible sires, and select only those of central German stock. By the time this book is made public he will probably have discovered that these also are no better than Jews or Poles, and much more pigheaded. But he will at least have tried the experiment very thoroughly, even at the cost of his own life if the surviving Germans whose relatives have paid the price with theirs turn on him and rend him.

Let us hope, however, that he will escape them to enjoy a comfortable retirement in Ireland or some other neutral country, as Louis Napoleon did at Chislehurst and the Kaiser at Doorn. What pedigree will he then advise us to breed from in the light of his experiment? He may of course despair of his species because all the races have failed him. But as he is an extraordinarily sanguine person he may realize that there is an alternative. Our geneticists are agreed that the secret of meliorist eugenics is the substitution of cross-breeding for inbreeding. It is the crossed stock that mutates. The future of mankind belongs to its mongrels and not to its handsome but brainless Borzois. The Führer is not himself a pedigree Prussian: genealogically he is a rank outsider picked by Nature as a winner. Chinese laundrymen and Irish colyeens (the Chink and the Biddy) are said to produce an excellent strain of children. English stock crossed with Italian is good both for big business and fine art. In Russia, where a whole generation of fine ladies and gentlemen have had to pretend that their fathers "worked on the land with their hands" and all sorts and conditions of humanity are promiscuously intermarriageable, civilization makes strides that leave the rest of Europe gasping miles behind. Meanwhile, in the remote villages where inbreeding is unavoidable for lack of invasion by strangers, and the population is one of not too distant cousins, the stock deteriorates; and congenital defects are common. Pedigrees begin by exogamous cross-breeding and end ignominiously as inbred endogamous caste selection of parasites by parasites.

The statesman must therefore abjure all forms of endogamy, whether of caste, nation, or color, whilst giving the fullest scope to natural selection between the sexes. This is not easy in our far flung commonwealth. We whites have signally failed to populate New Zealand, where we number only a million and a half instead of tens of millions in each of the two islands. When I was in Durban in 1935 the transport minister made an appeal for more British immigration to keep up the British population in South Africa. We have given up Australia as uninhabitable except in a few corners. Meanwhile the aboriginal blacks, the inventors of the miraculous boomerang, are not sterile, nor are the black tribes in Africa, nor the Maoris in New Zealand now that they have stopped eating one another. The remedy appears to be miscegenation. In Jamaica this has been so freely practised that when I was there in 1911 some of the whitest and most civilized men I met had brown fathers; and in Hawaii, where I wanted to hear some genuine native music instead of the British and American popular tunes with which our tourists are humbugged, I found that pure bred descendants of the old Sandwich Islanders are now human curiosities. Only the Japanese are endogamous. They also are trying the Hitlerian genetic experiment in the east; but I should bet on the mongrels for the long run if I were a sportsman.

In this as in every other department of public affairs we find the statesman brought up, not vaguely and generally against Science as an empty word beginning with a capital letter, but against living naturalists, physiologists, biologists, and philosophers, in their warring sects of natural selectionists and creative evolutionists (neo-Darwinians now voiced by Julian Huxley and Bergsonians by Joseph Needham). Also not against Art with a large A, but against very disputations schools of music, painting, sculpture, literature, and, above all, architecture. In most cases the statesman is helpless without the advice of skilled statisticians uncorrupted by anti-social commercial interests and unswayed by any passion stronger than mathematical passion, which in certain persons is the strongest and by far the most enduring of all the passions. The born mathematician is the phagocyte created by Nature to devour the profiteer.

CHAPTER XXX

STATE CORRUPTION

As the advance of Socialism from doctrine and theory to practice extends the activities and powers of the State it extends also the opportunities for corruption and the mass of the plunder. The Socialists advocate the nationalization of the means of production, distribution, and exchange: they exhort us to Educate, Agitate,

Organize with that in view. This is quite sound economically; but it will make Capitalism and Imperialism stronger than ever if the change from private to public business is made, as it is actually being made, by Capitalists and Imperialists fighting, like Wayland the smith, for their own hands, rather than by Communists aiming at the welfare of the community. For, I repeat, it is possible to nationalize the means of production, distribution, and exchange, and exploit them far more thoroughly than they are exploited at present, to increase unearned income and relieve its holders from taxation whilst increasing also the cost of living to the proletariat and reducing their means of defraying it. Our Optimists point exultantly to the rise of wages: for instance, the wages of women employed in war work have risen from twopence halfpenny an hour in 1914 to sixpence an hour in 1941, making six shillings a day for twelve hours work instead of half a crown. But when the woman takes her six shillings home the ground landlord immediately confiscates from eightpence to two shillings of it. With the rest she buys her food and clothes at considerably increased prices. The wages of skilled workmen have risen from £2 a week to between seventy and eighty shillings; but I read lately in the news that one of these aristocrats of labor was paying a rent of twenty-eight shillings a week. Yesterday (February 1943) the Government announced the building by the State of 6000 houses for agricultural laborers. The rent is to be thirteen shillings a week out of a wage of two pounds. Such rents would have been considered monstrous before wages rose.

I am not forgetting that there may be no landlords and no taxation of them as such when they have all been bought out by the State at their own expense as explained in Chapter Thirteen. But the bought out landlord, loaded up for the moment with spare money to invest, becomes a capitalist and calls his unearned income interest instead of rent, a change which makes no difference to the proletariat. The capitalists can be and perhaps will be bought out at their own expense on the same lines, leaving industry, like land, in the hands of the State. The old rich will be no longer landlords or capitalists; but what is to prevent their becoming perpetual pensioners on one pretext or another if the distribution of rent, interest, and profits is left in their own hands? Landlords and capitalists can be abolished easily enough; but rent and interest will remain at the disposal of the Government, which, controlling production and the markets, can profiteer if it chooses. In fact it cannot help making some profit in spite of itself if it is to remain securely solvent. The distribution of its profits, like the rents, will be at its discretion. It can pay enormous salaries and pensions to members of Parliament, including peers who are practically irremovable sinecurists, and institute a system of privileges graded from endowed nobility down to unskilled labor with starvation wages, making the change from private to public property a change for the worse.

The old Liberal craving for political institutions from which millennial prosperity will result automatically without restriction of individual liberty or State inculcation of political and religious views is natural enough; and it is powerfully reinforced by the Christian individualism which sets up the infinite worth of the divinely created immortal freewilling individual soul above the make-shift totalitarian authority of the artificial States of this world, our passage through which is only a brief and sinful episode in eternity; but there is no such thing as an automatic earthly paradise. A Socialist State can be just as wicked as any other sort of State. Eternal vigilance is the price of Socialism no less than of liberty; and unless it is well-instructed and well-informed vigilance it may do the utmost possible harm with the best possible intentions. It is safer to reject all automatic systems as excuses for political laziness, and to consider respectfully all systems involving daily direction and consideration. The belief in automatic salvation has wrecked Capitalism and extinguished Cobdenite Liberalism; and it will wreck Socialism quite as disastrously if we indulge in it.

Constitutional history has something to say here. A monopoly of land and capital by the Government is no new thing. It actually exists at present in law. There is no such thing legally as private property in land: it all belongs to the King and can be held by a private person only as an estate granted by him which he can "resume" at any moment. His right to tax his subjects has no legal limit; and he is at present confiscating the entire income of the richest of them and more, to be employed in defence of the realm. Thus the complete "expropriation of the expropriators" by making the Government the sole landlord, capitalist, and employer could be effected within the existing law. Henry VIII took the lands of the Church without a revolution just as the Chancellor of the Exchequer is taking as much of our money as he can squeeze from us without wrecking the whole Capitalist system. The law is ultra-Socialist, as indeed all constitutional law in its nature must be. Why, then, is government in practice anti-Socialist to such an unbearable degree that revolutionary discontent is seething everywhere except in Russia?

The answer is that the King and the Ministers who exercise his powers are not Socialists; and neither are those who elect them. They grant estates in land to private persons to exploit for personal advantage. They used to sell their taxing powers to tax-farmers who fleeced the taxpayers unmercifully. Exchequer Chancellors, in their Budgets, treat direct taxation of income as a last resort, to be imposed only when every other source of revenue has been exploited to the utmost. When private enterprise refuses to engage in necessary businesses which yield no profit, or for which it is not enterprising enough (the postal service, for example) governments do not supply it at cost price, but profiteer in it and use the profits to relieve or avert taxation on unearned incomes.

This is what has come so far of vesting the means of production, distribution, and exchange in the State and leaving the State in the hands of Anti-Socialist Ministers who have been taught that selfish private trade secures national prosperity. It has in sober fact produced poverty and slavery, prostitution and premature death, on a scale that has provoked the specific movement we call Socialism. And it is supported by popular movements called Liberalism, Peasant Proprietary, Anarchism, Syndicalism, or any name indicating mistrust of State.

Take the case of the boasted abolition of chattel slavery on British soil and in America. If I have a slave or serf for whose support I am responsible when he is past his work, and who is protected against the worst abuses of my powers by special laws regulating slavery, what does he gain by being thrown into the street to starve or sell himself to another master as "a free laborer"? He is assured that he can now choose his master; but when he must find employment or starve he soon finds that it is his master who can choose him. In losing his owner he has lost his rights as a chattel slave, and can be thrown on the scrapheap when he is no longer worth employing. When feudal serfdom was abolished in England deaths from starvation would have multiplied beyond social endurance but for the Elizabethan Poor Law. The industrial revolution made deaths by starvation a regular feature in the returns of the Registrar-General until the armistice which suspended the Four Years War, when millions of demobilized men, expert in the use of arms and hardened to slaughter and bloodshed, accustomed too to regular meals of bully beef, could find no employment. Lest they should revolt, the

Poor Law had to be supplemented by the dole, adding a horde of underfed poor parasites to the horde of overfed rich ones.

It has repeatedly occurred that State railways have been allowed to fall into ruinous disrepair and scandalous inefficiency through the Government using the money paid by the public for transport to reduce taxation instead of for necessary repairs and maintenance of the service at optimum efficiency, and devoting the profits, if any, to cheapening it or improving the condition of its operatives. Comparison of such State-owned and State-plundered railways with British and American privately-owned railways, greatly to the disgrace of the former, is often used to discredit Socialist proposals of railway nationalization, although our private competing railways are so absurdly ill adapted to the country's need that it is sometimes cheaper to send English goods to America by sea and then back again to their English destination than to send them directly across country in England by rail. In Italy trains never ran to time until the Duce, as absolute a ruler as Louis XIV, and in Spain Primo de Rivera, laid the hand of the State on them. In Russia Djerdjinski, as Minister of Transport, shot a sinecurist station master with his own hand; but as there were many more sinecurists than Djerdjinskis the Soviet had to organize a shooting police to establish discipline. Any State railway service can be made punctual, efficient, solvent, and profitable if the Ministry of Transport is determined to make it so. But if the Exchequer plunders it, and had rather make it a warning against State enterprise than an example, it can wreck it with the laziest ease. The people will not understand: they will know only that the railway system is rotten, and blame government management for it. And as Socialism involves government management, they will blame Socialism for it also, because their millennial vision of Socialism does not include the possibility that it may prove more disastrous in corrupt or ignorant hands than a simply selfish plutocracy.

In the hands of ignorant, unscrupulous, carelessly elected rulers (whether they call themselves Socialists or Conservatists matters not a jot) mismanagement of the currency may lead to national calamities. We all know what a railway train is, and can understand the railway system if we take the trouble to learn it. Nobody understands money. If you buy twopence worth of apples from a costermonger and hand him a silver sixpence he will hand you four bronze pennies as change correctly enough; and you may conclude that he knows what money is and all about it. He can even tell you, if you ask him where the coins came from, that they came from the Mint. But if you ask him why he should give you two eatable apples for two little discs of bronze, he is stumped. He knows the What, the When, the Where, and the How; but he does not know the Why. And the Governor of the Bank of England, in the late discussion of the Gold Standard, confessed himself equally stumped by that fundamental question.

Now imagine our costermonger becoming a Labor member of Parliament, as he may under existing conditions if he is a bit of a speaker, and has picked up all the abstract arguments for Socialism and against Capitalism by attending Socialist meetings and reading Socialist tracts. I have shared the platform with very eloquent costers who elicited thunders of applause by their speeches, though they dropped all their aitches and the Governor of the Bank of England has never been known to drop one. Imagine your coster a Cabinet Minister, a Prime Minister, or, if you like, a Duce, a Führer, or a Commissar! Such things happen nowadays. In that case he may see himself in the delightful position of being able to create un- limited wealth by simply printing scraps of paper marked ten shillings, a pound, five pounds, a hundred pounds. He can print them by the million, and make them legal tender in all business transactions. Revolutionary governments consisting of inexperienced men who know a good deal about poverty and halfpence and no- thing about millions almost always intoxicate themselves by this assumption, which is pure lunacy. No government can create a loaf of bread, an egg, a pair of boots, nor even repair a broken window by printing figures on paper. The bits of paper can be valid as title- deeds to bread and butter and boots and bricks and mortar or any other material objects or personal services only when the material objects and active servants are in existence. If not, the holders of the paper may go whistle for them. They might as well hold shares in an imaginary gold mine.

What happens at first is not a complete absence of the things that honest money can buy. Suppose the Government, accustomed to pay a penny apiece for eggs, and assuming that somehow or other there are always plenty of eggs to be had at that price, issues paper title-deeds to a dozen eggs for every half a dozen actually in the market! The price of eggs will go up to twopence apiece. This will infuriate the Government, which will accuse the sellers of profiteer- ing in a Black Market. To defeat this it will pass what is called a law of maximum, decreeing a fine of £100 or several years imprisonment or what not for everyone caught selling eggs for more than a penny. But the police cannot enforce such a law, because they cannot put a constable in every shop and at every street corner, nor a body of constables in every market-place, to see that the law is obeyed. The police can detect law breaking only when the aggrieved party calls them in. When both parties agree on a transaction there is no aggrieved party and no call for the police. Nothing can prevent a scarcity of eggs causing a rise of egg prices if the Government issues paper money in excess of the available supply of eggs whilst leaving the dealings in eggs to competitive commerce and private bargaining. In Germany after the Four Years War the postage of a letter from London to Berlin cost twopence-halfpenny. From Berlin to London it cost £12,500 in German paper money. As the postman's wages had to be on a corresponding scale it did not greatly matter to him; but people dependent on fixed incomes such as pensioners, annuitants, unmarried orphan ladies whose parents had provided for them by insurances, mortgagees, debenture holders, and creditors generally, were ruined. At the armistice in 1918 I was owed thousands of pounds by German publishers and theatre managers. The cry was "Make Germany pay." I still have the million mark notes with which Germany paid me. They are worth perhaps a few pence as curiosities. The same thing happened to rouble notes in Russia after 1917, to American paper dollars after the Civil War, to the assignats which served as currency during the French Revolution, and in hundreds of other cases in which paper money was used in excess of purchasable goods. This State misdemeanor is called Inflation. It is a variation of the confidence trick.

On the other hand debtors are relieved of their liabilities, which they can pay off with worthless paper; and trading companies relieve themselves of their debentures in the same easy manner. Speculators with longer heads and purses buy up existing goods for worthless paper and sell them to foreign customers for valid foreign money or keep them to sell at home when the Government can no longer deceive itself and is forced to return to a currency based on goods or gold. Thus there are always plenty of people who profit by State swindling. They egg governments on to inflate, and oppose all attempts to deflate. For them a year of inflation is a year of prosperity. A government which robs Peter to pay Paul can always depend on the support of Paul.

Inflation, however, soon defeats itself. In Germany when notes marked millions and even milliards of marks would not buy an egg or pay a tram fare, foreigners dealing with Germany stipulated that they should be paid in American dollars or in gold; and this forced the German Government to issue a new currency based on available goods. The return to normal prices rescues pensioners from destitution; but it ruins debtors, making the cure as calamitous as the disease, Paul being now robbed to pay Peter. Yet the illusion of paper money is still irresistible by financial ignoramuses raised to power by revolution or by adult suffrage. Such education as we give our rulers and voters does not help. The German and Russian inflations were the work not of upstart costermongers but of men who, having been through school and college, knew all that they could learn from books and business experiences. Henry VIII, one of the best schooled and accomplished men of his time, and no fool, adulterated his coinage before paper money was invented. He knew he was cheating; but he did not understand that the Exchequer would gain nothing by the fraud in the long run, and that meanwhile it would cause much suffering. Or perhaps he did but didnt care. A later monarch, Louis XV of France, met remonstrances on this score by his *"Après moi le déluge."*

To defeat inflation, the British Government, as I write these lines, has resorted to laws rationing necessary goods, fixing maximum prices for them, inflicting severe punishment for breach of the law ("Black Marketing"), but—and here comes the novelty—guaranteeing shopkeepers against loss through observance of the law by granting them subsidies. This is a comparatively intelligent measure; but as the taxpayers, including the shopkeepers, have to pay the subsidies, which in effect means paying the difference between the legal maximum price and the real scarcity value, the inflation is not defeated: its burden is shared by everybody instead of falling directly on the shopkeepers' customers individually. It might be called nationalized inflation: that is all.

Governments without currency illusions can nevertheless be dishonest. The French Government carried on the Four Years War by borrowing when the franc was worth tenpence. After the war it deliberately "devalued" its currency and ordained that the franc should be worth twopence. Accordingly the people who had lent France tenpences were paid twopences. This was done without any apology. The Government did what a bankrupt does when he confesses himself insolvent and offers to pay four shillings in the pound in discharge of his debts. But the French Government made no such confession and was not bankrupt. It simply repudiated four-fifths of its debt. The British investors in the loan were indignant and felt defrauded (as in fact they were); but the next thing of the kind was that Britain, having borrowed a vast sum from the United States, repudiated the debt on the ground that the Allied States for whom she had borrowed it had done the same. Finland, having borrowed directly from America, alone remained solvent.

So much for "government security," which depends not only on government solvency and honesty, but on Ministers' comprehension of what they are doing.

Private employers and landlords can appropriate the value of public services or pensions by raising rents or employing pensioners at wages that fall short of the standard wage by the amount of their pensions. When a new arterial road or a new public park creates exceptionally desirable frontages through privately-owned land, the landlord appropriates the increment of value by simply raising the rent. The employers and landlords need not take the initiative in these transactions. They have only to wait until the pensioners and builders themselves bid against one another for the jobs and the land by asking for them at lower wages and higher rents. The pensioners thus make the employers a present of their pensions, and the builders a present to the landlords of what is called "the unearned increment" though it has in fact been earned by the exertions of the whole body of taxpayers and ratepayers. This is not guilty corruption: it is the inevitable automatic consequence of private property in land and capital with enforcement of private contracts. But if the State or municipality purchases land to make new roads without taking care to purchase the frontages or municipalize the affected townlands, it is producing all the effects of corruption without knowing what it is doing. If it grants an insufficient pension, or, having granted a sufficient one does not stop it if the pensioner again works commercially for less than standard wages, this also produces the effects of corruption, intentionally or unintentionally.

Here the proletarian, confronted with these possibilities of corruption which are also strong probabilities, may well exclaim "So this is what comes of your nationalization and municipalization, your triumphant refutation of the Manchester School with its doctrine of *Laisser-faire,* your Fabian Society's demonstration of the enormous possibilities and economies of State enterprise and State control, your Socialization of the means of production, distribution, and exchange! Capitalists are to be richer than *Laisser-faire* could ever have made them; rents, already hardly bearable, are to rise on us;

and we are to be exploited as ruthlessly as ever. Thank you for nothing. Thank you for less than nothing. To the devil with your constitutional Socialism, which keeps the word of promise to the ear and breaks it to the hope! Strike up the Marseillaise. *Aux armes, citoyens!*"

But the Marseillaise will not save the situation. Sabotage and murder as a cure for political abuses have never proved permanent and have often aggravated the disease. The dread of them may have prevented corrupt governments from driving their subjects to desperation; but nowadays so much of the corruption is unintentional and automatic that governments know neither what is the matter nor how to remedy it. Faced with a violent revolt they set the police to work; call out the military; declare a state of siege in which all law is suspended except martial law; and pay the insurgents in their own coin. If the insurgents, as in the French Revolution, beat the Government at that game, they know as little how to better themselves as the Government did; so their rival Reign of Terror is as futile as the official Terror that provoked it. Terror produces nothing but counterterror and terror again endlessly, like a circulating decimal. When Fouquier-Tinville, the official agent of the guillotine, was himself sent to it to have his head cut off he met the execrations of the crowd by shouting from the tumbril, "Will your bread be any the cheaper tomorrow?" And it was dearer. The laugh was on the mob, not on Fouquier. In my native Ireland sabotage, arson, murder, and soldiers' songs were tried out to the bravest and utmost between Shinners and Black-and-Tans. Michael Collins, the insurgent hero, said, when the Black-and-Tans burnt the creameries, "For every creamery you burn I will burn two country houses." He kept his word, and thereby made Catholic Ireland nominally a Free State. Whereupon the Catholic Irish shot Michael, and made as hopeless a mess of their economic slavery as Dublin Castle and the old Grand Juries. For, having no instruction in citizenship, no economics, no philosophy of history, no defined aims, no mental stock-in-trade except romantic balderdash, they were soon groaning under higher prices and rents than ever, with vital statistics that would horrify Europe if Europe had not lost all the Quixotic interest it took in Ireland in the days when she was oppressed by England instead of by herself.

The moral is that of all these chapters. Heroic aspirations, devoted services, dauntless bravery, unsparing bloodshed are worse than useless when the combatants understand neither what is wrong nor how to set it right.

Yet many Socialists believe that Socialist government is incorruptible. It is in fact more corruptible than Unsocialist government, from which it differs in employing the power and riches of the State to develop industrial and agricultural production instead of letting them alone and confining itself to police work and to those indispensable services which are in their nature incapable of making commercial profits or are beyond the utmost resources of private capital. Clearly such an enormous extension of State power and activity carries with it a formidable extension of its possible abuse.

Fortunately no government, however corrupt, can be entirely unsocial. The making of city streets through which everyone may walk without direct payment is flat communism; but the making of the boots in which men walk along them can be left to private business. In the country the roads and bridges can be made by private enterprise and paid for by their users at toll-gates and turnpikes. The two systems soon get mixed. Tolls and turnpikes are a nuisance to people who do not like to be delayed by repeated stoppages and payments at closed gates, and are useless to proletarians who, their pockets being empty, must evade the tolls by trespassing into the fields and breaking the hedges. Therefore toll bridges and turnpikes are "freed": that is, paid for out of the rates and taxes: communized, in fact, as a necessary measure of convenience, in spite of their profitableness, when the State is sufficiently organized to understake such public services. How serious this limitation may be is shewn by the fact that it is hardly an exaggeration to say that from the time when the ancient Romans, who were great road-makers and bridge builders, left Britain in the fifth century until the nineteenth century, no new public bridges were built in England. Our rivers are still grievously under-bridged. Even in the middle of the city of Dublin one of my father's eccentricities was to shout "This infernal bridge will break me" when he crossed the river Liffey at the cost of a halfpenny by a toll bridge which was near his office.

But in spite of the cases in which private enterprise reduced itself to absurdity in practice as the turnpikes and toll bridges did, the world that I was born into held it as a sacred principle that the Government must not do anything that private profiteering enterprise could and would tackle. When I reached the age which was in my particular case the age of indiscretion, I was ripe for the discussion of the question why my father should pay a halfpenny to cross a cheap metal footbridge and yet be allowed to use the much more expensive and handsome stone bridges, with their roadways for horse and foot, for nothing. On reflection it became clear that my father did not enjoy the use of the public bridge for nothing: he was rated by the City Corporation for the cost of its maintenance; but his share of that cost was much less than a halfpenny a crossing, and less troublesomely collected. Thus there was Capitalism on one bridge and Communism on others a few hundred yards off, with Communism providing very superior accommodation at a lower price.

The further question why under these circumstances Communism should be abhorred as abominable and Capitalism extolled as the source of all prosperity was naturally raised by Karl Marx and other social philosophers. It was taken up in London by a little group of young people more or less of my own sort, who called themselves the Fabian Society. I joined it, and so provided myself with abler colleagues who filled up the gaps left in my culture by my exclusively aesthetic education, which nevertheless qualified me to impose on them histrionically as a capable platform leader and literary spokesman. One of them, Sidney Webb by name, greatly my superior in political knowledge, administrative experience, and that miraculous power of quick assimilation and unfailingly memorized mind storage which distinguishes Newtons and Napoleons, and in which I was and am wretchedly deficient, started such an avalanche of examples of the enormous economy and immensely widened scope of public enterprise with all its governmental powers and fiscal resources, that before the Fabian Society was ten years old *Laisser-faire* was knocked on the head, and a Socialist program imposed on the ultra-individualist Liberal Party even before Gladstone was in his grave.

This notable success achieved by the first generation of Fabians missed its mark very disappointingly. To make it available for the proletariat, for whose benefit it was intended, it seemed necessary to have Labor represented in Parliament by a new and independent party. Webb and I produced a tract entitled A Plan of Campaign for Labor; but its execution required money on a scale that was beyond the means of the little knot of Fabian Socialists. Only the Trade Unions could levy it easily. Webb, the first serious historian of Trade Unionism, had made its leaders "class conscious" as such, and thereby won their confidence and respect. He enlisted them in the new party readily enough, and even persuaded some of them to call themselves Socialists; but enlistment did not include conversion;

and when the new party won its footing in parliament in 1906 and soon ousted the Liberal Party as the official Opposition and in due time reached the Treasury Bench with a Prime Minister who had begun as a most intransigent Socialist, it was as a Labor Party which was only nominally Socialist. Its front benches denounced the Russian Communist revolution as virulently as any Die Hard.

The Conservative Party became so completely convinced that under the Labor Government nothing revolutionary would happen —indeed that nothing at all would happen—that it actually adopted the one-time intransigent Socialist leader as its own puppet leader. The Liberal Party very properly established salaries for members of parliament; but the effect was to make the House of Commons more and more an almshouse for retired Trade Union secretaries who called themselves Socialists only when they were told to, without knowing what the word meant. The supposed conversion of Britain to constitutional Socialism by the Fabian Society made even less change than the conversion of the Roman Empire to Christianity by Constantine. The triumph was not to the Fabian Society but to the dead Disraeli, who as Conservative leader had taken the first serious step in the enfranchisement of the proletariat, then called the working class, because in his early days as a revolutionist to whom the House of Commons refused a hearing ("The day will come when you shall hear me" was his slogan) he had learnt that the bulwarks of Conservatism were not in frivolous Mayfair but in poverty-stricken Mile End. The more the franchise was extended the more hopeless the situation became, until at last, when complete adult suffrage was consummated by the enfranchisement of women, votes for everybody made the oligarchical Victorian parliaments of Disraeli and Gladstone seem hotbeds of revolution compared to the parliaments of Baldwin and Ramsay MacDonald.

Now the negative side of this is accounted for by the general paralysis of parliament established by Sunderland's trick at the end of the seventeenth century. But other things were happening with very positive consequences. Not in England alone had the Socialist movement been side-tracked into a movement for the establishment of Labor Parties in parliament. The European lead had been taken by the German Social-Democratic Party in the Reichstag, captained by Wilhelm Liebknecht and August Bebel. But when, at an International Socialist Congress, Bebel, the most fluent orator in Europe, boasted of the electoral triumphs of his party, Jaurès, the French Socialist leader, equally eloquent but more concise, said, "If we had all those votes and seats in France, something would happen." As nothing parliamentary happened either in Germany or anywhere else, the proletariat became more and more disappointed and disgusted with parliamentary government without understanding what was the matter with it. Anarchists, Syndicalists, and Guild Socialists, crushed by Fabianism, raised their heads again and were able to shew that militant city mobs were more feared by despots than parliamentary Labor Parties by the Capitalist oligarchy. Despotic dictators came into fashion as fast as Lib-Lab prime ministers lost face. Peter the Great building a new capital city on the Neva; Napoleon sweeping out Augean stables, breaking rusty chains, draining marshes, making roads for world traffic, and opening a career to the talents in a blaze of revolutionary glory; his nephew Haussmanizing Paris and Mussolini rebuilding Rome; Primo de Rivera and Hitler covering their countries with up-to-date roads, were contrasted with the British parliament's helpless inability to build a bridge over the Severn, and the impotence of Liebknecht and Bebel under the heel first of Bismarck and then of the Kaiser. No parliament could either abolish unemployment, the most dreaded affliction of the proletariat, or treat the unemployed decently. The climax came in Russia, where Socialism and Democracy at last achieved real power by making the little fingers of its police thicker than the Tsar's loins, proving the wisdom of Ruskin's "old Tory" prevision that social salvation must involve, not less government and more liberty, but just the reverse. Adolf Hitler and Benito Mussolini found, as Cromwell had found before them, that with a New Model army, well paid, and a network of local prefects chosen by themselves and backed by this army (major-generals in effect), they could get anything they wanted done, and sweep all parliamentary recalcitrants into the dustbin, alive or dead. To the people it seemed that the dictators could fulfil their promises if they would, and that the parliamentary parties could not even if they would. No wonder the plebiscites always gave the dictators majorities of ninety-five per cent and upwards.

But the dictators were not so absolute as they seemed. The plutocrats were still masters of the situation, stronger and much richer than ever. For they had learnt the Fabian lesson and turned it to their own account. It is true that they understood their Capitalism as a system as little as the Labor Parties understood Socialism. But they needed no change of heart nor economic learning to convince them that by merely following their noses on the slot of profits they could become enormously richer and irresistibly more powerful by abandoning *Laisser-faire* and substituting State organization and State revenue for competing private firms and private savings. The gains had been earmarked by the Fabians for the benefit of the proletariat; but Providence was not a party to this arrangement; and State production and saving was as available for Pharaoh as for Fabius (or Shavius). The dictators, beginning as Socialists, were shot at and imprisoned until they could lay their hands on money enough to raise a New Model army in black or brown shirts; and just as the old Fabians had to become the instruments of the Trade Unionists and be politically extinguished by them after being exploited by them to get into Parliament, the dictators had to become the instruments of the plutocrats to get the funds without which Adolf Hitler was not dictating but lying in the street with the bullets of the plutocrats whistling over him.

And so it has been that when I began my political career the cry of the Capitalists to the State was "Hands off industry; hands off agriculture; hands off banking, shipping, mining; off everything but foreign policy and police protection of private property." When I assumed the necessity of land nationalization at a meeting of the British Association in Bath in 1888, Henry Sidgwick, a professor of political economy and ethics who had never before been known to lose his temper or raise his voice, sprang up and cried out that advocacy of land nationalization was advocacy of crime, and he would not countenance it by his presence. Thereupon he not only left the platform but actually slammed the door behind him violently. I have never been able to persuade those of his friends who were not present that he was capable of such an explosion; but the word nationalization acted as a detonator on this mildest of men.

Nowadays the Capitalist cry is "Nationalize what you like; municipalize all you can; turn the courts of justice into courts martial and your parliaments and corporations into boards of directors with your most popular mob orators in the chair, provided the rent, the interest, and the profits come to us as before, and the proletariat still gets nothing but its keep."

This is the great corruption of Socialism which threatens us at present. It calls itself Fascism in Italy, National Socialism (Nazi for short) in Germany, New Deal in the United States, and is clever enough to remain nameless in England; but everywhere it means the same thing: Socialist production and Unsocialist distribution. So far, out of the frying-pan into the fire. For though Fascism (to call State

Capitalism by its shortest name) has doled out some substantial benefits to the proletariat and given bureaucratic status to functionaries who were formerly only casual employees, besides tightening up the public services and preaching a worship of the State (called Totalitarianism) which will lead logically to genuine Socialism, it has produced a world war in which Anglo-American Fascism fights German and Italian Fascism because Fascism is international whilst the capitalists are still intensely national; for when Germany proposes to fashify the whole earth under the Führership of Adolf Hitler, and Italy the same under Benito Mussolini, the Anglo-American Fascists will see Germany and Italy damned before they will accept any Fascism that is not of their own making under their own Führers. They fight the foreigner as their forbears fought Napoleon when he aimed at a United States of Europe with the Buonaparte family and his marshals, especially those married to his sisters, in local command. The Fascists are further divided into those who want to fit Fascism into the old revolution-proof parliamentary Party System, and those who realize that Fascism involves new institutions because it cannot develop without swiftly active and efficient government, and must therefore get rid of the Party System and of civil services immobilized like ours with its traditions, its inertia, its rampart of irresponsible committees, and the security it offers to routineers who cannot move with the times.

If these purblind belligerents understood their position, or even had learnt the rudiments of politics, they would combine against the genuine democratic socialism of the U.S.S.R., and settle their own differences afterwards when they came to partition Russia among themselves. As it is, western Fascists are combining with Russia to destroy the central and mid-southern Fascists, and with Communist China to defeat Capitalist Japan.

Such contradictions and confusions will finally sort themselves out, and the belligerents fight for their own sides, plutocracy against democracy, Fascism against Communism; but Socialist production will suit both. How then is the citizen to distinguish between Fascist Socialism and Communist Socialism in daily practice? How, when he hands over a considerable share of his income to the rate collector and the tax-gatherer to be used productively as industrial capital, can he be assured that its yield will return to him in services, goods, wages or all three, and not be given to privileged spendthrifts to enable them to live unproductively in luxury at his expense? If he is himself one of the spendthrifts, or, hoping to become one of them, is willing to take his chance under Fascism, how can he enjoy the contrary assurance?

These demands cannot be satisfied by theorems in general terms, demonstrating the relative merits of the old Liberal *Laisser-faire* Capitalism, the new Fascist Capitalism, and Democratic Communism. When Fascist parties and Communist parties are advocating the same measures of municipalization and nationalization, the same substitutions of public for private capital and control so that it is agreed on all sides that a new mine cannot be opened nor a new big liner launched without State aid; when farmers and agricultural laborers as we know them are swept away by a wave of collective farming; when even *Laisser-faire* is no longer distinguishable from Lenin's "new economic policy" (N.E.P.) of 1921: in short, when the means are the same and the ends as distinct as black from white, theories will not help voters: they must have some knowledge of how corruption works in practice or they will soon find themselves voting their own heads off.

CHAPTER XXXI

MUNICIPAL CORRUPTION

MUNICIPAL corruption is at present rife and unashamed. The more corrupt it is, the more votes it gains. Now corruption cannot flourish as such. The bribery and jobbery which we associate with the word corruption are condemned by everybody. But they are negligible in comparison with the main swindle of municipal profiteering, which in our economic ignorance we are unable to distinguish from legitimate private profiteering. The more profit a municipality makes the more its enterprise is applauded.

Now a municipality should not make profits. In some instances it cannot, because its services are enjoyed by everyone without direct payment. Street lighting, paving, police protection, fire brigades, main drainage, water supply, cost a good deal; but they are paid for by rates imposed on all residents without regard to their individual use of the services. Their continual clamor to keep down the rates restrains the municipality from overcharging them. But when the municipality provides dwelling houses, electric light, gas, baths and wash-houses for private ablution and laundry, supplying them only to the actual immediate users and charging them individually for the service, then it is possible to charge more than the service costs as private companies do, and come out of the transaction with a profit. And what more customary and obvious when the profit is made than to hand it over to the Finance Committee to reduce the rates and appease the clamorers for such reduction?

But this is a corrupt proceeding. For instance, if I live on a County Council estate, paying the Council my rent and my electric lighting bill, and if the excess of what I pay above the cost to the Council is deducted from the rates levied from neighbors who light their privately owned houses with lamps and candles, then I am clearly being overcharged for their benefit, and in effect exploited and robbed by them.

Theoretically the remedy is simple. Do not overcharge: supply the service at cost price. Practically it is not so simple. Even when the municipality honestly keeps its charges down to the lowest figure on the safe side (and from commercial habit it is apt to do just the opposite), there is always a profit, minimum or maximum. The accounts, too, are complicated by the fact that the swindled consumers and the benefited ratepayers are to a considerable extent the same persons. Even when this does not balance the account it may still be highly desirable from the point of view of the public welfare to overcharge gentlefolk who live in squares to ease the poverty of proletarians who have to live in slums. A municipality may honestly make a profit on its swings to meet a loss on its roundabouts. Where mischievous inequalities of income exist, any arrangement that tends to equalize them is defensible. But here again we can approve only on condition that the municipality understands what it is doing. Mostly it doesnt. Being manned and womaned by people who are experienced in private business and utterly untaught politically, it takes it as a matter of course that profit should be maximized and made the test of success in municipal trading as in private trading. Those who insist that there should be no commercial profit are dismissed as unpractical theorists and dreamers.

All municipal profiteers can plead the example of the national Post Office. It carries my letters and postcards for me, and telegraphs my messages; but whereas it once carried my letters for a penny, my postcards for a halfpenny, and my messages for sixpence, I am now charged twopence halfpenny, twopence, and a shilling, with the result that a profit is made and used to reduce the income tax.

In my case it does not matter because, though I send many letters and postcards and telegrams, I also pay income tax; but it matters a good deal to a woman whose income is too small to be taxed, and who cannot send a letter to her absent relatives without paying the, to her, serious sum of twopence halfpenny to have it carried and delivered for her. As things stand at present it would be fairer to frank the few letters of the proletarians who pay no income tax directly (their underpaid labor pays most of it indirectly) and throw the cost on to the surtax.

These complications will disappear when and if genuine democratic Socialism equalizes incomes. As this comes nearer and nearer, public profiteering will become less and less excusable. When it is virtually accomplished, the rule must be to supply at cost price, the cost not to include profit.

Cost price, easily determinable by a shopkeeper, is not so simple for a manufacturer. When the Four Years War and the disastrous failure of private enterprise to keep the army supplied with munitions cost us thousands of lives and daily defeats in Flanders, the Government had to choose between making munitions itself in national factories and losing the war. It at once discovered that the private firms were overcharging monstrously, not only because they were charging as much as they could get without regard to any other consideration than that their duty to their shareholders and to themselves was to get as much as possible, but because they did not know in detail what their operations were costing, and did not care provided the dividends were satisfactory. The Government had to ascertain the price at which every material item could be bought in the cheapest market, and compel the private firms to charge for it at that price plus a fixed rate of profit sufficient to keep the firms in existence. It thus compelled them to ascertain their costings and keep account of them for the first time, which so vastly improved their business methods that when the war broke out again after a twenty-year armistice they were in a much stronger position.

Now cost of production is finally what it costs the producers to live and work and reproduce their kind, meanwhile making good all wear and tear of machinery and tools and providing spare subsistence for the establishment of new industrial adventures and experiments. And this is not a fixed figure. It varies from sex to sex, from age to age, from town to country. The fluctuations of supply and demand in the labor market may depress it below subsistence level, shewn by a high infant mortality and the shortening of adult life, or raise it to heights at which, as at the present moment, a few lucky boys are earning £12 a week for unskilled labor, journalists a dollar a word for ephemeral newspaper articles, surgeons sums of three figures for operations lasting an hour, and playwrights £20,000 for a film scenario. At the same moment the boy's parents may be living on less than quarter his wage; and the markets may be crowded with fabrics made by Chinese and Japanese workers who live on a penny an hour.

Consequently when a municipality makes a commercial profit there are other claimants for it beside the ratepayers. Municipal scavengers, who when I was a councillor were paid eighteen shillings a week, are now paid four times as much. The employees who are organized in trade unions not only secure higher wages when their sort of labor is scarce, but when it is plentiful refuse to be impoverished by uncontrolled operation of supply and demand, and claim "a moral minimum" wage to enable them to maintain their customary standard of living.

Under such circumstances the question of the cost of production includes the question of the worker's standard of living. What is the optimum standard of living within the limits of our resources, actual or possible? When reproached on the strength of fantastic newspaper reports for being a millionaire wallowing in luxury, I have always replied that nobody can ask less to live on than I. Give me a convenient flat in town and a comfortable villa in the country with a few acres of lawn and garden, a couple of cars for long and short distance travel, and a supply of pocket-money not necessarily exceeding a couple of thousand pounds, and there is not a more contented man on earth than I.

This passes off as a characteristic Shavian joke; and I enjoy the fun it makes; but the real joke is that I am quite in earnest. To enable me to devote myself entirely to my professional work I have everything else done for me as if I were a baby. Those who do it for me must also have their incomes to live on; and this I have to provide out of what I call my pocket-money. I can only hope I am worth the work they have to do to take care of me and of themselves. Mr Wells's estimate of £4000 as a minimum income is laughed at as long as it is thought of as the means of a single person. If you think of it as the family income of a citizen earning it by the exercise of a profession or craft which occupies all his or her working time and energy, your laughter will fade out, as Ecclesiastes puts it, "like the crackling of thorns under a pot." All the breadwinners' domestic work has to be done for them and paid for by them: they have not time to make their own clothes, bake their own muffins, cook their own meals, roll their own lawns, dig their own gardens, nor even polish their own shoes and make their own beds. I say nothing about their having to support and educate their children, besides surrendering an enormous percentage of their incomes to ground landlords who in return give them nothing but permission to live on the earth, because these are charges which may conceivably be undertaken by a Socialist State; but even when relieved from them the £4000 a year may have to support not one person only but half a dozen directly and a row of shops indirectly and partially. The £4000 a year per family becomes at most £600 per head. This may seem affluence to a laborer who is expected to bring up a family on £104 (when he can get it); but no State can be highly civilized with a majority of its citizens in such poverty: it needs family incomes of at least £15 a week, and must get them produced by hook or crook. It simply cannot afford £2 standards.

These figures are of course only suggestive in terms of present standards of living. Municipal trading and national and supernational organization, supplying subsistence at cost price with the natural sources of production communized, may reduce prices to a degree at which two units of a possibly duodecimalized currency will be ample for what we should now call a quite handsome way of living. For instance, if transport were communized (we should erroneously call it "free") and most of the things which everybody uses or benefits by were to be had for the asking, people would resent having to carry coins and notes about with them or calling at the bank as often as at present. Relieved of such bothers we should all live like gentlefolks without the intolerable boredom and demoralization of having no useful work to occupy us.

What, then, should the municipalities do for their constituents? What should they charge for it? How much revenue should be spent in wages and how much sacrificed to cheapening services? Should consumers be overcharged for them or undercharged at the expense of the whole body of ratepayers? Such questions cannot be understood, much less answered, by councillors without the special knowledge and capacity needed for intelligent dealing with them. I was expected to answer them in council with a collection of local shopkeepers, licensed victuallers (publicans), builders, auctioneers, and the like, with an occasional doctor or two and a Methodist minister, I being a playwright. Our ablest leaders were a greengrocer and a bootmaker, both of them much more capable than most members of Parliament; for it needs considerable character and ability to succeed as a shopkeeper, especially as a publican, whereas persons with unearned money enough can easily get into Parliament without having ever succeeded in anything. I found them excellent company, and liked and respected them for their personal qualities. In the hands of a town clerk or mayor who happened to be a Richelieu they could have achieved notable feats of municipal enterprise, and had in fact proved this in the past. But Richelieus occur seldom and are not immortal. And without a Richelieu we were absurdly unequal to the magnitude of our task of making the best of the local government of a quarter million people. Such training and education as we had was for private and personal profiteering, not for public welfare work. Not only could we not solve our problems: we did not know they existed. Of those that circumstances forced on us we knew only one side. I, a Fabian permeator, knew the questions and had doctrinaire answers ready for some of them; and my friend the Methodist minister (the late Ensor Walters) was a spiritual force that always acted in the right direction; but in the effective lump we were as ignorantly helpless politically as the mob of ratepayers who elected us, and who would never have elected me had they had the faintest suspicion of my ultimate political views.

In such conditions corruption was unconscious and automatic. It was practised with the best intentions in perfect honesty. The situation was often saved by the famous English intuitive wisdom so accurately observed and described by my friend Keyserling in his book on Europe fourteen years ago. We "muddled through." Keyserling, by the way, is a Baltic baron who has none of the Irish prejudices which make me a biased witness. He set up a university of wisdom in Darmstadt which was badly needed in St Pancras (my constituency). Now I know very well that the rational practice and training which my colleagues lacked, and which they mistrusted and even hated when they came up against it, sometimes leads to grave error when intuitive wisdom jumps instantly to the right conclusion. I have sufficient intellectual faculty and practice to laugh at the Jacobin delusion that reason is infallible. Intellect can blunder disastrously; but so can intuition when it is ignorant. Neither of them can reach sound conclusions without authentic facts; and if the known facts are too few, or, being imaginary, are not facts at all, the inferences and guesses will be alike unsound. Besides, facts do not always lead to reasoned inferences. They may provoke vindictive resentments, sentimental leniencies, hopes and fears, prejudices and cupidities, leading to explosions of emotion that sweep reason from minds that have not had stern judicial training and natural judicial consciences. Competent municipal councillors must be taught and trained as well as born.

All municipal corruption, however, is not innocent, though it is mostly too childish to matter much. And it is—at least within my experience—never straightforward, being usually expected and accepted as a customary perquisite rather than as a bribe. I should be surprised and incredulous if I were told that a contractor seeking the job of building municipal baths and wash-houses, electric power works or the like, had called on the chairman of the municipal committee in charge of the matter, and promised him £50 in cash if his tender was accepted. Both the contractor and the chairman would consider such a transaction as grossly corrupt. But if it were an established practice for contractors, on their being selected for a municipal job, to present the chairman with a service of silver plate (having covered its cost in his estimate, but not explicitly), the chairman could accept it with a clear conscience as a perquisite; and the contractor, to whom it had cost nothing, would thenceforth be *persona grata* at the municipality when tenders were under consideration.

Or suppose some big growing business wants to gain more space by having a street closed. It does not distribute ten-pound notes among the municipal councillors. Its manager gets elected to the municipality, and makes himself popular by entertaining his colleagues at banquets where champagne flows like water, besides being always ready with a subscription to this or that good cause in which the councillors are interested. A conviction soon spreads that the street in question is useless, dangerous, and ought to be abolished. It is closed; and the manager thereupon disappears from public life, and is seen no more in his aldermanic gown.

But it is not among councillors that corruption is rife. It is the employees who have to be watched. Everywhere the ordinary citizen, politically uneducated and undisciplined as he is, regards public service, not as a responsible job which it is his duty and his point of personal honor to make the best of without respect of persons (including his own), but as a sinecure in which his official dignity obliges him to be insolent to the public. Any disappointment of his expectation of having nothing to do disposes him to exact additional payment from the citizens for whom he has to do it. How this view percolates down from the haughtiest jobbers to the humblest municipal employees came to my notice early in my career as a propagandist of municipal Socialism.

One Sunday morning I walked in a public park in a provincial capital, and was pleased to see that the municipality had provided a dressing-room for the footballers and cricketers who played there. I went into this dressing-room to inspect it, and found myself witnessing a lively altercation between the municipal custodian of the room and a footballer who had not tipped him. The custodian made no secret of his expectations. He demanded loudly in the hearing of all present whether the player thought he could come there and use the place "without leaving something". And the only defence the player made was that he could not leave anything because he had nothing to leave. Thereupon he was told roundly that if he had no money he had no right to use the dressing-room. And this seemed to be the general opinion, including that of the supposed delinquent, who evidently did not know that he had only to complain to the municipality to have the custodian sacked for demanding bribes. This was the remarkable part of the business. Nobody present except myself had any conception of communal institutions. No doubt some of the footballers who had tipped or were going to tip the custodian, though they were poor enough themselves, were quite willing to pay a trifle for the exclusion of the absolutely penniless; but neither they nor the custodian himself saw anything dishonest or anti-social in the transaction. No doubt if a police constable had refused to allow them to walk through a main street of their city unless they tipped him, they would have been scandalized, because they were unused to such demands and thought of a street, however well lighted, paved, swept, and policed, as a gratuity of nature, like sunlight or rain water; but they had always paid someone for a dressing-room, and therefore regarded the grafter-custodian as quite in order.

That this limitation is by no means confined to the masses who have had no secondary education was shewn by a ridiculous incident which occurred during the premiership of the late Ramsay Mac-Donald. He had recommended a friend of his, on quite good grounds, for a baronetcy, which was accordingly conferred. Somebody then discovered that MacDonald's friend had once made him a present of a motor car. There was a tremendous fuss about it, rightly enough; for a Prime Minister should not accept costly presents from anyone who could conceivably have interested motives. Poor

Ramsay, who had not thought of this aspect of the affair and was quite innocent of any corrupt intention, had to get rid of his car. But the fuss was not about the valid point. What agitated the newspapers and the public was whether a Socialist (Ramsay professed himself a Socialist) could consistently with his principles own a motor car. A Socialist, they believed, was a sort of Franciscan who stripped off his gentlemanly clothes, sold all that he had, and threw the price into the street to be scrambled for by the poor. Apparently, if MacDonald had not professed himself a Socialist, he might have owned a dozen motor cars, all presented to him by prominent figures in the honors list, without being blamed in the least.

Anthony Trollope, a noted nineteenth-century novelist, was also an industrious civil servant. His literary model and hero was Thackeray. In spite of his reverence for Thackeray, Trollope was scandalized by the shameless persistence with which Thackeray tried to get a sinecure as such. If a man of Thackeray's mental calibre accepted sinecures as a natural part of our political routine the attitude of less brainy citizens can be imagined. A post in the Civil Service ("under Government" it was called) was a thing to be procured by a nobleman for his worn-out butler to save the expense of pensioning him, or given to a Parliamentary careerist whose eloquence or debating skill made him indispensable in Parliament. At last the abuse became intolerable in our island, where the present system of selection by competitive examination was instituted.

But the old system, and the public conception of it, still prevails. In the south of Europe, States can still be found in which every civil servant steals the salary of his immediate subordinate, who does the same until the bottom is reached and the lowest official has no one beneath him to steal from. He therefore refuses to perform his duties, or to abstain from performing them, unless he is tipped.

This ultimate device is by no means confined to the lowest officials: it is obviously open to the higher ones also. During the Crimean war a leading building contractor and timber merchant was driving through a Midland city with his wife. They passed one of his yards, where a huge store of timber was "eating its head off." The appalling sufferings of the soldiers at the front were just then coming to light and creating a wave of public indignation. The merchant's wife, who had been reading the papers, said, "Why not use the wood to make huts for the soldiers?" The merchant took the hint, and succeeded in planting much of his wood on our ally Napoleon III.

In due course he needed the price of his timber, but found it impossible to get it without going to Paris to collect it. He was received there by the responsible minister with the greatest civility, and was assured that the money was ready and would be at his disposal when certain formalities were complete. But the formalities seemed to be endless; for the merchant's visits produced nothing; and he was becoming seriously embarrassed when one day he met another leading contractor, who was an older hand at dealing with governments. On hearing of his friend's plight he asked, "Have you done the needful?" "What is the needful?" said the merchant. "A hundred-pound note dropped accidentally on the minister's desk, and forgotten when you leave" was the reply.

The merchant followed this instruction at his next visit, and at once received his cheque, which had been in the minister's desk all the time.

I once described to a philosopher from the south of Europe how a certain mining company seeking a concession there complained of having had to bribe a host of small people to get the business put through. He said the company did not understand how to do it: if it had bribed handsomely at the top there would have been no trouble with the smaller fry. When I was a child I heard my grandfather say that no man, however highly placed, could refuse a five-pound note if you crackled it under his nose; and though this old-fashioned Irish figure needs considerable correction for richer countries and modern money values, I still regard by grandfather's generalization as sound enough to be a useful guide in business.

Let nobody suppose, by the way, that corruption and jobbery are peculiar to the public services, municipal or central. In a plutocracy like ours every grade of the social structure inevitably gets worm-eaten by the tipping system. The first Lord Russell of Killowen in the course of his experience as barrister and judge was so scandalized by its prevalence and the mischiefs attending it that he initiated the Act prohibiting secret commissions and the like. But such Acts are of little use if neither of the affected parties will set it in motion. Were pickpockets and their victims to agree not to call the police, picking pockets would become a privileged custom, and as such, be practised by the multitudes of normally honest people to whom morality is nothing but custom. When palm oil lubricates business as other oils lubricate machinery, proficiency in its use is one of the necessary qualifications of the man of business.

In my sixteenth year an emergency made me very precociously

cashier-in-chief (there was no other) to a leading estate agent in Dublin. It was part of my duty to pay the metropolitan shopping bills of our country clients. I began by calling at the shops on my way from the bank, and paying them across the counter. To my surprise I was handed a percentage on the amount of the bill. Being then the greenest of innocents, I astonished the shopkeepers by refusing the tip. I did this not in the least because I had any scruple against being paid twice over for the same service. I did not think of it in that way. It was my class snobbery that could not brook the indignity of tips from shopkeepers. I stopped calling on them, and left them to call on me for their money.

This was before I had studied economics and learnt from Karl Marx that a tip does not under our system add to the tippee's income, as in his competitive struggle for employment at wages enough to live on he asks only enough to maintain his standard of living. If tips are to be had as well as wages or salary he reduces his demand accordingly, even to the extent of taking the place without any wage or actually paying for it. Besides, he has to tip others. The steward on a liner lives mostly on tips from the passengers; but he has to tip in the cook's department for speedy service. Tipping is virtually compulsory in a competitive system. It is sometimes compulsory by law: in Austria for example an untipped hotel waiter has a lien on the defaulter's luggage and can detain it until he is satisfied; and ten per cent is so customary that a cloakroom attendant will give change out of a tip when the proffered coin exceeds that figure. This convention relieves the tipper of all uncertainty and embarrassment as to how much he should give; but it also excludes both generosity and gratitude from the transaction; so in England we prefer to leave the amount uncertain and the gift legally if not really voluntary. The Englishman likes to feel generous and to be gratefully served; but before he has become an experienced traveller he suffers agonies of uncertainty as to when, whom, and how much to tip; and the tippee has no legal security for the price of his services. Add to this that in the long run tippees are no better off than their fellows who have no personal contacts with their customers and therefore get no tips, and you will understand why all the wisest leaders in attempts to organize waiters, stewards, taxi-cab drivers and tippees generally in trade unions are against the tipping system and would like to see their constituents refusing tips as haughtily as I did in my cashiering nonage, and demanding full standard wages instead.

When I broke loose from my cashier's desk and with desperate imprudence jumped overboard into the literary market in London only to find that nobody would publish my attempts at writing books, I made my living for some years as a critic of literature, painting, music, and the theatre. My good word was of some value then; but no painter, picture dealer, music seller, composer, actor, or manager ever offered me cash down for a favorable notice. One innocent youth in the provinces sent me a patent tobacco pipe with a letter asking me to be kind to his brother, to whom he was deeply attached, and who had taken to the stage as a profession. He had failed to ascertain that I do not smoke. I was touched by his brotherly devotion, and would certainly have paid a little special attention to the case if I had ever seen the brother acting or remembered his name. The methods of the theatre managers were less crude. They would consult me as an expert on the advisability of producing some foreign play of which they had purchased the performing rights. If I thought well of it, would I translate it and sell the option of performing my translation within six months, for, say, £50? If I had made a translation of some noted foreign play, preferably a French one, I believe I could have made a hundred a year by selling an option on it twice a year. One eminent actor-manager offered to accept an original play of mine, not committing himself to a date for production, but intimating that if at any time I desired an advance on account of royalties it could be arranged. At his theatre on every first night the stage was cleared after the performance for a banquet at which it was a coveted privilege to be a guest. The critics were invited discreetly by the box office chief as they entered. I always accepted the invitation as a courteous tribute to my influence; but I never went.

In the picture market nobody ever offered me hard cash, directly or indirectly, for a favorable notice. The picture dealers had personal contacts with the critics on the days they set apart for the Press before the opening of their exhibitions; and the older hands were experts in the art of personally humbugging reporters who, being only newsmen who could not tell a Greco from a Guido or a Frith from a Burne-Jones at sight, got on by praising the eminent painters and ignoring the beginners unless they were talked by the dealer into believing that his latest speculation in a beginner's work was the discovery of a new genius. At my first appearance at these "Press Views" I was addressed very flatteringly by a famous dealer, now long deceased, who expatiated to me rapturously on the marvellous qualities of half a dozen respectable but quite ordinary sketches in water-color by an unknown painter. I listened gravely and then said "Mr —: how can you talk such nonsense to Me? You know better." Without turning a hair he beckoned me confidentially and said, "Come with me" and led me to a private room in which he kept a few real treasures by old masters: mostly primitives.

His chief contemporary and rival in picture dealing, also long since passed away, had a subtler method. He invited me to see the latest picture by a well-known painter, and received me not very genially, like a man disgusted with the popular taste in art. "Oh!" he said, "Youve come to see this. Here it is. Pish! It is what you people like; and we have to provide it for you. Now here [pointing to a picture quite inconspicuously hung] is a picture to my taste worth ten of it. But it means nothing to you: you wouldnt know the painter's name if I told it to you. Look at his handling! Look at that sky. But you gentlemen of the Press pass it by without a glance." Of course the reporters who did not know chalk from cheese in painting would hasten to shew their connoisseurship by "writing up" the neglected genius for all they were worth. I was not taken in; but I had not the heart to spoil the old man's comedy by telling him so. I was soon recognized as a qualified critic and admitted to the inner fellowship that exists between the genuine critics and the dealers who are real connoisseurs. In that circle the tricks of the trade were dropped, with the result that many of the best critics knew nothing of the humbug and corruption practised on newsmen employed by editors who were ignorant of art and impatient of the convention that obliged their papers to notice it. They sent their worst and wordiest reporters to the galleries, the theatre, and the opera, reserving their best for political meetings and the criminal courts.

However, the relations of critics with dealers do not cover the whole field of possible corruption. I was never bribed by a dealer, and after my first appearances never humbugged. But I once gave up a valuable appointment as picture critic to a prominent weekly journal because I was asked to write flattering notices of the pictures painted by the proprietor's friends regardless of their merits, the argument being that as I was welcome to do the same for my own personal friends, I could not be so churlish as to refuse to do as much for my employer. Later on I obtained an equally desirable appointment, but had to give that up also, because the proprietress of the paper insisted on interpolating over my signature ecstatic little raptures about minor Academy pictures by painters who invited her to tea at their studios.

In the musical world no direct bribes ever came my way, nor did I ever hear of any. All I can say is that at the Opera as in the theatres and all other places of public entertainment it was far easier and pleasanter to praise everything, flatter everybody, and say nothing about shortcomings, than to write the critical truth. At the Opera my easygoing colleagues in the foyer between the acts would expatiate indignantly on the demerits of the new world-famous Italian tenor with the voice of a newspaper crier and the manners of a trooper who was that night proving himself utterly unpresentable in London as an adequate Manrico or Lohengrin. The conductor would have been in his proper place among the second violas; the cuts made in the score were unpardonable Vandalisms; the work was only half rehearsed or perhaps not rehearsed at all; in the love duet the soprano was sharp and the tenor flat all through; the Wagner Leitmotifs were phrased one way by the strings, another by the brass, and yet another by the wood-wind so that no one could recognize them as the same; the leaders of the chorus were in their seventh or eighth decades, almost voiceless and never in the middle of the note, but indispensable because they were "good starters," and so on through the series of impostures and makeshifts which make the Opera a hell for composers and for critics who know. "You must really shew this up," the easygoers would say to me. But they did not shew it up themselves. By their accounts the performances shone with all the brilliancy of the diamonds with which the ladies in the grand tier boxes were decked to advertize the riches of their financier husbands. Complaisant critics were welcomed in the theatre even when all the stalls were sold out and they had to be content as "rovers" without allotted seats, sitting or standing about wherever they could. From the agents and henchmen of the favored prima donna of that day I received hints that not only were unlimited tickets for her concerts at my disposal for the asking, but that invitations to her delightful castle in Wales were not beyond possibility for a critic who could be depended on not to mention that she was no longer sure of her high F and preferred to transpose and make it E flat. I was never a guest at that castle, even after I had asked the lady's accompanist in what key she sang "Ah, non giunge." He took it as a threat of exposure if I were not invited.

And so it went. The incorruptible critics were tolerated because their articles, being readable and controversial, kept up public interest in the art which the managers were exploiting. A readable unfavorable notice is a better advertisement than an unreadable or at any rate unmemorable puff. Also no doubt Awe was at work here: an able and independent critic could win authority and prestige. And the complaisant critics were not all corrupt: they imposed on the public because they were themselves imposed on, not knowing that there was anything to complain of, nor, when they had picked up a little knowledge, being sure enough of it to have the courage of it, or skilled enough to know exactly what was wrong.

These experiences of mine have apparently nothing to do with municipal corruption. I cite them here only to shew that in our society a high standard of private morality is no guarantee of even a glimmer of public conscientiousness. In the literary professions our social pretensions and our educational qualifications, combined with our specific talents, were held to be superior to those of the traders and shopkeepers who dominate municipal morals. But we were in fact utterly shameless in expecting and accepting favors from people whom we could advertize. If we did not take undisguised bribes in money we took money's worth without a blush. In an Italian city the manager of the fashionable hotel where I asked for rooms begged me to occupy his best suite as the honorary guest of the hotel for as long as I pleased. In other cases I had to dispute charges that were obviously nominal, and insist on full prices. And this was so customary that the most respectable journalists exploited it as a matter of course, and paid their way by puffs. They claimed discounts in shops and free admission to entertainments as a right, and would have been astonished and outraged if such proceedings were denounced as corrupt. They were not conscious delinquents. They had just not been politically educated.

In an honest world it would be a fundamental rule that justice and truth should not be bought nor sold, and that of all pernicious trades the trade in falsehood is the worst. In a commercialized world everything is bought and sold. The Catholic Church lost its hold on half Europe and provoked the Reformation by selling salvation. Judges no longer take presents from litigants as they used to do as a matter of course; but the bar is still venal, selling its services to the highest bidder with unfair advantage to the longest purse. This being so, is it surprising that municipal authorities have to stand on guard continually to protect their constituents from having to pay twice over, in tips and preferences as well as in rates, for all the services that its agents have power to render or neglect as they please? Payment twice over is the perquisite that few public employees can resist, especially as, being usually offered, it need not be explicitly exacted. Yet at no less solemn a temple than Napoleon's mausoleum in Paris, in the vestibule plastered with notices that tips are strictly forbidden, I have heard the attendants demanding them vociferously and abusively, just like the park official who enlightened my first preachings of municipal Socialism. No doubt they had competed for their jobs and were underpaid.

CHAPTER XXXII

COERCIONS AND SANCTIONS

WHEN dealing with the claims of the learned professions to be exempt from the prohibitions of the common law in their professional practice, and with their pleas that government itself in its treatment of criminals and its military activities has to organize and perpetrate the cruelties incidental to war and to the ancient and popular plan of securing the conventional behavior necessary to civilized society by dictation enforced by punishment for disobedience, I ruled out both punishment and cruelty from decent civilized practice, and thereby opened the question of what "sanctions" (as we now blasphemously call them) are to replace the smacking slipper, the cane, the birch, the bludgeon, the cat which disguises nine lashes as one, the prison, the gallows, the axe, the guillotine, the rack, the wheel, the stake, the slicing into a thousand pieces, the impalement, and all the other instruments of torture and homicide by which rulers enforce obedience to their decrees.

Let us carefully note to begin with that the abandonment of torture as a punishment, whether deterrent or vindictive, and of the death sentence as a penalty, does not involve what is commonly called the abolition of capital punishment. It does involve the abolition of punishment, but not of the capital sentence. The right to live in society is not unconditional: it cannot be conceded to persons who are unfit to live in civilized society and cannot be allowed to without wasting useful lives in restraining them. If a man is murderously violent we are not justified in turning his decent neighbor into a prison warder to keep him alive. If a woman is a poisoner or a vitriol-thrower no well-conducted woman should be wasted as a prison wardress for her sake. Such freaks should be pitied and painlessly killed without malice as a mad dog is killed. And so should all who are not worth their salt and are spoiling the lives of those who are worth their salt and a bit more, as all citizens must be if they are to deserve the respect and social consideration now given only to ladies and gentlemen.

This, then, is the final sanction that will never be abolished. The half thinkers who now wreck every discussion by proposing that we shall "reform the criminal" must be told, more or less patiently, to get out of the way or keep to the question; for a wrongdoer who can be reformed is not a congenital criminal and raises no problem: all we have to do is to reform him. He will then, if the operation has been really successful, make such amends for his misdeed as may be possible. The problem arises with the congenital criminal who cannot be reformed and cannot be tolerated. Let the reformers study methods of reform and they will soon drop the absurdity of trying to do it by inflicting cruel and malicious injuries on the culprit, and, having injured and exasperated him, turning him loose on society to commit more crimes.

Then there are people like Ibsen's Peer Gynt, who funk doing anything irrevocable, and will commit the horrible atrocity of imprisoning a human creature for life rather than mercifully kill him anaesthetically, and, if possible, without his knowing it. We can dispose of this phobia by pointing out to the abolitionists that a day's imprisonment is just as irrevocable as decapitation. If that does not silence them nothing will.

And now comes a conclusion that will take all Protestants aback. When we get rid of punishment and "judge not that we be not judged," admitting that two blacks cannot make a white, that Satan neither will nor can cast out Satan, and that after all Jesus was not quite the unpractical crank we have hitherto considered him, we shall have to revive the Inquisition. We need that institution very badly. It must be purged of the folly of punishment, but will probably have to commence operations by providing euthanasia for all our Torquemadas. Its capital function of getting rid of the unfit-to-live will revive all the more urgently when its old remedies that were worse than the disease are discarded. Its members should be selected from a panel of the highly qualified; for the question of life or death, though simple enough in crude cases of murderous violence or selfish unscrupulousness, may be difficult and subtle in cases of treason and heresy. But even if no such panels exist we shall have to do the best we can with whom we can get: the facts will not wait for the achievement of an ideal tribunal. Even a common jury is better than nothing. The Venetian Council of Ten, the Vehmgericht, the Star Chamber, the Politbureau with its Cheka, the Nazi Cabal with its Gestapo, the Ribbon Lodges and Ku-Klux-Klans, were and are all inquisitions; and it would be much simpler and more accurate to call them so instead of glorifying them as the old Inquisition was glorified by calling it the Holy Office.

The procedure, as far as we can foresee it, will be for the police to establish a capital case and bring the accused to trial by jury as usual; but the judge, instead of passing sentence, will report the case and the verdict to the Inquisition to consider whether the accused can safely be allowed to live at large in a civilized community. If the accused has married several times and his brides have all been found drowned in their baths, or burnt in the house stove, he will presently be found dead in his bed, having gone to sleep in perfect health expecting to wake as usual.

However painless euthanasia might be made by the Inquisition every citizen would know that it was waiting for the incorrigibly mischievous and dangerous. The convicted, knowing that the Inquisition was considering the case, could never go to bed with any certainty of being alive next morning. But this uncertainty would not concern the convicted only. It would concern everybody; for the question of fitness to live could be raised about anybody, whether an indictable crime had been committed or not. This would produce a sense of social responsibility which is not merely lacking at present but is actually discouraged and discredited by our clamorous insistence on our liberties as against the very still small voice in which we refer conventionally to our duties. Long ago I suggested that we should all be obliged to appear before a Board (virtually an inquisition) every five years, and justify our existence to its satisfaction on pain of liquidation. Quite lately I wrote a play called The Simpleton of the Unexpected Isles, ending with the Day of Judgment, which turned out to be a prosaic enquiry, on a fine summer morning without any apocalyptic terrors, into the question of whether we were pulling our weight in the social boat, followed by the mysterious disappearance of those who were not. But no London manager has yet thought the subject interesting enough to attract paying audiences. The recording angel would be described as a celestial Nosey Parker and resented and boycotted accordingly. Yet I cannot conceive a stable civilization without such an inquisitorial power and a constant general sense of responsibility to it. Nothing less can eradicate our carefully inculcated belief that labor is a curse, service a degradation, and gentility an inseparable attribute of opulent and unproductive leisure.

All cases, however, are not capital cases: that is, cases in which the right of the accused to live is in question. The American Declaration of Independence claims for every citizen the right to life, liberty, and the pursuit of happiness. But the gallows and the electric chair have made short work of the right to live; and the pursuit of happiness is the nearest way to frustration and suicide, happiness being a by-product of beneficial activity and comfortable circumstances. People so employed and circumstanced never bother about whether they are happy or not. Then what of liberty? Well, how much liberty? How little? Between life and death there are no degrees: between law and liberty there are many. Rousseau, whose Social Contract was the forerunner of the American Declaration, said that all men are born free: the most flagrant lie ever told by a sane man. All men are born helplessly dependent on their parents and guardians, and grow up to be dependent on their own labor, avoidable only by enslaving their neighbors. Every Government has to say to the vast majority of its citizens "Work or starve; for that is the Voice of Nature." And as nowadays few citizens can find work except as employees of an elaborate and costly industrial organization that is beyond their means the Government must find the work for them; whereupon the alleged right to liberty is knocked over by the discovery that without Socialism liberty means slavery or starvation; so away goes that liberty to live idly on the labor of others which is the main attraction of Capitalism.

Clearly, then, the Social Contract and the American Declaration are too thoughtless to be of any use to the Inquisition, which will be the final referee on the question of how much liberty a citizen can be entrusted with if he is good enough to be let live at all in civilized society. And it will have to deal with a considerable mass of people, now in prison as criminals, who, though unable to bear the responsibilities and withstand the temptations which beset normal freedom, can under special control and tutelage support themselves and live harmlessly useful lives without having to suffer any of the diabolical cruelties and privations now inflicted on them by our criminal code solely because Capitalist employers insist on their being made so miserable that their fellow proletarians will accept wretched wages and abject servitude rather than share their fate.

In Russia I have seen a humanely conducted convict settlement growing into a flourishing industrial centre because the convicts preferred to remain there after the expiration of their sentences of detention, just as many soldiers, who in the army have as nearly as possible no liberties at all, re-enlist and regard the expiration of their utmost term of service as the greatest misfortune that can happen to them. Even in British convict prisons the worst-behaved citizens are often the best-behaved prisoners. These exemplary prisoners should never be released; but they should be so humanely treated as never to desire release, and even to dread it. As we order things now, the "free" poor would all break windows to get into a humane prison; but there will be no danger of this when honest folk can be equally comfortable at large.

Nothing can limit the extension of public power over private life but an extension of individual power over collective power. If every individual could by a wave of the hand annihilate any force that the Government could bring against him, then Shakespear's vision of judicial Man as an angry ape dressed in a little brief authority would have no terrors; for his victims, without any authority at all, would be equally angry apes, quite as ready as any "pelting petty officer" to "use his heaven for thunder, nothing but thunder."

Let us look at the Utopias left us by our political prophets, and see whether they have been able to plan a perfect society without powers of life and death vested either in States or individuals.

Bulwer Lytton, a man of long political experience and outstanding literary eminence, has left us a Utopia entitled The Coming Race, in which every individual has an inborn power called Vril which can strike a dragon, or a dictator, or even an army dead. Consequently there are in that unfortunately fabulous land no dragons, no dictators, and an abhorrence of murder so overwhelming as to make it impossible. Mr H. G. Wells has written a tale in which war is abolished by the invention of a bomb which sets up a continuous atomic disintegration capable of decomposing the universe. Any ambitious conqueror attempting to arm his troops with it instantly produces a spontaneous League of Nations unanimous as to the imperative necessity for his immediate liquidation. Shakespear, having to account for the survival of the philosopher Prospero on an island where his only rival inhabitant was the primitive savage Caliban, who could and would have killed any normal philosopher, had to make Prospero a vulgar magician whose power of doubling up Caliban with cramps and agues must have reminded the unfortunate monster of his mother the witch Sycorax. Swift endowed the rulers of his imaginary Laputa with a flying island which they could dump down on the heads of rebellious subjects or any combination of them.

These fables throw no light on history because neither Vril nor Prospero's magic nor flying islands have ever existed, nor has the atomic bomb yet been invented. Their practical interest lies in their evidence that even the greatest poets and most inventive romancers have been unable to conceive a society in which the power of men to kill oneanother was not held in check. When I contributed my Utopia in a batch of plays entitled Back To Methuselah, in which mind reigned as irresistibly over muscle as Prospero over Caliban, I also had to find such a check; but I could not be satisfied with an imaginary one, as that would have taken me no further towards possibility and credibility than the older Utopians. There is no real hope in impossible Utopias. I had to resort to a power which, as it exists and is in daily operation, can easily be conceived as capable of evolutionary intensification.

This power is called Awe. It enables a head master to control masses of schoolboys who could mob him and tear him to pieces as de Witt was torn by a Dutch mob in 1672 if they were not restrained by Awe. The statesman has to exploit it because he has to give authority not only to superior persons who naturally inspire it, but to ordinary Yahoos who can be made to produce an illusion of superiority by unusual robes, retinues and escorts, magnificent liveries and uniforms: in short, by making animated idols of them. Uniforms, vestments, robes, maces, diadems, retinues, pageants, processions, cannon salutes, and codes of etiquette are artificial Awe producers to give authority to persons who are not natural Awe producers.

The reaction against this factitious Awe has produced the Roundhead, the British Quaker, and the American diplomat who appears at court among costumed peers and royalties in coat and trousers instead of in breeches, swordless and plain Mister; but these iconoclasts are powerless against the genuine natural awe inspirer. I am as irreverent and even derisive as any sane thinker can be; but I can remember an occasion (I was over twenty at the time) on which I was so overawed by a Jewish Rabbi that I could hardly speak to him. There was no reason for this: we had never met before, and had less than five minutes conversation on an ordinary matter of business which gave no occasion for embarrassment on either side of any sort; but he terrified me by some power in him, magnetic or mesmeric or hypnotic or whatever you like to call it, which reduced me to a subjection which I had never experienced before, and have never experienced since. I was simply discouraged by him. Since then my observation, and the stories I read about the dying-out of primitive tribes at the impact of civilized invaders, have convinced me that every living person has a magnetic field of greater or less intensity which enables those in whom it is strong to dominate those in whom it is relatively weak, or whose susceptibility to its influence, called shyness, is excessive. I have ranked this as a scientific fact in the fourth part of Back To Methuselah; but it will not be accepted as such by the professional biologists until one of them has succeeded in making a guinea pig overawe a dog in a laboratory. Someday an intelligent bio-physicist will perhaps find out how to measure this force as we now measure electricity. Meanwhile there is no denying that it exists and must be recognized and even exploited by every practical ruler.

In my Utopia I therefore fell back on Awe, both natural and artificial, as a means by which my Coming Race kept the Yahoos in subjection. And as age has to be naturally impressive so as to secure the necessary submission of children to their parents and guardians, I made my Coming Race exempt from natural death, in this following Weismann, who suggested that death is only Nature's remedy for overcrowding, and that men might be as immortal as amoebas if there were as much room for them on earth.

And so, without introducing any magic, I made it possible to accept a story in which by evolutionary development of purely natural forces wisdom had become awful to the extent of becoming lethal. For Awe operates through discouragement; and discouragement in the last degree is death.

Clearly the statesman must reckon with both natural and artificial Awe, and resort to the artificial sort when the natural runs short of what is necessary to maintain social discipline. Corresponding to Awe as a social force is Contempt, which can also be manufactured. Men are judged mostly by the clothes they wear. Our nudists sometimes forget that if navvies and kings went naked, the navvy would have to resume his cap and the king his crown as a matter of social convenience even if navvies had come to be considered more respectable than kings. The circus clown whose profession it is to appear lazy, cowardly, thievish, gluttonous, drunken, mischievous, and in every possible way ignominiously ridiculous, and to trip himself up and fall or be beaten and kicked, has to wear a ridiculous and ignominious costume and paint his face absurdly to achieve these effects. In the gaiters of a dean or the ermine of a judge, though in the lapse of time these have become hardly less quaint than the clown's motley, his clowning would be impossible even if the authorities would tolerate it. An actor having to play the part of a general on the stage must not wear the general's uniform: there must be some inaccurate detail to distinguish the real from the simulated. And this is not peculiar to the player: it is only the application to the art of acting of the general law that citizens must not put on the insignia of rank or sex other than those to which they are officially or naturally entitled.

Thus a government can manufacture Awe and Contempt to a prodigious extent, and can abuse this power proportionately. The feudal system selected its aristocracy by heredity, which at once produced in all directions barons who, being incapable of inspiring natural Awe, had to be made awesome by their clothes and riches and revenues. When the Black Death made proletarian labor so scarce that its price rose until common women could afford to buy silver ornaments, they were promptly forbidden to wear them by sumptuary legislation. When breeches were worn only by gentlemen, the insurgents of the French Revolution were called sansculottes, or the breechesless. When the American Revolution claimed the right to carry arms for everybody, it was grossly abused by the sort of American typified by Dickens in Mr Hannibal Chollop, who will finally oblige the American Governments to forbid anyone to carry a pistol just as the Italian Government was forced long ago to forbid any Italian to carry a stiletto. I may not possess a gun of any sort without a licence; and people are being shot at present all over Europe for being found in possession of arms. There is no end to the action and reaction which began in the need for artificial Awe created by a deficiency in the natural kind.

Now there is no reason to believe that this deficiency is itself natural. Nature, which is always incorrigibly prodigal, produces more than enough of natural born governors and organizers to fill all the panels of the necessary hierarchy with an overflow quite sufficient to give the governed choice enough to keep the elected under democratic control. But this generous supply comes from the entire population, and amounts to a percentage of it only. Moreover it is available only when the fullest culture and education are within the reach of everyone capable of profiting by them. Cut off nine-tenths of the population from such culture and education by proletarian poverty and you cut off nine-tenths of the natural supply of governing and organizing ability, and are forced back on dressing up "the tenth transmitter of a foolish face" to look like a natural aristocrat, and get through his public work by doing what was done last time, whilst his private affairs are managed by his butler, his bailiff, and his solicitor.

Empires finally die of such pretences. Democratic commonwealths will be rotted by them unless they secure access to culture and education, which means in practice equality of income, for everyone. The final sanction of such equality now that the priestly power to bind or loose in a future life is no longer effectively believed in, is the power of life and death possessed by the secular government, and not delegated to private duellists on any pretext whatever. Monarchs soon become accustomed to signing death warrants, especially in countries with large populations. Human life is certainly not more sacred in Ireland than in England; yet when I was a child in Ireland an execution occurred perhaps once in six months, and was conspicuous in the headlines for days, whilst in England, with ten times Ireland's population, Queen Victoria had to sign death warrants every week, and can hardly have felt more about it than about signing a cheque; so, as the late Gilbert Chesterton pointed out when he had to serve on a jury, it is well, when stern measures have to be taken, that there should be persons present with a voice in the matter who are not too insensitized by daily habit to the cruelty of such measures.

The powers of life and death necessary to civilized States find their widest exercise in the institution called War, through which a whole nation, or an alliance of nations, constitutes itself an international inquisition, and, if it decides that some other nation or alliance is unfit to live, proceeds to exterminate it. Such a decision is necessarily reciprocal, as the sentenced parties can hardly be expected to agree with the verdict, and their only way to escape execution is to exterminate the exterminators. And the powers of life and death must begin at home on both sides, because, as the armies, if they had any sense, would run away or fraternize instead of slaughtering oneanother at appalling risks to themselves, soldiers must be shot at dawn by their own comrades if they do not fight, kill, blow-up, burn and destroy: in short, behave like homicidal madmen.

All this extermination, though faultless logically, is finally impossible. Not only would it cost too much to carry it out to its bitter end, but its human agents, the soldiers and citizens, could not bear it: it would break down as it did in Germany in 1918. Besides, to exterminate a nation, you do not waste time killing its men, who can be reproduced by its women. You kill its women. Obvious as this is, no exterminator has ever dared to propose it as the object of a war. Even Adolf Hitler, whose anti-Semite phobia outdoes Joshua's anti-Canaanite phobia or the reciprocal rage of the Crusaders and Saracens, stops short of a general order to kill all the Jewish women and not bother about the men.

But the extreme cases settle nothing except the boundaries within which our choice must be made. Though we can neither exterminate hostile nations nor allow them to invade and subjugate us, we not only can but must exterminate individuals, and slaughter our enemies sufficiently to give us reasonable hopes of defeating them and imposing our own terms on them, wisely or unwisely. There is no golden rule by which rulers can decide when to kill or not kill without exercising their own judgment.

There is another limit to the power of the State over the individual. Sentences have to be executed as well as decreed and passed; and it may not be possible to find an executioner. But so far the most diabolical tortures have never been prevented in this way. The burning of women alive, the unmentionably abominable method of execution for rebels invented to intimidate such insurgent patriots as William Wallace, the Roman routine of crucifixion applied in the case of Jesus, the French routine of punishment for parricide which disposed of Damiens and Ravaillac, and the horrors specially invented to torment the Anabaptist John of Leyden (I have seen the cage in which what the torturers left of him starved to death still hanging on the tower of the cathedral in Münster) seem to exhaust the possibilities of human cruelty; and yet there is no recorded instance of any difficulty in finding persons willing to execute them for a very modest remuneration. Crowds came to see them carried out; and householders whose windows commanded the spectacle sold places at them for considerable sums. In fact an execution is also a popular entertainment. People assemble outside a prison in which a murderer is being hanged, though they can see nothing. The generation of Parisians that produced St Francis de Sales amused itself by watching criminals being broken on the wheel, a practice that lasted so far into the nineteenth century that when I was over twenty I numbered among my contemporaries persons who had witnessed it. I still abstain from circuses, though I should enjoy what in my childhood I called The Horsemanship, because I cannot endure seeing animals performing unnatural tricks at the command of trainers whom I should shoot at sight if I could be sure of a verdict of justifiable homicide.

Governments can and do still take advantage of such thoughtless sensation hunting and primitive ferocity to impose their will on their subjects; and this is why rulers should be very critically selected; for in every modern State there are blackguards enough to furnish a gangster government with coercive troops which the un-organized citizens cannot resist. Our best consciences are still far more humane than our criminal and military codes; and the gap between them can be closed only by giving our best consciences command of the situation. Otherwise we shall have what occurred in China: an exquisite civilization in the cultured classes whilst criminals were being sliced into a thousand pieces for the entertainment of the mob.

CHAPTER XXXIII

LAW AND TYRANNY

HISTORY has hitherto been too much occupied with the personal tyrannies of kings, usurpers, conquerors, and the Terrorist phases in revolutions. There is nothing to be said about them that has not been said a thousand times already. What needs notice urgently nowadays are the tyrannies imposed on us with the best intentions by rulers who are themselves imposed on by bogus Science and the blunders of half wits like Jenner, Lister, and Pavlov. I know this because I was imposed on myself in my nonage. The infallibility and authority I had been taught to ascribe to the Epistles of Peter and Paul I simply transferred to the lectures of Helmholtz and Tyndall. I scoffed at the first chapter of Genesis as an obvious fable only to accept Darwin's Origin of Species as Revelation. This is what everybody does more or less. St Thomas Aquinas and St John the Baptist believed that holy water, especially from the river Jordan, had magical properties; though I dare not say that they ever went as mad about it as our scientific people about radium when it was first discovered. John and Jesus, who substituted baptism for circumcision, were much less credulous and intolerant than Farmer Jesty and Doctor Jenner who substituted vaccination for baptism. We are so shocked by the African Medicine Men who smell out witches and have them killed that we stamp them out as resolutely as we stamp out Voodoo; yet we are raising a hue and cry against "carriers" of disease, with Typhoid Mary held up to us as more terrible than the witch of Endor.

Now I am not suggesting that all these transfers and transitions of our credulity are for the worse, though some of them are. We do not propose to burn Typhoid Mary: some form of humane killer is the worst that is implied by those who called for her segregation or destruction. Nor must it be inferred that because people believe in scientific discoveries as blindly as they formerly believed that the sun stood still for Joshua it follows that all the discoveries are mares' nests. All I insist on is that statesmen must not accept professional endorsement of a proposal as scientific as a proof of its soundness. It may be sound and it may not. Lister's antiseptic surgery, which won him a London statue and a shrine in the temples of medical science, proved a disastrous blunder; but the phagocytes less than a billionth of an inch long just made visible by the new electron microscope have none the less to be reckoned with.

It must be kept in mind, too, that blunders are not always, on balance, disastrous. Lister's mischievous antiseptic surgery was injurious not only to the patient but to the surgeon; yet it incidentally abolished hospital gangrene by enforcing scrupulous cleanliness where plague breeding dirt had reigned before. But when this point had been gained it was carried to such lengths that when war required prompt and speedy surgery wounded soldiers died while Listerious nurses were boiling water to sterilize everything. The Listerics had to be got rid of, much to their own surprise.

There is always a change which requires the most careful interpretation when a new law compels attention to matters previously neglected. I have myself, as a member of a Public Health authority, been a party to imposing on householders sanitary arrangements which were subsequently discovered to be much more dangerous to health than the old privies which they replaced. Yet their incidental substitution of attention for prudish neglect improved the vital statistics sufficiently to make our dangerous pan closets seem salutary until they were found out and we began to prosecute people for not discarding the very contrivances we had previously penalized them for not adopting.

I have just heard a Parliamentary secretary produce in support of the prophylactic inoculation of children against diphtheria what he considered the overwhelming figure in its favor of one death among the inoculated children and 418 among the uninoculated. Mr Everyman is convinced at once by such statistics. Far from proving their case they do not even clear the inoculation from the suspicion that, like vaccination, it may be more deadly than the disease it is meant to avert. For inoculated children are the children of well-to-do conscientious and educated parents who take anxious care of their children's health and have the drainage of their comfortable houses inspected by sanitary experts once a year. The uninoculated are the children of careless and uneducated or poor and overcrowded parents who cannot afford sanitary conditions, with a shockingly higher infant mortality from all causes than the inoculated. Statistics of resistance to infection as between well nourished children in handsome surroundings and underfed children born and bred in squalid homes, or even a whole population ninety per cent proletarian, always come out overwhelmingly in favor of the former. The inoculators claim the difference as the benefit of their nostrum; but our West End jewellers and outfitters might claim it equally for the wearing of a silk hat or the carrying of a gold watch by every father of a family. Qualified disinterested statisticians guard against such absurd inferences by what they call control experiments: for instance, if all the Eton boys were inoculated against a particular disease, and all the Harrow boys left untouched, any serious difference between the incidence of the disease in the two schools would at least prove that one of them was enjoying an immunity not shared by the other; but a comparison of either of them with poorer schools could prove nothing but that poverty and dirt are unhealthy.

Besides, statistics can be faked. My experience as a vestryman includes the last epidemic of smallpox of any seriousness in London. People rushed to be revaccinated; and as we paid half a crown for the operation the doctors rushed to revaccinate them. Presently we found that persons we had sent to the smallpox hospital as smallpox patients had been revaccinated. We instantly rediagnosed their illness as pustular eczema, or "varioloids," and moved them to the ordinary fever hospital. Accordingly, revaccination, as far as we were concerned, came out of the epidemic without a stain on its character, although it had caused considerable illness and temporary disablement even in the vestry itself. I omitted to be revaccinated. So did our Medical Officer of Health, though as a public lecturer he was an ardent Jennerian. We two unrevaccinated also proved immune from the epidemic. But we did not figure as such in the published statistics.

I have already described how diagnosis, which is believed to be an exact scientific classification of the causes of disease and death, is very largely nothing but nomenclature, and how easy it is to make diseases appear or disappear by giving them new names. We can reduce a thousand typhoid cases statistically to five hundred by listing half of them as enteric.

The bogus science created by this trick of passing off mere nomenclature as important discovery is so deceptive that those who can see through it are tempted to agitate for legislation to make the use of a new word felonious until it is authorized by Act of Parliament. As this remedy would be worse than the disease it is fortunate that the up-to-date scientific text books are so crammed with new words that they are in great part unreadable. When Mr A announces that he has produced such and such a result in his laboratory, and Mr B immediately declares that the result does not follow in his, there must be an error somewhere; but it is concealed by the simple expedient of announcing it as two important discoveries by Mr A and Mr B respectively, and giving them different names, as Greekish and polysyllabic as possible. Thus the textbooks sidetrack logic, and acclaim as notable discoverers gentlemen who have discovered nothing but their own mistakes. Statesmen who are duped by this procedure should be struck off the panels.

In dealing with public health as with diplomacy the statesman must never forget that, as Ferdinand Lassalle declared, "the lie is a European power." In sanitary matters it is a world power. Lying is privileged in commercial advertisements because commerce is rich and powerful, just as it was privileged for princes, as Machiavelli pointed out. Vaccination produced a lucrative trade in vaccines. Later on, the word vaccine was applied to prophylactics that had nothing to do with cowpox; and now we have a whole industry producing vaccines, pseudo-vaccines, therapeutic serums, gland extracts called hormones, antigens, antitoxins, in addition to the old-fashioned pills, purges, tonics, electric belts, and the like, all professing to avert or cure every known or imagined sort of illness, and some of them promising to rejuvenate their purchasers and prolong life by another fifty years or so. Scraps of Greek or Latin, with "ose" or "in" or "on" or "ax" tacked on to them, replace the old names or provide new ones, impressing the public just as the big word Mesopotamia is said to impress simple people as religious. We read the advertisements of these products, buy them, use them, cure ourselves by our *vis medicatrix naturæ*, and, attributing the cure to the medicine, send the manufacturers glowing testimonials which are duly published and sometimes duly paid for. A lady of my acquaintance received £800 for a letter ascribing the beauty of her complexion, which was entirely and thickly artificial, to a well advertized face cream. I have myself been offered a considerable sum to attribute my mental powers to an equally well advertized educational correspondence course. No doubt the cures are sometimes genuine, the testimonials disinterested, and the advertisers sincere enough to take their own medicines; but the residue of downright impudent venal lying is enormous.

Now when a lie is popular, as all fairy tales of miracles are, it is impossible to overtake it once it gets a start. However often and authoritatively it may be disproved, ignorant people keep repeating it, and journalists keep copying from one another, until they cease to want to believe it. Then, and not until then, it dies a natural death. But the death is a very lingering one: it may easily last a century and a half if I may judge from the number of lies found out and exposed in my boyhood which are still rampant at the end of my long life. The statesman must be on his guard against them. He may make use of lies for the purposes of government, like Caesar Borgia (to say nothing of our contemporary rulers); but if he believes them they may trip him up very disastrously. The Lord Melbourne who guided Queen Victoria when she came to the throne is reputed to have set his back to the door at a meeting of his Cabinet and said, "I dont care what damned lie we must tell; but not a man of you shall leave this room until we have all agreed to tell the same damned lie." Whether this tale be true or not, the most honest statesman has to govern the people by telling them what it is good for them to believe, whether it is true or not. If it is proved to be false next week it will not matter in England, as the English people never remember a political speech longer than the interval between the morning paper and the evening one. I once said in public (I was proposing the health of Albert Einstein) that religion is always right and science always wrong. Lord Melbourne would have put it differently. He would have said that the priests are always telling the same lie and sticking to it whilst the scientists have a new story every few years or so, and spend much of their time contradicting one another and finding out one another's mistakes. In astro-physics for example, the

book of Genesis has stood unchanged like a rock for tens of hundreds
of years whilst during my own lifetime the astral universe, beginning
with a dismal vision of a cooling sun that will presently freeze and
extinguish all life on our planet, is ending with the pleasanter assurance that as the retarding action of the tides must at last bring all
the revolving heavenly bodies to a standstill, they will then crash
together into a single mass of unthinkable magnitude, the crash producing a temperature so incalculably hotter than hell that nobody
can imagine what forms life and growth will take in it. Newton's
"law" of rectilinear motion bent by gravitation has been supplanted
by curve trajectory, which sets us suspecting the farthest star our
telescopes reach of being only our sun seen all round the universe.
We have had an expanding universe with all the stars receding from
us at terrific speed as proved by the shift of the red in the spectrum;
it has then been proved on the same evidence that some of the stars
are approaching us with similar velocity and that someday Sirius
may hit us as a cricket ball hits a wicket or score a wide as the case
may be, making the expanding universe really an erupting volcano.
Our simple notion of the atmosphere as a mixture of three gases has
been upset and complicated by the discovery of argon and its train of
new gases. Tyndall, who staggered the world by announcing that he
saw in matter the promise and potency of all forms of life, is forgotten and succeeded by the brothers De Broglie, who convince us that
there is no such thing as matter, only motion.

All this is intellectually very amusing: it gives Science that charm
of novelty without which sustained attention is boring and finally
impossible; but the statesman cannot govern without stability of
belief, true or false; and this is why he must confine himself to vir-
tual certainties and be very suspicious of variable speculations. There
are such certainties: for instance the sun will rise and set tomorrow;
and a citizen deprived of food and drink for twelve hours will become dangerously ravenous and unphilosophical, and will weaken and
die or rebel and steal if the privation is prolonged. Here the statesman is on sufficiently solid ground to tackle the agricultural problem with some assurance. Yet without a science of agricultural
chemistry the most fertile soil will become a Sahara, as some of
my friends who have bought American ranches are discovering
just now. In Russia prodigious progress in agriculture has been
achieved by collective farming and mechanized cultivation; but both
will finally change Russia into a Gobi desert without scientific re-
fertilization, which brings the statesman up against the scientist

who assures him that all the land requires is a dressing with vitamin A or B or C, or X or Y or Z; and the statesman can hardly reply "This is Science; and Mister Shaw says that Science is always wrong."

The statesman is ever in this same dilemma, unable to govern without a conservative stability that forbids progressive change, and yet warned by Mr Wells that a community is doomed if it will not adapt its institutions to the changes made by invention and discovery, quicker communications, mechanization of labor, house-to-house distribution of electric power enabling workshops to knock out factories as factories knocked out cottage industries, harnessing of the tides, tapping the earth's central volcanic steam as the Italians are doing (there is a natural blow hole in New Zealand wasting power enough to turn the world upside down), all multiplying the production of uneatable things whilst obsolete peasant farming keeps food production at its old level; so that men ask for bread and are offered tons of steel; and, as aforesaid, Saharas and Gobis threaten to destroy us faster than ever the icecaps did. How to be conservative enough to govern without being too stagnant to adapt government to changes that are beyond its control is not a job for Tom, Dick, and Harriet in the lump. It can be done only by the pick of them duly and carefully empanelled as qualified for such work.

Improved production and communication and the like are not alone in forcing revolutionary changes on conservative politicians. While Sahara and Gobi are striking at the roots of production, cancer and diabetes and malaria are striking at the roots of human life. Maddening but delightful poisons, from gin to cocaine snow, can demoralize whole civilizations and wipe out tribes and races if the trade in them is left uncontrolled. The statesman must deal with these perils; and this necessity is the opportunity of the science merchants, who press their cures and prophylactics on the legislators as fanatically as the Inquisition pressed masses, absolutions, christenings, churchings, sacraments, and prayers. And the laboratories have their torture chambers like the Inquisition, and claim the same privileges and powers to bind and loose. Naturally, the priests and the scientists, being rivals, are at mortal strife for the formation and control of our minds.

The statesman has his own torture chambers on Dartmoor and elsewhere. As I write these lines two robbers are receiving 108 lashes each (nine at each stroke) in addition to sentences of imprisonment. As I revise them a sick conscribed soldier has just been man-handled to death in the British army on suspicion of malingering; and though his slayers have been court martialled for going too far, the sentence has been much less severe than would have been passed in a civil court on civilians, who would possibly have been hanged. We reprobate German terrorism of this kind very loftily; but the European relapse from the comparative humanitarianism of the nineteenth century has infected us so notably that we cannot too urgently remind ourselves that cruelty, retributive or sadist or both, sets in rapid operation the Gresham law that a base coinage drives out an honest one. It holds as good in morals as in money.

CHAPTER XXXIV

JURIES AND MINISTERS OF GRACE DEFEND US!

LAW is no respecter of persons or circumstances: otherwise it would not be law. Yet as it deals always with persons and circumstances it would produce intolerable injustices and outrages if it were inflexibly and inexorably administered. The law itself must be inflexible; but there must be between the law and the citizen some institution which is elastic and is moved by mercy, compassion, respect for persons, consideration of circumstances, and pressing political expediency. The hand that signs the death warrant must have the alternative of signing the pardon. There must be a covenant of grace as well as a covenant of law.

In the British Constitution the two main agencies of grace are the sovereign's prerogative of pardon and the jury. The sovereign has many other duties: the jury exists solely as a buffer between the citizen and the law. Unfortunately this is so generally misunderstood that in practice it is often nullified. I should say that at least 99.9 per cent of the British citizens on the jury list believe that when the police have established the facts and the judge has instructed the jury as to the law, its verdict of guilty or not guilty must follow automatically. If this were so there would be no need for a jury: the case could be settled by the police and the judge without the interference of twelve promiscuous ratepayers. But it is not so. The function of the jury is quite separate from that of the police and that of the judge; and it does not begin until theirs is ended.

To illustrate, take the case of a trial for murder, as that always makes popular reading. Tom is in the dock, accused by the police of having murdered Dick. First, the police must convince the jury that Dick has been killed. Next, that Tom intentionally killed him. If they fail there is no case: jury, judge, police, and prisoner may pack up and go home to bed. If they succeed, then begins the judge's task, which is to lay down the law for the instruction of the jury. This done, the jury is in possession of the facts and of the law. It withdraws from the presence of the judge and the police, and addresses itself to its own special and sole task of deciding whether Tom's intentional killing of Dick was malicious or laudable, necessary, or excusable. Shall Tom be hanged; or does he rather deserve a title with a Parliamentary gratuity of £20,000? Is he guilty or not guilty?

Thus the verdict does not follow from the mere facts. The twelve ratepayers, all correctly informed as to both the facts and the law against homicide, may differ as to whether Tom was justified in doing what he did. If Dick has seduced Tom's wife whilst Tom was away fighting for his country, they will acquit him. If he is a fanatical revolutionary agitator and Dick was a popular statesman, Tom will be found guilty. Even when the police have failed to convince the jury that Tom killed Dick, but have succeeded in proving that Tom is a dangerous character whom it would be safer to hang or lock up, he may be found guilty; but if the case for the actual murder is too doubtful the Home Secretary as the sovereign's minister will probably cancel the death sentence and substitute imprisonment for life. In all cases, if the jury is capable of thinking for itself and not merely doing what the judge directs or the barristers persuade, the verdict will give effect to the education and consequent moral principles, prejudices, and sentiments of the jury, facts or no facts, law or no law. It will be an act of conscience under the covenant of grace.

What is needed to give effect to the jury system is the restriction of the jury list to qualified persons: that is, to persons who understand the function of the jury, and know the history of its long struggle for independence of judge and king. Payment of juries should be sufficient to make a place on the list coveted as a privilege instead of dodged by every available trick. I blush when I recall the shifts by which I succeeded in shirking jury service until I was superannuated, my best excuse being that our way of dealing with criminals by retributive punishment and deterrent example is in my opinion so wrong that I should be impossible as a juryman.

Why should it not be sufficient for the judge to instruct the jury as carefully in its peculiar function as in the law concerned? The reason is that experience of the ignorance of promiscuous juries, and of their susceptibility to the venal eloquence and sophistry of the bar, soon convinces the average judge that all cases can be better decided by any judge than by any jury. In this conviction he does everything in his power to get the decision into his own hands. And the readiest way to effect this is to confirm the jury in its error of believing that their verdict must follow the law and the facts. Our judges went so far in this direction that an Act of Parliament, known as Fox's Act, had to be passed to establish beyond question the right of the jury to return a general verdict: that is, of guilty or not guilty, or for or against the plaintiff or defendant, instead of answering questions and leaving the judge to interpret them, or obeying his direction instead of taking it into account without being in any way bound by it. But it is nearly a century and a half since that Act was passed; and it has been so effectually suppressed and forgotten that as I write perfectly innocent persons who have omitted to comply with certain technical war finance regulations of which they had no knowledge and could not have guessed on moral grounds, have actually pleaded guilty and been heavily fined under the impression that they were only saving the time of the court by admitting the facts, as to which there was no dispute. They must have done so on the advice of their solicitors, who ought to have known better.

As to the police, it is not their business to instruct the jury or to enlighten the accused. On the contrary it is their business to secure a conviction by every means in their power, because it is officially held that the object of the criminal code is to deter citizens by fear of punishment from breaking the law; and from this point of view every crime must be followed by a punishment whether the person punished has committed the crime or not. Hanging an innocent person is just as deterrent and exemplary as hanging a guilty one, provided the public can be persuaded that he is guilty. It is therefore possible for a chief of police to believe conscientiously that when a murder has been committed it is better to hang the wrong person than to hang nobody. The philosopher who declared that the whole duty of a jury is to find against the judge and against the woman took it for granted that it should find against the police. I do not endorse this extravagance; but it was at least a reminder that the power of the jury on occasion to deliver an accused person from both the police and the letter of the law is the sole reason for its existence as an institution.

Above the jury stands the King with his power to pardon when even the jury condemns. This power is administered by the Home Secretary. When I first came to London in the year 1876, I used to read murder cases, not as thrillers, but because I have something of a legal mind. I still remember one in which a man and a woman were accused of murdering the man's wife. Both were found guilty by the same verdict and duly sentenced to death. The Home Secretary overrode both verdict and sentence by sending the man to penal servitude for life, and pardoning the woman, who immediately obtained employment as a barmaid on the strength of her brief celebrity.

Sometimes the pressure of political expediency protects the law-breaker without any overt act of grace. It would be perfectly legal and reasonable for a Belfast chief constable to prosecute a Roman Catholic priest for obtaining money by false pretences on the ground that persons with deceased relatives had paid him for masses to be said for their souls, the consideration being the shortening of their terms of penance in purgatory. But it would not be a wise proceeding, as it might lead to a civil war comparable to the Thirty Years War in Germany. Neither is it wise, however, to leave obsolete laws on the statute book on the ground that nobody would dream of enforcing them. There are laws at present unrepealed against apostasy and against homosexual indecencies, in which the penalties are so monstrous that in normal states of public feeling no jury would convict under them, the refusal being not an act of grace but because the prescribed punishment would be unbearably cruel. When conviction for high treason involved confiscation of property, thus punishing the traitor's innocent dependents, the question whether the accused had any property was put to the jury, who always replied "None" even when he possessed ducal estates. The worst barbarities of our criminal code, such as the hanging of children for trivial thefts and the burning of women, have been abolished in this way; but it is a very crude expedient because it leaves the jury no middle course between condemning accused persons to a horrible punishment and acquitting them even in cases where, as the great Duke of Wellington said of military discipline, "Anything is better than impunity." Distinctions between murder and manslaughter, and between unlawful entry and burglary, help a little; but a jury often finds itself unable truthfully to find the accused not guilty, and yet unwilling to endorse the prescribed punishment.

They evade the difficulty by appealing to the sovereign for an act of grace less drastic than an acquittal by adding to their verdict of guilty a recommendation to mercy.

These makeshifts prove the need for periodical revisions of the statute book. They prove also a more fundamental need: to wit, the complete riddance of cruelty and punishment from our criminal code. Neither jury, judge, nor sovereign should have to consider whether a convict should be tormented or not. Our prisons are artificial hells for which there is no excuse: all the physical brutalities of concentration camps and torture chambers are trivial and temporary compared to the routine of imprisonment described by Mr Fenner Brockway after twentyeight months of it, and of penal servitude as described by Mr Jim Whelan after thirteen year of it. Both of them would have been extremely lucky if they had been let off with a flogging, however savage, as a public entertainment.

This detestable cruelty is not British. It is not human: it is capitalistic. In society we have to deal with people who, being unfit for civilized life, are intolerable nuisances. They should be painlessly and apologetically killed. There are persons who can support themselves and do no harm under tutelage and discipline, but without such restraint and guidance, cannot go straight. They should be employed, guided, and restrained accordingly and made as happy as possible meanwhile. This would oblige employers to raise wages to a point at which their employees would be as well off as the convicts, and more free, as otherwise the poorest wage slaves and "the reserve army of unemployed" would break the law to escape from their half starved "freedom" into the convict colonies; and the product of their work there would compete with and probably undersell the commercial products. Besides, the convict industries would be established with capital provided by taxing the capitalists, who would be obliged to finance their competitors as well as themselves. Thus under totalitarian ` Capitalism, however abject proletarian misery may be, prison misery must be worse. When British capitalism was at its summit of propertied prosperity Karl Marx was able to say that British prisons were the cruellest in the world, and that capital in pursuit of profit was absolutely merciless. Yet the British are not the most cruel people on earth. If some understanding of the situation could be knocked into their heads they would say, "If we must choose between kindly Socialism and ruthless Capitalism, Capitalism must go."

It must not be forgotten that neither juries nor constitutions nor prerogatives of grace are panic proof. In political emergencies such as those created by rebellion or war all expedients to humanize the law are abrogated without scruple. In Ireland under British rule the Habeas Corpus Act, which forbids imprisonment without trial, was suspended so regularly whenever the Nationalist movement became troublesome that it can hardly be said to have existed. In Eire under Irish rule, five military officers in council can hang anybody whose political views displease them. In India the British Government does not even trouble to suspend trial by jury: accused persons acquitted by the jury are sometimes sentenced exactly as if they had been convicted. The fact that elections never seem to be affected by these lawless episodes, even when political parties and newspapers use them noisily as sticks to beat the Government with, shews how useless promiscuous democracy is in a politically uneducated and systematically hoodwinked electorate as a safeguard against even the most barefaced excesses of State power or the grossest desuetude of popular rights.

CHAPTER XXXV

CONSCIENTIOUS OBJECTION VERSUS GENERAL STRIKE

GOVERNMENT by Anybodies elected by Everybody, calling itself Democracy, has given us rulers who, without taking the trouble to understand what they are doing or considering its inevitable consequences, decree anything that will tide them over an immediate difficulty. To disarm the opposition to compulsory military service, which in the nineteenth century was held to be a Napoleonic tyranny that no free-born Briton would submit to, they have decreed that anyone who has conscientious scruples against soldiering shall say so and be exempt. A more thoughtless anomaly can hardly be conceived. Only those who have never learnt the difference between laws and constitutional rights would resort to such an expedient. When Moses brought down from Mount Sinai the ten commandments, he did not add to each "You shall not" the saving clause "but you may do as you think fitting." A law is a law: a right is a right; and if the two cover the same subject they cancel one another. No matter: our legislators made no more bones about the anomaly than good Queen Bess did about the 28th Article of the Church of England, which first affirms and then denies transubstantiation, thus satisfying both Prelatists and Puritans. There is nothing new in this: it is a compromise in the eternal conflict between public authority and private judgment which raged long before the Reformation, and will be aggravated by the great extension of public authority involved by Socialism, and foreseen by Ruskin when politicians of all parties were assuming, like many of the Bolsheviks in 1917, that civilization always moves towards individual liberty. As long as laws are made by people whose proceedings make our more intelligent citizens wonder at the lack of wisdom with which the world is governed, conscientious objection will persist; and authority will have to maintain itself by persecuting it. There is therefore something to be said for the registration of conscientious and reasonable objection to obey a law, and, on examination of the cases, the considered exemption of individuals from its obligations. I, for instance, am exempt from military conscription on the ground that I am too old to be of any use as a soldier. I am not exempt from war taxation on the ground that my political conscience revolts against most modern wars as senseless and mischievous. I pay partly because I have no power to withhold, and partly because if I were on a ship which had sprung a leak I should take a hand at the pumps even if I knew that the damage to the ship had been caused solely by the incompetence of the captain and his navigating staff. My exemption from first-hand killing is shared in all directions by able-bodied people in reserved occupations. There is no apparent reason why the tribunals which deal with these exemptions and reservations should not deal also with the plea of conscientious objection to fighting and killing as such. There is in fact no serious difference between the improvised tribunals which specialize between combatant and noncombatant cases. When I say that in my private opinion I am better employed in writing books and plays than in forming fours in a barrack square or playing battles as a Home Guard, or stabbing and shooting young persons who may be incipient Goethes or Beethovens, I am on the same footing as any woman who pleads that she is better employed in domestic work than in filling shells, or a man who claims a return of deducted income tax on the ground that he is too poor to afford it.

Surely the worst way of smoothing out such difficulties is to pass a law with a clause to the effect that it need not be obeyed by anyone who conscientiously objects to it. For as the authorities have not the smallest intention of releasing anyone capable of military service from the obligation to defend the country directly or indirectly, they interpret the word conscientious in their own way; and as nobody can prove that the appellant for exemption is a conscientious objector and not a hypocritical coward, or perhaps an unpatriotic shirker and liar, the results of his appeal are unpredictable. A friend of mine who, far from having any objection to military service, had voluntarily gone through a course of Officers' Training, appealed to the tribunal for exemption on the ground that though quite ready to fight in a war of which he approved, he did not approve of the particular war (the Four Years) for which he had been called up. He was exempted at once, whilst obviously sincere Pacifist Christians who pleaded the Sermon on the Mount were forcibly enlisted and sent to prison mercilessly. No ordinary criminal can be tried twice for the same offence, nor can sentences of imprisonment with hard labor exceed two years; but the un- fortunate Conshy, as he is called, could be and was charged again and again for the same offence (refusing to obey orders) and pun- ished by successive sentences of two years which made them practi- cally perpetual and dangerously injurious to his health. Thus the law to exempt him has resulted in his being punished more severely than other criminals.

This revolting discrimination against conscience is quite logical; for denial of the social right and duty to kill ungovernable assailants of civilization, whether in individual cases as criminals or in bulk as hostile armies, is much more immediately dangerous than an objection to some particular case in which this right and duty, though fully admitted, clashes with the objector's particular policy. If, as is not impossible, the Western Powers were to declare war on the U.S.S.R., which would mean a war of State Capitalism against Democratic Communism, the number of conscientious objectors might run up to millions and make such a war impossible. The so- cial organization of such conscientious objection is the only method now available of preventing a war. So far, the only preventive recommended is the Trade Unionist one of a general strike. This has been tried over and over again, and has always broken down, as it always must break down; for it is nothing but the latest form of the ancient plan of bringing the oppressor to reason and justice by starving on his doorstep. It fails because Lazarus dies of starva- tion before Dives misses a meal, which serves Lazarus right for being such a fool. The way to make a strike successful is to confine it to one trade whilst all the others work full time, and overtime if necessary, to support it. The conscientious objector does not starve himself: he asserts himself in the practical form of a flat refusal to fight; and if he is numerous enough there will be no war.

Compulsory State service, when, as in the fighting branches, it involves State boarding, lodging, and medical treatment, may bring about very serious conflicts between the State and the individual. We are so preoccupied just now with being ordered by the State to fight whether we think it right or not, that we forget that if we submit, we shall be ordered to share our sleeping room with scores of other persons, to eat certain foods whether we think them healthy or not, to wear certain clothes whether we like them or not, to take certain drugs when we are ill whether we believe in drugs or not, and, when we are well, to endure certain inoculations, supposed to prevent disease, though we may be convinced that they are dangerously mistaken. Few of us fuss about these matters because we are so used to have them settled for us by custom that most of us never think about them, and do just what our neighbors do. It seems to us that there can be no difference of opinion about them.

But some of us do think about them and study them, with such various results that conscientious objections spring up. There are people like myself who drink neither beer nor even tea, and will eat neither fish, flesh, nor fowl. There are invalids who will take drugs homeopathically but not allopathically, and others who will not take drugs at all. Anti-vaccinationists are now only one of several sects of antis who not only practise their beliefs but propagate and suffer for them with the zeal of martyrs.

Up to a certain point the State can vary its regulations to suit these sects. There can be vegetarian messes as well as carnivorous ones; barley water can be provided as well as beer and rum; even some segregation of non-smokers is possible. But there remain questions on which the objectors are irreconcilable.

In the seventeenth century John Bunyan was imprisoned for twelve years because he conscientiously objected to be a member of the Church of England; but today there are so many who share his objection that our prisons could not contain them; so anyone may now belong to no Church at all with impunity. The new Conshy is the old Dissenter, who, when he was new, was the old Heretic. Now the modern compulsion to be a soldier is immensely worse than the obligation to go to church instead of chapel on Sundays.

In Bunyan's day it was bad enough to besiege a city, storm it, and sack it; but to destroy a city by fire and high explosive, incidentally blowing its inhabitants inside out or into fragments without discrimination of age, sex, or combatancy, as has just happened in Stalingrad, Kharkov, Hamburg, Cologne, Naples, Berlin, Bermondsey, Coventry, Plymouth, the old City of London, and elsewhere, is a horror compared to which the worst that Tilly did at Magdeburg and Suvarov at Ismail shines out as merciful. The British frightfulness of 1943 has left the German *Schrecklichkeit* of 1915 far behind, though the use of poison gas has been discontinued because high explosive and incendiary shells are more destructive and lethal. The only plea for frightfulness that can appeal to any humane person is that though its effect in slaughter and demolition may be confined to the enemy it frightens both sides impartially; for what London did to Berlin yesterday (as I write) Berlin may do to London tomorrow. Bomb weight, which used to be measured in pounds, is now measured in tons; and their contents explode more violently, wrecking streets where only single houses suffered formerly. Conscientious objection to their use in war grows with their atrocity, and is reinforced by the business objection that whereas when Tilly or Suvarov sacked a city they had the city for their pains when the few days of slaughter and rapine and loot ended, when Stalingrad and Kharkov were recaptured there was nothing left of them for the victors but heaps of rubble, corpses to bury, and enemy prisoners to feed. The use of high explosive does not pay. Even the builders and glazers could be better employed building new cities than rebuilding senselessly demolished old ones.

As demolished houses can be replaced in a few months, and could be in a few weeks if the vested interests in old methods were summarily dealt with, and as it takes twenty years to replace an adult, modern military slaughter reduces available labor much more seriously than when the slain were mainly soldiers, and war was held up as a remedy for overpopulation just as bombardment is now incidentally beneficial as a method of slum clearance. Tilly and Suvarov, Wallenstein and Gustavus Adolphus, Marlborough, Saxe and Wellington, could sacrifice battalions without fearing that their countries would be any the poorer in the lump, or that the slain would not be soon replaced by the irresistible urge of the reproductive instincts and the exemption of women and children from the perils of the trenches. But nowadays soldiers and civilians, children and adults, mothers and fathers, are slaughtered indis-

criminately; and the mothers who survive have learnt a technique
of birth control by which they can refuse to travail merely to supply
generals with cannonfodder. I have already pointed to the significant
fact that wars used to break out when the interest on safe investments fell to $2\frac{1}{2}\%$, and stopped when it rose again to 5%; but modern warfare is not so easily stopped: it may in a single week or so
overshoot the 5% mark and produce exhaustion, inflation, and ruin.
Though fortunes are made by war, and unemployment is cured by
it while it lasts, yet commerce will not now face war without a mora-
torium; and this is followed so soon by price control, profit limitation, and confiscation of incomes and excess profits on a scale un-
dreamt of by Victorian statesmen, that conscientious objection to
war is being strongly reinforced by commercial and financial interests. A majority of objectors is not necessary: an organized minority
could stop war, as it stopped Prohibition in the United States.

Still, conscientious objection as a legalized institution is an anomaly too absurd to last: a law must be either obeyed or repealed
unless it is disused and forgotten. As the State becomes more and
more Socialized, civil service will be imposed as military service is
at present: every ablebodied person will have to work, as every man
of military age now has to drill and fight, whether he is a penniless
tramp or a millionaire. Can anyone imagine Conscientious Objection being extended to allow Manchester School Individualists to
escape national service on the plea of a conscientious objection to
Socialism? Everyone could if Socialism were to do the mischief that
war does, and become abhorrent to humane people. But as Socialism
has so far proved as enormously productive as war is destructive,
this is not likely to occur. Even if it does, the remedy will not be a
return to Capitalism any more than the triumph of conscientious
objection will necessitate a return to unmitigated militarism.

In short, the legalization of conscientious objection is only an
expedient for making bad laws tolerable until they are repealed. It
is really a variety of sabotage, and always means that there is something wrong with the law. Its purpose could be achieved more easily
and sensibly by placing exemption on Christian grounds on the
same footing as all the other grounds.

The time may come when people who have no conscientious
objection to war will be treated as the Conshies are treated now, or
worse; for they could not plead, as the Conshys can, that if everybody acted as they do (the Kantian test) the world would be much
more comfortably prosperous than it is at present.

CHAPTER XXXVI

OUR ATTEMPTS AT ANTHROPOMETRY

THE most elaborate tests of intellectual capacity we have yet established by law and custom are the university and civil service examinations. They are, certain adaptations apart, alike in character.
They are better than nothing inasmuch as they ensure a body of
civil servants who can at least read, write, cipher, and even use the
binomial formula; but as the questions available for the examination papers, with the acceptable answers, are limited in number and
soon become known, the coaching of candidates for examination becomes a profession by the aid of which any blockhead who has a
good memory and has been broken-in to school drudgery can be
crammed with a list of questions and readymade answers which will
enable him or her to deal with a sufficient percentage of those
actually chosen for any particular examination. The majority of
civil servants and university graduates have won their posts and
degrees in this way. It actually excludes thinkers whose memories
will not retain things not worth remembering, and who cannot
stomach school books, though their appetites for books which are
works of art or helps to criticism of existing life are insatiable.
That is to say, it excludes the very people it should select.

But let not examinations therefore be condemned. Any examination system can be reduced to absurdity and ignominy by a wrong
method or by irrelevant questions with dictated answers many of
which are obsolete or false. Such mischief is in the method and in
the questions and answers, not in examination as a necessary part of
any test. The remedy is not to abolish examinations and take our
chance now that chance has become a branch of mathematics, and
the mathematical chances are that the public services will be staffed
by average routineers and not by nincompoops. Unfortunately, the
mathematical chances make it equally unlikely that they will be
staffed by supermen (or shall I, following Aldous Huxley and Dr
Sheldon, call them cerebrotonics?). For without some cerebrotonics
a political machine as complicated as a modern democratic State
cannot be kept in order.

Now it is extremely dangerous to leave political supermen unemployed: they see things going wrong which they could set right
if they had the necessary power. If they are men of action they are

impelled to upset the Government and appeal to the discontented sufferers to support them in a *coup d'état* to give them that power. If, like myself, they are not men of action but men of letters, they engage in a propaganda of sedition and revolution which is very bad for the political health of the State. Voltaire, Diderot and Rousseau made Robespierre and Napoleon possible. Lassalle and Marx, Engels and Richard Wagner, made Hitler and Mussolini possible as well as Lenin, Stalin, and Ataturk. Carlyle and Ruskin, Wells and Shaw, Aldous Huxley and Joad, are making possible the devil knows who in England: probably someone of whom these sages would vehemently disapprove. Democracy must find better auditors than its literary malcontents or else face their disruptive restlessness as best it can.

Besides the examinations there are the intelligence tests which have engaged psychologists so much during my lifetime. They are capacity tests instead of the mere memory tests which enable so many teachers and scholars to be certified as proficient when they should have been certified as mentally defective. I have never yet come across an intelligence test that I could pass, or an examination paper that I could fill up, except on a few questions my answers to which, not being the expected ones, would have secured my angry disqualification. Whether this is a high recommendation of them or a disparagement it is not for me to say.

Then there are blood tests, endocrine tests, bacteriological tests, electronic tests. The laboratory folk believe that they are the only scientific authorities, and that some day scientists will be able to diagnose potential political ability, and perhaps even take babies and qualify them as future prime ministers by a suitable inoculation; but so far they are too inexperienced and irresponsible politically, and their discoveries have too often proved to be mares' nests, to win confidence as well as credulity. Still, there are possibilities in this direction which are at least worth mentioning. Lord Samuel has even suggested a surgical possibility. In his Utopia the islanders have their sutures manipulated to make room for bigger brains, and thus make them all cerebrotonics. Someday we may have Cabinets in which all the hats measure ten. My own hat is only seven and an eighth.

The mathematical biologists, working at tests of vocational aptitudes, are more interesting than the vivisectors, and far more brainy. But they have got no farther at present than attempts to classify children between $11\frac{1}{2}$ and $13\frac{1}{2}$ as potential soldiers, mechanics, and accountants. Secretaries of State, and cerebrotonic supermen generally, are still below their horizon, though their language is mostly above the heads of the readers for whom this book is written, to say nothing of my own head occasionally. Those who would like to hear more of their regression and correlation coefficients, their multivariate and univariate selections and weightings, must subscribe to the British Journal of Psychology, which continues the work begun by Karl Pearson in *Biometrika*. Their work, bloodless, painless, and untroubled by Druidic or Aztec reflexes, is not, like physiological laboratory work, open and even attractive to every callous dunderhead. Statesmen should keep acquainted with its progress; for a good deal may come of it yet.

In the religious orders, and in the latest political parties, we have probations, novitiates, and disciplines operating as qualification tests for spiritual and political leadership, and for charity work done for its own sake. We have the Sister of Charity, who wears an obsolete but attractive dress such as ordinary respectable women wore in France in the sixteenth century. It was prescribed for her then by Saint Francis de Sales so that she should be personally undistinguished and unpretentious; but it is now the most distinguished uniform in the world. She may not take vows for longer than a year; so that she is free to return to the world as an ordinary citizen once in every twelve months, and therefore never suffers from "cold feet." In Russia there is the Communist Party with its rules and disciplines and frequent purges of the cold footed. The Russian League of the Godless is as devout in its worship of Marx as the Trappists in their worship of Christ, and enormously less egocentric and unsocial. But here again the waters are deep. The relation of the statesman to Religion is as important and complicated as his relation to Science. Both are not only deep social forces but very dangerous ones, and yet also infinitely hopeful ones. I shall deal with them presently.

I have already dwelt sufficiently on the ease with which the object of our present examination papers can be dodged by the coaching system, and on the fact that they exclude candidates who think for themselves instead of simply memorizing and believing their textbooks. But it should not be impossible to ascertain by better devised examination papers and conversations the mental range of an examinee. A practised university tutor soon finds out whether an undergraduate should be encouraged to study for honors or is hopelessly incapable of anything beyond the bare pass which is kept within his reach rather as the hallmark of a gentleman than as a certificate of fitness for any occupation demanding higher educational qualification than that of his college bedmaker. A professional coach for the Civil Service can advise his pupils whether to read for the Foreign Office or for the Excise.

It is true that an opinion on a postulant's chances of passing this or that examination is relevant only when the aim is to keep up the supply of university dons and gentlemanly civil servants; yet it is a human judgment; and human judgment, however fallible, is not limited to any particular examination system, and is, anyhow, the only instrument at our disposal when we have collected the available facts. Were we to discard a bushel or two of our existing examination papers as worse than useless, we could do nothing until we had devised better ones. The single decisive examination, with its possibility of coaching, should be scrapped, and a series of tests, taken over a period of apprenticeship under critical observation (as in the army, navy, and merchant marine) substituted.

Also, as all serious universities should be places for adults, not for schoolboys, a period during which the postulant ought to earn his living in the wide world on an adult footing should come between school and university. Academic degrees should not be obtainable by technical proficiency, nor technical proficiency be assumed on the strength of an academic degree. Nobody should be dubbed Master of Arts without specifying what arts, if any. The college don who knows everything and can do nothing should not be lumped in with the handy man who knows nothing and can do everything. To put it learnedly, the cognitive type should be distinguished from the conative as far as that can be done in view of the fact that as these extremes do not exist, real human persons can be placed only somewhere on the scale between them.

There are so many directions in which new ground can be broken that the rule "When in doubt do what was done last time" should be discarded for doing nothing that was done last time. We can only do the best we can as a beginning for the moment. The task is quite beyond me; but I may as well have a shot at a few items to begin with.

Should a public councillor of any sort be a mathematician? Yes and no. Technically no. It cannot be too often repeated that technicians, though indispensable as experts and assessors, are not judges. A Prime Minister may be unable to add up his washing bill; but he must comprehend mathematics sufficiently to know that their public endowment may be enormously more important than a duty on pickled onions. We do not want to be governed by the sort of people who cut off Lavoisier's head with the comment that "the Republic has no need of chemists," or who exiled and robbed Einstein because all they could understand about him was that he is a Jew. At present we have persons in authority who at the least threat of war try to clear out the British Museum and the Royal Observatory, and use them for military offices and stores, besides conscribing their staffs. The safeguard against this is not technical efficiency but comprehension. When it is comprehension we have to test, not executive facility, fifteen minutes conversation should be amply sufficient; but the conversation must not be in abstract terms, popularly called fine words; for in abstract terms the views of our rulers are all correct. Fine words are like letters of the alphabet used as algebraic signs, useless to the practical politician until they are attached to definite things in definite forms, definite quantities, for definite durations. Statesmen may be agreed that a pint equals twenty fluid ounces; but if they infer that a pint of milk is equal to twenty fluid ounces of gin they will be dangerous when the feeding of children is in question. One may understand the law of economic rent as thoroughly as De Quincey and Ricardo and yet be unconscious of the fundamental question of how much of the national land and capital should be used for agriculture and how much for industry. On this the theory of rent throws no light; but if the statesmen go wrong on it they may produce a nation of farmers with plenty of fields but no spades nor ploughs nor tractors to cultivate them with, or a vast superfluity of tools and machines and nothing to eat. We are always somewhere between these two extremes. In Russia the finding of the right place by trial and error gave trouble which would have wrecked the Soviet Government but for the overwhelming dread the peasants had that if they destroyed the Soviets their old landlords would come back. Food perishes if not immediately consumed, whereas hardware may last a lifetime. I carry my keys on a ring which I bought for fourpence in Dawson Street, Dublin, seventy years ago; and it is as serviceable as ever, though of all the bread baked and the beef slaughtered then not a scrap remained eatable for seven days.

No less important than the theory of rent is the theory of value. Here the danger is not, as in the case of rent, that the statesman has no theory, but that he is obsessed by a wrong theory, especially if he is a devout Marxist Socialist; for Marx took over his theory of value, by which he set great store, from the classical economists, from

Petty to Adam Smith and Ricardo, who held that the value of a commodity could be measured by the labor needed to produce it, and that, in effect, labor could create value. This was knocked on the head by John Ruskin, one of the greatest English artist-philosophers, when he pointed out that the exchange values of articles produced by labor for commercial use are no index to social values and are often inverse to them. The *coup de grâce* to the labor theory was given when the study of economics was taken up by the mathematicians. Common sense had always felt that the value of an article was another name for its desirability. The labor theorists admitted that there was what they called use value or utility, but that it was variable and therefore incalculable and immeasurable, whereas labor value was calculable and measurable by its duration. The mathematicians laughed at the notion that variables cannot be measured and calculated. Such calculation and measurement is their daily business. They cited the case of a man dying in the desert of thirst and hunger. He values a glass of water and a bunch of dates at all he possesses; but for a twentieth glass and bunch he will give nothing. It is equally true that every loaf by which a London baker increases the supply of bread is worth less than the preceding one. The labor theorists dismissed the difference as infinitesimal and immeasurable. Nonsense, said the mathematicians: we can measure infinitesimals as you can count beans: it is our specialty: that is why we are called higher mathematicians.

The labor theory is as dead as a doornail. A Government convinced that keyrings and loaves must always be equally valuable if they embody equal labor might conceivably flood the country with keyrings and leave it nothing to eat. Nowadays governments have to fix prices; and prices cannot vary from keyring to keyring and from loaf to loaf as their value does. There cannot be two prices for the same article in the same market, because no good housewife will pay twopence for an article that she can buy for a penny. Prices therefore cannot reflect value. The most necessary things, sunshine for example, have no price: we get them for nothing from Nature. Diamond rings, though unnecessary until we are glutted with everything else, are priced at thousands of pounds.

In commercial practice—and here Marx's theory works as well as Ricardo's—prices are concerned with cost of production in labor. That cost varies greatly over the whole field of cultivation. A lump of coal may in one place cost the labor of picking it up off the ground and carrying it to the fireplace, and in another digging a tunnel to a seam several miles out under the sea. A bushel of wheat may cost a day of labor on one farm and an hour or two on another. But no relatively remote coal seam or barren farm will be mined or cultivated until a scarcity of coal or wheat has raised the price to a point that will support the extra labor needed to produce it. Thus when the mines and farms are separately and privately owned, and the owners are competing for customers, the cost of production under the worst conditions fixes the price. But a government owning all the mines and all the farms, good and bad, can fix the price at the cost of production averaged over the whole field: that is, at the Marxian "value," which thus becomes an indispensable specific practical factor in the Socialist plan in spite of its rejection as an abstract theory, making the product much cheaper to the consumers, and distributing among them the rent of the more productive mines and lands, now appropriated by the fortunate owners, who are firm believers in equality of income for everybody but themselves. So farmers' incomes are equalized by high and low rents; and laborers are paid at the same rate whether the mines and fields they are working at are highly productive or only just barely worth cultivating, whilst we, the consumers, pay the same price for our coal and wheat (and everything else that is saleable) whether it costs an hour's labor or a week's, and are thus hugely overcharged for the product of the best mines and farms, and buy the products even of the worst at a profitable excess over their cost.

Every increase in the labor cost of production will, by raising wages, throw the worst mines and farms out of cultivation unless the miners and farmers work harder and enjoy less leisure to keep the supply at its former level. An increase in productivity beyond this point by improved methods, accelerated transport, or how not, will on the contrary bring still worse mines and farms into exploitation without finally reducing prices or increasing wages or bringing gain to anyone except the landlords!

All this must be thoroughly learnt and understood by the rulers of modern States in which government is for the welfare of the whole community and not merely for policing the private property and freedom of the landlords and capitalists, who meanwhile resort to Communism to the very considerable extent of carrying on the many services and industries in which private property and profiteering are impossible, though they depend on them for their existence.

We see then that statesmen should know as well as Ruskin did that commercial prices and profits are no index to social values, and in private hands are often inverse to them. They should know that labor, though necessary for their realization, cannot create them: rather may value be said to create labor. They should know that rent, which Marx called Surplus Value, far from not entering into price, as our universities teach, costs us part of every penny we spend (sometimes an enormous part of every pound) and can be distributed only by fixing prices at the Marxian value and thus "nationalizing" it: a measure possible only when land is public and not private property. They should know that interest is rent of capital and should be handled similarly. In short, they should know a good deal that nobody can learn without deeply interested study of political economy, which most voters loathe as intolerably dry. Also that sale of goods at their averaged cost will not supersede our present communism in roads, bridges, street lighting, water supply, police protection, fire brigades, school meals, sanitary and factory inspection, naval and military service, etc., nor be applied to intoxicating drinks and dangerous drugs.

To make democracy real, capably directed productive employment at the highest wage the country can afford must be guaranteed by the State and regarded as a fundamental right of every citizen and family; and as on this condition private employment and individual enterprise for profit or otherwise, duly chartered, can do no harm and may open new paths, both may not only be tolerated but encouraged and occasionally subsidized. It follows that though shareholders test commercial balance sheets by the magnitude of the profits and losses recorded in them, statesmen must test them by the vital statistics of the Registrar General.

The theory of economic rent applies to personal ability even more urgently than to land. The difference between the rents of two acres of land, one in the middle of Salisbury plain and the other in Lombard Street, is not as great as that between the profits of a Carnegie and of an average Scots shopkeeper. And as the use of a plot of land for growing wheat, or as the site of a cathedral or college, may be less lucrative to its private owner than its use as the site of a totalizator, an able merchant may make more money out of the vices of mankind than an inventor or philanthropist out of its needs and virtues. In England a surgeon can earn hundreds of pounds by a major operation, and three guineas by declaring it to be unnecessary. A doctor who cures his patients loses them. A victualler's "good bar customer," meaning one who drinks more than is good for him, is a bad citizen. The prudent plumber takes care not to make his repairs

too permanent. It is therefore disastrous from the public point of view
to give any person a pecuniary interest in disease or in mischief of
any sort. I am not forgetting that people have consciences as well as
selfish interests; but consciences depend on beliefs; and there is no fact
better established than that most people believe what they profit by
believing and therefore wish to believe. Under Freedom of Contract
and *Laisser-faire* the English nation was wasted and ruined, starved
and murdered and prostituted, on an appalling scale; but because its
manufacturers and mine owners made fortunes then deemed colossal,
Laisser-faire became the political religion of the English bourgeoisie,
which was nevertheless a highly conscientious class. "Wishful thinking" is not a recent discovery: thought is always wishful, and cannot
occur until a wish prompts it. Fortunately human wishes include
the evolutionary wish to do good and ascertain truth as such. Rulers
in whom this appetite is not very keen are dangerous. Cobdenite
Laisser-faire is a terrible example of wishful thinking by profiteers.
Trade Unionism and factory legislation have prevented it from doing
its utter worst; but there are still firms who refuse to negotiate with
Trade Unions or tolerate production committees or shop stewards,
or even to employ workers who belong to a Union. A hawker with
a conscience so far out-of-date would be deprived of his license.

The statesman confronted with rent of ability may tolerate it or
confiscate it as the case may be. If a prima donna with three octaves
can fill an opera house or concert hall with people paying from a
guinea to a shilling to hear her sing, she may make a hundred thousand pounds whilst her dresser cannot make a hundred thousand
pence. No sensible statesman would bother about this for a moment.
Nobody would be impoverished by tipping the lady a shilling or a
guinea. She would have to sing her scales and learn her songs and
opera parts and keep herself in training as a worker much more
arduously than most city men. She would have to give full value for
money willingly and even enthusiastically paid. She could buy rings
and sables and ropes of pearls (if there were any in the shops) just
to keep up her spirits and help her to imagine herself a queen of
song; but she could not create a plutocracy of prima donnas and
upset the balance of the State, nor could she live more comfortably
than her neighbors even if she had half a dozen picturesque castles
built for her to live in. She would have to be content with an ordinary husband or else marry a rival in the person of a popular tenor
as harmless socially as herself. It is actually desirable to have individuals here and there with money to throw about not only on stone

castles but on castles in the air, an important branch of building in which governments cannot indulge. If they threaten mischief they can always be dealt with by surtaxation and death duties. It does not matter whether they are prima donnas or champion pugilists: as long as they are scarce they do no harm except occasionally to themselves. Gracie Fields and John McCormack, Gene Tunney and Joe Louis, Charles Chaplin and Greta Garbo may pile up hundreds of dollars for every cent the rest of us can earn, with nobody the worse and their fans highly pleased. Even the few authors and playwrights who make more than a very ordinary and precarious livelihood by their pens may be left alone to keep literature alive by luring others into making a profession of it.

All these art workers get their money by sweating themselves, not by sweating other people. They get it by amusing, entertaining, cultivating the leisure of their industrial neighbors, and may be left to make their own bargains, provided always that the right to ordinary employment and leisure remains open to them whilst they are making their artistic reputations or losing them. Their social value is great; but it is so incalculable and disorderly that the Government can do little but look on and let them have their own way, subject, of course, to the general police regulations, which in their case need not be too vigilantly or rigidly administered. Rent of artistic ability may be classed as politically negligible; but statesmen must understand this, and not be simply ignorant in the matter.

They must bear in mind also that above the level of income at which all classes are intermarriageable a few incomes in excess of this figure are not politically dangerous. They are in fact a burden rather than a joy to their owners. They confer on their possessors no power over others. At present the power of A with a few thousands a year over B with a few pounds a week may be a tyranny; but give B a few thousands and A a hundred thousand and B may snap his fingers at A. Sensible millionaires unload themselves on to Carnegie Trusts, Rockefeller Trusts, Pilgrim Trusts, Nuffield Trusts, Peabody Trusts, Guinness Trusts, Nobel Prizes, and the like, or build cathedrals and turn castles in the air into solid bricks and mortar. The fortunes of the half-witted ones are soon scattered and squandered by themselves and their children. When we all become socially intermarriageable we shall be for all political purposes equal, even though a few of us may be unlucky enough to have fifty thousand a year instead of five thousand.

Commercial fortunes are very far from being politically negligible. If only five per cent of our population can or will manage business, still, five per cent of forty millions is enough to constitute a class of a couple of millions whose immediate pecuniary interests are anti-social, inasmuch as the less they pay their proletarian employees the more there is left for themselves. It is equally true that the less they pay to their landlords and financiers the more they have left for themselves; but as they intend to establish themselves and their heirs finally as landlords and capitalists: that is, as gentry, they throw their political weight overwhelmingly on the side of private property in land and capital. The combination of proprietors of commercial managing ability with the proprietors of land and capital levies a tax on the proletariat so enormous and in many ways so mischievous that at a certain stage of civilization it threatens to wreck the commonwealth. That stage was reached in England in the nineteenth century; and would-be rulers who are not yet fully conscious of this should be disfranchised and listed as ineligible for public affairs.

This brings us back to the citizen's right to employment for his own support when there is no commercial profit to be gained by it. As private commercial enterprise exists only in view of commercial profit, this national defence against starvation must be organized and managed by the State like the other national defences. At present the combination of the renters of commercial ability with the renters of land is so rich that it can afford to buy off the proletarians whom it cannot profitably employ by giving them a dole sufficient to keep their bodies and souls together in a condition of demoralizing idleness and degrading poverty, whilst much neglected public work, from bridge building, road making, town planning and slum demolition to tidal and volcanic electrification is left undone. People who are incapable of grasping the waste and wickedness of this may be harmlessly stupid in private life; but politically they are public enemies and should be disqualified accordingly.

It must be borne in mind that the relative scarcity of business ability is produced not only by lack of capacity for it but by a very strong and prevalent distaste for it, accompanied by an overwhelming preference for more interesting occupations. Take the case of Shakespear. He left school early to spend his teens helping his father, who was a Stratford tradesman of some standing. Shakespear's subsequent career proves that with this much business training he could easily have prospered as a tradesman in Stratford.

But having an irresistible literary and histrionic vocation he broke loose and migrated to London (I did the same myself) where he obtained a footing and authority in the theatre by organizing the business of attending to the horses of the equestrian playgoers. Marlowe of the mighty line was king among playwrights then; but when he presently died, Shakespear had proved that he could write not only mighty lines by the bushel, but sensible and amusing ones too. He was set to rewrite old plays and dramatize old stories; and he transfigured them so amazingly that only once in his short life (52) did he take the trouble to invent an original story for himself. But though this became his main occupation he kept up his business habits as a side line with so much success that in his forties he was able to return to Stratford, not as Shaxper the runaway poacher, but as William Shakespeare Gent., landed proprietor with a coat of arms, living in the finest new house in the main street. His fellow playwrights were mostly university scholars who, never having been forced to acquire business habits, and having acquired instead the very unbusinesslike habit of writing their stage directions in Latin, suffered greatly from poverty, even, as in the case of his chief rival Chapman, living and dying in comparative indigence. Could John Shakespear have afforded his son a university education William would have had a hard time of it.

The fact to be borne in mind here is that the attraction of commerce, which lies in its lucrativeness, is rare and feeble compared to the attraction of the arts and crafts, the sciences, and the open air pursuits which involve daily contact with the miracles and the visual beauty and adventure of nature. It is not the ability for money-making that is rare, but the taste and the selfishness for it. It would be ridiculous to imply that Lawrence of Arabia could not have done the work of a merchant or moneylender; yet he deliberately chose the lowest rank in the Air Force as a means of livelihood to high command, diplomacy, or literature. Shakespear handled his money capably enough; but he made it by turning bad plays into better ones at the risk of making them too good for his audiences. Dickens, in his last complete book, made a character, narrow and mean and greedy and cowardly enough to think of nothing but how to make money for himself, become much richer than the better citizens for whom money making was only an irksome necessity. Commercial ability is often really mere spiderishness. Deprived of the support of landlords and capitalists with spare money to invest, and of illiterate and destitute labor to exploit, it would become cheaper than skilled mechanical and manual labor. It has already done so in Russia, and for a long time past in petty commerce even in Capitalist States.

INTERMEZZO

I HAVE not come to the end of what should be known and understood by citizens before they can be empanelled as qualified to meddle in public affairs. To complete the list, or foresee future additions and deletions, is far beyond my knowledge and capacity. I can only demonstrate the unchangeable economic foundations on which all States must be built, and the inevitable results of building feudal, capitalist or communist political structures on them, illustrating them by samples within my limited knowledge or personal experience. I have omitted much that has been dealt with by other writers, aiming rather at reminders of the overlooked, and views from new or neglected angles, than repeating what is already on record in extant literature. I have as far as possible kept to matters of fact, historical and contemporary, the existence of which, however partially they may be selected and cited, is not in question.

I now leave this comparatively solid ground for the shifting sand of opinion and hypothesis, passing on from physics to metaphysics; from natural history to philosophy; from the facts and the sequences in which facts occur regularly enough to be predictable, to the thought plans (frames of reference) in which we have to arrange them before we can apprehend them; from the disorder of their actual happenings to the legends and dramas by which born story tellers arrange them intelligibly; and in general, passing from rational inference in which every effect has a preceding cause (Determinism) to evolutionary guessing, in which desire for the effect, sometimes in defiance of all reason and prudence, is itself the cause, and we escape from the Determinist dungeon of Giant Despair to the path that leads to the Celestial City.

CHAPTER XXXVII

CREED AND CONDUCT

I SHALL not now propose more examination subjects. Enough is enough for a beginning. Comprehension of them can be ascertained by examination, conversation, and correspondence. They are elementary and indispensable. Their mastery requires a degree of natural political capacity far in excess of even the pretences of the plutocrats and careerists who govern us today. And they leave the examinee free to advocate any policy he may judge best in view of them. There must be no dogmatism on this point: no dictated answers to the questions nor orthodox tendencies prescribed for the essays and conversations.

Nevertheless certain axioms and postulates must be accepted: it must be agreed on both sides that two plus two equals four, and that the language used shall be customary and syntactic; for without such agreement human intercourse is not possible. If the examiner says "Two and two equal four. You agree?" and the examinee replies "No: I dont hold with that," the examinee must be dismissed as unexaminable. But if the examiner says "We are agreed that we write down two dozen eggs as 24 eggs," and the examinee replies "No: the figure ought to be 20; for my arithmetic, which will, I hope, be the official arithmetic of the future, is duodecimal," the answer must be taken as satisfactory, as it proves that the examinee not only knows the multiplication table but understands that our arithmetical notation, like our spelling, is a convention that can be changed and bettered. But the examiner must not go on to ask "Are you in favor of a change?" and to treat Yes (or No) as a disqualifying answer. In the same way, when land and industry are in question, if the examinee denies that there is such a thing as economic rent, or a proletariat, or class war, or that there was ever any such thing as the feudal system or the capitalist system, he must be dismissed as ignorant and illiterate. But if he proves that he knows as much about economic rent as Thomas De Quincey and Henry George did, and as much about the Industrial Revolution as Karl Marx, he must not be asked whether his conclusions are the Conservative ones of De Quincey, the Single Tax of George, or the revolutionary ones of Marx. He must be free to draw his own conclusions provided he knows the ascertained relevant facts: in short, knows what he is taking about.

Democracy, however, cannot commit itself to give power to all who can prove that they comprehend the theory and know the history and practice of the political systems with which they will be concerned if so empowered. An examinee may pass all the tests with flying colors, and yet leave the citizens whom he proposes to govern completely in the dark as to whether he (or she) is a saint or a scoundrel, a fool or a sage. He may be highly intelligent and very well informed without the smallest intention of using these advantages for the benefit of the community instead of for his personal selfsatisfaction. John Bunyan, one of our leading authorities on human nature, consigned Ignorance pitilessly to hell; but he makes it clear that Mr Worldly Wiseman and Mr Badman will join him there, though they are better men of affairs than Christian or Hopeful or Faithful. Some good men have been disastrous rulers. Some infernally cruel blackguards have been great rulers. Peter the Great did so much for civilization in Russia that even a humanitarian saint like his countryman Peter Kropotkin had to admire this side of him. Tolstoy, another Russian saint, could not manage his own affairs: his "world-bettering craze" as his children called it, spoilt his private life. Aknaton, in the 14th century before Christ, and Amanullah yesterday, came to grief as monarchs as hopelessly as our pious simpleton James II. Louis XI of France, pious as James but capable, left his country solvent enough to bear the follies of his successors before, on the verge of collapse, it was set up again by Henri Quatre, who, far from being pious, changed Churches with a jest. His sexual conduct, like that of his equally sagacious grandson, our Charles II, was scandalous. Comparatively blameless kings have been exiled, beheaded, or shot. When Napoleon was finally smashed at Waterloo, the best brain in England (Byron's) was "damned sorry" and the mightiest soul in Germany (Beethoven's) dismayed. For Napoleon, vulgarly ambitious as he was, did more for France, and indeed for Europe, than the Abbé Sieyès, a much more virtuous character. Napoleon's conquerer, the Duke of Wellington, was not only a much more original soldier, but a nobler character; yet as a politician he lacked foresight and faith in the possibility of changing human nature by improving its circumstances. Robert Owen had both foresight and faith; but he could not handle the world outside his own factories. Once when I was advocating Socialism at a meeting, I was opposed by a speaker who said that he did so not because he disagreed with my arguments, or those of the Owenite apostles, but because their personal conduct and characters did not harmonize with their professions.

It follows that though candidates must be disqualified for ignorance or political stupidity, qualification must not ensure election or appointment. All it should ensure is registration on panels of the citizens most capable of political work in its various grades, and available for election. When a candidate applies for a post or presents himself for election the questions that the examiners may not ask are the very first ones that the electors or civil service commissioners will want to have answered. Adolf Hitler might leave George Washington nowhere in an examination (his book Mein Kampf contains a good deal of sound doctrine); but as his conclusions include German hegemony, subjugation of "non-Aryans" as such, extirpation of Jews, with hostage slaughter and military terrorism as his method, the wisdom of entrusting him with political power is so questionable that the objection to it has produced a world war. He has neither done justice nor loved mercy nor walked humbly with his god. Neither have we nor any of our Allies; but that is not a reason for tolerating Herr Hitler: it is a reason for reforming ourselves as well as dethroning him.

We must be governed by good men and true as well as by capable and knowledgeable ones; and on this account would-be politicians had better be exemplary in their personal conduct. Yet how is this to be judged? It is easy to ascertain whether an examinee understands rent or banking or insurance or feudalism or the precession of the equinoxes; for no matter what conclusions are drawn from them, they are matters of ascertainable fact. But conduct is a matter of very variable opinion. The scoundrel of today may be the saint of tomorrow. In the nineteenth century, Shelley, Tom Paine, and Mary Wollstonecraft were ostracized as enemies of God. They are now famous for their public virtues. But in private they behaved scandalously. Why have they been forgiven, and even admired, for this?

Clearly because our notions of exemplary private conduct, for all their ethical pretensions, are continually passing out of date. In the Roman Catholic Church people must not marry their first cousins; and priests must not marry at all. Under the Mosaic law a man must marry his deceased brother's widow on pain of public ignomiy. In the play of Hamlet a king who has done this is execrated as incestuous. Such marriages, having recently been made legal, are now regarded as convenient and natural; and the play would be unintelligible were it not that the King happens to be a murderer as well. There are societies in which much closer consanguinity makes marriage almost compulsory. When we were fighting Napoleon we were depending on two commanders: Wellington and Nelson. Of Wellington Tennyson could write "Whatever record leap to light he never shall be shamed", whilst Nelson left his wife and shared Sir William Hamilton's quite ostentatiously; yet Nelson was the more popular of the two. Daniel O'Connell was a famous Irish patriot and very devout Catholic; but the people of his native Kerry said of him that you could not throw a stone there without hitting one of his bastards. Nevertheless young ladies were not allowed to read or even mention Shelley or Byron; and Parnell and Dilke were politically annihilated for unconventional sexual conduct.

What are we to say to the extraordinary case of my namesake St Bernard of Clairvaux? His temper was so controlled, his disposition so sweet, his intellect so penetrating, his values so divine, that in the turbulent twelfth century he, a mendicant monk promoted Abbot, was able to make warring emperors and robber barons see reason and ensue peace. When I learned his life, I wrote "We teach history from the lives of our scoundrels: when will we begin to learn it from the lives of our saints?" He was really one of the great statesmen of history. When he went wrong, as he did when he preached the second crusade, he was religiously wrong, misled by his devotion to the deified Christ of his Church. But his rule of personal life was not exemplary. If everybody lived as St Bernard lived the human race would soon be extinct. His celibacy was a social crime, his self-mortification suicidal.

This last drawback raises a question of vital high importance. Was St Bernard a suicidal masochist or a healthy voluptuary with a finer sense of values than Falstaff or Anacreon? Is the notion that virtue consists in selfdenial, to which God, through William Law, sent us a "Serious Call," a pernicious traditional error, corruptly inculcated by profiteers to keep the thoughts of the poor on eternal happiness in an imaginary next world and off Trade Unionism and Socialism? Is self-mortification a Christian practice? St Bernard starved himself, wilfully exchanging wine for water and luxury for poverty. But Jesus exchanged water for wine; refused to fast; feasted with the officials of the Roman Government; and complained that he was called "a gluttonous man and a winebibber" because he would not practise the austerities of John the Baptist. Nowhere in the Gospels is there any mention or suggestion of his denying himself any indulgence within his reach and consistent with his vocation. Why, then, did St Bernard make himself uncomfortable, and institute the Cistercian order imposing discomforts and abstinences on all whom he could persuade to take the cowl? And why was he so successful that Cistercian monasteries sprang up like mushrooms all through Christendom, and even beyond it?

It seems to me that people to whom a decent life is a life of self-denial must be classed as born voluptuaries who, being also born masochists, would impose their craze for torturing themselves on people whose natural impulse is to enjoy themselves. A really good man is one who is good because he likes being good. His good life is a life of self-gratification, not of self-denial. He is made that way; and the credit for it belongs not to himself but to his maker, whether we call his maker God or Creative Evolution.

It happens that I resemble my sainted namesake in refusing to eat flesh, fish, or fowl, to smoke tobacco (or anything else), or to stimulate myself with drugs or spirits. I do not go about in a monk's frock and rope-girdle; but I spend no more on clothes than men with a twentyfifth of my income, if so much. For nearly fifty years past I have had at my disposal an unearned income sufficient to enable me to live comfortably without doing a stroke of work; but I work daily like any proletarian. If saintliness consists in these abstinences and exertions I may claim a place in the Communion of Saints beside St Bernard or any other hero of the hagiographers.

On this a ridiculous legend has grown to the effect that a stern Puritan bringing-up imposed Law's Serious Call on me from my childhood. No fable could be farther from the truth. The only belief impressed on me in my Irish Protestant childhood was that all Roman Catholics go to hell as such when they die, and all Protestants to heaven if they are good children. I grew out of this when I was promoted from petticoats to knickerbockers; and the rest of my development was in a family atmosphere so sceptical, Bohemian, anarchic, and on its educational side aesthetic, that in my teens I was a professed atheist, with no reverence whatever for the Trinity, but a profound and lasting respect for Michael Angelo and Raphael, for Handel, Mozart and Beethoven. To literature I took without enthusiasm or ambition because it was in my lifeblood. At all events, I am the last man in the world to be cited as ascetic either in theory or practice. In refusing to drink maraschino and drinking apple juice instead, I may seem to thoughtless topers as heroically selfsacrificing

as St Bernard and St Thomas Aquinas when they refused archbish-
oprics; but the truth is that I like apple juice and would as soon
drink petrol as maraschino. May not the truth about the two saints
be that as their tastes were different from those of Becket and Wol-
sey and Richelieu they rated mitres, red hats, and riches infinitely
below the solitude and simple life and ecstasies of the monk and
scholar? The late Lawrence of Arabia, whom I knew pretty well, deliberately chose the lowest rank in the army, refusing to give orders
and classing himself as illiterate, not in the least because he was
humble, modest, and self-sacrificing, but because he felt that he
would be in a stronger position and much freer as an aircraftman
than in the officers' mess, which was equally open to his choice. Stalin
outdid Lawrence by rising from social nothingness to the summit of
political power in Russia without a handle to his name or even a
Cabinet portfolio. Not until years later, when he had to sign treaties
and concert military operations with his western allies, had he to let
himself be dubbed Premier and Marshal.

We should consider these cases without prejudice; for the discussion of personal righteousness in abstract terms is waste of time.

Granted that St Bernard and St Thomas were as resolute egoists
as I, having equally disregarded the interests and wishes of our
families in our determination to go our own ways, and choosing
always the course of life most congenial to us at all costs to ourselves
and others, why did they go so far as to kill themselves at half my
age by overwork and privation? It was not because they believed
themselves to be the servants and instruments of God; for I believe
myself to be the servant and instrument of creative evolution, which
comes to the same thing, and entitles me to rank equally with them
as a religious person: that is to say, a person to whom eating, drinking and reproduction are irksome necessities in comparison with the
urge to wider and deeper knowledge, better understanding, and
greater power over ourselves and our circumstances. So far, there
is no reason why I, too, should not be canonized some day. Perhaps
I shall.

But there is a difference. St Bernard believed in an eternal personal life after death for everybody. He believed that happiness in
that after life, though it could not be deserved by us as sinful creatures, was possible on the assumption that all our sins were ex-
piated in advance by the torture and death of Jesus, on whom God
had laid the iniquity of us all. I not only do not believe this, but
should regard it as in the last degree ungentlemanly on my part to

allow anyone else to suffer for my sins. And the notion that the very unsatisfactory product of creative evolution known as G.B.S. will persist for ever instead of being depersonalized and replaced by something better, is not only incredible but as unbearable in my imagination as it must be in everyone else's. There I am sharply at issue with the Abbot of Clairvaux both as to the facts and the morals to be drawn from them.

Again, St Bernard got his courage and his humility from his belief that he was the servant of God; and I get mine (such as they are) from my kindred belief that I am the servant of creative evolution and that my supreme appetite is an evolutionary appetite. But here again there is between us the tremendous difference that he conceived God as omnipotent, omniscient, all-righteous and infallible, whereas it is plain to me that creative evolution proceeds by trial and error, which should perhaps be called trial and failure. The world is so full of its failures that much of our time is occupied in killing them lest they should kill us. Thus for me there is no Problem of Evil, whereas for Bernard of Clairvaux there was an insoluble one, only to be got round by the fiction of a devil disputing the rule of the world with God, who tolerates him as a test for our virtues.

The advantage of my version of the situation from the political point of view is that there is no danger of my imagining that because I regard myself as an instrument of creative evolution I must therefore be right in my way of doing its work. As it works by trial and error so must I. The advice I am giving in this book is the best I can offer at my age; but it may be a mischievous mistake. Certainly I had rather be writing a play instead. But a servant of God, though he may confess himself a miserable sinner, is apt to think that when he is mortifying his flesh and acting solely for God's sake he must be right because he is directed by God's righteousness and exercising God's supreme autocracy. St Bernard, most fortunately, thought of God as a god of mercy and of Christ as the prince of peace. That conception made him a saint. But it was as a servant of God that Charlemagne killed all his prisoners of war who refused to embrace Christianity on the spot; that Torquemada became one of the most abominable tyrants known to history; and that the highly conscientious and pious Christian emperors Charles V and his son Philip II are execrated for their cruelties in the Netherlands. When the Victorian Samuel Butler preached Laodiceanism, and warned us to hold our convictions lightly, he had in view so many missionary rulers, from Charlemagne to Robespierre and Hitler, whose "sanctions" were in effect atrocities, that, like his great Norwegian contemporary Henrik Ibsen, he saw civilization as a melodrama in which all the villains are pious idealists.

Thus we see that British mistrust of the servants of God, and preference for sceptically circumspect opportunists as Prime Ministers, is rooted in bitter experience. But a mere opportunist cannot create opportunities, he can only seize them when other people create them, and even then may either not notice them or else mistake them for public dangers. He may be qualified intellectually for the top panel; but unless he can not only grasp opportunities but create them without mistaking himself for a Jehovah or "a tin Jesus" he had better be left in private life.

As I see the world, the statesman must be religious; but he must discard every element in his religion that is not universal. He may have a vision of the whole human race bound together in a worldwide Catholic church; but he must not be either an Anglican Catholic or a Roman Catholic. If he personifies the creative factor in biology as God he must not nationalize it as Jehovah or Allah, Buddha or Brahma. Above all he must not look to God to do his work for him. He must regard himself as the fallible servant of a fallible God, acting for God and thinking for God because God, being unable to effect His purposes without hands or brains, has made us evolve our hands and brains to act and think for Him: in short, we are not in the hands of God; but God is in our hands. A ruler must not say helplessly "Thy Will be done": he must divine it, find out how to do it, and have it done. His God must not be an existing Omnipotent Omniscient Perfection, but as yet only an ideal towards which creative evolution is striving, with mankind merely its best attempt so far, and a very unsatisfactory one at that, liable to be replaced at any moment if creative evolution gives it up as hopeless. He must face the evil in the world, which apparently reduces the goodness of God to absurdity, as but the survival of errors originally well intended. He must treat life as everlasting, but treat his contemporaries as ephemeral mortals having no life beyond the grave to compensate them for any injustices they may suffer here and now.

Now it would be easy enough to formulate all this and more in a creed and catechism, and make it a condition of prime ministership that the postulant must know the catechism by rote and make an affidavit to his belief in the creed. An Act making apostasy a felony could be added. It is the method we use to guarantee permanent Christianity at present. In the Church of England we have elaborated it into thirtynine Articles of Religion. No sane person can possibly believe them all; yet every time an ordained clergyman is inducted into a Church living, and asked by the bishop in the face of the whole congregation whether he believes them, he has to tell a flat lie which the bishop knows to be a lie (having had to tell it himself), and which the few members of the congregation who have ever read the Articles know to be a lie. It is the price beneficed clergymen have to pay, quite unnecessarily, for following their vocation. And it is an exceedingly scandalous one, though it makes sure that our clergy shall be Laodicean enough to tell a thumping lie on occasion, and that Quakers and other troublesome zealots shall be excommunicated: for a Church that has not enough spiritual energy to cut the dead wood out of its ritual, and lead its people instead of lagging centuries behind them, is no real Church at all. And the fact that it has no difficulty in obtaining these sworn professions of faith from scholars and politicians who know better, must be taken as an experimental proof of the futility of creeds, catechisms, and vows as tests of conduct and character.

The political parties prove this as fully as the Churches. Their programs and principles are swallowed and vomited just as the Articles are: parliamentary ministers who have risen to power as intransigent Socialists use their power only to do nothing but prevent any change; and Conservative pets of the Primrose League find themselves bringing forward the very Bills they have been elected for opposing. I am not blaming them for this. Progress is impossible without change; and those who cannot change their minds cannot change anything. Creeds, articles, and institutes of religious faith ossify our brains and make change impossible. As such they are nuisances, and in practice have to be mostly ignored.

However, they raise the question as to whether, though policies may and must change, there are not eternal truths which nothing can change. If not, none the less must not a statesman and his constituents act, if they are to act at all, on provisional assumptions as if they were eternal truths? Did not Voltaire say that if there were no God it would be necessary to invent one; and did not Robespierre, exercising the political power which Voltaire never possessed, arrive by trial and error at the same conclusion? Is a ruler who hates justice, loves cruelty, and tramples proudly on his god, to be tolerated because injustice and cruelty and faithlessness are sometimes not only expedient and even unavoidable, but imposingly logical?

Must we not draw a line somewhere, logic or no logic, as a matter of pure sentiment?

The reply to this is that whether we must or not, we do, and always will. No matter though a citizen were at the top of all the panels, we would and should, before electing or appointing him, find out where he draws the line. I do not know of any method that will help us here. A century ago anyone professing Freethought or Republicanism, or even Co-operation, was reprobate. Later on, doubts as to the existence of such a place as a brimstone hell, and whether the Resurrection really ever occurred, came gradually to be tolerated. Men lived openly with their deceased wives' sisters without being ostracized as monsters of depravity. Laws to prevent apostasy, sedition, and obscenity, though they were not repealed as the obsolete clauses in them should have been, were relaxed or tacitly dropped and supplanted by new Acts. It became more and more observable that sceptics, heretics, rebels, were often good men and true whilst rigid conformists were quite as often gentry whose only number was Number One. In drawing the line between good candidates and bad ones, which every voter does, reasonably or unreasonably, as inevitably and naturally as he breathes, labels are hopelessly untrustworthy. There are British electors whose rule it is to vote against the Jew, against the Jesuit, against the Irish Roman Catholic, the Atheist, Socialist, Republican, Teetotaller or who not, and others whose rule it is to vote for them. Such lines are the only ones they are capable of drawing. This would not greatly matter if they had to choose from a panel; but they should be disfranchised anyhow.

Usually, however, electoral choice cannot be instinctive in England at present; for our rulers are mostly elected by people who have never seen them and know nothing intimate about them, voting therefore according to Party labels, religious creeds, and social prejudices, under pressure of more or less vigorous propaganda and canvassing.

Behind the occasional propaganda of the hustings there is the ceaseless propaganda of the Churches, the professions, the movements of one sort or another, each trying to make proselytes by persuading the public that it is, on its own subject, the sole authority on the eternal truths. Some of them go so far as to be the sole authority on all truths on all subjects. And we are obliged to accept these pretensions because as some individual or council must decide we have to treat these deciders as infallible for the moment. The Pope, *ex cathedra*, is infallible; the Judicial Committee of the House of Lords is infallible; the Royal Academy of Arts is infallible; the General Medical Council is infallible; the Bible is infallible; the Cabinet is infallible; the Men of Science are infallible; drumhead courts martial are infallible; and the King can do no wrong. We have to assume the truth of these propositions in the teeth of thousands of instances in which all these authorities have been wrong over and over again.

CHAPTER XXXVIII

COLLECTIVE SCOUNDRELISM

A SCOUNDREL is a person who pursues his or her own personal gratification without regard to the feelings and interests of others. Perfection in scoundrelism is never attained by individuals, though many have achieved it nearly enough to make it necessary to liquidate them. Cartouche, Titus Oates, and those who adopt as their means of livelihood the practice of marrying for the purpose of insuring the lives of their spouses and then murdering them, no doubt act kindly on occasion; but no statesman fit for his job would hesitate to order their deaths. Pending the discovery of some means of changing their natures they must be left to the executioner as certain morbid physical growths must be left to the surgeon.

With men in the lump it is different. Organized as States, Churches, professions, or commercial companies, they not only commit the worst atrocities but claim the right to commit them on principle and glorify them as national triumphs. Christendom is supplanted by Scoundreldom; and in the realm of Scoundreldom statesmen find themselves obliged to contrive and sanction villainies in the interests of the State from which they would recoil horrorstricken on their private account. Unofficial sectional organizations, if numerous enough, misbehave in the same way, each asserting that its interests are, like those of the State, totalitarian. Imperialist conquests with their bombardments and blockades, offensive and defensive, the fires of Smithfield and the Inquisition, the criminal codes, the cruelties of the physiological laboratories, the shortening and embitterment of proletarian life by commercial profiteering, all go to prove that public morals differ from private ones.

This is where Machiavelli comes in. Nothing could have been easier for him than to have told Caesar Borgia that his duty was to do justice, to love mercy, and to walk humbly before his God. Such counsel would have been pious, but not to the purpose of Borgia, which was, as he put it, "to swallow Italy bit by bit like an artichoke" so that he might then unify it as a single Catholic State. In this he was no more wicked than Garibaldi or Cavour, than Abraham Lincoln unifying the North American States, than Joseph Chamberlain and Lord Randolph Churchill maintaining the union of Britain and Ireland, than Bismarck unifying Germany, or than Adolf Hitler unifying Germany and Austria and, like Napoleon, finally aspiring to unify the Eurasian continent. Now Caesar Borgia could not unify Italy by simply doing all that God required of him according to Micah the Morasthite. There were hostile princes to be overcome, and ignorant and superstitious populaces to be enthused. What Borgia wanted to know was how, under the circumstances, to outwit these princes and humbug these populaces, they being what they were, and he, Caesar Borgia, being what he was. Deceit was necessary. Bloodshed was necessary. Treachery was all in the day's work. Hypocrisy was a matter of course. Assurances that victory and fulfilment of the will of God were the sole objects of Borgia's policy were indispensable. Machiavelli applauded him for his sagacity in knowing this, and his practical ability in acting on it. Why blame Machiavelli for not lying about it? It is true that by substituting candor for hypocrisy he gave away the show; but then, being a deeper man than Caesar Borgia, he wanted to give away the show. I myself have meddled in public affairs, and am in fact doing so at this moment in the manner of Machiavelli by writing a book about them. Meanwhile the Big Powers are engaged in bombing cities, torpedoing ships, cutting off food supplies and mining the seven seas: all of them actions which are not merely scoundrelly but diabolical. I would do anything in my power to have them classed as criminal by supernational law, and barred from civilized practice as duelling and piracy are barred; yet I am obliged by the circumstances to urge their continuance and extension until the Nazis are defeated and their Führer politically outlawed. And so are we all, friends and foes alike.

Now nothing is more puzzling than having to work with a double set of morals. The king of Brobdingnag found Gulliver a very amiable little pet until Gulliver rashly boasted to him of the glories of English history, whereupon the king was amazed to find that his amiable little pet was also a most pernicious little scoundrel. Mr Wells found Pavlov charming, humane, and intelligent, with a striking resemblance to me who denounced him as a monster of cruelty. He was a man with two natures and perhaps several more of which we know nothing; for human nature is manifold not only in the sense that men differ from each other and "it takes all sorts to make a world," but in that every one of us is not a simple single character but a bundle of characters under one hat. Yet for public purposes we blacklist one man as a coward, and inscribe the name of another on the roll of honour as a hero. The Victoria Cross has been won by men abjectly afraid of ghosts, dogs, and dentists. Lawrence of Arabia, in the one full dress pitched battle at which he was present, had an attack of pure funk which troubled him for twenty minutes and then passed off completely. In 1815 no one would have been so shameless as to confess to such a lapse. In 1915 nobody was so shameless as to pretend that he felt no misgivings when the enemy's barrage was finding the range.

What makes legislation and government such a difficult and uncertain business is that laws cannot vary as individuals vary. They must assume that everybody is exactly like everybody else, although no two people are alike; that everybody is consistent although everybody is in fact a sackful of contradictions; that all marriages are alike, all love affairs alike, all children alike, all parents alike, all consciences alike, and all capacities alike, although they are all as different as fingerprints. The petty legislators of the professions are in the same dilemma as the political ones. Clifford Allbutt, a famous physician, is quoted as saying to his students ranged round a hospital bed "This, gentlemen, is what is called scarlet fever; but all the cases are different." Another eminent doctor, Bland Sutton, was treating typhoid fever without drugs when a friend of mine suffering from it swallowed prescriptions containing half a dozen different poisons. She actually recovered. But in law and in the medical schools it must still be assumed that scarlet fever is scarlet fever, and that there is only one proper treatment for typhoid. No matter in what direction we turn we find that we must "draw the line" somewhere. The medical staff of a hospital may test a new drug by trying it on a ward full of sick children (sometimes most of them die); but a law making the killing of children in the course of experimental research a privileged scientific activity, has not yet been passed by any legislature.

In the laboratories the drugs are tried on the dog, the guinea pig, the rat, the mouse, and the drosophila fly. We do not waste any sympathy on the fly: indeed our sanitary laws aim at the extermination of flies, bugs, lice, cockroaches, and other pests. People who live in the country and cultivate the land very soon discover that a necessary part of their business is the ruthless slaughter of keas, foxes, rabbits, and squirrels, though squirrels are quite attractive creatures, and rabbits are kept as pets when they are white. A French fencing-master said to me, when he was told that I never eat meat, "But, sir, if we do not eat the animals the animals will eat us." Eating, however will not keep them all down; for we refuse to eat cats as the Chinese do and frogs as the French do, whilst the Germans refuse to eat rabbits as we do, and all Europeans refuse to eat beetles as Africans do. The Roman Catholic Church and some of the Indian Churches may not take life under any circumstances; and we have people who object to killing murderers, though the substitution of lifelong penal servitude leaves them quite satisfied. Such people are impossible as politicians. Killing is a necessity, a duty, which no State, however humanitarian, can escape or leave unregulated. A parent who finds a cobra in the garden where his children play, and hesitates to kill it, is unfit to have charge of children. Wolves and man-eating tigers must be exterminated. There are men and women quite as dangerous. They also must be killed, not in the least as punishment or expiation, but simply because they are unfit for civilized society, and the lives of fit people must not be wasted in restraining them. Our killing must extend from the weeding out of unbearable individuals to the extinction of whole species. The capital punishment abolitionist must draw the line somewhere.

When we consider not only the birds, beasts, and fishes, but the insects, the obligation to destroy or be destroyed is terrifying. As I write, the human species is busy on its own destruction: half the world's population is doing its best to kill the other half; and though that end is unattainable, being beyond the slaughtering power of either, yet the dead are counted by millions. Many pious simpletons are asking why God does not stop this. But how?

Well, if I were an Omnipotent Creator I could stop the war in a week by letting loose a few billion locusts and white ants in every acre of territory in the countries of the belligerents. Next day they would be fighting, not each other, but armies of tiny creatures advancing on them heroically wave upon wave over the bodies of their dead comrades in countless numbers with indomitable discipline, and making an end of human food and human furniture so fast that even the pallid spirochete and the anopheles mosquito would be forgotten in the general terror. There would be no Semites and anti-Semites then, no British and Germans, no Americans and Japanese, no proletarians and proprietors, no democrats and plutocrats, Moslems and Hindus, blacks and whites, yellows and reds, no Irishmen even, nothing but men and women fighting frantically for human life against a war of aggression known before only by little samples of its possibility.

However, as it might be too troublesome and too messy to create insects in the necessary numbers I am not sure that I should not try another method. Suppose the papers tomorrow appeared without a single headline about the war, and one very big one to announce that the Polar icecaps had begun to spread! That has occurred before and may occur again at any moment. Our empires, our great national destinies, our glorious pasts, our jealously guarded frontiers, would not count then for much more than the dinosaurs and pterodactyls do now.

I imagine such things when I wish to see all our patriotic and militaristic bunk and guff and bugaboo in their proper insignificance; but as my present business is rather to reveal the importance of killing as a necessary department of political and personal activity, and to convince you that our statesmen have to deal not only with Moses's "Thou shalt not kill" but with Nature's "Thou must kill or perish" I must leave the white ants and icecaps and pursue Scoundrelism into its possibilities when government is not collective but individual, as our inveterate idolatry of Great Men tends continually to make it.

CHAPTER XXXIX

GOVERNMENT BY GREAT MEN, SO-CALLED

It is generally assumed in political harangues and discussions that there are only two methods of government to choose from, the first being, as Lincoln phrased it, government of the people, for the people, by the people, called shortly, Democracy. The second is government by single great men, called dictators. I hope I have already made it clear that democracy thus defined is romantic nonsense. "The people" have obstructed government often enough:

they have revolted; but they have never really governed. The Great Man idea will bear a more detailed examination, which I undertake with some authority, as I happen to be classed by the sect of Shavians as a Great Man myself.

The two methods are impossible extremes, not inevitable alternatives; but the vulgar assumption that they are is useful to both at elections. "Are you, free Britons, going to vote away all the liberties your fathers have won, and be the slaves of a dictator and his bureaucracy?" cry the democrats. "Have you not had enough of parliamentary futility and anarchy?" cry the idolaters. "Vote for effective responsible government by our great leader!"

For government, as for other human activities, the means must exist as well as the ends; and we must make the best of what rulers we can get instead of howling for all we would like. Government by the people is not possible if the people do not know how to govern, and desire to be governed as little but as spectacularly as possible. Government by Great Men (so-called) needs capable pretenders, who are not always forthcoming. When they are, they are not all of the same sort. The late Ignaz Paderewski was classed as a Great Man because he was an extraordinary piano player: he was actually made President of the Polish State. Napoleon won a similar eminence as a military genius. I am classed as a dramatic genius; but I have not yet been invited to govern the British Empire or even my native Ireland; nor was Shakespear, though great "not for an age but for all time," made Emperor of the Earth. Benito Mussolini and Adolf Hitler, self-classed as Great Men, have invited themselves to rule their countries as a preliminary to governing all the other countries, and had their invitations endorsed with enthusiasm by their fellowcountrymen. Titus Oates had many persons executed in England in spite of the royal power of Charles II; and Rasputin exercised despotic influence in Russia over the official hereditary despot. Cromwell, Richelieu, Frederick William of Prussia and his son Frederick the Great, reorganized the State in their respective countries to their individual liking by completely tyrannical methods. So did Peter the Great. Julius Caesar, Genghis Khan, and Attila won enduring fame as Great Men before Jesus Christ, who promised to rise from his tomb and reign over the kingdom of heaven on earth: a promise which, though unfulfilled, still numbers many believers.

This is very far from being a complete list; but as a collection of samples it shews that the supply of Great Men is not providential, and has been adulterated by cads, halfwits, snobs, scoundrels, black-guards, and undesirables of all sorts to a degree so discreditable that the reaction against it has made a romance of democracy, and a conditioned reflex of Anarchism, just as these extravagances have in turn provoked counter reactions into feudalism, oligarchy, divine right of kings, or a now prevalent romance called Totalitarianism or the complete subjugation of the individual by the State. But all, Democrats and Anarchists no less than Caesarist militarists and churchmen, have their leaders and heroes and are like lost sheep without them.

A party without leaders and a State without rulers is like a ship without navigators; and the problem for the political philosopher is how to keep the leaders and rulers in moral harness. The French were probably right when they chose Napoleon as the man most capable of restoring order. He did restore order, and ruled more ably than the Directorate which he superseded; but he presently crowned himself, forced the Pope to accept him as Holy Roman Emperor, and made the rulership of France hereditary in his family. Though he passed as the world's greatest realist, he quarrelled after his downfall with Sir Hudson Lowe in St. Helena because Sir Hudson realistically refused to accept him as the emperor he no longer was, and addressed and treated him as General Bonaparte. The few devoted adherents who voluntarily shared his exile had to stand in his presence and address him as Sire, though realisti-cally he had become a complete nobody. When he became bank-rupt as a glory merchant, leaving France under the feet of the enemies he had made for her, there was nothing left of him but a rather pitiable Borkman dreaming vainly of an impossible restora-tion, and resuming his early efforts as an author by whitewashing himself in volumes which only the most industrious professional historians have ever read. Even at the height of his fortunes he kicked Volney (another realist) for saying that what France wanted was to have the Bourbons back again. He kidnapped and shot D'Enghien in a fit of temper which made him technically a mur-derer, and made D'Enghien dead worth a thousand times more to Napoleon's enemies than ever he was when alive.

It is therefore quite in order to call Napoleon a snob, a cad, an assassin, and a scoundrel. Contrasted with equally famous and more original generals like Marlborough, Marshal Saxe, and Wellington, he was no gentleman. Contrasted with his subordinate Bernadotte, whose heirs still hold the throne of Sweden, he was a failure. Those of his detractors who imagine that dauntless personal courage on all occasions is the leading characteristic of great generals can please themselves by pointing out that in two crises in his fate he was so frightened that in the first he owed his life to his brother and in the last he described his own conduct as that of a poltroon. Contrasted with his schoolfellow and valet-secretary Bourrienne, who discharged himself from his service after calling him unprintable names, he was a beggar on horseback who rode hard to the devil. He not only landed himself in St Helena, defeated and politically smashed, but, it is said, reduced the average stature of the French nation by a couple of inches through the wholesale slaughterings of young men in his battles. And all this, which I jot down offhand as common knowledge, can no doubt be aggravated by anyone who cares to compile a fuller dossier.

Now it would be the greatest mistake to infer from these facts that Napoleon was not what we imagine when we call him a Great Man. What they do demonstrate is that he was not an anthropomorphic god; so, as divinity and nothing less is what his devotees claim for him, it may safely be concluded that Great Men and anthropomorphic gods are alike fabulous.

All men, Lord Acton said, are corrupted by irresponsible power. Sometimes, as in the cases of Nero and Torquemada, it produces horrible excesses of cruelty and bigotry. Sometimes men like Julius Caesar, Mahomet, Cromwell, and Washington make the best of their power or at least not the worst of it. On the whole I should say that the absolute rulers who have not abused their authority intolerably must be in an enormous majority. But they have ruled on established moral, legal, and ritual lines which have served as a constitution, though, like the British constitution, they have never been written down as such. The Cadi under the palm tree, though apparently a despot, does not provoke a revolution. It is when reformation is in hand that despots make trouble, and the Great Man finds his chance. Cromwell, the country gentleman brewer, becomes Lord Protector: plain Tsar Peter becomes Peter the Great: Lieutenant Bonaparte, an artillery officer, becomes Emperor Napoleon: Kemal, another subaltern, becomes a Supersultan: Benito Mussolini, a proletarian journalist, reigns as Archduke: Hitler and Stalin, both of them social nobodies, rise by sheer gravitation to powers that no Holy Roman Emperor ever exercised. Of these only Cromwell with his Bible and Covenants of Grace, and Stalin with his Marxist philosophy, held themselves within constitutional limits (as we say, had any principles); and they alone stand out as successful rulers. Napoleon began as a Jacobin instrument of the French Revolution and the colleague of Sieyès who specialized in constitutions; but he soon threw Sieyès over and went his own way, like Shakespear's Richard III, whose final profession of faith was "Our strong arms be our conscience, swords our law."

Of Kemal Ataturk I know too little to classify him; but the permanence and solidity of his success, and the consistency of his reforms, convince me that he had a mental framework which served as a constitution. Peter, a terrific blackguard personally, was a Westernizer, like our own government in British India; and westernization, even when blindly overreached, takes its leaders beyond mere selfishness and gives them a creed. And as the creeds are of all sorts, it matters not whether a ruler is Atheist or Plymouth Brother, Jain or Mussulman or Buddhist, Confucian or Lâotist, Catholic or Protestant, Anglo, Roman, or Greek Catholic, Ritualist or Quaker. Provided he (or she) be militant and not merely ovine, the rule will be to that extent extra-personal and predictable; and if it be also acceptable, capable, and popular, it will endure, however undemocratic it may be in form. As the phrase goes, you know where to have such rulers, meaning that even if you cannot guess what they will do next you feel sure as to what they will not do. Mussolini and Hitler have failed in this respect. They have won their eminence by doing certain things that everybody wanted to have done, and been idolized accordingly; but having no established and generally intelligible creed, no one can feel any assurance of where they will stop; and so, to keep their supremacy, they have to feed their idolaters with military glories and their financiers with commercial successes, which is not continually possible. Napoleon was able to hold on as a glory merchant for fifteen years, his nephew for twenty, Mussolini for twentyone. Hitler, in spite of dazzling conquests, is already badly shaken after ten years. Possibly Napoleon in St Helena may have felt that his transient successes had lasted long enough to have been worth while, and that he had done more good than the rulers he had supplanted; and the others may make out an equally good case for themselves. But this does not excuse the futility and corruption which gave them their chance, nor the bloodshed and destruction and demoralization which the glory merchant has to substitute for "the grace of our Lord Jesus Christ." All the good that Great Men have done could have been done without them had the governments they supplanted been either efficient or reasonable.

There are two more snags in government by Great Men. Their work soon wears them out. Napoleon considered that a general is used up in six years; and he himself was certainly not the same man at Leipzig, nor even after his rest in Elba at Waterloo, as at Austerlitz. Yet the direction of a war is simpler than the civil government of a commonwealth; for every opposing interest, every moral and constitutional safeguard, has to give way to the need for victory, whereas in peace they are all in full play and cannot be extinguished by violence. The American Presidency lasts for four years only; and a second term, deeply grudged, is granted only under war pressure or as the better of a choice of evils, though, as four years is too short, a second term when the presidency has worked well will probably become customary.

The other objection to Great Man rule is that it is too totalitarian to be really possible. As the ablest autocrat would be worked to death in a few months if he attempted to direct everything in the country, he has to leave the local work to a host of deputy autocrats chosen from his most subservient followers rather than from his ablest rivals. In the days when the President of the United States and the Tsar of Russia represented the two extremes of responsible government and autarchy, it was notable that the credit of the President and his Secretaries of State, commercial and political, was enormously higher than that of the Tsar with his provincial governors, any of whom could knock down a factory to please a mistress who did not like the look of it.

There is no getting over these inexorable facts. There is no hope for civilization in government by idolized single individuals. Councils of tested qualified persons, subject to the sternest possible public criticism, and to periodical (in pressing cases even summary) removal and replacement, is our safest aim. The purpose of this book is to urge the necessity for panels of the qualified, and to suggest items in the testing curriculum.

It must not be inferred that absolute authority, ranking as infallible, can be dispensed with by any State. There must be authorities in all directions whose decisions are final, from those of the housekeeper in the kitchen to those of the Pope in the Vatican. But the Pope ranks as infallible only when he speaks *ex cathedra:* that is, in council with his cardinals, and with the Vatican library at his disposal for historical research. The remarks dropped by Alexander

Borgia in the course of his somewhat scandalous diversions were not pontifical. In England the Judicial Committee of the House of Lords is Pope; but it also is ranked as infallible only in council: the small talk of the judges who compose it has no more authority than yours or mine. Not that either the Pope or the Judicial Committee, the Vatican or the House of Lords, is really infallible; for there is no such thing in nature as an infallible human authority; but somebody must have the last word: that is all. It should, however, be *ex cathedra:* the last word of a council, not of an individual. Leaders in council may have influence enough to be virtually dictators; but as no leader can know everything, if the decision really rests with him personally he should work with assessors, and hear all sides and be informed of all the local facts as far as possible. Assessors, however, can never replace councillors; for all the facts never become accessible until years after the event. The best informed statesman must be also a good guesser *a priori;* for, as Wellington put it, he never can see what is happening on the far side of the hill.

We must not think too exclusively of how to guard against government being unbearably bad. It may also be unbearably good. From Amenhotep IV in ancient Egypt to Amanullah Khan in modern Afghanistan enlightened cerebrotonic monarchs have tried to impose on their subjects reforms and new institutions that were too high over their heads. They failed, and were more hated than Nero or Tsar Paul. When the temperance movement in the United States culminated in total prohibition of the drink trade, the direct results were excellent, and are still being achieved under Local Option here and there in Great Britain, and nationally in Sweden and elsewhere; nevertheless such an amazing reign of gangsterdom grew out of the illicit trade in intoxicants that Prohibition had to be eliminated from the Constitution. If I were an omnipotent despot I should enforce such a distribution of the material conditions of natural vitality as to make my subjects independent of analgesics, intoxicants, stimulants, tobacco, fish, flesh, and fowl for their endurance of life. I should try to abolish trade in these things. Cackle about Freedom of Diet, and cries of "Better England drunk in freedom than sober in slavery" would not move me in the least. But I neither aspire to be a British Tsar nor care to risk being lynched. I am properly classed as too good to govern a nation too poor to stand the strain of combining goodness with poverty. A genial goodnatured connoisseur in whisky, cigars, and horses, with plenty of energy and no intellect, would be much more popular than I can ever hope to be. He would not provoke a regicidal revolution as I probably should. Even if I died a natural death, it would be followed by a reaction compared to which the one that followed the death of Cromwell would seem trifling. True, the licentiousness of the Restoration court did not affect the entire nation, which is still as Puritanical as New England; nor, though Calvin and Knox were unco guid like Cromwell, has their moralizing work ever been wholly undone; but they provoked a considerable reaction by not giving the Devil his due. Had they done so they would not have mistaken the Divine Artist for the Prince of Darkness. Yet these Puritan Philistines had glimpses of the light, thanks to the word-music of the English Bible. Cromwell thought that stage plays were wicked, but approved of operas. A Cabinet minister, whom I was pressing for an educational grant to a school of dramatic art, said "Couldnt you put in an organ?" The possibility of this saved the situation: I got the grant. That minister presently distinguished himself as a leader of the opposition to an attempt in Parliament to revise the Book of Common Prayer, a document hopelessly out of date in some essential matters, but casting its spell as a work of art.

It happens most blessedly that the Bible is not only the supreme example of English literary art. Dangerous and barbarous as much of it is, it is also inspired in its constant association of the spiritual plane with music, thus exempting this most enchanting of all the arts from the scriptural damnation of the simulative arts which persist in making graven images and likenesses of everything in the heaven above and on the earth beneath and in the water under the earth, even going to the length of dressing up histrionic vagabonds to simulate sacred personages.

The moral of this is that leaders and rulers should be cultivated aesthetically so as not to be liable to the popular error of confusing recreative art with the debauchery and pornography of its prostitutions. Government by ignorant good men may be worse than by cultivated bad ones. Cromwell found that though the Reign of the Sinners was so bad that it provoked him to cut off King Charles's head, the Reign of the Saints made government quite impossible. Twentyfive years ago, Russia abolished God; suppressed the Bible; and copied from the Abbey of Thelema the precept Do AS THOU WOULDST, with the result that Russia is now the most Puritanical country in the world, without as yet any perceptible reaction.

If I had to choose between government by zealots and government by Laodiceans I might vote for the Laodiceans. But I prefer sensible manysided men to either.

CHAPTER XL

FOR THE REVIEWERS

THE pressing need for breaking off this unfinishable book has now become imperative. It consists largely of things often said before by myself and others. They will have to be said again and again, oftener than a nail has to be hit by a hammer, before they get effectively knocked into Mr Everyman's consciousness.

I have another reason for repeating them here. I have to consider the reviewers. When I first began to live by my pen I did so as a reviewer; and I know well that whether a reviewer can afford to read the book he is reviewing depends on how much he will be paid for his review. Sometimes the blurb on the dust jacket must suffice; and as this is always laudatory, authors are fortunate when the reviewer gets no farther. I shall take care accordingly that an appetizing blurb is provided. But there are reviewers who, being better paid, can afford to be more conscientious. Though to go through the whole book would take up too much of their time they would like to have it condensed for them.

Then there is the general reader, who actually pays to read the book as a privilege instead of being paid to read it as a job. He (or she) is often so bewildered by the time the thirtieth chapter is reached that a reminder of the first is needed to restore selfpossession. Let me therefore attempt here a rough conspectus of the field as I have surveyed it.

There are five main directions in which a civilization can go wrong, mostly by falling out-of-date and being overgrown with superstitions through not weeding the garden. The five are its economics, its politics, its science, its education, and its religion. I maintain that in all five we are dangerously behind the times, and will go to pieces like all former civilizations known to us unless we give our institutions a thorough overhaul pretty frequently.

The question immediately arises, from whose point of view are

we out of date? From the point of view of Everyman and his wife
our institutions are not only not behindhand but considerably beforehand, because the Everymans are so ignorant or miseducated
economically, politically, scientifically, and religiously that they can
neither govern themselves nor choose their governors wisely. Their
unwisely chosen rulers land them in such messes that in desperation
they fall at the feet of selfchosen dictators who get corrupted by
absolute powers which no single man could exercise singlehanded
even if he were uncorrupted. These despots presently age and die,
leaving their idolaters in their former helplessness until some new
adventurer arises to be idolized by them.

The only radical cure for this is a completely up-to-date education
within everyone's reach, technical and compulsory up to a certain
point (every child must learn the multiplication table), and beyond
that point voluntary, rational, and aesthetic to the limit of human
knowledge and capacity. This limit varies so much from individual
to individual that our attempts to impose the highest education indiscriminately on average minds (let alone primitive ones) is not
only waste of time but injurious cruelty, like setting a child to
stroke in the University Boat Race, whilst to deny it to an Einstein
or a Gilbert Murray is to waste or handicap a talent of inestimable
value to civilization. It should be within the reach of everybody
and forced on nobody. People who are neither over nor under
educated take their places in the world cheerfully, and are the first
to admit that the notion that everybody can be taught at school to
become a higher mathematician, a grammarian and epic poet writing in ancient Greek and Latin, an epochmaking philosopher, a Pope
or Primate, a competent Prime Minister or member of the Cabinet,
a victorious admiral or field-marshal, a Lord Chief Justice, a successful shopkeeper or factory director, much less a qualified judge and
elector of all these, which is the theoretic aim of our Boards of Education and Adult Suffragists, is pedantic poppycock. Rulers must
be persons born with relevant special aptitudes and special abilities,
and acquire an executive technique as carpenters and cooks do.
In their various grades they should therefore be chosen from panels
of persons who have satisfied the best available tests of their capacity, and not merely at random from telephone directories or
election registers of common ratepayers.

Nature miraculously provides the necessary number of persons
thus specially gifted, and always provides them in excess, giving their
electors a choice which makes democracy possible when the supply

is not cut off by withholding the indispensable education from nine-tenths of the population, as at present. This special operation of Nature is called Divine Providence. It has been denied or ignored for a century past by professional scientists just as the Diabolical Providence that produces our percentage of idiots is denied or ignored by doctrinaire democrats. It has been idolized by our party democrats and by North Americans generally, who maintain that in politics there is no such thing as political specialization, all majorities being equally and infinitely wise as social philosophers and infallible as electors. This of course is nonsense: majority rule was simply a peaceful acceptance of the probability that if the parties fought for supremacy the bigger battalions, not the brainier, would win. Nature, or Divine Providence (whichever or whatever you choose to call it) is all for minority government, competent Cabinet ministers being in a much smaller minority than tinkers and tailors. There are no vocational majorities; and wise government is the most highly specialized of vocations. The professed scientists and democrats who do not know these facts are treated in this book with the most complete disrespect as public nuisances. And both sorts very naturally retort by denouncing me as an enemy of Science and an old Tory. But however we may squabble, the facts are the facts; and the reader will do well to look at the world and not listen to our reciprocal vituperations.

And now to my summaries.

CHAPTER XLI

ECONOMIC SUMMARY

TWENTIETH-CENTURY sociologists must begin with an emphatic repudiation of the eighteenth-century Rousseau-Jefferson and pre-Marxian delusion that all men are born free. They must rub in the fact that we are all born in a slavery to Nature which compels us to work x hours a day, as cows are compelled to graze, on pain of death by hunger, thirst, cold, and exposure. No one can shirk this burden of work except by imposing a double burden of it on somebody else, or, if this is impossible, a tenth of the burden on ten other people. This can happen only when the shirkers are the political masters of the workers, and the workers the political slaves of the shirkers as well as the slaves of Nature.

Everyone, worker or shirker, must sleep for eight hours out of the twentyfour, and reserve two hours more for meals, dressing, washing, and the locomotion that cannot be shifted to horses, cars, or the back of Sinbad the sailor. However, as eating, drinking, sleeping, and moderate exercise are agreeable, nobody wants to be relieved from them; and as, anyhow, they cannot be materially altered by legislation, the statesman is troubled only with the fourteen hours left available for productive or serviceable work.

Thus, though Man as the slave of Nature must work, his dislike of compulsory work urges him to a constant effort to reduce it and leave him free to do what he likes, or to do nothing but amuse himself. This freedom is called Leisure. It is, like labor, transferable. When tools, division of labor and mass production, machines, machine tools, and the harnessing to the machine tools and machines of horse power, steam power, electricity, and volcanic pressure make labor power so productive that, say, 14 hours of labor by one worker can produce a day's subsistence for several families in addition of that of the worker's family, it can maintain a single chieftain's family in royal splendor alongside fewer workers' families with barely enough to live on, or any distributive arrangement between these two extremes. And when there are, say, fourteen millions of workers available, they can, by working as hard as ever, and consuming only what is barely necessary to keep them living and reproducing themselves, make it possible for a million families to have fourteen hours of leisure daily in the greatest purchaseable luxury without contributing a stroke of work for the community except the childbearing of their women.

No sane person would propose or expect such an arrangement *ab initio*. The original intention of all human societies except bands of robbers was to make sure that "if a man will not work neither shall he eat." But when civilization began by agriculture, the readiest means of securing this moral end was to give every man the land he cultivated as his private property, and make laws to prevent anyone from trespassing on it without obtaining his permission by grace or by purchase. Whilst there was enough equally fertile land for everybody this worked fairly enough; but when the best land, and finally all land within reach, was appropriated, and populations increased from hundreds to millions, the very anomaly which property in land was instituted to prevent was automatically produced by it: that is, the proprietors took all the leisure and the rest did all the work.

As under these conditions the landless were serfs with barely enough to live on, and the landlords had much more than enough, the monopoly of land created a monopoly of spare money. Spare money made factory industry possible, and when used to establish it was called capital. The proprietors came to be called capitalists, and the serfs who had no capital to be called, classically, proletarians, and *en masse*, the proletariat. This class monopoly of capital made schooling and aesthetic culture also a class monopoly. These monopolies passed from generation to generation by inheritance or bequest because there is no other way of disposing of them until the State develops into a Commune equipped for owning, conducting, and administering land and industry for the public benefit.

Simple inheritance subdivides land and scatters capital into smaller and smaller parcels until they are not worth owning. To prevent this the proprietors instituted primogeniture, by which estates descended intact to the eldest son, thus producing a new class of younger sons with the education, culture, and expensive habits of their class, but without bread and cheese, which they had to earn by engaging in the businesses and professions from which the proletariat were excluded by their illiteracy.

Thus automatically, without anyone knowing what was happening, a Three Class System established itself: upper class, middle class, and illiterate lower class. The lower class outnumbered the two others combined; but, being too poor, ignorant, and leisureless for political work, and having no weapons but sticks and stones, nor any tactics except strikes and riots, they could do only what their masters planned and ordered, receiving just enough money to save them from extinction as a class in spite of frightful infantile mortality and brevity of adult life.

Such a state of things inevitably produces a chronic class war, in which the middle and upper classes are in league against the lower; for the men of business, being the active instruments of the exploitation of the proletariat, live by sharing the plunder, leaving legislation and diplomacy to such members of the propertied class as have any fancy or capacity for it, whilst the rest live unproductively on rents, and in France are frankly called renters.

Protests and revolts against the Three Class System and against its iniquities were made long before anyone understood it as a system. Sages, seers, prophets, agitators, and demagogues of all classes have denounced it. Many of them were martyred, perhaps the best known of these being Jesus, who declared that it was easier for a camel to pass through the eye of a needle than for a rich man to enter the kingdom of heaven. He should have taught that it was quite easy for the rich men to be virtuous, and desperately hard for the poor men; but not understanding the capitalist system he was led by his compassion for the poor and his indignation at their treatment to attribute all virtue to the poor and all villainy to the rich, the fact being that "the poor in the lump is bad" and the rich in the lump comparatively good, poverty and not wealth being the evil to attack and abolish.

By the eighteenth century the capitalist system had become so complicated that it had to set to work seriously to understand itself. In France the Physiocrats (notably Turgot) tackled the problem and studied it to the point at which it was taken up in Scotland by Adam Smith in his Wealth of Nations, and carried to its final elucidation by Malthus, Ricardo, and De Quincey. They convinced people as intelligent and benevolent as John Austin, Macaulay, Harriet Martineau, Cobden, and John Stuart Mill (who finally became a Socialist) that with all its evils, which they fully admitted and faced, it was the best of which human nature is capable. It became the standard political economy of the first half of the nineteenth century; but as by sheer force of circumstances it soon had to be patched up by communistic measures everywhere, it is now so discredited in England as a theory that the last Cobdenist doctrinaire who ventured to contest an election as such forfeited his deposit. Yet Cobdenism is still taught as classic in the universities. It may yet recover its shattered prestige when communist legislation produces a country in which poverty and slavery no longer exist, and everyone has a fair share of the available leisure and spare money. Cobdenism may then revive sufficiently to republish Mill's essay on Liberty; canonize Benedetto Croce beside Karl Marx; and dominate our minds as Free Trade did in the heyday of Cobden and Bright.

For Cobdenism never converted the sociologists who could see beyond their class, and knew the world they were living in. The facts were too horrible. Ruskin, Carlyle, and Dickens would have none of Macaulay's cheerful meliorism and progress-boosting: they saw that Capitalism was the robber's road to ruin, and would not study its theory. Therefore they never understood it, and could not find the political remedy. Then there arose Karl Marx, a prophet

who had read the reports of the factory inspectors, and knew more
than any of them about the condition of the working class. Being a
Jew, he felt about it like Jeremiah, and could hate as passionately.
Being a trained Hegelian thinker, he picked up enough of the
Ricardian thought plan to turn its guns on itself. In Germany
Ferdinand Lassalle, another educated Jew, did the same. These two
between them provided what Jeremiah, Jesus, and Ruskin lacked:
an alternative political economy to that of Ricardo and Cobden.
This economy, called Socialism, solved the problem of mass production and its possibilities of leisure, by State ownership of land,
State control and practice of industry, and State allotment of the
product between consumption, capital, and investment, in the ex-
tremest contradiction to the Cobdenist restriction of State action
to police work, diplomacy, episcopacy, and enforcement of private
contracts.

The struggle between the two policies has produced an attempt to
mix them. Our Manchester and Midland Cobdenists have had their
eyes opened by the Fabian Socialists to the enormous possibilities of
commercial enterprise aided by the financial resources and political
power of the State. To achieve this without State ownership of land
or confiscation of rent and interest, would make the capitalist class
rich beyond the dreams of avarice, and enable it to be generous
enough to the proletariat to keep a decisive majority of voters
satisfied. This policy, called Fascism in Italy, National Socialism
or Nazidom in Germany, is in growing and vigorous practice in
England and the so-called Western democracies, where it is left
unnamed. Properly it is State Capitalism; but, as it still passes as
the old private Capitalism, its advocates daily denounce Italian and
German Fascism as the blackest political villainy and its leaders as
the last foes to be overcome. This is an example of the present
general confusion of tongues, in which, as the theories of Capitalism,
Fascism, and Socialism are understood by only a very few specialists,
they are continually misplaced by politicians and journalists who do
not know what they are talking about. The few who do know find
that nineteenth century Socialism was too much preoccupied with
the abolition of poverty and too little with the employment of
leisure and culture. The word Socialism jars on them as shopsoiled
bad English; and they are substituting Scientific Humanism, which
is more comprehensive, better English, and free from the Inhuman-
ism which has so horribly shopsoiled the name Science during the
last hundred years.

Meanwhile the tyranny of Nature dominates all Party considerations and policies; and the problem of organizing human society so as to secure the utmost possible welfare for everybody through a just sharing of the burden of service and the benefit of leisure remains fundamental. Until this is not only demanded but achieved in effective practical operation, all Constitutions, platform slogans, and political programs, from the commandments of Moses and the Sermon on the Mount to the Atlantic Charter and the Teheran Declaration, count for little more than phrasemaking and hot air. Benedetto Croce is right when he teaches that Liberty is a key to history; and Benito Mussolini is equally right when he describes Liberty as a stinking corpse. In the world war we claim to be fighting for democracy; and Adolf Hitler retorts unanswerably that British democracy is nothing but Anglo-Semitic plutocracy. Liberty and Democracy mean nothing to the citizen who has no leisure. Where 90% of the people have all the work and no leisure, and 10% all the leisure and no work (or thereabouts), Liberty is a will-o'-the-wisp; Magna Charta, the Petition of Rights, the American Constitution, and the French motto of Liberty and Equality are mere scraps of paper; and no fresh Declaration of rights can be implemented. Class war under such circumstances is endemic; and, as it has proved in Spain and Russia, frightfully bloody and destructive. The old Party labels of Democrat and Republican, Labor and Nationalist, Left and Right, Whig and Tory, Liberal and Conservative, are no longer to the point: what we should ask is whether candidates are pre-Marx or post-Marx, Capitalist or Fascist or Communist. And whilst the distribution of labor and leisure remains corrupt, all governments, central or local, inevitably act as the instruments of that corruption, no matter how democratic the principles and programs of their members may be.

This view of the economic situation is basic in modern politics.

CHAPTER XLII

POLITICAL SUMMARY

UNLESS the people can choose their leaders and rulers, and can revoke their choice at intervals long enough to test their measures by results, the government will be a tyranny exercised in the interests of whatever classes or castes or mobs or cliques have this choice. And until popular choice is constitutionally guided and limited, political ignorance and idolatry will produce not only Hitleresque dictatorships but stampedes led by liars or lunatics like Titus Oates and Lord George Gordon. The choice should therefore be limited to panels of persons who have passed such tests as we can devise of their wisdom, comprehension, knowledge, and energy. For legislative purposes adult suffrage is out of the question, as only a small percentage of any population has either the requisite faculty or knowledge; but for ventilation of grievances, questioning of ministers and criticism of Cabinets, suggestion of remedies and new methods, moving of resolutions and votes of confidence or the reverse, and generally for keeping the government in touch with the people, a representative popular parliament of men and women in equal numbers is necessary.

Such a Parliament alone may properly be called a House of Commons. It should not have any direct power to legislate, because legislative capacity is not common. Nature provides only a percentage of persons uncommon enough to be able to devise, revise, or add to the Ten Commandments and administer them. But unless these persons are chosen and removable by the common people, the people, not feeling that they are being governed by their own consent, will become seditious. Fortunately Nature always provides for real needs excessively and even extravagantly. When the chances are a thousand to one against a fish's egg surviving the perils of the sea, Nature provides a million eggs to balance the odds. And when one Prime Minister, one First Consul, or one President with a dozen Secretaries of State, is needed to govern a country, Nature, if not thwarted by avoidable poverty and ignorance, provides a hundred. The percentage of capable legislators in a fullfed and fully educated population is thus sufficient to give the electors a choice of rulers; and a choice is all that is needed to give them as much control of their government as is good for them. To achieve this in practice the capable must be ascertained, tested, and empanelled in their various degrees, making government in this respect a profession like any other profession. The empanelled legislator or administrator will be on the footing of the ordained clergyman, the enrolled lawyer, the registered doctor, and the university graduate. The unempanelled agitator can still have his fling in the Commons. There may even be ways of evading the tests, such as honorary degrees or qualifications conferred on *"bona fide* practitioners" whose competence has been established in the course of events; but such irregular qualifications and evasions should be conferred and allowed by tested rulers only. The tests should be revised at intervals short enough to keep them up to date, and regarded as provisional and changeable, not as sacred and infallible.

The British Party System should be scrapped ruthlessly. It was invented two and a half centuries ago to nullify the House of Commons by obliging the King to select his ministers from the Party commanding a majority in it, and to dissolve Parliament and inflict a costly election on its members whenever that Party is defeated on a division; so that members never vote on the merits of a measure but always on the question of whether the reigning Party is to remain in office, both sides risking the loss of their seats and incurring heavy expense and trouble if they unseat the Government.

Parliamentary business should therefore be conducted as in our municipalities, where members are elected for a fixed term and serve on standing committees which consider all questions appropriate to their departments and report their conclusions and recommendations to the whole body. The reports can be discussed and accepted or amended or sent back for further consideration on their merits wholly; for no member gains any personal advantage or suffers any disadvantage whichever way he votes, nor does the rejection of any recommendation involve an immediate dissolution and election, nor displace the chairman of the reporting committee. At present, municipal councillors play at party politics by organizing the ovine members who do not know how to vote until a Party Whip tells them, and opposing independent candidates at the elections. The remedy for this is the exclusion of ovines from the municipal panel. All others are independent of party considerations in their votes on the reports.

But parliaments and municipalities do not cover the whole political ground, nor will they when they multiply by fission until instead of one parliament we have several. What Dr Johnson inserted in Goldsmith's poem

> How small of all that human hearts endure
> That part which kings or laws can cause or cure!

remains true to this day; for trade unions, professional associations, the Inns of Court, the General Medical Council, the Bishops, the

Stock Exchange, to say nothing of private employers and financiers
and their federations, hold rights of admission and exclusion over
so many breadwinning callings that abolition of all direct government control, if that were possible, would leave our livelihoods
still at the mercy of bodies over which we have no control. They
are controlled only by their own *esprit de corps* (called in England
professional ettikett), which may conflict with their regard for the
public welfare, as it gives the clergyman a vested interest in sin,
the lawyer in litigation, the policeman in crime and conviction, the
doctor in disease, the Stock Exchange in gambling, the empire in
poverty and slavery, and the employee in doing as little as possible
for as much as he can get. All organizations of these anti-social
interests tend to become conspiracies against the public. They maintain scarcity of professional services to keep up their prices, making
entry difficult by unnecessarily prolonged apprenticeship, and examinations in discarded techniques, obsolete languages, and irrelevant
academic subjects. They resist all new techniques that supersede
their own and impose new acquirements on them. They persecute
outsiders ruthlessly. The skill and knowledge they guarantee is, as
to the skill, untested and often imaginary (for example, it is possible
to obtain the highest surgical degree without having ever performed
an operation); and the knowledge is often academic only, and out
of date at that.

To leave bodies with such potentialities and actualities of mischief
uncontrolled by the State whilst giving them powers and privileges
which none of the Estates of the Realm now dare claim is plain
political madness; yet we do it as a matter of course, and denounce
as the most horrible tyranny their national integration by State
departments under modern Fascist regimes on the Continent,
though nothing can be more democratic than a refusal to establish
a Vocational State on the ground that the laity should control the
vocations politically and not the vocations the laity. A medical
service in which its patients have no voice, a clergy with powers
to bind and loose the souls of the congregations, a legal profession
unrestrained by its clients, an industrial system in which the producers are represented but not the consumers, will create a vocational
tyranny as dangerous as any other sort of tyranny; yet we all hold
it to be selfevident that the clergy should be controlled by clergymen, the doctors by doctors, the courts by lawyers, the landlords
by landlords, the stockbrokers by stockbrokers, the miners by
miners, the engineers by engineers, and so on. If associations to

control burglary and murder were tolerated we should take it for granted that the members should all be burglars and murderers. Even when the association is a Committee of the Privy Council, as the General Medical Council is, I had to agitate for many years for the representation of the laity (the patients) on it before a single layman was appointed, and then only because the persecuting policy of the Council had been openly scandalous.

This thoughtless practice, however, is not a deliberate policy. It just occurs because producers organize themselves before consumers do. Organization is much easier for them because they are relatively small compact bodies with their livelihoods at stake, whereas the consumers, being in the most important cases the whole nation, must be organized nationally, which means that until social organization has developed to a point at which such national organization is possible the consumers are not organized at all, and so are governed by the producers; for the unorganized are always governed by the organized in millionfold modern populations, whether consciously and intentionally or not. The Socialist State on its Marxist side is an organization of the consumers in selfdefence against the organized producers.

Until this organization of consumers is complete enough to dominate the organized producers, the natural differences of talent will make democracy impossible, because some of the most precious talents are not lucrative, whilst others—some of them so base as to rank as vices rather than talents—are enormously lucrative. The superpoets, the superphilosophers, the supermathematicians, must either starve or take university chairs and pretend to impart their talents to young people quite incapable of them but needing to know how they should fill examination papers about them, unless, indeed, like Morris and Richardson, they wisely prefer to keep a shop and let the shop keep them. At the same time persons with some cunning in planning combined with abnormal acquisitiveness make fortunes in commerce and finance. The career is never open to all the talents under Capitalism: its door is wide open to certain talents and double locked against others. William Morris, eminent among the greatest poets of the nineteenth century, told me at the height of his fame that he made £100 a year by his poems. He lived comfortably by managing a factory and a shop producing furniture and decorations of extraordinary artistic quality; but his profits were not so large as those of his competitors who dealt in the commonest fashionable trash. Robert Browning, being assessed for income tax at a guess on the hundred a year scale for his poetry, threatened to leave the country, and actually did so for many years. He lived on his private unearned income. Newton was not paid as much for the infinitesimal calculus nor Einstein for Relativity as I have been paid for a single performance of a play in which I took no part. Thus even among the exceptionally talented there is gross inequality of income, without counting the inequalities produced by private property in land and capital.

Now equality of income up to the point at which all sections of the community are intermarriable is a fundamental necessity for a stable civilization; and it is made natural and easily feasible by the simple fact of natural history that geniuses, saints, heroes, conquerors, and cerebrotonics generally, cost no more to keep alive and active than Tom, Dick, and Harriet. This utterly defeats the pretensions commonly made—more commonly in fact by Tom, Dick and Harriet than by our Homers and Pythagorases—that when less skilled or poorer persons than they are paid more for their work (get a rise, as they say) they also must get a rise to maintain their inequality of income as their badge of superiority. Such selfish political shallowness must be stamped out by education instead of inculcated as it is at present. Taking the sort of life now represented by an income of a few thousands a year as standard, all incomes should be levelled up to this; and as the case of our poorest is the most urgent, the lowest income should be raised first to the grade above, and the two grades thus equalized then levelled up to the next grade above, and so on until finally the intermarriable level is attained. The skilled artisan must allow the income of the unskilled laborer to rise to his own, and then, but not until then, combine with him to gain the next step up equally for both. Let him by all means cherish his conviction that he is a superior being and be proud of his skill; but let him not forget that the hodman is as necessary as the bricklayer; that at any moment the invention of a machine may make both of them unnecessary, or make him unnecessary whilst leaving the hodman still necessary; and also that the wellbeing of his neighbors is an inseparable part of his own wellbeing; for the most luxurious palace becomes dangerous and undesirable if a slum with a high death rate grows up round it. Above all, he must get rid of the notion that the long scale between unskilled labor at the bottom and the rarest technical accomplishment at the top can be calibrated with a scale of wages, salaries, fees, or any other form of money quantities. If he doubts this, ask him to express in pounds, shillings and pence the difference between the social service of an archbishop and a turf bookmaker, or to fix a just wage for poets laureate and sausage makers.

But it is possible to assess two hours of any man's time as worth twice as much as one hour of it, and to vary his periods of service and leisure, and his age of retirement, in cases outside factory, office, and military routine. Playwriting, for instance.

CHAPTER XLIII

RELIGIOUS SUMMARY

It is time to tell our Fundamentalists bluntly that they are the worst enemies of religion today; that Jehovah is no god, but a barbarous tribal idol; that the English Bible, though a masterpiece of literary art in its readable parts, and, being the work of many highly gifted authors and translators, rich in notable poems, proverbs, precepts, and entertaining if not always edifying stories, is yet a jumble of savage superstition, obsolete cosmology, and a theology which, beginning with Calibanesque idolatry and propitiatory blood sacrifices (Genesis to Kings), recoils into sceptical disillusioned atheistical Pessimism (Ecclesiastes); revives in a transport of revolutionary ardor as the herald of divine justice and mercy and the repudiation of all sacrifices (Micah and the Prophets); relapses into sentimentality by conceiving God as an affectionate father (Jesus); reverts to blood sacrifice and takes refuge from politics in Other-Worldliness and Second Adventism (the Apostles); and finally explodes in a mystical opium dream of an impossible apocalypse (Revelation): every one of these phases being presented in such an unbalanced one-sided way, that the first Christian Catholic Church forbad the laity to read the Bible without special permission. When the Reformation let it loose on Mr Everyman, it produced a series of wars of religion which have culminated today in the Hitlerized world war. In this the campaigns of Joshua for the conquest of his world have broken out again with the difference that the Germans and not the Jews are the Chosen Race (*Herrenvolk*) who are to conquer and inherit the earth; and the lands flowing with milk and honey which they are to invade and put to the sword are not only the patches of North Africa which used to be called the land of Canaan but virtually the whole five continents. It is one of the paradoxes of the situation that Joshua Hitler, born in comparative poverty into the bitter strife of petty commerce in which the successful competition of the Jews is specially dreaded and resented, and for which he is himself unfitted by his gifts, hates the Jews, and yet is so saturated by his early schooling with the Judaism of the Bible that he now persecutes the Jews even to extermination just as the first Joshua persecuted the Canaanites, and is leading his country to ruin not through anti-Semitism, but through Bible Semitism with its head turned.

Yet from my reading aloud of all this writing on the wall, Mr Everyman, who never reads the Bible, and never listens critically to the ritual of having the lessons read to him every Sunday in Church (when he goes to Church: a habit which he is dropping), gathers nothing but that I am a damnably irreligious man who will certainly go to hell when I die if there be any such place as hell, which Mr Everyman is beginning to doubt, because it has uncomforting possibilities for himself as well as certainty for me.

If we must canonize some collection of writings as evolutionarily inspired, which is what we have done with the budget of selected samples of ancient Hebrew literature we call the Book of Books, surely we had better canonize our own modern literature, as it is equally inspired evolutionarily, and much more up-to-date socially and scientifically. The Bible in its canonical aspect is not helping us: it is obstructing us and making us dangerously irreligious. Rousseau said in the eighteenth century, "Get rid of your miracles and the whole world will fall at the feet of Christ"; and this was seasonably said at the moment; but he was wrong: the whole world has become indifferent to the Bible miracles, and instead of falling at the feet of Christ has fallen at the feet of Pasteur and Pavlov, and set up a new canon of miracles which it calls miracles of Science.

Yet it has not discarded its old Fundamentalist superstitions and taboos and mental habits. No longer ago than the end of the nineteenth century Stewart Headlam, a clergyman, got into trouble with his ecclesiastical superiors by saying that what the Church needs is to bury the Bible for a hundred years, and let it then be discovered for what it really is. I cannot agree that we should bury the Bible only: we should burn the Prayer Book also. It is saturated with blood sacrifice beyond all possible revision; and its constant reiteration of "through Jesus Christ our Lord" grows more and more unbearable by its essential falsehood as more and more people

realize that what is true in the Prayer Book would be equally true
if Jesus had never existed, and that his martyrdom does not relieve
us of a jot of our responsibility for our sins. For instance, though a
thief can redeem himself by becoming honest, until he does so he
remains none the less a thief, and a damned one at that, though
Jesus had died a thousand times. Jesus never said "Sin as much as
you like: my blood will wash it all off": he said "Sin no more."
The Prayer Book, by incessantly holding him up as a scapegoat,
discredits him and undoes the civilizing value of the Church. In this
way the Prayer Book is keeping Mr Everyman away from church,
though he still thinks he perhaps ought to go when in fact he
doesnt. He certainly often spends his Sunday in a much duller and
more expensive way than he would in a church brought honestly
up to date.

The Roman Church, more worldly wise than the Church of
England, and served by trained and professionalized priests instead
of by casual amateur British gentlemen wearing slightly unusual
collars, is even more handicapped because it will not admit that it
has ever made mistakes, and refuses to make experiments although
modern science has made it impossible to believe in God at all
unless with the admission that God has made experimental mistakes.
The world is full of them; and it is our job to correct them or get
rid of them. For a familiar practical instance, the Roman Catholic
must "suffer his holy ones to see corruption" by the horrible
practice of earth burial because his Church began by committing
itself to the childish notion that a buried body can be resuscitated
but not a burnt one, reminding me of an uncle of mine who, believing that he was about to be taken up to heaven like Elijah in
a celestial chariot, took off his boots to facilitate the operation.
The Roman Catholic Church, if it is to compete successfully with
rival catholicisms for the faith of men better instructed than my
uncle must rise above his level and admit that the law of change is
the law of God.

For another instance, its refusal to allow divorce has forced it to
annul marriages, sometimes on grounds that would not pass in a
Dakota divorce court.

Quakers and saints can be religious without ritual, and compose their own prayers; but there are others who if they do not
go to church will forget their religion and go to the devil, or worse,
to war. And in the long run they will not go to church if what they
hear there is incredible and unreasonable. Dogmatic Sanctions and

Prohibitions must be kept up to date fast enough to avoid a disastrous clash between Dogma and Pragma. But when I say these things, all that Mr Everyman gathers is that he had better lock up his spoons when people like me are about. Yet he would dislike me still more if he discovered that I am religious enough to have spent a great part of my life trying to clean up the heavily barnacled creeds, and make them credible, believing as I do that society cannot be held together without religion. An incredible religion is also an uncomfortable one: that is why Mr Everyman dislikes religion and religious people. I began in my early teens by maintaining that it was not the Bible and its Ten Commandments that made people good, but their sense of honor: a recent acquirement of my own which had cured me of childish lying and stealing. My numerous uncles thereupon concluded that I was an atheist, and that something ought to be done about it. But as nothing was done I accepted the epithet as due to my intellectual integrity, ranking me with Giordano Bruno and the noble army of martyrs whom Science placed above the glorious company of the apostles. I submit that when quite respectable young gentlemen like Shelley and myself boast of being heretics, and clubs of them are formed at the universities, Mr Everyman is right in concluding that there must be something very wrong somewhere; for as heretics are clearly traitors to civilization, they should be liquidated (not necessarily burnt) by The Inquisition, not now so-called, but always in active operation, were it only to extinguish the heresies of Thuggee and Voodoo. When The Inquisition is out-of-date, and the heretics up-to-date, there is the devil to pay.

But nowadays institutional religion and the habit of churchgoing have so lost their hold on Mr Everyman that my criticism of the creeds has never been resented as Shelley's was by the indignant Englishman who is said to have knocked him down at sight in a post office. Once, when I was a guest in a Manchester club, I was insulted by one of the members so offensively that I had to lecture him severely on his breach of club manners, and warn him that my host might complain to the Committee. What annoyed him was not my uncompromising refusal to accept Jehovah as a god, but that I had denied the omniscience and infallibility of Shakespear. On another occasion I was present at a meeting addressed by a gentleman who was devoting his life to combating the modern heresy that the earth is globular, and maintaining that it is flat. The debate that followed was quite the funniest I have ever attended. Opposition such as no atheist could have provoked assailed him; and he, having heard their arguments hundreds of times, played skittles with them, lashing the meeting into a spluttering fury as he answered easily what it considered unanswerable. When he was asked whether he had ever watched a ship through a telescope and seen it sink beneath the horizon he blandly inquired whether the questioner had ever used a telescope in this manner. Apparently nobody present except myself and the lecturer ever had. The lecturer went on, "I have myself witnessed this interesting illusion. My questioner, though he admits he has spoken from hearsay about the ship, has no doubt often stood on a railway bridge and seen the two parallel tracks converge and meet in the distance. May I ask him whether he believes that the two lines do actually converge and meet as they seem to him to do?" Thereupon another questioner, boiling with rage, rose and shouted, "Can you deny that if you start from Liverpool and keep travelling due west or east you will find yourself in Liverpool again?" "Of course you do," said the lecturer, and traced a circle on the flat table top with his finger. The next questioner, confident that he was cornering the lecturer this time, played his ace of trumps with "In an eclipse the shadow of the eclipsing body is round: how do you account for that?" "So is the shadow of a griddle, which is the flattest thing on earth," was the reply.

I joined in the debate to declare that the lecturer had answered and silenced all his opponents, who had only picked up and parroted a string of statements they had never thought out nor verified. I added, however, that having followed the lecturer's argument closely, I thought it led to the conclusion that the earth is in shape a cylinder.

For the rest of the week the Everymans showered comminatory letters on me, renouncing friendship with me, and demanding my expulsion from all societies of advanced thinkers and even of decent people. They assumed that I believed the earth to be flat, and concluded that this indicated not only gross ignorance of science, but abhorrent moral delinquency. It was evident that the writers would have seen me, if not burnt at the stake, at least imprisoned for a year, with entire satisfaction. I might have written the leading article in The Freethinker for twenty years without provoking a single abusive postcard. Mr Everyman is often as credulous and bigoted in his modern scientific scepticism as his grandfather was in his Evangelicalism.

Mr and Mrs Everyman never seem to doubt that if anyone disagrees with them in any matter upon which they feel strongly, they have the right to injure the dissenter to any extent within their power short of *heretico comburendo*. It seems to them as natural a right as their right to inflict the most mischievous and prolonged torments on lawbreakers, or to cuff and flog their naughty children and share that right with the school teacher. If they pleaded in justification that their tempers are so explosive that they would wreck civilization without a safety valve one could argue with them; but they pretend instead that two blacks make a white, and that they are acting with judicial calm in the best interest of society. When I tell them that they have no right to punish anybody (except perhaps themselves); that when Jesus told them so he was giving them sound practical advice; and that our treatment of criminals is diabolical, they dismiss me as a dreamy sentimentalist; but when I add that far from sympathizing with those who demand the abolition of capital punishment and the substitution of a penal servitude worse than death, I demand the liquidation, as kindly as possible, of all incorrigible living nuisances, I muddle and amaze them as much as when I profess myself a democrat and yet demand the disfranchisement and disqualification of political nincompoops from every political activity except that of ventilating their grievances and choosing between rulers of proved competence.

I was present once at the induction of a rector into a Church of England living. Although I knew beforehand that the bishop would have to ask the postulant a question to which the answer would be a deliberate lie, known to be such to both of them, and was prepared to admit that they were both doing this under duress, having to do it or have their vocations closed to them, it was none the less shocking to see and hear it actually done. The best brain among our Church dignitaries has given it to us in writing that if the Thirtynine Articles (the subject of the lie) were taken seriously the Church would be staffed exclusively by fools, bigots, and liars. Until we have a Church and a Government righteous enough and strong enough to discard the Articles, rewrite the Prayer Book, and put the Bible in its proper place, we shall not get our civilization out of the murderous mess in which it is at present staggering. Science and religion at loggerheads are reflected politically in a suicidal world war. The popular notion that one of the two must be all right and the other all wrong is what I call Soot-or-Whitewash reasoning: it is not reasoning at all, but thoughtless unobservant jumping at conclusions. Both our science and our religion are gravely wrong; but they are not all wrong; and it is our urgent business to purge them of their errors and get them both as right as possible. If we could get them entirely right the contradictions between them would disappear: we should have a religious science and a scientific religion in a single synthesis. Meanwhile we must do the best we can instead of running away from the conflict as we are cowardly enough to do at present.

Anthropomorphic Deism will remain for long as a workable hypothesis not only for children but for many adults. Prayer consoles, heals, builds the soul in us; and to enact a Prohibition of Prayer, as some Secularists would if they had the power, would be as futile as it would be cruel. But there are all sorts of prayers, from mere beggars' petitions and magic incantations to contemplative soul building, and all sorts of divinities to pray to. A schoolboy who witnessed a performance of my play St Joan, told his schoolmaster that he disliked Jesus and could not pray to him, but that he could pray to Joan. An Ulster Orange schoolmaster would probably have given him an exemplary thrashing to make a proper young Protestant of him; but this schoolmaster was wiser: he told the boy to pray to Joan by all means: it is the prayer and not the prayee that matters. To the Franciscan, Francis and not Jesus is the redeemer; and to countless Catholics and not a few Anglicans Our Lady is the intercessor. To the Jains God is Unknowable; but their temple in Bombay is full of images of all sorts of saints, from nameless images of extraordinary beatific peace to crude elephant-headed idols. As a Protestant child I was taught that my Roman Catholic fellowcountrymen would all go to hell because they said Hail, Mary! At the same time my English contemporary Arthur Conan Doyle was being taught at Stonyhurst that I should be damned for not saying it. I have lived to see modern Germany discard Hail, Mary! and substitute Heil, Hitler!; and for the life of me I cannot bring myself to regard the change as an improvement. It looks too like a revival of the worship of the ancient Egyptian god Ra, whose head was the head of a hawk. Still, I think the Church of England wrong in imposing Jesus, whom many people dislike as my schoolboy devotee of Joan did, as the sole form in which God can be prayed to. Every Church should be a Church of All Saints, and every cathedral a place for pure contemplation by the greatest minds of all races, creeds, and colors.

CHAPTER XLIV

THIS book can never be finished any more than the Annual Register can. But each of its successive writers must stop somewhere, not always because they have no more to say, and certainly not because there is no more to be said, but because they are tired of saying it, and their readers of reading it, not to mention the limits of available time and space. I must stop, leaving much unsaid.

When I was a child my governess made me read a book called The Child's Guide to Knowledge. When I was at the height of my adult powers I wrote a play called As Far As Thought Can Reach. The present book, written in my second childhood, is not meant for people who want to know how far political thought can reach: it is just a Child's Guide to Politics. For my political experience has convinced me that though in this department everybody nowadays seems to know the $x\ y\ z$ of everything, nobody knows the $a\ b\ c$ of anything. In politics especially, though Democracy is staked on the monstrous assumption that Mr Everyman and Mrs Everywoman, being Omniscient, must be made Omnipotent, neither of them knows anything of what Herbert Spencer called Social Statics as such, though they may know them from often bitter experience through having had to live them. They think of politics as something outside life, though politics are either the science of social life or nothing. When our newspapers set us talking, and perhaps quarrelling, about words like Socialism, Fascism, Communism, Capitalism, Nationalism, and romantic Utopianisms of all sorts, we connect them with the real world as little as Don Quixote connected knight errantry with it. We can take a private house and keep an office or a shop by simply imitating our neighbors; but of economics and finance in the national lump we know nothing. Elections we can throw ourselves into because elections are contests, like dog races; but we choose our side because our fathers chose it and brought us up to it, or sometimes in rebellious reaction because our fathers took the opposite side. When, as may happen, we have dreams and visions of a better world under a new order we are unable to make them practicable by hooking them on to existing institutions because we know nothing of the technique and theory of these institutions, nor suspect that our dreams have been dreamt before, and that much human history is of attempts at their realization, sometimes by mistaken and frightfully disastrous methods.

Now a chemist may have the most thrilling dreams and visions of the future of chemistry, and the most public-spirited industry in furthering its latest developments; but if he knows nothing more about antimony and manganese than that they are both black he will blow himself and his neighbors up instead of contributing to a New Order. A Chancellor of the Exchequer may read the most abstruse mathematical studies and speculations of Sir Arthur Eddington and Sir James Jeans with intense interest; but if he has no grasp of the fact that $2 + 2 = 4$ and not 8o, he may wreck the nation's finance and industry with every intention of building Jerusalem in England's green and pleasant land.

Let us not, however, rush to the conclusion that statesmen must know everything, and build a perfectly scientific policy on a perfectly scientific basis. Of the real world in which we dwell it is not possible for anyone to know more than the fragment that is within our personal experience or hearsay at any moment. Even that negligible fragment we see, not in the perspective of history, but as a distorted close-up. When the German so-called Historical School in the nineteenth century repudiated classical, dramatized, apriorist history, and called for masses of recorded facts and years of dryasdust searches through libraries for documents, they were overlooking the cardinal fact that their method is physically impossible, because most of the facts are hidden or out of reach, and such records as exist are mostly lies, or at best wishful guesses. Therefore when facing contemporary situations and acting on them the statesman has not the alternative of omniscience: he must be guided by his knowledge of how human nature reacts to external pressures. He must be apriorist to the extent of being a psychologist and physicist guessing with very imperfect data to go upon. He cannot wait until he has read a thousand books and all the documents in the Record Office: the Opposition is at the gate, and sometimes the bayonet at his throat; and he must act at once.

But this does not justify the shallow Opportunism of our old parliamentary hands, who react to the shocks and surprises of social evolution as unintelligently as a cricket ball reacts to the stroke of a bat. To say that we know little is not to say that we know nothing; for that little may make all the difference between peaceful constitutional changes and civil wars that leave the country half ruined. In economics we have the law of rent and the law of value, both of them as well established as the axioms of our mathematicians and astronomers; yet out of our six hundred-odd members of Parliament I know of one only who shews any sign of having ever heard of the law of rent; and he is not in the Cabinet. Though history is adulterated with lies and wishful guesses, yet it sifts and sheds them, leaving finally great blocks of facts: for instance, though the contemporary records of revolutions are at best onesided and at worst frantically mendacious and vituperative, we in England can ascertain with sufficient truth the history of the Norman Conquest under William, the Commonwealth under Cromwell with its sequel in the conquest of both Crown and Commons by the plutocracy, the French Revolution under the Jacobins and Napoleon, our futile restoration of the Bourbons, the Russian Revolution of 1917 under Lenin, and the German *coup d'État* of 1933 under Adolf Hitler. Macaulay's history of England and the Communist Manifesto of Marx and Engels are not infallible scriptures; but persons who have never read them nor comprehended the change in historical outlook from one to the other should be eligible for the Foreign Office, or indeed any Downing Street office, only as porters or housemaids. Yet we never dream of asking whether a Secretary of State has ever heard of Macaulay or Marx, nor even whether he can read the alphabet.

My Everybody's What's What is only an attempt by a very ignorant old man to communicate to people still more ignorant than himself such elementary social statics as he has managed to pick up by study and collision with living persons and hard facts in the course of a life (long as lives go, but too short for this particular job) spent largely in discovering and correcting the mistakes into which his social antecedents and surroundings led him. I certainly have not corrected them all; but those to which my peculiar intellectual constitution makes me refractory I have gone into as far as I am able. The rest I must leave to my betters.

As to the future, beginning with the year 1944—

(*to be continued by them that can*)

INDEX